BRITAIN IN 2010

BRITAIN IN 2010

Jim Northcott
and PSI Research Team, as listed in acknowledgements

Economic forecasting in association with
CAMBRIDGE ECONOMETRICS

Research Funding

Funding for the project was provided by the following consortium
of private sector companies and government departments
led by an independent foundation

JOSEPH ROWNTREE FOUNDATION
EMPLOYMENT DEPARTMENT GROUP
DEPARTMENT OF TRADE & INDUSTRY
IBM UNITED KINGDOM
GLAXO
NATIONAL WESTMINSTER BANK
INLAND REVENUE
UNILEVER
DEPARTMENT OF ENVIRONMENT

The project is the work of the PSI research team and, as with all PSI
studies, the Institute is responsible for the study and the report setting
out its results and conclusions. Neither the selection of the
information presented nor the inferences drawn from it may be taken
to reflect the views or opinions of any of the organisations that
provided research sponsorship.

Special support for production of graphs
JOSEPH ROWNTREE FOUNDATION

BRITAIN IN 2010

THE PSI REPORT

The publishing imprint of the independent
POLICY STUDIES INSTITUTE
100 Park Village East, London NW1 3SR
Telephone: 071-387 2171; Fax: 071-388 0914

ISBN 0 85374 492 0 (Hardback); ISBN 0 85374 493 9 (Paperback)
PSI Report 704, January 1991

A CIP catalogue record of this book is available from the British Library.

How to obtain PSI publications
All bookshop and individual orders should be sent to PSI's distributors:
BEBC Ltd., 9 Albion Close, Parkstone, Bournemouth BH12 3LL
Books will normally be despatched within 24 hours.
Cheques should be made payable to BEBC Ltd.

Credit card and telephone/fax orders may be placed on
the following freephone numbers:
Credit Card Orders: FREEPHONE 0800 262260
TeleFax Orders: FREEPHONE 0800 262266

Booktrade Representation (UK & Eire)
Book Representation Ltd
P O Box 17, Canvey Island, Essex SS8 8HZ

PSI Subscriptions
PSI Publications are available on subscription.
Further information from PSI's subscription agent:
Carfax Publishing Company Ltd
Abingdon Science Park, P O Box 25, Abingdon OX10 3UE

Cover Design/Graphics/Layout: Russell Stretten Design, London NW1
Graphs: 4i Collaboration, London W1
Type: Laserset by PSI
Printed in Great Britain by BPCC Wheatons Limited, Exeter

Acknowledgements

Jim Northcott led the project and drafted the report. But the project was also a *team* enterprise and its strength has been founded on PSI's ability to bring together a multidisciplinary group of researchers with relevant experience in a number of different areas.

The work of the project was organised through a core group of PSI researchers who brought together the research material on which the report is mainly based in a number of major working papers covering the following subject areas:

Richard Berthoud	–	social policy
Michael Carley	–	urban and rural development
Charles Carter	–	macroeconomic and production issues, changes in consumption patterns
Bernard Casey	–	population, labour force
Ian Christie	–	science and technology
Mayer Hillman	–	energy, transport
Michael White	–	employment and training
Peter Willmott	–	social structure, values and styles of life

In addition to preparing the material in their own subject areas the members of the PSI core group also worked closely together to plan the project, organise the analysis, interpret the findings and improve the early drafts of the report. In particular, Ian Christie played a key role in bringing the different strands of work together, as well as contributing from his own area of research.

A special role in the project was played by Charles Carter: it was on his initiative that the project was undertaken; as chairman of the *Participants' Committee* he provided a link with the supporting organisations; and throughout the project he was a constant source of ideas, suggestions and constructive comments.

Additional major working papers were provided by experts not on the staff of PSI:

Christopher Ham	–	health care
John Pinder	–	Europe
Simon Webley	–	United States

A particularly important contribution to the project was made by Terry Barker and his colleagues at *Cambridge Econometrics*. Their special projections on the Cambridge model provided the figures used in the main economic forecasts and in the three scenarios illustrating the impact of different policy options.

The core group at PSI were greatly helped by Susan Johnson, PSI's librarian, and by inputs of various kinds from other researchers at PSI, including Isobel Allen, Rex Baron, Tonya Berthoud, Colin Brown, John Cassels, Andrew Feist, Michael Fogarty, Robert Hutchison, Elizabeth Perkins, David Smith, and Annette Walling.

Final preparation of the report was the work of another team: Alex Quero and Michael Warry who prepared the charts; Malcolm Russell Stretten who designed the cover and page layouts; and Karin Erskine and Clare Morgan who handled the desk-top publishing and typesetting. As always, especially important contributions were made by Eileen Reid and Nicholas Evans in the roles of editor and publisher respectively. With valuable help from Peter Willmott, they ensured that the book read well, looked good and was produced on time to a tight schedule.

Valuable help was also provided in various ways by many others outside PSI, including Gerald Barney, H. Brech, G. Caraca, Martha Garrett, J. Gershuny, Hugues de Jouvenel, Ian Miles, Riccardo Petrella, and Graham Vickery.

While much of the report is based on PSI's own research, extensive use has also been made of the reports, papers and articles of the many other individuals and organisations in Britain and other countries which are listed in the sources section at the back of the report. Their contributions were mostly unwitting, but nonetheless essential.

Finally, we are glad to put on record our gratitude to the organisations that supported the project and to their representatives on the *Participants' Committee* whose information, ideas, comments and criticisms did much to enhance the project and improve the report. Without their participation the project would have been weaker; and without their funding it would not have been possible.

We should make it clear, however, that, PSI is an independent research institute and, as with all its projects, takes responsibility for the published report. It follows, therefore, that while the contributions of the participant organisations and others outside PSI were most valuable and much appreciated, it should not be supposed that the selection of the information reported or the inferences or conclusions drawn from it reflect their views.

C *ontents*

THE WORLD IN 2010

Global developments

Regional Developments

Britain in 2010

Charts

17   Life in Britain in 2010

18   Three Scenarios

Foreword

There are plenty of speculative books about the future, but we hope this one is a little different. It is not produced with the tunnel vision of enthusiasts for one particular development, who tend both to overestimate the impact of their own enthusiasm and to forget the importance of developments in other fields. It is a cooperative venture between researchers in a wide variety of subjects, contributing their ideas about developments in their own special fields, and then coming together to consider the interactions. It is intended to be a sober forecast of what seems likely to happen, not a statement of what *ought* (in the opinion of particular individuals) to happen. So we hope that it will have a serious and practical use in government, industry and commerce, and will be of interest to many members of the general public.

A book of this kind is liable to the faults of works designed by a committee, but happily it has had the unifying influence of a single author, Jim Northcott, whose skill in presenting complex matters with clarity and deceptive simplicity we all value. But he would be the first to acknowledge his debt to many other contributors, including the representatives of the bodies which have funded the whole enterprise – Government departments, major firms, and a charitable trust – and who have met in committee to consider each stage of the work. A special mention is needed for Cambridge Econometrics, who contributed invaluable economic forecasts to the work of the research team.

In the year 2010, the Policy Studies Institute will no doubt have a conference to discuss what went wrong; for, of course, many of our judgements of the future will certainly be proved wrong. All we hope is that this picture of the future will be recognisable and, in the intervening years, of value in the development of wise policies.

Charles Carter
Chairman, Participants Committee

Preface

This report is very much a product of the Policy Studies Institute and incorporates many of the distinctive characteristics of PSI. First, it is interdisciplinary. It draws on the work of a range of groups inside and outside the Institute. Secondly, it is problem-oriented. The groups on which it draws are themselves organised to confront problem areas rather than to advance academic disciplines. And so the New Technology Group, the Employment Studies Group, the Family Finances and Social Security Group and the Environment and Quality of Life Group have all made substantial contributions to the study. Moreover, the criteria for evaluating and selecting their contributions have been quite simply the principal author's judgement of how useful they were in answering the questions that the project posed. Thirdly, the approach has been empirical and pragmatic. The project has not been driven by any great vision of how the future should be or any great fear of what it might be. It has been inspired quite simply by the Institute's mission 'to inform policy by establishing the facts'. In this instance that has involved painstaking research on what is happening now in the different areas of the project's field of enquiry and how that has been changing; and making informed judgements of the likely changes in the future, taking into account other likely developments.

Fourthly, the project received multiple funding from the private, public and voluntary sectors. When we embarked upon that system of funding research projects it was principally to tap new sources of money for PSI strategic research. But as this project progressed we were increasingly struck by a range of other benefits. When I attended meetings of the *Participants' Committee* I could imagine few other circumstances where representatives of the government departments and of the major companies present would meet together with policy researchers for joint problem-solving. We received invaluable information and comment from the participants that would never have been available had they themselves not had a stake in the enterprise. Perhaps we were occasionally inclined to feel that the contributions of the representatives of government departments were a little constrained by immediate problems and perspectives. But it was a good discipline for us to have to confront those perspectives, and the representatives properly accepted that the report ultimately reflected the judgements of the Institute. Now that the report is published we confidently expect that the involvement of the different funders will be as valuable in the dissemination of the report as it was in its assembly.

Overall, then, the project was the product of an organisation where different subject groups are able to come together collaboratively to help solve problems and inform policy debates. Each contributes what it can to the subject and the criteria for judging its contribution are the quality of the information and its practical usefulness. The work is done in a framework where the contributions of policy-makers and practitioners are evidently valued. Such arrangements would seem to be so self-evidently desirable that it is astonishing that the Policy Studies Institute is one of the few bodies dedicated to them.

Finally, although the report was built on the institutional strenghts of PSI, the work was principally done by one man, Jim Northcott. It was a herculean task to which he brought a rare set of research, intellectual and literary talents. It is a further feature of the Institute that its distinctive approach enables it to attract such distinctive talents.

W W Daniel
Director, Policy Studies Institute

1. **I**ntroduction

How will Britain change over the next two decades? This report aims to give an informed and objective assessment of likely developments to the year 2010 in many different areas, and of the interactions between them, and of developments in the rest of the world that will have particular impact on Britain. It is based on the work of a two-year research project undertaken by a multidisciplinary team of the independent Policy Studies Institute (PSI).

Purpose of the study

Perhaps the first question to be addressed should be: why attempt to study the future? Surely the future is not only unknown, but inherently unknowable? Even short-term forecasts usually turn out wrong, so why waste time with longer-term predictions?

The notion that the future is something predetermined and fixed and that, by diligence of application and refinement of technique, we may hope to prise open its secrets and predict, with certainty and precision, what is going to happen in many years to come is clearly not an approach that is likely to give useful results. But it does not therefore follow that *any* attempt to look ahead into the longer-term future can be of no possible use. On the contrary, there are many areas where we can be fairly confident, at least about the *range* within which future events are likely fall and the *general shape* of the picture likely to emerge. And if we are content to work in terms of *degrees of probability* rather than absolute certainties, in *main features* rather than in fine detail, the result, while less than ideal, may still be of considerable interest and usefulness. The aim has therefore been to collect and analyse the best information available in order to get a considered and consistent view of the prospects ahead and to bring out the most significant factors affecting them.

Value of the study

Such an exercise can be valuable in two ways. First, by providing a more systematic foundation for expectations about the future, it can improve the basis on which decisions on longer-term questions are taken. And second, by highlighting the issues that will need to be addressed, and the factors affecting them, it can stimulate constructive thinking about the choices to be made. If as a result of sensible forward thinking people make better choices than they would have done otherwise, the effect will be to *change* the future for the better. Thus what is involved is not *predicting* a future that is fixed, but making possible better-informed *choices* so that the future can be made better than it would have been otherwise. These potential benefits of helping decision taking and enhancing the scope for choice apply alike to government, business and individual citizens.

Value to government

There are many areas where government policies have long-term effects for example, in energy, transport, housing, social security and environmental conservation. Policy makers are at a disadvantage if they have to focus on short-term considerations and to consider each area in isolation from the others. Policies can be better based if they have the benefit of a longer-term perspective of the wider context in which they will operate – for example, of changes in the structure of the population and the shape of the family, in the operation of the labour market and the nature of work, in the pattern of consumption and attitudes to social provision.

Value to companies

Business policies work through the market, and market outcomes are the result of many separate decisions by many different organisations. Each decision can be as good only as the information it is based on. Hence, the better the information, the better the decisions, and the more efficient the working of the market system is likely to be.

There are many kinds of business decision for which good information about the medium- and long-term future is likely to be relevant. Firms need to make investments in plant and buildings which will take time to produce a satisfactory return; to undertake research and development work for new products and services to meet future demands; to build up labour and management skills so as to be able in the future to use improved methods of production of goods and provision of services. To keep competitive they need to plan well ahead, and they will be better placed for doing this if they have a clear view of the wider 'market' in which they will be operating in the longer term – for example, of the changes in total demand due to economic growth; of the changes in consumer spending patterns due to movements in tastes, incomes, and family structure; and of the changes in staff availability due to developments in education, work practices and population age distribution.

Value to individuals

For many individuals the longer-term future is a matter of great interest and curiosity. It can also be a matter of practical utility. Many of the big choices in life – in education, career, marriage, family, home, retirement – are made for intensely personal reasons; but since their consequences can be very long-lasting, there is the possibility of better-informed choices sometimes being made if more is known, for example, of future prospects for incomes, employment, social security and patterns of family life. For some of the most important personal decisions, no less than for government and corporate ones, a well-founded picture of the future can be not merely interesting, but also useful.

The report

The report aims to present the findings of PSI's *Britain in 2010* project within a manageable length and in an easily readable form so as to focus attention on the issues of central importance. Inevitably, therefore, it does not set out in full all the detailed work underlying the findings; however, it is expected that some of this will be incorporated in other reports to be published later in the course of a continuing programme of research on longer-term changes.

Method

The chapter following this introduction explains the method and approach used for the study and clarifies the basis of some of the assumptions adopted for it.

The international context

The next group of chapters set Britain in the context of developments expected in the rest of the world. Chapters 3-5 describe three areas in which there are important developments which are essentially global in their impact: war and peace, the world economy, and the global environment. Chapters 6-11 consider likely developments in six different regions of the world: the United States, Japan, the Third World, China, the Soviet Union and Europe.

Population

Consideration of developments in Britain itself starts, in Chapter 12, with population: changes in birth rates, death rates and migration and the changes in total size and structure expected to result from them. Population is taken as the starting point because this is an area in which the data provide a better base for projections than in many other areas and because it is people who generate the needs to be met and who provide the main resource for meeting them.

Resources

The next chapters are concerned mainly with the resources for the generation of wealth and the ways in which they are likely to be used. Chapter 13 considers the human resources likely to be available: changes in the potential labour force, in the operation of the labour market, in levels of employment and unemployment, in skills, in training and education needs, and in occupation structures.

Chapter 14 looks at the resources of the physical environment: at changes in agriculture and the countryside, at urban development and settlement patterns, at housing and shopping, at transport, energy and water, and at the problems of pollution and waste management.

Chapter 15 examines developments in science and technology and the impact they may make in changing production processes and in providing new kinds of goods and services.

Output

In the light of the developments expected in these different areas, Chapter 16 analyses the prospects for future economic growth, including changes in investment, government spending, imports and exports and the differing growth rates likely in different economic sectors.

Life in 2010

Chapter 17 looks at the ways in which the fruits of economic growth are likely to be used and the changes in life-styles and attitudes. It outlines some of the likely changes in daily life in 2010 in people's work, incomes, homes, food and clothing, leisure and recreation, health and social care, family and social life and social attitudes.

Different scenarios

The analysis up to this point aims to identify the course of developments that seems most likely to happen. However, in many areas what happens depends to an important extent on what policies are pursued by the government. There is, therefore, scope for choice between options.

Accordingly, Chapter 18 sketches briefly some possible implications of three different scenarios based on three different policy approaches: a market-oriented approach, characterised by deregulation, privatisation, reduced public expenditure and lower taxes; a more interventionist approach, with more government involvement in education, training and R&D and greater expenditure on the welfare state; and a more strongly environmentally-oriented approach, with higher priority for pollution prevention and a carbon tax at escalating rates to reduce emissions of greenhouse gases.

Conclusions

Finally, Chapter 19 sums up briefly some of the main conclusions which emerge from the report as a whole.

Sources

The object of the report is to highlight the more important developments in prospect – to outline the broad shape of the wood, not to define the details of individual trees. It has therefore been necessary to keep it relatively short and set out only a small part of the information on which it is based. However, for those wishing to probe beneath the tip of the iceberg, a list of the principal sources used is given at the back of the report, with reference numbers in the text to indicate the points to which they relate.

2. Method and Approach

There are many factors affecting the way things will develop in the longer-term future, and many complex interactions between them. It is therefore important to approach matters in a systematic way, limiting the coverage, simplifying the complexities, assessing the probabilities and highlighting the key issues, so as to make the analysis manageable, the report intelligible and the findings useful. There is no ready-made methodology universally acknowledged to be appropriate for a study of this kind, and there are many possible approaches reflecting differing aims and circumstances. The approach we have adopted as most suited to our particular purpose and situation, and the reasons for doing so, are described below.

Selectivity

It would not have been practicable to undertake major new research in each of the different subject areas and the approach has therefore been to rely mainly on the information already available in each area, concentrating on identifying the developments of greatest significance and analysing the interactions between them. It has been necessary to be rigorously selective in the range of areas covered, giving most attention to the key areas which are of particular interest, either because of their importance in their own right, or because of their influence on other areas; while other areas which seem less important have had to be treated more cursorily or even ignored altogether. However, we hope to rectify some of these unavoidable omissions in the course of further work in the programme of research and to publish the findings in later reports.

Causes and effects

There is, of course, no clear-cut and tidy division between two discrete categories, causes and effects: almost all the subjects we are dealing with can be considered as both causes and effects, interacting with the others in highly complex ways. Even so, some may be regarded as mainly 'causes' in the sense that their future is sufficiently autonomous to be usefully predicted independently; while others may be regarded as mainly 'effects' in the sense that their future can best be predicted as the consequence of changes in the 'causes'. We have, therefore, as far as practicable, considered earlier the subjects which are more 'causal', and used the results to help make forecasts later in the areas which are more 'consequential'.

Reliability of data

There are some areas in which the available factual evidence is reasonably solid, and others in which it is much more unsatisfactory. Accordingly, we have given attention earlier to areas in which there is evidence to provide a fairly firm basis for long-term forecasts, and left until later areas where the evidence is weaker. This way it has been possible to use the findings in the stronger areas to reduce the uncertainties in the weaker ones.

Quantification

It is clearly desirable, wherever possible, to use figures to show relative orders of magnitude and differing degrees of probability. However, it would not have been fruitful to attempt to construct some grand model which would work out a numerical value for everything at once. There are many areas in which there are few firm data available and there are many more where the relationships between the main variables are not reliably established. Hence the construction of a comprehensive mathematical model would have been a very considerable exercise and one which could not realistically have been contemplated within the framework of the present project. It was therefore necessary to concentrate on getting broad figures for the main variables and to see the relationships between them in terms of an informal model rather than a precisely calibrated one. It seemed better to put more emphasis on clear thinking than on elaborate calculation to ensure the validity of the findings.

There is, however, one important area in which further quantification has been found feasible and valuable: the future of the economy. By working in close partnership with *Cambridge Econometrics*, it has been possible to draw on econometric projections from one of the largest and most advanced models of the economy, which have been specially extended to the year 2010, and which have been integrated with the findings in other areas of the study. It has thus been possible to have the benefit of a full set of internally consistent economic data which take account of developments in a broader range of areas than are normally allowed for in macroeconomic forecasts.

Objectivity

It must be stressed that, although we are inevitably dealing with probabilities rather than with certainties, the need for objectivity remains paramount. What we have sought to clarify is not what we most *want* to happen, nor what we want *not* to happen, but what is *most likely* to happen. It is thus not a matter of postulating a number of ideal goals for the future and speculating on how we might reach them, but rather of seeking to come to a coherent view as to what it is most realistic to expect in the light of current trends and relationships and the government policies in force and in prospect.

Ranges of uncertainty

In most areas, however, there is a wide range of uncertainty about what it is most realistic to expect. This can be made more manageable if, instead of considering a wide spectrum of values, attention is focused on a limited number of options. For forecasts of future population, for example, it is possible to work on the basis of a high birth rate and a low birth rate to indicate the range within which the future birth rate is thought likely to fall, and a middle birth rate to indicate the point within this range near which it is thought particularly likely to fall. The three different rates can then be followed separately and their different implications explored.

This approach ceases to be manageable, however, if there are many different variables to be considered, giving rise to a larger number of combinations of options. Again using population forecasts as an example, if in addition to the high, low and middle birth rates, there are also high, low and middle death rates to be examined, and net inward, outward and neutral migration flows as well, there will be altogether 27 different combinations of options giving 27 different possible future population sizes and structures.

And if these different sets of population figures are used for different estimates of future workforce, with separate high, low and middle activity rates for each sex and each age group in each of these populations, the number of potential combinations becomes manifestly far too large to handle.

For the purposes of the study, therefore, the only practicable course has been, while considering briefly the main possible options at each point in each area, to come to a view of the *most probable* outcome and to use that as the basic assumption to be carried forward into the consideration of other areas.

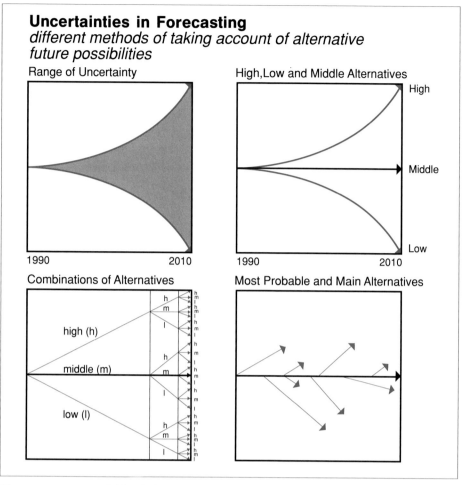

Uncertainties in Forecasting
different methods of taking account of alternative future possibilities

Range of Uncertainty

High, Low and Middle Alternatives

High

Middle

Low

1990   2010   1990   2010

Combinations of Alternatives

high (h)

middle (m)

low (l)

Most Probable and Main Alternatives

There are many variables in forecasting, and major uncertainties with each. Calculating separate high, low and middle values clarifies the range of uncertainty – but keeping them for a series of variables generates unwieldy numbers of combinations. The main emphasis has therefore been put on the 'most probable' outcomes.

Kinds of uncertainty

However, it is important to bear in mind that future uncertainties are of different kinds. Some uncertainties arise from developments which are largely independent of the policies of government in Britain: for example, changes in population, or in the price of oil or in developments in China. Other uncertainties arise from developments which are largely influenced by government policy: for example, changes in pensions, in income tax rates, or in the numbers of people attending university. A very important difference between these two kinds of uncertainty is that the outcomes of the first kind are largely beyond our control, while the outcomes of the second kind are largely the result of policy decisions. Accordingly, with the first kind it is useful to try to assess the *most probable* outcomes. With the second kind, also, it is useful to consider the most probable outcomes; but even more important will be the identification of policy options and their likely consequences, so as to highlight the *choices* that can be made between them.

Different scenarios

In view of this we have made the main forecasts on the basis of assumptions about the government policies that seem most likely to be followed in the future, taking account of the changing circumstances expected to apply; and in the areas where outcomes are particularly dependent on the policy decisions of government, we have drawn attention to this.

We have then gone also to set up three different scenarios to illustrate in outline some of the implications of different policy approaches. There are, of course, a very wide range of possible shades and combinations of policies, and to keep the discussion manageable we have therefore illustrated possibilities in the form of three bundles of policies representing three different general approaches: the first, a market-oriented one, the second a more interventionist one, and the third a more environment-oriented approach.

In considering different policy approaches it is necessary to bear in mind two kinds of limitation. The first is the extent of change in political attitudes which it is realistic to envisage. Party-political preferences, as reflected in opinion polls, are highly volatile, often shifting appreciably from one month to another. But these fluctuations are largely in response to the perceived competence or correctness of the government's handling of the issues of the day. Underlying basic political attitudes tend to change much more slowly, and it is these underlying attitudes which, in the longer term, have most influence on party programmes, election outcomes and government policies.

The second kind of limiting consideration is that future governments, probably even more than past governments, will be faced by numerous external constraints. Inevitably, these will in practice restrict their freedom of action in many important ways.

Nevertheless, despite these limiting considerations, there will still be sufficient room for manoeuvre for different policy approaches to lead to significantly different outcomes. There is therefore the possibility of meaningful choice, and some of the options are briefly set out in order to help make the choices better informed ones.

Thus the method has consisted of making base forecasts on the 'most probable' assumptions and then going on to outline scenarios to illustrate the effects of different policies. It is hoped that this approach will have two important advantages. For the decision taker needing an informed view of what is most likely to happen, it delineates the range of uncertainty and sets out the factors likely to determine where within this range the actual future will lie. And for the policy maker seeking an informed basis on which to make policy decisions that will influence the future, it postulates viable sets of options and brings out the implications of their adoption. Thus it can help meet the dual aims of the study: to narrow the range of uncertainty and clarify the areas of choice.

Global

Developments

GLOBAL DEVELOPMENTS

Some developments are specific to a single country and there are others which cross national frontiers to affect a number of different countries. There are others again which are essentially world-wide in their operation and effects; and it is appropriate to consider some of these in global terms before going on to give attention to developments that affect mainly certain groups of countries, or to the developments specific to Britain in particular. The three sections which follow deal with three of these global issues: war and peace, the world economy, and the world environment.

World Security

The present century has seen two world wars which have brought destruction and loss of life on an altogether unprecedented scale. They have been followed by a period of Cold War tensions between the two superpowers, the United States and the Soviet Union, and this has ensured that security from war has remained a major concern for most countries in the world.

Cold War

Over most of the postwar period it is doubtful whether either superpower seriously contemplated making a direct attack on the other; but if it had been so minded, it would almost certainly have been deterred by its awareness of the mutual destruction that would ensue if the two superpowers' nuclear weapons were used against each other.

Maintaining the balance of deterrence has not been an ideal solution, nor even a comfortable one. It has involved both superpowers, and their allies, in very considerable expenditure on defence, year after year; and as the nuclear arsenals have built up, the stakes have gone up with them. It is no longer a matter of the certainty of inflicting unacceptable damage on the other side: there is now the possibility that a full nuclear exchange would bring the total extermination of human life on the planet through the blasts themselves, an ensuing nuclear winter, and the longer-term radioactive contamination.

Nevertheless, the balance of terror has proved successful in providing the ultimate safeguard against a third world war for more than four decades, despite the strains put on it by events such as the Berlin blockade, the Cuban missiles crisis, the Hungarian attempt at independence, the Prague spring and the wars in Korea, Vietnam and Afghanistan. Until quite recently there seemed every prospect that it would continue to do so for years to come, although there remained the risk that *eventually* a global catastrophe would result from one or other of a number of possible circumstances such as:

- an unstable or irrational leadership coming to power in the Soviet Union or the United States;

- brinkmanship in a crisis leading to a misjudgement of the other superpower's response;

- technical faults in radar or computer systems leading to a false alarm and launching of missiles before discovery of the error;

- use of battlefield nuclear weapons to avoid defeat in a conventional war escalating to a full exchange of strategic weapons;

- use of nuclear weapons by other nuclear powers (Britain, France, India, China) entangling the superpowers and escalating to a full nuclear exchange;

- proliferation of nuclear weapons capability to additional countries (Israel? South Africa? Pakistan? Argentina? Libya? Iran? Iraq?) which might at some time have irresponsible leaders, unstable political systems and unresolved disputes with neighbouring countries.

Arms reduction and redeployment

Whereas a few years ago the continuation of the Cold War, possibly with a degree of détente, seemed the most probable course of events to be expected through to 2010, the prospects have since been radically transformed by a series of proposals by President Gorbachev and the response made to them by Presidents Reagan and Bush.

- *Strategic nuclear missiles*
  Soviet proposal for 50 per cent reduction; American acceptance in principle; negotiations in progress

- *Intermediate-range nuclear missiles*
  Soviet proposal for complete abolition; American acceptance; implementation in progress

- *Short-range nuclear missiles*
  Soviet proposal for early mutual reductions, leading to abolition; NATO deferment of plans to modernise weapons and agreement to start negotiations on reductions after agreement is reached on reduced levels of conventional forces

♦ *Chemical weapons*
Soviet proposal for complete abolition; American agreement in principle

♦ *Conventional force levels*
Soviet announcement of unilateral cuts and proposals for major reciprocal reductions; American counter-proposals for major reciprocal reductions; provisional agreement reached on reciprocal cuts to achieve parity at greatly reduced levels

♦ *Redeployment of forces*
Soviet announcement of change in strategy, away from forward deployment for pre-emptive strike into Western Europe to rearward defensive deployment further east; agreements to withdraw Soviet forces from East Germany, Poland, Hungary and Czechoslovakia

♦ *Foreign policy*
Soviet abandonment of Brezhnev doctrine of intervention in Eastern Europe and adoption of less interventionist policies in Third World, with withdrawal from Afghanistan and reduction of involvement in Ethiopia and Angola; US-Soviet cooperation in seeking solutions to problems in Southern Africa and in joint response to Iraqi invasion of Kuwait

The outcome of these developments has been a marked relaxation in international tensions and more progress in arms reduction in four years than in the previous forty. If the pace and direction of change continue, long before 2010 the Cold War will be merely a distant memory and the risk of world nuclear war will have become very remote indeed.

This prospect raises two key questions. First, is the rise of East-West détente likely to continue? And second, if it does, what implications will it have for the world in general and for Britain in particular?

Factors in disarmament

Soviet Union

There are a number of cogent reasons why the Russians are likely to press further down the road to disarmament.

♦ Soviet backwardness in technology means it cannot realistically hope to keep up with America, the world

Cold War
1985

NATO Countries

Warsaw Pact Countries

Powerful Soviet forces confront NATO face to face in Germany.
Soviet and Warsaw Pact armies outnumber and outgun
NATO in Europe.
Red Army tanks and bombers within 150 miles of Bonn, within
400 miles of Paris and within 500 miles of London.
Iron Curtain, confrontation, tensions, capability for sudden
massive attack on Western Europe.

Détente
1995

NATO Countries

Russia

Independent republics ?

Major Soviet and NATO force reductions in Europe.
Former satellites now democracies, forming neutral block separating
Soviet Union from Western Europe, with armies likely to resist, not
assist, any Soviet attack.
Red Army at least 500 miles further east, more than twice as far away from
Paris and London, more than five times as far away from Bonn.
Open borders, friendly relations, economic assistance, no possibility
for invasion of Western Europe.

leader in technology, in an arms race increasingly centred on high-tech systems such as 'stealth' aircraft, unmanned vehicles and 'smart' weapons.

• The poor performance of the Soviet economy has failed to deliver the consumer goods people want and diversion of resources (particularly scarce technical ones) from defence is needed to help revitalise the civil sector.

• The success of the perestroika reforms will be judged largely by the extent to which they bring a marked improvement in economic performance – quickly.

• The glasnost reforms mean that the government must be far more responsive than before to demands for a higher standard of living, and also for the newly articulated demands for protecting the environment.

• The many changes under way at home make it more important than before to avoid foreign entanglements and minimise defence burdens.

United States

The United States is far richer than the Soviet Union and has a much larger and more dynamic economy. Its leaders are therefore under less pressure than the Russians to undertake major reductions in defence. Even so, there are a number of reasons why, after a suspicious initial response, they are likely to react in an increasingly positive way.

• The budget and overseas payments deficits are a central problem, tax increases are unpopular, and defence is one area in which substantial spending cuts are potentially possible without undue pain to any large body of voters.

• Much of American public opinion has long held that US military deployments in Europe should be reduced and the Europeans made to shoulder a bigger share of the costs of their own defence.

• The Soviet arms cuts already made or proposed, the shift to a more defensive deployment of conventional forces, the change to less aggressive foreign policies, the abandonment of the Brezhnev doctrine in Eastern Europe, the effective ending of the Warsaw Pact alliance, the underlying weaknesses in the Soviet economy and political system, and the fundamental shift in the Soviet foreign policy stance, all combine to make the possibility of a major Soviet attack almost inconceivable – and hence the perceived *need* for the present level of US defence expenditure more questionable.

The degree of over-kill implicit in existing levels of nuclear arsenals and the improved possibilities for verification by satellite and on-site inspection make the risks of default on agreed reciprocal reductions much smaller than before.

Europe

Similarly, there are factors encouraging arms reduction in the countries of both Eastern and Western Europe.

The countries of Eastern Europe are no longer ideologically opposed to the West, they are no longer constrained to participate in a Soviet-dominated military alliance, and pressing economic and environmental problems give them strong reasons for cutting military expenditure as much as they can.

The NATO countries in Western Europe must weigh up the new situation following the 1989 revolutions: Russian tanks will soon be 500 miles further away; there will be far fewer of them; they will be separated by a band of countries sympathetic to the West; the armed forces of the former Soviet Warsaw pact allies will be largely disbanded; and the armed forces of East Germany are already absorbed in a reunified Germany. NATO has formally acknowledged that, even if there were the will, the *capability* for a Soviet invasion of Western Europe no longer exists – and all these countries have electorates which are likely to press for resources to be shifted from maintaining defence forces to meet a threat which is no longer there.

Risks of reversal

In these new circumstances, the main concern in the NATO countries is: what is the likelihood of Gorbachev being overthrown and his policies reversed? Certainly there is some possibility of a change in the top leadership, but much less likelihood of a renewal of the military threat to the West.

The Soviet economic problems are deep-seated and difficult to correct, the *perestroika* reforms have not produced quick results in the form of higher living standards, and this has been giving rise to increasing disappointment and discontent.

Glasnost has allowed expression to many previously suppressed views, and this has already led to more open and active political opposition to the government, to the disavowal of the leading role of the Communist Party, and to the growth of vigorous, at times violent, separatist movements among the minority nationalities in the Soviet Union.

These developments could lead to the fall of the present political leadership. However, if this happens, the new leaders may well be reformers wanting speedier liberalisation of the economy and radical dismemberment of the Soviet Union in its current form – and this group will neither be interested in, nor capable of, renewing the Cold War.

There now seems little likelihood of a return to power of conservative-minded people in the Party and the bureaucracy committed to a reversal of the recent changes. While their dissatisfaction is not in doubt, their chances of regaining power get weaker month by month as the influence of the Party is diminished, as old-guard officials are moved from their posts, as policy reforms are put in place and as democratic processes become more strongly established. Changes have long passed the point where it would be easy to put the lid back on again.

Why USSR cannot restart Cold War

- Soviet forces being drastically cut

- Red Army moving 500 miles further east

- Warsaw Pact effectively dissolved

- Likely breakaway of some Soviet republics

- Army likely to be needed for internal security

- First priority the raising of living standards

- Weakening of ideological basis of east-west tension

There remains the possibility of a military coup; but even if a coup were successful, the new leaders would still be subject to the same underlying factors – the economic failure and the technological backwardness – which caused the top leadership to perceive the need for radical changes and led them to give power to Gorbachev in the first place. It would also lose any chance of economic and technical assistance from Western Countries. It is therefore very likely that, even if a military government were capable of imposing discipline on radical groups and separatist republics, it would ultimately prove unable to resist the underlying pressures for reform – as happened after the imposition of martial law in Poland.

Thus there is much uncertainty about what will happen in the Soviet Union, and although the possibilities include a period of violent internal upheavals which could spill over into neighbouring countries, they do not seem likely to include circumstances in which there would be an *interest* in renewing the Cold War or in posing a military threat to the West.

Thus the prospect for the next two decades is for the avoidance of a third world war, the ending of Cold War tensions, and a large measure of superpower disarmament.

Local wars

Even though the risk of a third world war has greatly diminished, it is no more than realistic to expect that the next two decades will still see *other* wars, albeit wars which, for the most part, do not involve the use of nuclear weapons and do not involve the participation of the superpowers. For while the relaxation of Cold War tensions will reduce one cause of wars, other causes are likely to remain.

Since the last world war there have been a succession of other wars between countries – for example, India/Pakistan, Israel/Egypt, Iraq/Iran, Britain/Argentina – as well as others within countries for example, Lebanon, Chad – which were not primarily the result of superpower rivalries. Even after the end of the Cold War, there will still be a number of reasons why further local wars are very likely to happen.

Nationalism

Nationalism remains a powerful force often leading to war, and there are a number of circumstances in which it could give rise to hostilities in the coming decades.

Many Third World countries are based on colonial territories the boundaries of which in some cases split tribes and nations between different countries and in some cases enclosed a number of different tribes and nations within a single country, thus giving rise to friction when divided groups seek reunification and minority groups seek a separate identity.

Similarly in Eastern Europe a number of nationalities are seeking a greater degree of independence and in the Soviet Union itself several of the minority nationalities are seeking to have their separateness recognised in the form of greater economic and political autonomy or outright independence.

Religion

Religious differences have played a part in many recent disputes. Differences between sunni and shia muslims have been a factor in the Gulf War; differences between christians and muslims have been a factor in the troubles in Lebanon and in Cyprus; and differences between judaeists and muslims have been a factor in the quarrels between Israel and its neighbours.

Religious tensions, particularly those associated with the rise of militant Islam, may well give rise to wars in the decades ahead; and some may be difficult to bring to an end because disputes arising from religious differences tend to be less amenable than others to solution through pragmatism and compromise or the intervention of outsiders.

Dictatorships

Many countries are ruled by authoritarian regimes whose leaders enjoy little popular support and are maintained in power mainly by military force. Such countries provide an ever-present risk of war, either through uprisings of their own people or through military adventures against neighbouring countries.

Natural resources

Many wars have been undertaken with a view to securing the natural resources of neighbouring countries – most recently the invasion and plundering of Kuwait. The dangers are particularly great where, as with the oil states in the Persian Gulf, relatively weak countries have exceptionally valuable resources regarded as vital by a number of other more powerful ones.

Environmental calamities

In the coming decades we may also have to contend with the possibility of wars arising from new combinations of causes. In some Third World countries there is the possibility that population expansion will lead to overcrowding which, combined with the effects of economic difficulties, and possibly also of environmental disasters, may lead the stricken nations to try to force a move into neighbouring countries which appear to be better favoured. This could widen into more general confrontation between the poorer nations of the South and the richer nations of the North.

For these and other reasons it seems realistic to expect that in the course of the next two decades there will be further wars, particularly in regions like the Middle East where several of these factors are present in combination – dictatorial and ruthless régimes, militant religions, major unresolved territorial grievances and the presence of massive oil resources considered vital to them by many different countries.

However, the ending of the Cold War should mean that, over the period as a whole, wars will tend to be fewer and smaller than otherwise. There are unlikely to be any in Western Europe; and the risk of one of them bringing about a world war with a nuclear exchange between the superpowers will be much less serious than hitherto.

Implications

The ending of the Cold War will have considerable implications for both the form and the scale of defence programmes.

In the recent superpower disarmament negotiations, the independent deterrents of Britain and the other secondary nuclear powers were regarded as marginal and largely ignored because they are so small compared with the nuclear arsenals of the two superpowers. However, as the stockpiles of the two superpowers are steadily reduced, the disparity will narrow until the time comes when Britain's deterrent is no longer inconsequential and its retention is seen as a factor impeding further reductions by the superpowers. There is then likely to be pressure on Britain and the other nuclear powers to reduce *their* deterrents too in order to allow the superpowers to make further reductions while still preserving an adequate margin over the others; and the Soviet Union has already made it clear that Britain's nuclear capability (planned to be *increased* 16-fold with the replacement of Polaris by Trident) will need to be brought into the negotiations for the next round of strategic arms cuts.

Later on, a major consideration inhibiting the superpowers from yet further nuclear weapons reductions is likely to be the fear of proliferation to new nuclear powers, and increasing attention is therefore likely to be given to trying to prevent this happening. Since many of the prospective new nuclear powers apply to themselves the same arguments as are used by Britain to justify its possession of an independent deterrent, there is likely to be increasing pressure on Britain to give up its independent deterrent altogether in order to give more weight to measures to prevent nuclear weapons spreading to new countries and thereby jeopardising the stability of the nuclear balance.

Later still, it is probable that concern will extend to reducing the incidence and gravity of *non*-nuclear wars, with in future the superpowers normally cooperating in pursuit of a common interest in reducing tensions instead of fomenting conflicts in the pursuit of Cold War objectives. Since most of the countries most likely to precipitate local wars depend for their armaments mainly on a handful of suppliers, there may well be moves to get the supplying countries to cut off supplies. And since Britain is currently one of the world's leading exporters of arms, it is possible that there will be mounting international pressure for a drastic curtailment of these sales which at present make an important contribution to Britain's export earnings.

It should be noted that the end of the Cold War will mean not only that Britain will not be involved in a third world war, but also that for most of the next two decades it is not likely to be heavily involved in *any* war. For it will mean that there will be no war in Western Europe; and most wars in other parts of the world are unlikely directly to involve Britain. While there are still some potential trouble spots where there is a British commitment – Hong Kong, Falklands, Gibraltar, Belize – it would seem not very likely that any of them will involve Britain in a war in the course of the next two decades.

The one major exception, as events in 1990 have demonstrated, is the Middle East, where the risk of a major part of the world's oil resources being seized by a belligerent and unstable régime has resulted in large-scale intervention from outside the region. The invasion of Kuwait and the international reaction to it have shown that the prospect of major wars is not yet a thing of the past. They have also shown, however, that the ending of the Cold War implies a much less dangerous world in the next two decades than in the previous four. A crisis which even a few years before could have involved a superpower confrontation, and hence the ultimate risk of world war, has instead been met with an unprecedented degree of superpower *cooperation*, under the auspices of the United Nations, and with the military muscle provided predominantly by the United States. Britain's military contribution has been only a very small part of the forces based in Western Europe.

> ### The end of Cold War could mean for Britain
>
> - Potential 'peace dividend' of up to £20 billion
>
> - Release of R&D resources from defence to civil applications
>
> - Pressure to cut back British nuclear deterrent
>
> - Pressure to cut exports of arms
>
> - Reduction or removal of US military bases

It is not yet clear how large a defence capability may be desirable to enable Britain to make an appropriate contribution in any future crises in other parts of the world. What *is* already clear is that the size will be considerably less than was felt appropriate to meet the threat of a Soviet invasion of Western Europe.

It follows, therefore, that over the two decades to 2010 as a whole, the area where the impact of the end of the Cold War and the removal of the Soviet threat is likely to be most felt in Britain is in the opportunities provided for major reductions in the level of defence expenditure for which it is felt necessary to make provision. Since defence is one of the largest items in the government budget, accounting for more than one eighth of the total and nearly half of all government-funded R&D, it implies the release for alternative uses of very substantial resources, including technical skills which are scarce in civilian industry.

This should, during the course of the two decades to 2010, make many problems more amenable to solution. At the same time it will also create problems of its own in securing the transfer of highly specialised and localised resources to alternative uses without the disruption and unemployment which in the past have often been associated with the decline of other major industries.

While the ending of the Cold War implies considerable future savings in defence expenditure, this is an area in which it would be imprudent to count chickens until they are hatched; and the possibilities which may lie ahead are not yet reflected to any great extent in government defence policies or forward budgets. Consequently, *for the purposes of the study*, we have in later chapters assumed only modest relative cuts in defence (with spending held at present levels in real terms instead of increasing in line with economic growth). It should therefore be remembered that in reality the end of the Cold War is likely to make possible savings in defence considerably greater than those that have been allowed for, and that this in turn is likely to have important implications for what is likely to be feasible in other areas.

If, as seems quite probable, by 2010 defence spending were reduced to about half the present level in real terms, it would amount to somewhere in the region of £20 billion less than if it had continued at today's percentage of gross domestic product. This is big money by any standard: of the same order of magnitude, for example, as the *total* level of annual government expenditure today on health or on education, and far greater than total government capital expenditure of all kinds. It is also equivalent to about 15 times the current level of expenditure on overseas aid.

4. World Economy

There are two developments in the world economy that are of particular relevance to the future of Britain. One is the long-term decline in Britain's relative size and importance in the world. The other is the more recent and very important shift towards a single world economy, working in ways which cross national boundaries, increase international interdependence and reduce the extent to which national governments are able separately to act effectively in economic affairs.

Britain in the world

Over a very long period Britain's military, political and economic influence in the world has been declining.

Power

A century ago Britain was the world's strongest power, with an empire covering nearly a quarter of the planet's land area and population. Half a century ago Britain was still one of the greatest world powers. Now Britain is one of the five major powers in Western Europe but has much less influence than before on developments in the rest of the world.

Output

Two centuries ago Britain was the only industrial country. One century ago Britain was the leading industrial country. Half a century ago Britain was one of the leading industrial countries. Since the second world war Britain has remained a major industrial country, but one of steadily diminishing

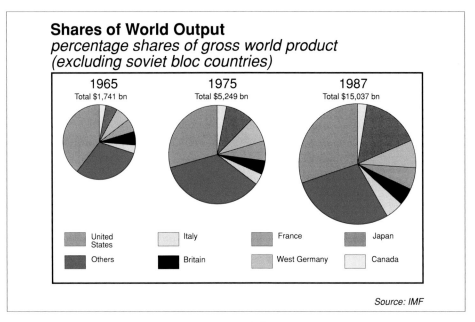

Shares of World Output
percentage shares of gross world product
(excluding soviet bloc countries)

1965	1975	1987
Total $1,741 bn	Total $5,249 bn	Total $15,037 bn

Legend: United States, Others, Italy, Britain, France, West Germany, Japan, Canada

Source: IMF

Britain was the first country in the world to industrialise – two centuries ago. Since then other countries have industrialised too, and Britain's early industrial pre-eminence has dwindled to less than 5 per cent of the world economy now.

importance in the world, with its share of the total output of the market economy countries falling from 5.8 per cent in 1965 to 4.6 per cent in 1987.[1]*

Trade

Britain was once the world's greatest trading nation. It has since been overtaken by the United States, Germany, Japan and France and its share of total world trade has fallen from about 20 per cent of the total in 1950 to about 11 per cent in 1970 and about 8 per cent in 1989.[2]

Income

A century ago Britain was the wealthiest country in the world. but by 1950 average income per head was already higher in the United States, Canada, Switzerland and Sweden; by 1970 in West Germany; by 1980 in France and Japan; and by 1990 in Italy.[3]

---

* *Figures in superscript in the text in this and subsequent chapters refer to the sources listed at the back of the report.*

Implications

It must be stressed that these changes record not an *absolute* decline, but merely a decline *relative* to other countries; they indicate not so much *failure* by Britain as *success* by other countries. Britain was the first country in the world to experience an industrial revolution and it was therefore inevitable that, as other countries followed, Britain's initial pre-eminence would not last. In the postwar years Britain's relative decline has continued, partly because the economies of other industrial countries have expanded more quickly than Britain's, and partly because an increasing share of the world's output and trade has been accounted for by Japan, whose share of world trade increased from 5.2 per cent in 1965 to 15.9 per cent in 1987,[1] and by other newly industrialised countries.

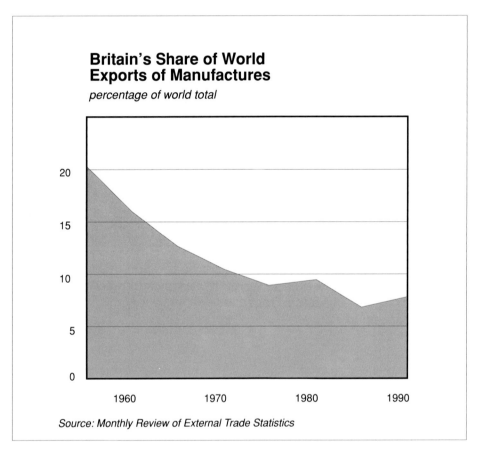

Britain's Share of World Exports of Manufactures

percentage of world total

Source: Monthly Review of External Trade Statistics

Britain's share of world trade in manufactures has fallen from 20 per cent in 1955 to 8 per cent in 1989 – but the long decline may be levelling off.

In the next two decades it is quite probable that the economies of some of the other industrial countries will continue to grow more rapidly than Britain's, and it is certain that new countries will industrialise. It is therefore realistic to expect that these long-term trends of *relative* decline will continue, although this will not be incompatible with continuing *absolute* growth of the UK economy. The significant point is that by 2010

Britain is certain to account for well under 5 per cent of the world's economy, perhaps for as little as 3 per cent, and therefore cannot expect to have such a major voice in the economic councils of the world as in earlier times when its economy had a more leading position.

The global economy

Far more important, even for Britain, than Britain's declining importance in the world economy is the way in which the world economy has been undergoing major changes which are causing it to function increasingly as a single market with not only sales, but also production, investment, research and development and financial operations increasingly managed in an international context by large companies.

Trade

Since the second world war, indeed some say since as far back as 1800,[4] world trade has grown faster than world output. For example, between 1970 and 1986 total world merchandise trade has risen by an average of 4.4 per cent a year compared with a rise in world production of 3.1 per cent a year; and exports of manufactures have risen by an average of 6.3 per cent a year compared with a rise in production of manufactures of 1.3 per cent a year.[5]

This has meant that in all the industrial countries, including Britain, imports of manufactures have been accounting for an increasing proportion of total consumption and exports for an increasing proportion of total production. For the industrial countries as a whole it is estimated that total merchandise trade rose from 12.7 per cent of aggregate output in 1960 to 30 per cent in 1984.[6]

Most services do not lend themselves to international trading as readily as goods, but with those which can be traded there has been an even faster rise in trade than with physical merchandise. Currently, world exports of services are estimated to total more than $500bn, equivalent to about one quarter of the value of exports of goods.[6]

Production

It is not only international trade in finished goods which is growing; production itself is also becoming increasingly internationalised. First, plants are sited at the locations considered most advantageous, with far less regard than before for national boundaries. Hence direct international investment has been rising rapidly. For example, in the seven years between 1979 and 1986, the stock of US direct investment in the rest of the world rose by over a third, from $188bn to $260bn, while the stock of foreign direct investment in the United States nearly quadrupled, from $55bn to $209bn.[7]

The other way production has been internationalised is in sourcing. Increasingly, components are brought in from overseas and processes are carried out in other countries. Likewise, increasing use is made of imported machinery and technologies.

Finance

Financial markets also are becoming increasingly international. The pool of savings is now a global one, with the savings of people in one country channelled though financial institutions for investment in many others, and vice versa. An indicator of the increase in financial interdependence is the rise in net international bank credit from $12bn in 1964 to $1,485bn in 1985, a compound growth rate of over 25 per cent a year, about double the growth rate of trade in goods and services (in both cases in terms of current prices without adjustment for inflation).[8]

Shares in leading companies are now traded in stock markets around the world and these are closely linked in the way they reflect, not only major economic developments, but also changes in market sentiment. This was vividly illustrated on 'Black Monday', 19 October 1987, when, within hours of each other, all the leading stock exchanges in the world recorded a similarly dramatic fall in share prices.

International financial transactions are undertaken not only by financial institutions but also, increasingly, by industrial companies operating in a world market. They switch funds frequently between currencies, partly to meet the needs of operating in different countries and partly to hedge against changes in exchange rates and to take advantage of differences in prices and interest rates. Total foreign exchange transactions currently amount to more than $200bn a day.[9] Thus in a single *week* they are equivalent to more than the value of total gross domestic product in Britain for a whole *year*.

Another aspect of greater world financial movements has been the build-up of the total of international debt from $200bn in 1975 to over $700bn in 1987.[1] Much of this represents borrowing by Third World countries, many of which have had extreme difficulty even in servicing interest payments and have little prospect of ever being able to contemplate repayment of the principal. This has given rise to serious economic, social and political problems for many less developed countries, and these have fed back to the more developed countries in the form of bad debts for lending banks and intensified regional and global environmental problems.

Factors in globalisation

The rapid movement towards a more global economy is largely explained by interrelated factors such as the removal of barriers, major developments in transport, communications and technology, changes in financial institutions, the growth of multinational companies, and changes in market characteristics.

Removal of trade barriers

Successive rounds of cuts under the auspices of GATT have led to widespread dismantling of tariff barriers to trade. The average tariff level of the industrial countries has been reduced from about 40 per cent in the mid 1930s to about 6 per cent now.[10] Within the European Community and the countries associated with it tariff barriers have been removed altogether.

The reduction of tariff barriers has often been accompanied by the erection of new obstacles to trade: for example, import quotas, subsidies for domestic producers, preferential public procurement policies, health, safety, environmental and consumer protection regulations and standards, and tax, financial and legal complications. It has been estimated that about 27 per cent of all imports of the industrial countries, and 34 per cent of their imports from developing countries, are affected by non-tariff barriers.[11] These other barriers can often have a greater effect on trade than traditional tariffs. However, the current GATT Uruguay round aims to reduce these barriers on a world scale; and the EC single market after 1992 aims to remove them altogether for trade within the European Community.

Developments in transport

Over the past three decades there has been a revolution in transport technology which has cut dramatically the cost of international movement of goods and people.

- Between 1960 and 1990 typical ocean tanker sizes have increased more than ten-fold and the real cost of oil shipment has been drastically reduced.

- Bulk carriers for grains, ores and heavy chemicals have also risen in size and brought much lower costs.

- Containerisation, with giant ocean carriers, roll-on/roll-off vehicle ferries and special trains and lorries has brought spectacular improvements in costs, speed and reliability for shipments of manufactured goods; and turn-round of ships at ports has become much quicker.

+ Larger lorries, using modern motorways, have reduced costs for journeys at either end of international shipments.

+ The replacement of steam locomotives by diesel and electric ones has improved the speed, cleanliness and reliability of rail transport and reduced costs.

+ Jets have shortened international journey times for goods and people, and larger aircraft and more economical engines have lowered costs.

Developments in communications

Improvements in instruments and switchgear and the use of cable networks and VHF and satellite links have brought great improvements in the reliability and convenience of telephone and computer links and greatly reduced the cost of using them. New services like telex and fax have been introduced and opportunities have been opened up for using a whole range of new kinds of interactive computer systems.

These improved communications links have made it far more feasible than before to integrate the operation of international production and marketing operations and to manage them from a distance. It has also provided the means for rapid, secure and economical international transfers of funds and for the provision of international links between stock exchanges and other financial institutions.

Changes in financial institutions

The removal of barriers to physical trade has been accompanied (if less widely) by the removal of obstacles to international financial dealings. Many countries have reduced or abolished foreign exchange controls and restrictions on movements of capital, thereby making it more feasible to move funds from one country to another to take advantage of market opportunities, while improvements in communications have made international transactions much easier and cheaper.

There has been a tendency in most industrial countries for savings to be increasingly institutionalised in banks, insurance companies and pension funds, and these large organisations are much better equipped than most individual investors to make effective use of the increasing opportunities for placing and switching investments on an international scale. In some countries there has been a reduction in restrictive practices and a loosening of the regulations affecting the operation of the financial institutions, which has led to rationalisations and mergers, often including international link-ups, and this has further increased the proportion of the business handled by large organisations in a position to trade internationally.

Financial deregulation, improved communications and increased use of computer systems have often been followed by greater fluctuations in exchange rates and greater volatility in stock markets, and this has given not only financial institutions but also industrial companies reasons for undertaking an increasing range and value of international financial transactions in order to hedge the risks.

Growth of multinationals

All these developments have encouraged the growth of multinational companies which are well placed to make use of the removal of barriers and the improvements in transport and communications to build up their transnational operations. Having no particular reason, other than the efficiency of their own operations, for preferring one country to another, they have shifted production, sales, R&D, investment, funds and personnel between different locations, often on a global scale, with a view to minimising costs of capital, production and taxes and maximising growth and profitability.

They have done this on a very large scale. It has been estimated that as much as half of the world's exports of non-agricultural products are probably made by multinationals, while possibly as much as a quarter of the total is actually 'internal' exchanges between different units within the same multinational group.[12] The multinationals are thus a very important feature in the growth of world trade.

Technology transfer

The findings of pure science have long been treated as an international resource, openly published for use around the world. The growth in volume and the use of different languages has made the international transfer slow and imperfect, although this is increasingly being overcome by improved information and communication services.

In recent decades the applications of science in the form of technology have also increasingly been transferred around the world and have become an aspect of international economic links of growing importance.

The effective use of new technologies in manufacturing production and design, and in the products themselves, has become a decisive factor in industrial success. However, R&D expenditures have been rising, the pace of technological change has been accelerating, product life cycles have been shortening, the rewards of being first with a winner have been mounting, and the penalties of being second best or too late have also

The world is increasingly becoming one economy

Forces behind globalisation

- Removal of many trade barriers
- Removal of restrictions on financial flows
- Revolution in transport and communications
- Growth of multinational companies
- Increase in international technology transfer
- Increase in movements of people

Forces behind further integration of global economy

- Single European Market after 1992
- European Monetary Union in late 1990s
- Uruguay round of tariff cuts
- Development of market economies in Eastern Europe, USSR and in developing countries
- Further development of global telecommunications

Features of the integrated world economy

- Global range of choice for investment locations
- Global sourcing for production
- Global markets for products and services
- Large-scale movements of employees within multinationals
- Global flows of investment funds and profits
- Global interaction of capital markets
- Global interaction of national economies

Implications for national governments

- Diminishing power to control their economies unilaterally
- Increasing need to enter international partnerships and build new supranational institutions

increased. There have therefore been mounting pressures on those with technological resources to spread the costs by getting them used more widely; on those without them to get access to them quickly; and hence on both to get together to arrange for technology transfer. And since technology is blind to nationality, international boundaries present no barrier to transfer; indeed, in negotiations for international investment projects the transfer of technology is often a matter of much greater concern than the transfer of the investment funds themselves.

International technology transfer takes several different forms. Probably the most important (accounting, for example, for an estimated 78 per cent of foreign receipts for technology by American companies in 1983) is cross-border transfers within multinationals between different companies in the group located in different countries.[13] Another is transfers between separate companies on a licence basis. A third is through joint research and development projects involving companies in different countries. And a fourth is the more informal transfer which takes place through individuals going to other countries for technical education or training. For example, there are currently nearly 200,000 foreign students studying technical subjects in universities in the United States.[6]

The scale of technology transfer has become very large. It is estimated that receipts from the export of technology by firms based in five leading countries (United States, Japan, West Germany, France and Britain) rose from less than $2bn in 1965 to around $11bn in 1983.[14] In the key fields of electronics and information technology it has been increasingly dominated by exports from two countries, the United States and Japan, so that the rest of the world has become increasingly dependent on these two sources of supply.

Cultural convergence

A further factor which also has helped accelerate the growth in international trade is underlying cultural changes which have the effect of breaking down the barriers between different national markets.

After countries reach a certain level of prosperity there seems to be a tendency for consumer demands to become similar, and the growing internationalisation of news and entertainment media tends to encourage a convergence of tastes and fashions and a break-down of prejudices against foreign goods – indeed with high income consumers the quest for novelty and variety sometimes leads to an actual preference for imported goods precisely because they are foreign and different from the familiar local product. This can increase the scope for manufacturers to achieve economies of scale by supplying a similar range of products to markets in several different countries.

A further factor tending to internationalise markets is the increasing movements of people between countries. Growing numbers of young people go to other countries for part or all of their higher education. Increasing numbers of managers and specialist staff are posted to other countries by their multinational employers. And very large numbers of people visit other countries more briefly for foreign holidays. These experiences may often lead to a new familiarity with foreign products and to a wish to continue consuming them after returning home.

Finally, the growing dominance of English as the international language has probably also played an important part in facilitating increased trade and technical transfer and the drawing together of the world economy in other ways.

Prospects to 2010

Most of the factors which have been moving the world towards a single economy over the past two decades seem likely to continue to apply over the next two decades also, and there are a number of further developments which could add to their influence.

◆   Trade barriers should be greatly reduced within Europe with the establishment of the Single Market after 1992; and more slowly in the rest of the world as a result of further GATT rounds. Political and economic changes should lead to much increased trade with the Soviet

Union and Eastern Europe and, more uncertainly, with China.

* The construction of the Channel Tunnel and other major tunnels and bridges, and the development of more high speed train links, should stimulate more trade within Western Europe; and there is also the possibility of further improvements in air and sea transport.

* Communications networks and associated computer systems are certain to improve further, lowering costs and extending the speed, range and quality of the international links used by multinational companies and, in particular, of financial institutions.

* The growth of the multinationals seems likely to continue, together with closer internal integration of their activities.

* The importance of technology in manufacturing and service sector competition is certain to increase, and with it the importance of international technology transfer.

* The adoption of market-based economic systems by the Soviet Union and the countries of Eastern Europe will lead to their fuller integration into international economic organisations such as OECD, GATT, IMF and the World Bank and to a consequential reduction in obstacles to trade.

* The reduction of economic and political barriers around the former Soviet bloc countries, and possibly later those with China also, together with increasing movements of people between countries and the increasing internationalisation of the media, should lead to further erosion of the cultural differences dividing national economies.

There are likely also to be important factors operating against international economic integration: for example, the revival of nationalist separatism and militant forms of religion in some parts of the world. The balance of probability, however, is that many of the forces which have already brought the economies of different countries much closer together over the past two decades will continue to have an important influence over the next two decades, so that by 2010, to an even greater degree than now, there will be in many ways a single world economy.

Implications

The movement towards a global economy which has already taken place, together with the further developments in prospect, imply an increasing degree of interdependence between different countries; and Britain's smaller place in the world economy implies greatly diminished scope for action in directions which diverge from those taken by other countries.

Macroeconomic effects

When imports account for a high proportion of consumption, and particularly when they account, at the margin, for a high proportion of *increases* in consumption, some of the effects of macroeconomic policy measures undertaken by a government in one country tend to spill over into the economies of its international trading partners. For example, if a government seeks to accelerate growth or reduce unemployment through expansionary fiscal or monetary policies, this tends to suck in greater volumes of imports, thereby diluting the expansionary impact on the home economy and at the same time giving an unintended boost to other economies through additional stimulus to their exports. This has the consequence that when countries follow economic policies which are more expansionary than those of their main trading partners (as did France in the early 1980s and Britain in the late 1980s) they tend to run into overseas balance of payments difficulties and pressures on the foreign exchange rate. And conversely if, in order to combat inflationary pressures, countries adopt macroeconomic policies more deflationary than those of their trading partners, they tend to experience an unintended build-up of payments surpluses and appreciation of the exchange rate.

As a result of the increasing difficulty of using macroeconomic policies to regulate any one economy alone, governments in many of the industrial countries have been giving increasing attention to finding ways for governments of different countries to coordinate their economic policies with a view to all achieving non-inflationary expansion together.

In the next two decades, the substantial further increases expected in the proportion of consumption accounted for by imports, and of output accounted for by exports, in all the industrial countries, may be expected to add further to the difficulties of succeeding with go-it-alone national macroeconomic policies, and also to the frictions and instabilities consequent on attempting to do so. Accordingly, it seems very probable that this will lead to the development of much stronger arrangements for the international coordination of macroeconomic policies.

Location effects

The effects of increasing economic globalisation are likely to extend far beyond the area of policies for overall macroeconomic regulation.

Companies will take decisions on locations of investment and R&D, on transfer of technology, on levels of production, on exploitation of markets, on movements of funds, with decreasing regard for national boundaries. In some areas, such as financial flows, the resulting changes may be very large and sudden. In others they may be more lagged: for example, changes in locations of fixed investment will normally apply only at the margin to *new* investment, and changes in production levels are only possible, in the short run, within existing capacity limits. However, the cumulative effects over a period will still be considerable.

These changes may be expected to bring the benefits associated with a free market:

- economies arising from specialisation and concentration of activity in the most competitive units;

- efficient production with lowest costs;

- effective use of new technology and other resources;

- high return on capital employed;

- location at most cost-effective sites.

These should be advantageous for the multinational companies taking the decisions. All else being equal, they should also bring advantages for the consumers using their products and services. However, all else may *not* be equal in the sense that the companies' pursuit of the most cost-effective locations puts pressures on national governments to make their countries attractive in ways which may be to the detriment of other objectives. For example:

- pressures to keep taxes low may restrict the scope for provision of public services and other activities requiring expenditure from government funds;

- pressures to keep marginal rates of income and corporation taxes as low as possible may force more dependence than otherwise on indirect taxes;

- pressures to keep labour costs low may inhibit making arrangements for ensuring good labour market and working conditions;

- pressures to minimise government interference may limit the feasibility of imposing regulations for company law, for health and safety standards, for consumer protection and for the preservation of the environment.

These kinds of consideration may often be offset in varying degrees by other considerations seen by multinational companies as offering competitive location advantages, for example: political stability; availability of a skilled and educated labour force; good financial, legal and accountancy services; strong transport and telecommunications infrastructure; common language and similar culture; and an agreeable physical and social environment.

> ## The globalisation of the economy can mean for Britain
>
> - Reduced control over interest rates, exchange rates, investment flows, production locations
>
> - Greater difficulty in preventing inflation, balancing overseas payments, securing steady economic growth
>
> - Need to join in European Community moves towards supranational economic policies

Government strategies

Even so, to the extent that the economy becomes increasingly a global one, the opportunities open to companies to switch locations will *increase*, and the ability of national governments to control them will *decrease*. Hence there will be increasing pressures on governments to modify their policies in order to make their countries the most attractive locations for the siting of activities in the competitive world economy. And just as in the world of shipping there are some countries which offer 'flags of convenience', which are attractive to ship-owners but not always to all the other parties involved, and in the financial world there are others which offer 'tax havens', so in the future there are likely to be countries which seek to under-bid rivals by offering more unregulated conditions in areas such as company law, health and safety requirements, consumer protection, labour conditions and environmental protection.

This will intensify the classical debate between the *general* benefits of free trade and the *particular* advantages of specific departures from it; between the advantages to be gained from a market-determined allocation of resources and the need for interventions in cases where the market does not provide for externalities or for macroeconomic aspects.

However, there will be an important difference. It used to be the case that, where the unfettered working of the market was considered not to provide the most satisfactory outcome for a country, it was possible to override it by intervention by the government. In a world economy, however, there is no world government to override the working of the market, and the powers of national governments to do so are becoming less and less adequate for the purpose. Faced with increasing globalisation of the economy, there are, broadly speaking, three possible ways in which national governments may respond.

Some governments may adopt a 'flag of convenience' approach, going all out to make their countries attractive locations to investing companies so as to maximise the benefits of economic growth, but at the expense of adverse consequences in other spheres and in other countries.

it from international forces, but at the expense of losing many of the economic benefits from global specialisation.

The third approach governments may adopt is to seek to do together what they cannot any more do separately: making arrangements for increased cooperation and coordination of their policies, working through existing international organisations such as GATT, the IMF, the World Bank, the ILO and the OECD; through more ad hoc inter-government links such as the group of seven financial countries and the various international research projects and conferences addressing environmental problems; and, in Western Europe, through development of the various mechanisms of the European Community.

So far, most of the major industrial countries have adopted mainly the third of these approaches. As economic globalisation continues over the course of the next two decades, it seems very likely that the first of the approaches will be thought to be unneighbourly and likely to incite counter-measures; and the second one will prove to be unpopular and ineffective; so that the main emphasis is placed on the third approach of regulating the operation of the international free market by building up machinery for concerted action by governments as a group with, in Western Europe, by far the most important role being that of the EC.

World Environment

The impact of humanity on the physical environment in pre-industrial times was mostly very local. With population growth and industrialisation, the impact has become greater and extended over whole countries. Recently it has often extended across national borders; and in the coming two decades many of the most important environmental problems will be largely international, or even global, in the extent of their effects. And because what is done in one country often affects other countries also, in some areas national environmental policies are becoming increasingly a matter of international interest, concern and even regulation as countries seek to avoid their environments being damaged through the inadequacy of policies adopted by their neighbours.

Likely environmental developments in Britain are considered in Chapter 14, and some of the possible consequences of more strongly environmentally-oriented policies are outlined in Chapter 18. However, there are four areas in which what happens in Britain will be particularly influenced by international considerations and where it is therefore appropriate to consider first the wider context. These four areas of international concern are the avoidance of nuclear hazards; the prevention of acid rain; the preservation of the ozone layer; and the checking of global warming. Of these, the last is by far the most difficult and important and is likely to be a central issue in international relations throughout the coming two decades.

Nuclear waste

Since the end of atmospheric testing of nuclear weapons, the main international concern over radiation risks has been focused on the disposal of waste products from the large number of nuclear power stations around the world and the possibility of accidents.

Waste disposal

The operation of nuclear power stations inevitably involves the generation of radioactive waste products. The greatest volume, about 60,000 cubic metres a year in Britain, is low level waste which is bulky to store but not particularly hazardous. The 6,000 cubic metres a year of intermediate level waste presents rather greater problems. It used to be dumped at sea, but concern at possible contamination of fishing grounds gave rise to international concern which led to a complete ban on sea dumping since 1983. However, there is the possibility of storing intermediate level waste until its radioactivity has fallen to levels similar to that of the low level waste.

High level waste, which could still be a significant hazard after a century or more, presents more worrying problems. Proposals have been made for storing it permanently in secure containers in deep shafts on land, or submerged on or in the seabed, but the difficulty of ensuring that the storage is secure against earthquake, corrosion, terrorism and other possible risks has led to local opposition to suggested land sites and international opposition to sea dumping, with the result that no national or international agreement has yet been reached. Costs are also a problem. High level waste has been estimated to cost in the region of £500 a litre to dispose of,[15] and it is expected that by the year 2000 there will be more than 3,000 cubic metres of it in Britain.[16]

There will also be problems in decommissioning nuclear power stations that have come to the end of their operating lives, which is expected to be very costly, and in disposing of the reactors in obsolete nuclear powered ships and submarines: plans to dump them on the seabed have aroused strong international opposition.

Accidents

In principle, a well-designed, efficiently-run nuclear power station should involve no risk of accidental discharge of radioactive products into the environment. In practice, the near-accident at Three Mile Island in the United States and the major accident at Chernobyl in the Soviet Union gave rise to concern that cumulative human error could result in disaster. The power station at Chernobyl was of a design which would not have been accepted as safe in other countries, but it demonstrated that an accident in a power station in a country with inadequate safety standards can bring damaging consequences in other countries a considerable distance away.

Environmental advantages

Nuclear power has the environmental advantage that it does not involve the generation of the gases which cause acid rain and the greenhouse effect, and thus offers the possibility of large increases in energy supply without adding to air pollution or global warming. However, this consideration has not been sufficient to prevent local opposition and high costs (due in part to designs intended to meet environmental objections) leading to the halting of nuclear power construction programmes in many countries and to plans for phasing out the capacity installed already in some countries, and there is likely to be continuing international concern over storage problems and accident risks while nuclear power plants remain in operation.

Acid rain

Emissions of sulphur dioxides and nitrogen oxides undergo changes in the atmosphere and fall as sulphuric and nitric acids in rain, mists and snow, causing damage to trees, vegetation, lakes and buildings. It has been estimated that the loss of timber to acid rain in Europe's forests may be more than 15 per cent of the potential harvest and that a reduction of at least 80 per cent in emissions of acid pollutants will be needed to deal with the problem.[17]

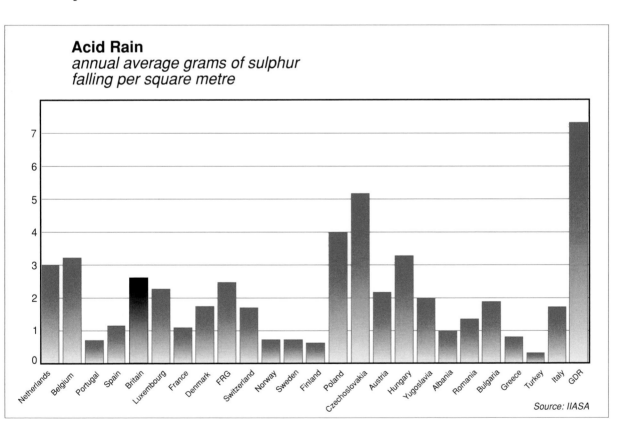

Acid Rain
annual average grams of sulphur falling per square metre

Source: IIASA

Each year acid rain falls on Britain at the rate of more than 6 tons of sulphur per square mile — much of it from our own power stations. Several countries in Central Europe get more still.

The problems are international ones in that the emissions of gases from one country commonly fall as acid rain in other countries. Consequently, there has been mounting international concern leading to a number of measures to limit emissions of gases from the two main sources, power stations and vehicles.

Power stations

The European Environment Council reached an agreement, to which Britain is committed, which provides for a phased reduction of sulphur dioxide emissions from large combustion plants (mostly power stations) of 20 per cent below the 1980 level by 1983, 40 per cent below by 1998 and 60 per cent below by 2003; and in nitrogen oxide emissions of 15 per cent below by 1993 and 30 per cent below by 1998. To meet these obligations Britain planned to spend about £2bn, much of it on retrofitting flue gas desulphurisation plant to some of the largest coal-fired power stations and low-NOx burners to all 12 major coal-fired power stations.[18] Subsequently, however, it appears that the plan has been changed and it is now intended to meet the targets more cheaply by securing part of the reductions through using imported low-sulphur coal and new gas-fired power stations.

In a wider international move in 1988, 24 countries, including the United States, the Soviet Union, Britain and most of the countries in Western and Eastern Europe, agreed by 1994 to cut their total nitrogen oxide emissions back to the level reached in 1987.

Road transport

Cars are one of the main sources of nitrogen oxide emissions and the EC has set limits for large cars which are similar to those in the United States and can be met only by the fitting of catalytic converters to vehicle exhausts. Subsequently, it has set limits for smaller cars of less than 1.4 litres engine capacity, which will apply to new cars from 1992 and all cars from 1993. They have been set at levels which, it is believed, can be met by the use of new 'lean-burn' engines. However, an OECD study has claimed that the EC measures are not the most cost-effective way to reduce nitrogen oxide emissions in Europe; several EC countries would prefer the adoption of tougher standards; and the Netherlands has announced its intention of introducing unilaterally a package of measures designed to encourage the use of smaller cars and bring about a substantial reduction of the car population.

The balance of probability would seem to be that in a few years' time the EC regulations will be further tightened and that Britain will be required to conform to them; and that, possibly a few years later still, similar controls will be imposed in Eastern Europe, where vehicle densities are currently much lower, but likely to grow in the future.

Ozone layer

The use of chlorofluorocarbons (CFCs) in aerosols (62 per cent), foams (18 per cent), solvents (12 per cent) and refrigerants (8 per cent) has led to a depletion of the protective ozone layer in the upper atmosphere, bringing increased UV solar radiation and incidence of skin cancers and possible risks to animals and plants.[18] The gases also make a major contribution to the 'greenhouse effect'.

The problem has only recently been identified, but was quickly seen to be serious and global in its effects – but also capable of solution by concerted international action without excessive costs. In 1987 a conference in Montreal, supported by most of the leading CFC-using countries, agreed a protocol providing for a 50 per cent reduction in CFCs by the year 2000. However, it was subsequently established that even a reduction of this magnitude would still result in a doubling of the level of chlorine in the upper atmosphere by the year 2000 and, because of time lags in the process, even a cut of 85 per cent would entail levels continuing to rise for several decades ahead.

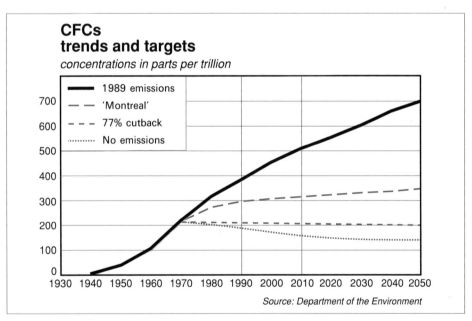

CFCs trends and targets
concentrations in parts per trillion

— 1989 emissions
— — 'Montreal'
- - - 77% cutback
········· No emissions

Source: Department of the Environment

CFC gases are destroying the ozone layer which protects the earth from dangerous ultra-violet radiation. At Montreal in 1987 agreement was reached to cut emissions by 50 per cent. Since then it has become clear that a complete ban will be needed to stop the deterioration.

In view of this, a further conference was held in 1990 at which it was agreed to cut emissions of CFCs and other ozone-depleting chemicals by 50 per cent by 1995 and by 85 per cent by 1997 and to phase them out altogether by the year 2000. Several countries have pressed for earlier targets: a group of 11 European countries plus Canada, Australia and New Zealand have agreed to phase them out by 1997.

Doubts have been expressed as to whether even the new targets are sufficiently stringent. The 'bank' of CFCs and other ozone depleting chemicals trapped in products already produced, such as refrigerators and fire extinguishers, is estimated to be the equivalent of more than four years' consumption;[19] the size of the Antarctic hole in the ozone layer has continued to grow;[20] and Joe Farman of the British Antarctic Survey, who discovered the ozone hole, has estimated that the volume of chlorine in the atmosphere will grow by a further third by the year 2000 and it will not be until about 2030 that the chlorine will drop to the 1986 level.[21] It has been agreed to hold another conference in 1992 to review the situation.

It is expected that substitutes will soon be available for most, perhaps all, CFC applications, but some of them are more costly and require the use of new technologies. Moreover, some of the substitute chemicals (HCFCs) may also contribute to a lesser extent to global warming and ozone depletion, and will themselves need to be phased out in the long term. This presents serious problems for developing countries such as India, China and Brazil which had plans, for example, for large-scale production of refrigerators using large volumes of CFCs, but which have neither the money nor the technology to use instead some of the prospective substitutes. As India's environment minister put it:

> The developed countries have created the problem, they must pay for cleaning it up.[22]

Accordingly, a fund of $160-240m has been set up to help less-developed countries adopt the substitutes, and they have made their acceptance of the targets conditional on the necessary technologies being made available for them to use.

Global warming

Global warming presents problems on a much greater scale. The past decade has seen the five hottest years of the century[23] and exceptional storms, floods, droughts and crop failures. This has stimulated concern that the planet may be warming at an unprecedented rate with potentially disastrous consequences.

The scientific evidence

In recent years increasingly many scientists have been coming to the conclusion that a build-up of gases in the atmosphere is intensifying the natural 'greenhouse effect' – allowing short-wave solar radiation to reach the earth, but preventing infra-red heat from escaping into space – and causing a long-term rise in temperatures which, if continued unchecked, will have seriously damaging effects.[24,25,26,27,28,29] Since the increase in

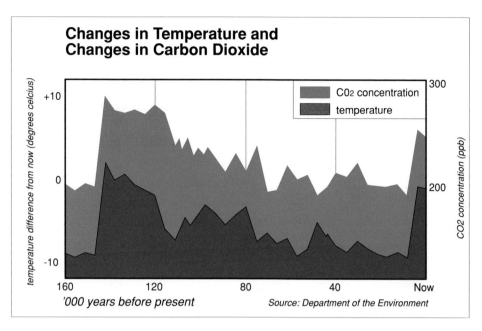

Changes in Temperature and Changes in Carbon Dioxide

'000 years before present

Source: Department of the Environment

Over thousands of years changes in carbon dioxide levels have been associated with changes in world temperatures.

these greenhouse gases – principally carbon dioxide (CO_2), methane (CH_4), chlorofluorocarbons (CFCs) and nitrous oxide (NO_x) – is largely the result of human activities, in particular the burning of increased quantities of fossil fuels due to economic growth and rising population, their conclusion has been that major changes in human activities, particularly in energy use, will be needed in order to prevent damaging climatic changes.

Other scientists, however, have argued that recent climatic experience has been within the range of past short-term fluctuations, has a precedent a century ago when there was a similar decade of hot weather, and may be due to other causes, for example the effect of sun-spots. Accordingly, they have argued that no drastic action should be taken until more conclusive evidence is available.

The conflict of expert advice, with predictions ranging from moderate inconvenience to terminal disaster, has presented government policy makers with a problem; understandably, most have been reluctant to take difficult and potentially unpopular measures to reduce greenhouse gas emissions until the need for them is demonstrated beyond doubt.

They responded, therefore, by setting up the largest and most ambitious assessment of this issue ever undertaken, with some 80 countries joining in the Intergovernmental Panel on Climate Change (IPCC), sponsored jointly by the United Nations Environment Programme and the World Meteorological Organisation. The IPCC has now produced its report,[30] and its conclusions are very clear cut:

Conclusions of the world's leading climate scientists according to the International Panel on Climate Change (IPCC)

Man-made global warming is happening and will increase

IPCC forecasts

- Loss of nearly one third of world grain production

- Rising sea level threat to homes and livelihoods of up to 300 million people

- Desertification threatens millions more people

IPCC recommends

- Immediate cut of 60 per cent or more in greenhouse gas emissions to stabilise concentrations at present levels

Action so far

- Cuts of 20-30 per cent by 2010 planned by some countries

- Stabilisation at 1990 levels planned by Britain by 2005

- No targets yet set by USA or Soviet Union

Future developments

- Steadily growing pressure:
    - to accept increasingly tough targets for cuts in gas emissions
    - to give aid to developing countries to help them cut emissions

Measures likely before 2010

- Promotion of energy economy in industry, business, homes and transport

- Increased prices for energy and use of cars

- Switch from coal to natural gas in power stations

- Development of renewable energy sources such as wind, wave and solar power

- Greater investment in public transport

We are certain emissions resulting from human activities are substantially increasing the atmospheric concentrations of the greenhouse gases: carbon dioxide, methane, chlorofluorocarbons (CFCs) and nitrous oxide. These increases will enhance the greenhouse effect, resulting on average in an additional warming of the Earth's surface.

Based on current model results, we predict under the IPCC 'business-as-usual' emissions of greenhouse gases, a rate of increase of global mean temperature during the next century of about 0.3 °C per decade (with an uncertainty range of 0.2 °C to 0.5 °C per decade), greater than that seen over the past 10,000 years; under the same scenario, we also predict an average rate of global mean sea level rise of about 6 cm per decade over the next century (with an uncertainty range of 3-10 cm per decade).

It should be noted that the report was the work of more than 200 scientists from all the world's leading research organisations in this field, and that its conclusion was unanimous and unequivocal: 'We are certain...'. Thus there is no longer serious doubt about the reality of global warming from man-made causes.

Remaining uncertainties

There remain, however, many uncertainties. As the IPCC report points out, the scale and complexity of many of the processes involved, and the limited information and understanding of their working, mean that much uncertainty remains about the size, timing and distribution of the temperature changes in prospect, and still more about their consequences for humanity and other species.

There is the possibility that the effects of the increasing volumes of greenhouse gases will be damped in various ways, for example, if plants and plankton adapt to absorb more carbon dioxide, or if bacterial action leads to reduced emissions of methane when previously waterlogged tundra dries out.[31]

On the other hand, there is also the possibility of *positive* feedback leading to *faster* rises in temperature if, for example, climate changes diminish the capacity of plants and plankton to absorb carbon dioxide,[32] or if changes in ocean currents reduce the effectiveness of deep ocean heat-sinks,[33] or if melting Arctic ice sheets bring higher sea levels and air temperatures,[34,35] or if the thawing of previously frozen tundra releases increased quantities of methane.[36]

Thus, while there is some possibility that negative feedbacks will dampen the greenhouse effect, it is notable that the majority of the feedbacks mentioned in the IPCC report are *positive* and more likely to *enhance* the greenhouse effect:[30,37]

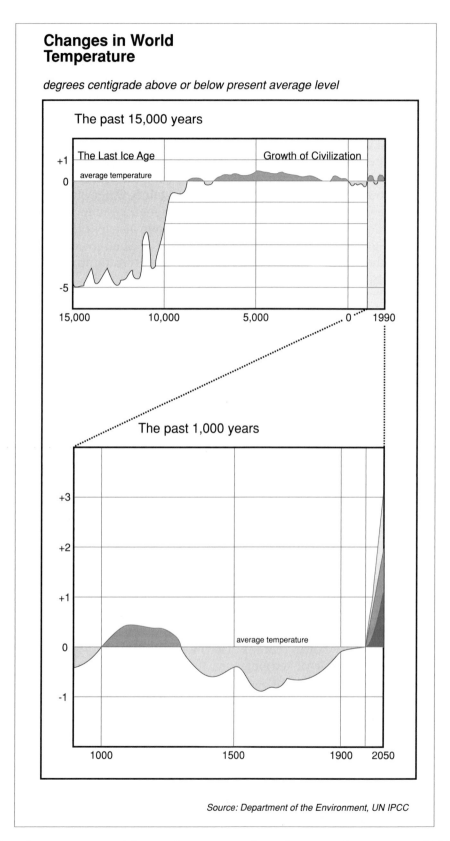

Changes in World Temperature

degrees centigrade above or below present average level

The past 15,000 years

The Last Ice Age   Growth of Civilization

average temperature

The past 1,000 years

average temperature

Source: Department of the Environment, UN IPCC

Greenhouse gases are raising world temperatures faster than at any time in the past 10,000 years. If it goes on it will bring storms, floods, droughts and loss of homes and livelihood for millions of people; by the end of the next century the world will be its hottest for 2 million years; eventually the planet will cease to be habitable.

Although many of these feedback processes are poorly understood, it seems likely that, overall, they will act to increase, rather than decrease, greenhouse gas concentrations in a warmer world... and hence that climate change would be more rapid than predicted.

More ominous still is the consideration that little is known about the forces which in past eras upset periods of relatively stable balance, suddenly 'flipping' the planet into and out of periods of rapid change. There is at present no means of knowing whether we are approaching a threshold the passing of which may trigger a 'runaway greenhouse' process leading to early catastrophe. Thus the uncertainty arising from the limitations of present knowledge means that risks, which may be great, cannot be reliably assessed and it will accordingly be prudent in these circumstances to adopt the 'precautionary principle' of seeking to avoid actions which result in serious and irreversible damage.

Predicted effects

The IPCC report[30] predicts that, if we continue on a 'business-as-usual' basis, there will be a mean global temperature increase of 0.3°C a decade (with an uncertainty range of 0.2°C to 0.5°C), giving total increases above present levels of 0.6°C (0.4°-1.0°C) by 2010, 1.5°C (1.0°-2.5°C) by 2040 and 3.0°C (2.0°-5.0°C) by 2090.

These increases are faster than in any previous period in human history and by the end of the next century will make the world hotter than at any time in the past two million years.

The IPCC report forecasts very serious effects from a 'business as usual approach', both on natural ecosystems and on human activities and welfare:[30]

Rapid changes in climate will change the composition of ecosystems; some plant and animal species will benefit while others will be unable to migrate or adapt fast enough and may become extinct.

In many cases the impacts will be felt most severely in regions already under stress, mainly the developing countries.

The most vulnerable human settlements are those especially exposed to natural hazards, e.g. tropical or coastal flooding, severe drought, landslides, severe storms and tropical cyclones.

In the course of the next 50 years warmer temperatures may bring a more Mediterranean climate to parts of Northern Europe and extend the range of cultivation in Canada and the Soviet Union, but they are also likely to make the Mediterranean countries and the grain-growing states in the United States much more arid, and to give rise to severe difficulties in already arid regions such as the Middle East and the Sahel. World grain production could fall by nearly one third, and total food output by 5-10 per cent.[38]

The IPCC report predicts a rise in world mean sea levels of 1 metre within about a century and a half and foresees this could mean:[30]

> Hundreds of thousands of square kilometres of coastal wetlands and other lowlands could be inundated, while ocean beaches could erode by as much as a few hundred metres... Flooding could threaten lives, agriculture, livestocks and structures, while saltwater would advance inland into aquifers, estuaries and soils, thus threatening water supplies and agriculture in some areas. Loss of coastal ecosystems would threaten fishery resources.

> Some nations would be particularly vulnerable to such changes. Eight to ten million people live within one metre of high tide in each of the unprotected river deltas of Bangladesh, Egypt and Vietnam. Half a million people live in coral atoll nations that lie almost entirely within three metres of sea level...Other states in the Pacific and Indian Oceans and the Caribbean could lose much of their beaches and arable lands.

Adaptation

One response to these prospects is to accept them and adapt to them. Indeed, adaptation must be a necessary part of any response since, even if the increase in greenhouse gas emissions were stopped immediately, an increase in temperatures of about 1 °C is anyway now *inevitable* due to the lagged effects of past increases in greenhouse gases.[39]

The problem is that many ecosystems cannot adapt to changes in climate faster than about 1 °C a decade (about one third of the predicted rate of increase) and adaptation of human activities would involve many problems and costs. For example, it is estimated that to protect existing developments from a 1 metre rise in sea level would require the construction of more than 200,000 miles of coastal defences at a cost of about $500bn;[30] while to abandon low-lying land would involve giving up some of the world's most productive food growing areas and moving and rehabilitating up to 300 million people.[40] In other areas desertification would destroy the livelihoods of millions more, giving rise to high economic costs and possibly also to major migration problems.

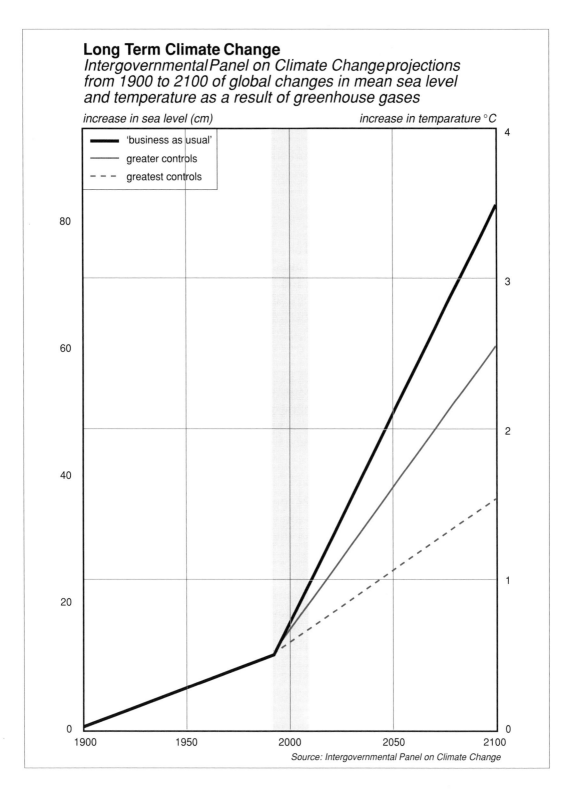

Long Term Climate Change
*Intergovernmental Panel on Climate Change projections
from 1900 to 2100 of global changes in mean sea level
and temperature as a result of greenhouse gases*

increase in sea level (cm)   *increase in temparature °C*

- **'business as usual'**
- greater controls
- - - greatest controls

Source: Intergovernmental Panel on Climate Change

*With 'business as usual' the world is likely to be 0.6˚C hotter by 2010 and 3.3˚C hotter by 2100 – with grave
consequences. To prevent this the world's leading climate scientists have unanimously recommended
cutting emissions of greenhouse gases by at least 60 per cent.*

There is a more fundamental difficulty. While adaptation may be feasible for a while, the warming process is predicted to go on *indefinitely* – until eventually the planet becomes uninhabitable.

Prevention

Accordingly, the IPCC report strongly recommends that action should be taken to check the build-up of greenhouse gases in a number of different areas.

Forestry

Deforestation accounts for about 9 per cent of human generated greenhouse gases.[30] The annual rate of tropical deforestation in the eight main countries has quadrupled since 1981-1985 and in Brazil alone the area cleared is more than 25,000 square miles, three times the area of Wales, *each year*.[41] The IPCC report urges stopping deforestation, starting new planting and harvesting existing forests on a sustainable basis.

Agriculture

Agriculture accounts for about 14 per cent of human generated greenhouse gases, mainly through methane from livestock and rice paddies and nitrous oxide from nitrogen fertilisers. The report recommends changes in agricultural practice to reduce this.

Industry

CFCs account for about 24 per cent of the total of human-generated greenhouse gases, and phasing out of their use is already planned as a result of measures to protect the ozone layer.

Energy

The burning of fossil fuels, mainly in power generation, heating, transport and industrial processes, accounts for slightly more than half of total human-generated greenhouse gases, and is disproportionately concentrated in the industrialised countries. The IPCC report points out that there is no technological 'quick-fix' option for this, and recommends that reductions should be made through fuel substitution, improvements in efficiency and conservation, changes in transport and changes in behaviour patterns.

It is mainly the proposed measures to reduce greenhouse gas emissions from the use of fossil fuels for energy that will affect Britain, and these are considered in Chapter 14 in the context of other factors affecting the future environment of Britain.

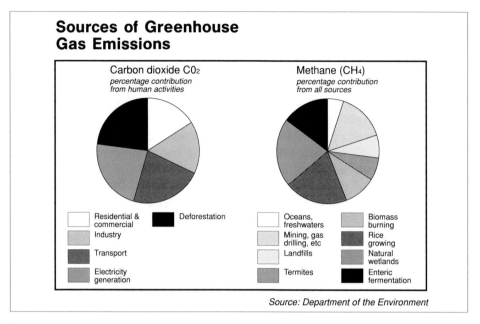

Sources of Greenhouse Gas Emissions

Carbon dioxide CO$_2$
percentage contribution from human activities

Methane (CH$_4$)
percentage contribution from all sources

Residential & commercial	Deforestation
Industry	
Transport	
Electricity generation	

Oceans, freshwaters	Biomass burning
Mining, gas drilling, etc	Rice growing
Landfills	Natural wetlands
Termites	Enteric fermentation

Source: Department of the Environment

Carbon dioxide emissions account for half of all global warming. Nearly one quarter come from deforestation in tropical countries; the remainder from burning fossil fuels for power, transport, industry and heating – mainly in the industrialised countries. Methane emissions are largely from 'natural sources'.

International targets

The extent and timing of any measures taken in Britain will be much influenced by what is done in other countries (since the problem is a global one) and, in particular, by any specific targets adopted internationally.

The IPCC scientists estimate that to stabilise concentrations of greenhouse gases at today's levels would require an immediate reduction in global emissions of over 60 per cent,[30] and similar estimates have been made by other research groups.[42,43,44] The IPCC has also prepared scenarios based on less ambitious targets for emissions reductions. While the 'precautionary principle' suggests that the safest course will be to initiate preventive measures as soon as possible, and the sooner they are begun the smaller the adjustments which will need to be made, the reality is that it is the targets actually agreed internationally which will be the main determinant of the scale and speed of measures likely to be undertaken, and no targets approaching the IPCC stabilisation one are in early prospect.

In 1988 an international conference in Toronto proposed the target of reducing global emissions of carbon dioxide to 20 per cent below 1988 levels by the year 2005, and the possible economic implications of meeting this target for Britain are illustrated in Chapter 18.

The initial responses of governments to the suggestion that internationally agreed targets are required has varied greatly. The United

States and the Soviet Union, the two countries responsible for the largest emissions of greenhouse gases, have opposed the setting of *any* international targets at this stage. Most of the less-developed countries have argued that the main reductions should come from the industrialised countries (which account for the bulk of current emissions), and that anyway they are not in a position to meet targets unless they get help in finance and technology.

Britain has proposed bringing emissions back to 1990 levels by 2005. The European Community's environment and energy ministers have agreed to stabilise emissions at 1990 levels by 2000 'in general' – with Spain, Portugal and Greece not making any commitment, Britain committed to stabilise by 2005; the Netherlands by 1995 and France planning to cut emissions to 20 per cent below current levels and Germany to 30 per cent below. Sweden, Norway, Finland, Switzerland, Canada, Australia and Japan have also announced that they will stabilise emissions by 2000.[45]

These national positions are very varied and changing, and were not reconciled at the United Nations conference on World Climate attended by 30 countries in Geneva in November 1990. The conference did agree, however, to the starting of negotiations designed to culminate with the signing of an international convention on global warming in 1992. The most likely outcome is that agreement will be reached, successively, and over a number of years, on:

♦ recognition that the greenhouse phenomenon is real, presents dangers and requires a response;

♦ acceptance of the principle that targets for reductions in emissions need to be set on a basis that is realistic, equitable and acceptable to the great majority of the countries with substantial emissions;

♦ acceptance, initially, of targets far less ambitious than most of those currently proposed (but with some countries unilaterally choosing to go beyond them);

♦ acceptance, by stages, of successively more stringent targets, the pace of progress being determined largely by the balance between perceptions of the need for tougher targets and of the difficulties experienced in implementing earlier targets.

Implications

Because problems from nuclear waste, acid rain, the destruction of the ozone layer and global warming do not stop at national frontiers, international concern, pressures and regulations are likely to assume increasing importance in the years ahead, and what is done in Britain will be greatly affected by the provisions of international agreements.

Nuclear waste, acid rain and the destruction of the ozone layer have not diminished in importance, but many internationally agreed measures for tackling them are already in place. The problem of global warming will become much more important than any of the other three, because of the seriousness of the threat it poses, but its existence has only recently been recognised, and the process of preparing international response measures has only just begun.

Global warming will be more difficult to deal with than the other three main international environmental issues because of:

- inadequate scientific understanding of the complex processes involved;

- the wide variety and economic importance of the activities that cause the emission of greenhouse gases;

- the enormous scale, and perceived costs, of the corrective measures likely to be required.

At issue also are clear conflicts between current benefits and the welfare of future generations, as well as sharp conflicts of interest between different countries and between different groups within each country.

The industrialised countries, including Britain, are likely to be particularly affected in three ways.

- As the heaviest users of the fossil fuels which generate many of the greenhouse gases, they will have the largest absolute adjustments to make in order to achieve any particular percentage reduction.

- Because developing countries are contributing much lower levels of emissions, they will not expect to make reductions in emissions as large as those of the heavier polluters; and because they will want in the future to be able to develop to nearer the economic levels of the industrialised countries, they will expect to be allowed some *increases* in emissions in the future. For both these reasons the industrialised countries are likely to be expected to make reductions *greater* than any overall global percentages that may be agreed.

Global warming: policies in Britain

Measures likely by 2010 include

- Promotion of energy efficiency in all sectors of economy

- Higher prices for energy and private transport

- Increased investment in public transport systems

- Switch from coal to natural gas in power stations

- Increased development and use of renewable energy

◆ Because many of the less-developed countries will not feel able or willing to undertake the investment needed for changing to new methods, or to give up low-cost existing methods, or to forego the use of indigenous fossil fuel or forest resources, they are likely to provide the cooperation required of them only if they get financial and technological help from the more developed countries. This is likely, in one way or another, to involve substantial transfers of technology and investment capital from the richer countries to the poorer ones.

While international agreement will be essential, the scale of the problem and the conflicts of interest will make agreement particularly difficult to reach. There will also be the need to devise suitable policy instruments and institutional arrangements for implementing them. Fortunately, the need for agreement is not immediate: there is concern about tripping unknown thresholds but, essentially, it is a problem not of weeks or months, but of decades and centuries. This combination of high stakes, conflicting interests and lack of immediate urgency means that international bargaining will be long, difficult and important – most probably the central issue of international negotiations throughout the two decades to 2010.

The WORLD in 2010

Regional Developments

REGIONAL DEVELOPMENTS

In addition to the developments that are essentially global in their operation, we also consider briefly some of the main developments expected in particular regions of the world and their possible implications for Britain. In the next six sections we consider the following regions.

United States The world's largest economy and a major trading partner of Britain.

Japan The fastest growing of the major economies and a world leader in many areas of automation and electronics.

Third World A diverse group of developing countries which includes the great majority of humanity and has many of the most serious problems.

China The country with the largest population and potentially the largest economy eventually, but with many uncertainties about the directions that will be followed in the next two decades.

Soviet Union and Eastern Europe A region undergoing fundamental changes with uncertain outcomes.

Western Europe The region that Britain is part of and which is developing closer economic and political links between states.

6. United States

The United States is the world's strongest military power and the largest national economy. Future developments there are consequently of great importance to the rest of the world, not least to Britain which regards itself as having a 'special relationship' with the United States based on ties of history, language, culture, trade and defence.

Military position

Since the end of the Second World War the United States has been the world's strongest military power, with a superiority based on its lead in nuclear weaponry and the strength of its economy and technology.

There is little reason to doubt that this superiority will continue over the next two decades. It will be enhanced, first, by the US lead in microelectronics and defence software, the keys to the 'smart' weapons systems likely to be of increasing importance in the future; and, second, by the ending of the Warsaw Pact as an effective military alliance as a result of political changes in Eastern Europe and the Soviet Union itself (considered in Chapter 10).

The US military dominance, however, is likely to be in the context of a much lower level of armaments in the two world military alliances as a result of the ending of the Cold War (see Chapter 3).

In 1988 US defence spending was running at the rate of $281bn a year – about three times the level in each of France, West Germany and Britain – and representing 6.8 per cent of American gross domestic product, compared with 5.1 per cent on defence spending in Britain, 3.9 per cent in France, 3.1 per cent in West Germany and 1.0 per cent in Japan.[46] These differentials are likely to be narrowed, partly by the lower general level of defence expenditure and partly by the probability of a partial, and possibility of a complete, withdrawal of the American military presence in Europe by 2010, leaving the European countries to carry more of the burden of their own defence.

Political and social developments

With a democratic tradition stretching back over more than two centuries, the United States has a history of political stability matched by few other countries, and this is not likely to come to an end. There are, however, a number of areas where social changes may give rise to increasing political problems in the course of the next two decades.

- *Drugs*
  The extent of drugs abuse appears to be greater than in most other industrial countries and a matter of growing domestic concern.

- *Violence*
  The incidence of violent urban crime is one of the highest in the industrial countries, and still rising.

- *Population change*
  Demographic change is leading to an increasing proportion of people aged over 65, with high pension expectations, and aged over 85, with needs for intensive medical and social care, and there is increasingly vigorous political activity to give expression to their interests.

- *Changes in the family*
  More marriages are ending in divorce and divorces are happening earlier in marriage: over half of first marriages of women aged between 35 and 39 are projected to end in divorce; one quarter of women at present in their mid-thirties were already divorced by the age of 29.[47] In 1984 21 per cent of all births were to unmarried women. About one child in six is living in a single-parent family.[47]

- *Social division*
  A proportion of the population, unemployed or in unskilled, casual, low-paid jobs has failed to share in rising national prosperity.

- *Ethnic tensions*
  The black and Hispanic minorities already comprise more than one tenth of the population and are expected to comprise more than one fifth of it by 2010.[47] They are concentrated in particular areas: they already account for the majority of the population in major cities like New York and Chicago and by 2010 are expected to do so in major states such as Texas and California. The ethnic

minority populations have a disproportionate share of single-parent families and of the unemployed and of those with low educational attainments and low incomes.

These problems are serious and interrelated and could have explosive consequences in major cities with high concentrations of ethnic minorities and poor and unemployed people. However, the great wealth of the American economy and the underlying cohesiveness of American society should provide the means for dealing with them. Thus the balance of probability is that, despite a number of difficult problems, the basic social and political stability of America will be maintained over the next two decades.

Economic performance

Given the likelihood of continuing military and political stability, the aspect of future US developments of greatest interest to the rest of the world is likely to be the economy.

Since the end of the Second World War the US economy has occupied a position of central importance in the world. It has been of particular importance for Britain, both for trade and for investment. The United States has been Britain's largest single trading partner, accounting for about 10 per cent of Britain's imports through most of the past three decades and for a share of Britain's exports rising from 9 per cent in 1958 to 14 per cent in 1987.[48] US investment in Britain has been substantial over a long period and now stands at more than $44bn, more than in any other country except Canada. More recently, there has been an even larger flow of UK direct investment into the United States. This now totals more than $80bn. In the past few years more than two-thirds of all UK direct foreign investment has gone to the United States, where Britain is the largest source of foreign direct investment.

However, despite the continuing strength and importance of the American economy, in recent years some domestic observers have detected in the United States symptoms of a 'mature', 'tired', 'declining' economy similar to those already observed in Britain.

- ◆ *Output*
  The US share of world output (gross domestic product of the market economies) has fallen from 39 per cent in 1965 to 30 per cent in 1987.[1]

- ◆ *Trade*
  In 1960 the United States was the world's largest exporter. Since then it has been overtaken by West Germany and Japan and its share of world exports has

shrunk from 19 per cent in 1970 to 15 per cent in 1988.[1] Imports have increased from 3 per cent of gross domestic product in 1960 to 8 per cent in 1986.

+ *Overseas payments*
The deficit on the overseas balance of payments has risen to nearly $140bn a year, much the highest in the West and equivalent to about 2.5 per cent of gross domestic product.[49]

+ *Overseas debt*
US overseas debt has risen to an expected $600bn at the end of 1990, equivalent to about 11 per cent of gross domestic product; the world's leading creditor has in the course of a few years become the world's leading debtor.[49]

+ *Budget deficit*
The federal government budget deficit has risen to the equivalent of 3 per cent of gross domestic product in 1989.[49]

+ *Inflation*
Throughout the 1980s, and most markedly since 1987, price inflation has been higher in the United States than in West Germany and Japan, its two leading competitors.

+ *Industry*
Industry, which used to keep competitive through high investment and its lead in technology, has increasingly been moving south, or off-shore, to compete through lower labour costs.

+ *Employment*
Employment growth has been partly in professional occupations, but also in low-tech or no-tech activities using unskilled, female, casual or part-time labour.[50]

+ *Technology*
The world lead in technology has become less secure. In the key sector of microelectronics and information technology Japan has in some areas caught up with the United States and in some areas has taken the lead.

+ *Saving*
Private saving has declined from an average of 9.7 per cent of gross domestic product a year in the period 1971-1980 to 7.7 per cent a year in 1981-1988, while

government dissaving has increased from 2 per cent to 4.5 per cent over the same period, with the result that total net saving has declined from an average of 7.7 per cent to 3.2 per cent.[3]

♦ *Investment*
Net domestic investment has declined by less – from an average of 7.5 per cent a year in 1971-1980 to 5.2 per cent in 1981-1988 – but this has only been possible because net foreign investment has increased from 0.3 per cent in 1971-1980 to 2.1 per cent in 1981-1988 (2.9 per cent in the last three of these years).[3]

♦ *Incomes*
Incomes have been rising more slowly than in other industrial countries, with the result that international gaps in income levels have been narrowed. Between 1960 and 1987 average income per head (on the purchasing power parity basis of calculation) in Japan rose from 29 per cent to 72 per cent of the American level; in Germany from 61 per cent to 73 per cent; in France from 53 per cent to 70 per cent; and in Canada from 73 per cent to 95 per cent.[3]

These developments have led to some modifications in economic policy: concern about the 'twin deficits'; more inclination to erect protective barriers against 'unfair' foreign competition – the Reagan administration increased the share of American imports subject to official restraints from 12 per cent to 23 per cent; moves to provide subsidies to support key industries important for defence; and reduced willingness to spend on such a large scale as before on international institutions and aid programmes. However, they have not so far led to a serious undermining of self-confidence or to a major reorientation of economic policies.

The limited extent of concern is probably because these indicators, like similar ones in Britain, are signs of *relative* decline. Although some other countries, most notably Japan and West Germany, have been growing more rapidly, the United States economy also has been growing in *absolute* terms – by average rates of about 3.8 per cent a year in the 1950s and 1960s, 2.8 per cent in the 1970s and about 2.3 per cent in the 1980s. The average rate of growth has been slower than it used to be but, even so, cumulatively over the past two decades it has produced an increase in gross domestic product of two-thirds. The general improvement in incomes and living standards has therefore been substantial.

Economic prospects

Much of the debate on economic policy in the United States in recent years has been focused on the problem of the 'twin deficits' and the efforts to find relatively painless ways to eliminate them. Certainly they present a number of difficulties, particularly in the short term, but there are three main reasons for expecting that in the longer term they will not be a major impediment to continued economic growth, let alone lead to an economic collapse.

First, they are *popular*. People do not like either higher taxes or cuts in spending on public services and appear happy to go on consuming more than they produce.

Second, they are *sustainable*. While overspending now must be to some extent at the expense of the future, America is so large and rich that it can go on for many years before any day of reckoning is reached. Its continuance depends on the size of the reserves, which are large, and on the willingness of the rest of the world to invest part of its surplus savings in the United States – a willingness which seems likely to continue to be forthcoming because investment opportunities in the United States are so plentiful and offer higher returns and lower risks than most of the alternatives available.

And, third, the deficits seem likely to *diminish* in due course without the need for distressingly painful measures. A weaker dollar is likely to reduce the overseas deficit by restoring the competitiveness of American industry, many parts of which are basically efficient but unable to compete internationally at a high dollar exchange rate. And the major cuts which are likely in defence spending should over a period provide a relatively painless way of reducing the federal budget deficit. (Total defence spending is at present more than twice the size of the budget deficit.)

In the longer term, the ageing population structure and the various social problems may bring a requirement for higher government expenditure on education, health and other government social programmes, and these may require higher levels of taxation, but need not necessitate a slower rate of economic growth.

There are, however, two internal factors which may be expected to constrain the rate of economic growth over the next two decades. One is the decline in the growth of the labour force as a result of demographic changes. The other is the slower rate of capital accumulation in the 1980s which is expected to constrain the growth in productivity in the 1990s.

Despite these constraints, the probability is that the economy will continue to grow, at slower rates than in some previous periods and in some younger and more dynamic economies, but nonetheless at rates which are far from insignificant – maybe at an average of between 2.5 and 3 per cent a year in the 1990s and about 2.5 per cent a year between 2000 and 2010. Growth at these rates should produce a total increase over the next two decades of about two-thirds.

Implications

The United States is likely to continue to be the world's strongest military power, providing ultimate security for its allies, but in a world with a much lower level of armaments and a substantial degree of disengagement between the two superpowers.

Internal social problems are likely to produce difficulties, but not sufficient to upset the underlying political stability.

Economic growth over the next two decades is unlikely to be completely smooth, but there is little risk of economic collapse. There may, however, be serious problems of deflation and readjustment during the period in which the massive defence industry is scaled down and resources transferred to other areas.

By 2010 the United States economy may be about two-thirds larger than now, presenting problems for the world environment and depletion of resources.

While the United States will still be by far the largest national economy in the world, faster economic growth in a number of other countries will mean that its share of the world economy will be less great and its influence in world economic councils will be less dominant.

Reduced competitiveness and possible overseas payments difficulties resulting from it may bring some return to more protectionist trade policies and more reluctance to pay the lion's share of the costs of international institutions and programmes.

The United States will remain an important trade partner for Britain, but will probably become less important to Britain economically than West Germany and France.

With the shift of population, prosperity and political influence from the East Coast to the West and South, and the growth of the Hispanic population, it is likely that the main focus of American foreign policy will be less towards the Atlantic and more towards Japan, the Pacific and Latin America; and, in Europe, interest is likely to concentrate more on Germany and France, perceived as more positive and central forces in the changes taking shape there. In these circumstances, the 'special relationship' with Britain may be expected to continue to diminish in importance.

7. **J**apan

Japan, like Germany, lost the war but has been winning the economic battles subsequently and this has made its economic performance and prospects a matter of particular interest to other industrial countries competing with Japan in world markets.

Economic performance

Japan's industry was largely destroyed in the war, but in the postwar period Japan's economy has grown markedly faster than those of the other main industrial countries. Between 1965 and 1975 Japan's gross domestic product became greater than that of Britain, and by 1987 it was nearly as great as the economies of Britain, France and Germany combined and about half the size of that of the United States. Its share of the total world economy (excluding the COMECON states) trebled from 5 per cent in 1965 to 16 per cent in 1987.[1]

Much of the rise in output has gone into exports, which have also risen much faster than in the other main trading countries. Since the early 1970s Japan's exports of manufactures have been much higher than those of Britain and France; since the early 1980s they have been substantially higher than those of the United States; and in the late 1980s Japan has been rivalling West Germany as the world's greatest exporter. Japan's share of world exports of manufactures has risen from 12 per cent of the total in 1970 to 18 per cent in 1988.[1]

At the same time, unlike in almost all the other main trading countries, Japan's imports have remained low (equivalent to about 5 per cent of gross domestic product) with the result that in recent years Japan has been building up overseas payments surpluses greater than in any of the other OECD countries.[51]

Japan has become one of the world leaders in some industries, such as vehicles and electronics, and this has been based largely on effective use of new technologies. In some areas of microelectronics Japan has overtaken the United States and in a number of other new technologies Japan is also challenging the previous US dominance.

In recent years the rate of growth has been less rapid than before (an average of about 5 per cent a year in the six years 1983 to 1989) but still far faster than in most other industrial countries.[51] It can be calculated that, if the differential rates of growth of the past two decades were to continue in the next two, by 2010 Japan's economy would be larger than that of the United States or that of the combined total of the present 12 members of the European Community; Japan would account for more than one quarter of total world exports of manufactures; and it would have a commanding lead in many key new technologies. But how likely is it that this will actually happen?

Factors in economic performance

In 1945 Japan was faced with a number of major disadvantages: the aftermath of defeat in war; shortage of land; poverty of energy supplies and mineral resources; remoteness from main existing world markets; a reputation for poor quality products; a culture which made little use of the female half of the population; and a language little used in other countries with an orthography which is unsuited to use on keyboards and takes several years of school to learn. Despite these disadvantages, success has been achieved in a number of key industries, largely as a result of the following factors.

- *National strategic planning*
  The sectors offering the best opportunities for Japan were identified and resources channelled into them.

- *Long-term investment*
  High levels of investment were undertaken with a view to achieving long-term improvements in competitiveness and growth in market share. This was made possible by access to cheap capital on a secure long-term basis, without threat of take-overs or market pressure to maintain dividend levels in the short term.

- *Technology*
  Heavy investment was made in R&D and automation to establish a technological lead and use it to improve product performance and production efficiency.

- *Management*
  High standards of managerial competence and technical qualifications were set in order to ensure efficient engineering and workplace organisation.

♦ *Education and training*
High educational standards (90 per cent stay at school to 18, 40 per cent go on to higher education) and systematic in-company training and retraining ensured a well-qualified industrial workforce.

♦ *Worker attitudes*
A well-motivated workforce, loyal, flexible and actively cooperating to improve quality and raise productivity, was ensured by life-long job security, non-hierarchic management and participation of workers in the fruits of higher productivity.

♦ *Subcontractors*
Long-term links were built up with subcontractors to ensure consistent quality standards and reliable deliveries to make possible reduced inventory levels.

♦ *Consensus*
Industrial relations and commercial links were based on consensus, cooperation and a team approach designed to give long-term results, as opposed to relying on competition between individuals in a company or between suppliers from outside it to give the most immediately cost-effective outcome. (At the same time competition between groups for shares of final markets has been fierce.)

These factors have applied mainly in the large industrial combines, less in smaller companies; mainly in a few key industries, less in other manufacturing industries or in the service sector. But where they have applied, it has been to good effect, giving Japan a leading world presence in a number of important sectors.

Economic prospects

Most of the factors which have brought Japan success in the past are likely to continue to work in its favour in the future (at least to the extent that competitors do not copy them). However, there are a number of new factors which may make it difficult to keep up such exceptional performance in the future.

♦ *Cost levels*
The exchange rate, previously low, has become much higher, making Japanese production costs high in international terms – at recent exchange rates Japanese

industrial workers are some of the most expensive in the world. Japanese manufacturers have reacted, so far with success, in two ways. First, they have introduced yet more automation and further improvement in methods in order to bring costs down. And second, they have invested in neighbouring countries, using their cheaper labour to provide lower cost sources of components or sites for assembly.

- *Import restrictions abroad*
  Some of Japan's trading partners have responded to Japan's export success by imposing bans, quotas and other barriers to keep out what they claim to be 'unfair' competition. These restrictions have to some extent been circumvented by setting up Japanese subsidiaries to manufacture behind the barriers inside the United States and the European Community.

- *Import restrictions in Japan*
  Increasing international pressure has finally resulted in the removal of some of the barriers to imports of foreign manufactured goods into Japan, and this may be expected to lead to some increase in imports, although important cultural and institutional obstacles will remain.

- *Competition from newly industrialised countries (NICs)*
  Some neighbouring countries, such as South Korea and Taiwan, are offering increasing competition by using methods similar to those used by Japan – but starting from a much lower level of labour costs. Japanese companies are responding partly by moving up-market into areas where their advanced technology and design skills give them an advantage, and partly by themselves investing in the NICs in order to get the benefit of their lower labour costs.

- *Innovation frontiers*
  Much of the progress in the past has taken the form of catching up with the world leaders, principally the United States. Now that in increasingly many areas Japan itself has become the world leader, further gains depend on pioneering innovations from out in front. The Japanese used to think that they were strong on copying others and applying their innovations efficiently, but weaker on original, creative ideas. Efforts are now being made to build up Japan's strength in basic scientific

research. It remains to be seen how far this will be successful.

- *Breadth of economic base*
  Japanese economic growth, particularly in exports, has been based largely on a limited range of industries, in many of which Japan already has a significant share of the world market. As the scope for further expansion in these markets becomes exhausted, possibilities for further growth will depend on moving into other sectors in which Japan has fewer advantages and in which up to now it has not been so successful.

- *Cultural changes*
  There have recently been a number of developments that may be signs of major cultural changes which will have an impact on the economy. Political opposition to the government party has become stronger and more successful; the press has become more critical of government and business and more active in raising questions hitherto left undiscussed; women are beginning to play a bigger part in education and the civil service and also, more surprisingly, in industry and politics; high-income consumers are becoming more interested in products imported from abroad; people are beginning to attach a higher priority to better housing, better public services and better environmental standards. In short, in many ways, attitudes and behaviour are becoming more similar to those in the other advanced industrial countries.

- *Demographic structure*
  In the long term, probably the most important single consideration is the changing demographic structure. After the war fertility rates fell sharply in Japan, dropping below replacement levels in the early 1950s, two decades earlier than in the United States and most of the other industrial countries. The result is a population which is unlikely to grow significantly over the next two decades; and which has a structure that is ageing more than in most of the other industrial countries. The percentage of the population aged over 65 is expected to rise from 11 per cent in 1990 to 17 per cent in 2010 and there will also be increases in the proportions over 75 and over 85.[52] Thus there will be more old people expecting pensions and more very old people needing care services and fewer young people in the labour force to support

them, a combination which does not help economic growth.

The implication of these changes seems to be that Japan is likely to become stronger still in the areas in which it is already powerful; and that the economy will continue to grow, although probably not as quickly as in the past two decades. More investment will go into housing, environmental measures and improvements in public services, and more of it will flow away into other countries; and more of the current spending will be on health care and pensions – and on imports.

Thus while continued growth of the economy is very probable, it is likely increasingly to take forms that are not reflected in physical exports and which therefore do not have so much direct impact on the rest of the world. In many areas Japan will be the most important competitor in world markets, but will not necessarily go on to dominate them. Economic growth rates in Japan will probably continue to be faster than in the older industrial countries, but not by sufficient margins to make Japan's economy as big as those of the United States or the European Community.

Japanese economic bloc

There remains the possibility that, even if Japan on its own does not grow large enough to equal the other two economic blocs, in the future it may join with newly industrialising countries in the region so that together they form an economic bloc which is similar in size but considerably more dynamic than the existing two in Europe and North America.

Certainly, Japan's trade and investment links with neighbouring countries have been expanding (although the main orientation is towards North America and Europe). But there is as yet little sign of this leading on to a more formal structure such as the European Community. Differences in culture and institutions are greater than between members of the European Community. The countries are not contiguous and the distances between them are greater: Singapore is as far from Tokyo as London is from New York. There is also a problem of balance. In the European Community there are five major countries and seven smaller ones, so that no one country has a potentially dominant position; even Germany after reunification accounts for less than one quarter of the total population of the present European Community, and for less than 30 per cent of its total gross domestic product.

Japan, however, is much bigger and stronger than its most likely partners, South Korea, Taiwan, Hong Kong and Singapore. Its population is nearly double that of the four others combined and its economy is more than six times as large. Any economic bloc made up of these alone would inevitably be dominated by Japan to a degree most unlikely to be acceptable to the others.

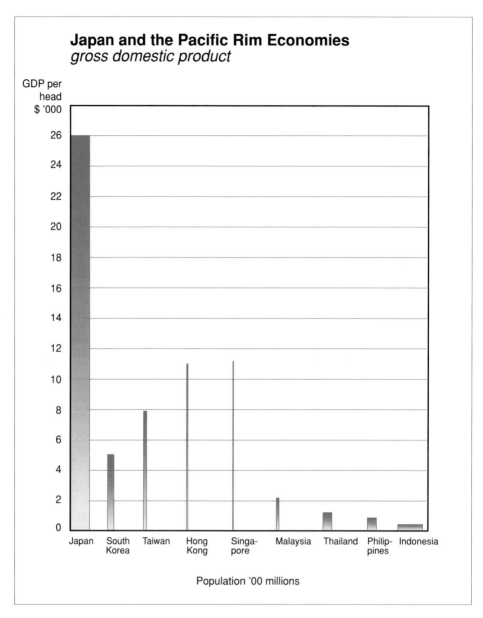

Japan and the Pacific Rim Economies
gross domestic product

South Korea, Taiwan, Hong Kong and Singapore have been doing well, but they are not as rich as Japan and their combined population is less than half that of Japan. Other countries in the region have larger populations, but less prosperous economies. Japan's economy is four times as large as those of the other eight countries combined.

There are other countries in the region that might make possible additional partners – Philippines, Thailand, Malaysia, even Indonesia – but they have not yet shown the dynamism of the other four, their economies are less developed and less internationally competitive and, even with their addition, Japan's economy would still be four times as large as those of the other eight combined. It is highly improbable that such an unbalanced union would be attractive to the other potential partners. Moreover, even if it were attempted, it would take considerable time to build up working structures comparable in effectiveness with those which have taken more than three decades to build in Europe.

Accordingly, it seems likely that by 2010 Japan will have developed much more extensive bilateral economic links with some of the other countries in the region, but that these will stop short of the formal structures needed to form an 'economic bloc' comparable with the European Community.

8. **T** *hird World*

At present about 4 billion people live in the countries of the Third World.[53] They comprise more then three-quarters of the world's total population and most of them are very poor – average income per head (measured in terms of GDP) in the less-developed countries is less than one fifteenth of that in the more developed countries.[52] For many of them the recent past has seen a decline in already poor living standards and prospects for the future are much less favourable than for the more developed countries.

Differences between countries

The Third World is spread over three continents – Latin America, Africa and much of Asia – and includes countries which vary greatly in size and in economic and social development. There are very considerable differences between them, both in their experiences in the past and in their prospects for the future. All want faster economic development, and capital investment and foreign exchange with which to achieve it but, depending on their circumstances, they have chosen a number of different routes in trying to get them.

Oil exporters

The countries with large oil exports have become very much richer since the OPEC oil price rises in the 1970s and, for those of them with small populations, the main problem has been how to spend the money fairly or invest it wisely.

Exporters of other primary products

Some countries, particularly in Africa, have had to rely mainly on the export of minerals to earn the foreign exchange and accumulate the capital needed for their economic development. In common with the oil exporting countries, they have the disadvantage that in the course of exporting they are depleting their primary resource; but unlike the oil countries, they have had the problem that for much of the past two decades world mineral prices have mostly been low and their earnings have in consequence been depressed.

Other developing countries have relied primarily on exports of agricultural products; and they too have been hit by low world prices and also by systems designed to protect domestic producers in the two largest markets, the United States and the European Community.

Exporters of manufactures

Some of the less-developed countries, lacking major natural resources or large home markets, have sought to develop their economies by building up manufacturing industries designed to make products for sale in world markets. Some, in East Asia, have done so with notable success.

South Korea has followed a path similar to that of Japan and has now become a significant competitor to it in a number of areas. Between 1964 and 1983 its gross domestic product rose at an average of more than 8 per cent a year – a rate faster even than Japan's and more than twice as fast as the United States or the main industrial countries of Europe.[54] With a population of 44 million, three-quarters of Britain's, its gross domestic product has risen to nearly one quarter of Britain's.

Taiwan also has achieved very rapid growth, averaging nearly 9 per cent a year between 1964 and 1983.[54] With a population of only 20 million, its total gross domestic product is much smaller than South Korea's, but average income per head has risen to nearly half that in Britain.

Hong Kong grew between 1964 and 1983 at an even faster rate (over 9 per cent a year) and *Singapore* faster still (11 per cent a year) and both have an average income per head of more than two-thirds Britain's.[54]

In the most recent years the rate of growth in these four countries has been not quite so rapid, but in most years they have continued to grow at a faster rate than Japan and at a much faster rate than the United States or the countries of Western Europe. In most ways these countries now have more in common with the industrial countries than with the less developed countries from which they have been emerging.

Other countries in South East Asia – *Philippines, Thailand, Malaysia* – have been seeking to follow a similar course, building up new industries based on export markets. In the past two or three years they have achieved high rates of growth but, with their differences in culture and temperament, it is still very uncertain whether they will succeed in sustaining high rates of growth over long periods like the other four countries.

Other newly industrialising countries

There are other industrialising countries, such as *Brazil* and *Mexico*, which are following a somewhat different path of development. They too have built up a substantial industrial base but, at least until recently, aimed not so much at exporting to world markets as at import substitution in their home markets. They are large countries, with substantial natural resources, including petroleum, and with large populations (150 and 89 million) providing large home markets potentially capable of supporting a wide range of manufacturing industries.

Their growth rates have been less spectacular, averaging respectively 6.5 per cent and 5.7 per cent a year between 1964 and 1983,[54] and their average income levels are still much lower than in the Pacific rim countries, but they have the potential to become significant world economies in the course of the next two decades.

Other Third World countries

Other Third World countries differ greatly. Some, such as *China* (considered separately in Chapter 9), *India, Pakistan, Indonesia* and *Nigeria*, have large populations and some industry; others are much smaller, with little or no industry. Many have few resources around which to build up their economies other than the labour of their people. It is in some of these countries that poverty is the most acute and development the most difficult to achieve.

Obstacles to development

Each Third World country has had a different experience, but in the past two decades there have been a number of features, several of them interrelated, which have presented obstacles to development in many of them:

* rapid population growth;

* soil deterioration due to overgrazing, drought or climate change;

* depletion of indigenous mineral and forest resources, often with little local value added;

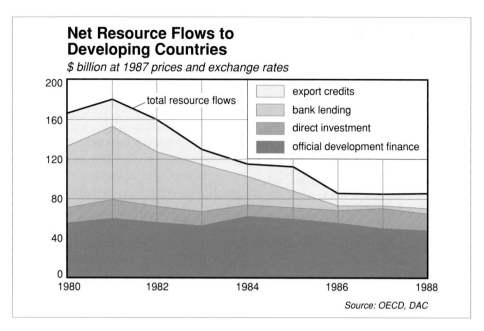

Net Resource Flows to Developing Countries

$ billion at 1987 prices and exchange rates

Legend: export credits, bank lending, direct investment, official development finance — total resource flows

Source: OECD, DAC

Since 1981 western bank lending to developing countries has virtually dried up and export credits have fallen, but official development aid has not been increased, so resource flows are now half what they were.

- ◆ weaknesses in local physical infrastructure and industrial support services;

- ◆ limited skills availability due to inadequacies in local education and training facilities;

- ◆ increasing automation in the industrial countries adopted as an alternative to imports of manufactured goods made with low-cost labour;

- ◆ protective barriers in North America and Western Europe restricting the volume of exports of primary products and manufactures to them;

- ◆ low world prices for primary products (except oil) leading to worse terms of trade and greater difficulty in paying for imports;

- ◆ difficulties in accumulating savings locally to provide capital for investment;

- ◆ build-up of debts from capital raised abroad, together with high interest rates, pushing up debt-servicing costs to more than $130bn a year[55] – some countries have found that payment of interest on their debts has used up a large part of their export earnings;[56]

- drying up of the flow of lending from western banks from $70bn in 1981 to less than $10bn a year since 1986,[56] together with pressures to repay earlier loans;

- decline in value of credits on exports to one third of their peak level;[57]

- official development finance not increased to cover these gaps[57] and aid often not to where it is needed the most or will be used the best, frequently tied to bilateral supply sources and geared to trade, political or military considerations;

- sub-optimal use of the opportunities available as a result of political instability, technical and managerial incompetence, corruption, excessive income inequalities, communal and tribal pressures, or spending on 'prestige' projects;

- military spending a total of over $130bn in 1987, more than on health and education combined;[53]

- war.

Consequences for development

The result has been that many Third World countries have not been well placed to achieve economic development by their own unaided efforts. The various natural and market obstacles have not been offset by external aid: net transfers of resources *from* the less developed countries *to* the more developed countries totalled $20bn a year in 1984-86 and $40bn a year in 1987-89;[55] and in many countries the development achieved has been swallowed up by increases in population.

Hence, there has been progress, but it has tended to be slower in the 1980s than in the 1970s, and uneven – in many of the poorest countries with the most difficult problems and the largest debts, average incomes have actually been *falling* during the past decade.

In consequence, massive problems remain among the billion people constituting the poorest fifth of humanity, who dispose of a mere 4 per cent of the world's wealth, compared with the richest fifth's 58 per cent.[53] There are still estimated[53] to be more than:

- 500 million malnourished people;

- 250 million children not in school;

♦ 850 million adult illiterates;

♦ 1700 million people without safe sanitation.

Moreover, all these numbers have been *increasing* during the 1970s and the 1980s.

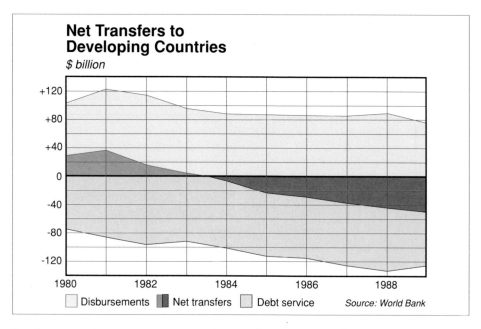

Net Transfers to Developing Countries
$ billion

☐ Disbursements ■ Net transfers ☐ Debt service   *Source: World Bank*

Debt interest and repayment costs have become bigger than development aid – net transfers from Third World countries to developed countries have risen to $48 billion a year.

Future prospects

The prospects ahead, like the experiences before, vary greatly in different countries and regions, but a basic factor underlying most other considerations is population change. In the less-developed countries as a whole there has been enough development to ensure that the *percentages* of people malnourished, illiterate, without sanitation and impoverished in other ways have been *declining*, albeit only slowly; but increases in population have meant that the *absolute* numbers in poverty have continued to increase. And the countries with the fastest rates of population increase have tended to be the ones experiencing the most intractable social and economic problems. A crucial factor in future prospects will therefore be the changes which occur in population.

Population

In most of the industrial countries both fertility rates and mortality rates have been falling over the past century and the net effect has been to produce populations which are now ageing and no longer growing in total size. In most of the Third World countries, in contrast, the fall in death rates has come later, and the fall in fertility rates much later still. This has resulted in a much younger age distribution and a high rate of population increase.

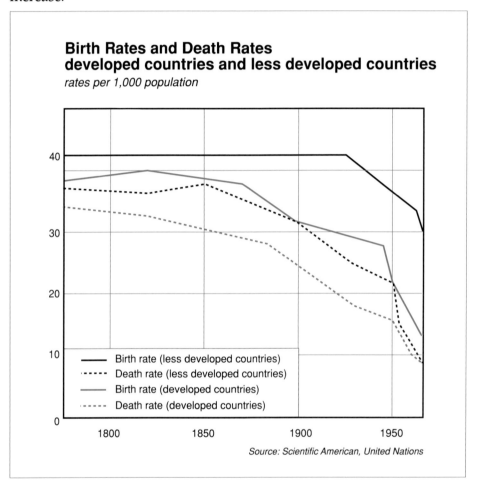

**Birth Rates and Death Rates
developed countries and less developed countries**
rates per 1,000 population

Birth rate (less developed countries)
Death rate (less developed countries)
Birth rate (developed countries)
Death rate (developed countries)

Source: Scientific American, United Nations

Death rates tend to fall as countries become richer; and, after a time, birth rates fall too. However, in some of the less developed countries birth rates have not been falling as soon as had been expected.

UN demographers expected that, in time, population change in the less-developed countries would follow a pattern similar to that already experienced in the more-developed countries – with increasing prosperity and wider use of family planning, birth rates would decline and populations level off. In many countries this has been happening, but in others change has been slower than expected, and population is still rising at about 2 per cent a year in Southern Asia and South America and at more than 3 per cent a year in Africa; and there are indications that future fertility rates may not drop as quickly as was expected.

For example, it is now estimated that by the turn of the century only about two-thirds of women in Latin America, half those in South Asia and one quarter of those in Africa will be using contraceptives.

In the light of this, there has been an upwards revision of the UN forecasts of world population. It is now expected that over the next two decades world population will increase by more than 90 million people

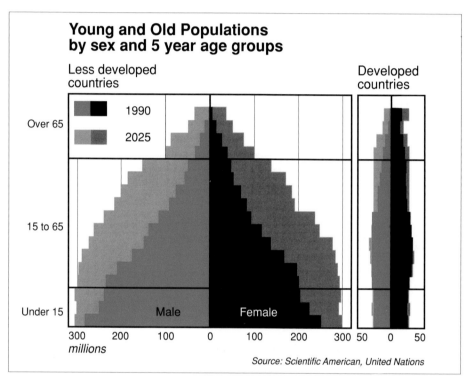

Young and Old Populations by sex and 5 year age groups

Source: Scientific American, United Nations

In most of the developed countries low birth rates and low death rates have brought stable populations with even age structures. In the Third World high birth rates and high death rates have brought a much younger age distribution – with more potential for further rapid population growth.

(one-and-a-half Britains) *each year,*[53] and most of the increase will be in the countries of the Third World. Hence the population of the Third World countries is expected to increase in the course of two decades by more than one half, a *total* increase of about 2 billion people (another China and another India). The Third World *increase* will be far greater than the present *total* population of all the more developed countries.

It should be noted that even apparently well-founded long-term population projections often turn out to be wrong. The UN projection foresees increases in population mainly as a result of continuing high fertility rates in some regions. It is possible that fertility rates will drop sooner than expected and the population increase will, in consequence, be

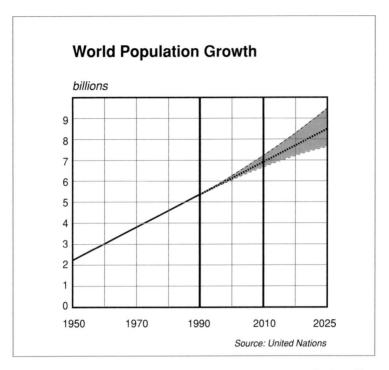

In the next two decades world population is forecast to grow by 90 million people (one and a half Britains) each year. By 2010 there will be 2 billion more people (another China and another India.)

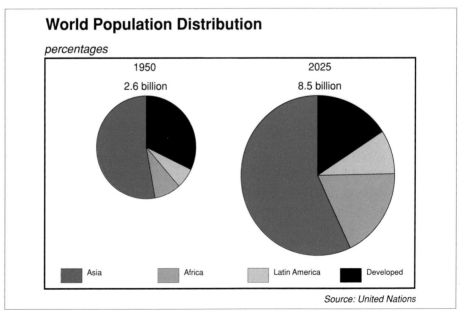

Between 1950 and 1975 total world population will have more than trebled. Population in the developed countries will have increased by only a half, so their share of the world total will have fallen from 32 per cent to 16 per cent.

less. In some areas there is also the possibility that AIDS will cause an increase in death rates, on a major scale in parts of Africa, perhaps.

Another consideration is that a rising population, while undoubtedly causing problems, may also help in their solution. If there are more mouths to feed, there are also more hands to grow the food for them. And the young age-structure in the countries with rising populations gives them a more favourable dependency ratio – more people in the economically active age groups relative to the numbers in the dependent age groups.

Nevertheless, the very large increase in population expected in the Third World countries will give rise to a number of serious problems.

Food

Large increases in population were projected, and actually experienced, in the past two decades, and also in the two before them; and anxieties were felt beforehand about whether it would be possible to feed so many more people. In the event, however, there has been a revolution in agricultural methods and productivity and world food production has been increased by the amount required.[58] Indeed, some countries have surpluses they are unable to find markets for. (There have been famines, but people have starved because war and other political factors prevented food being grown or relief supplies getting though, not because the food was not available.)

Further substantial improvements in agricultural productivity are expected and there are accordingly grounds for believing that it will be possible to increase food output by the amount required. However, there are already increasing problems with chemical pollution, soil erosion and desertification, and it would be rash to take it for granted that food production can be increased indefinitely without fear of running into difficulties.

> ## Prospects for Third World countries
>
> ### The poorer Third World countries face huge problems
>
> - 500 million people under-fed
> - 1700 million people without safe sanitation
> - 2000 million more people expected by 2010
> - development aid more than offset by debt burdens
>
> ### Some of the poorer countries face
>
> - Huge shanty cities larger than London
> - Growing food and water shortages

Urbanisation

The combination of rising total population, rising productivity in agriculture in the countryside and expanding employment in industry and associated services in the towns is already leading to a large-scale movement of people from the countryside into the towns in nearly all Third World countries, and this is expected to continue. The proportion of Third World population living in towns has risen from 17 per cent in 1950 to 33 per cent now, and is expected to reach about 46 per cent by 2010.[52] While this proportion is low compared with the more-developed countries, where more than 70 per cent of the population already live in towns, the large population densities in some Third World countries imply the growth of some very large cities.

On present trends, it is expected that by 2010 Mexico City and Sao Paolo will each have a population of more than 25 million; Bombay, Karachi, Calcutta and Seoul more than 15 million; and Rio de Janeiro, Buenos Aires, Jakarta, Manila, Delhi, Teheran and a number of others populations of more than 10 million – larger than London at present.[53,59] The problems of providing a tolerable living environment in these very large Third World cities are already formidable and will probably become even more severe in the course of the next two decades.

Water

In many countries fresh water supplies will become a problem, with not only more people but also rising levels of consumption and increasing problems with pollution. In the more-developed countries, where water consumption per head is high and use tends to be extravagant, there will often be scope for using water more economically. In many Third World countries, however, the most important use is in irrigation and there is often only limited scope for improving efficiency of use or for recycling because of losses from run-off, evaporation and salination. In some countries water supplies are already fully committed. Egypt, for example, already uses 97 per cent of the available water resources, although its consumption per head is only one fiftieth of that in Britain.[53]

Energy

Third World countries are, in general, expected to have a faster percentage rate of economic expansion than the industrial countries, and with it a steeper rise in energy requirements. Difficulties in securing energy supplies, particularly where they have to be imported and paid for in foreign exchange, may present a serious impediment to growth in some countries.

Environment

Industrialisation and urbanisation in Third World countries, as elsewhere, is bringing pollution and higher emission levels of greenhouse gases. In some of them, the destruction of forests is presenting additional local problems, as well as adding significantly to global problems of climate change.

Implications

The pace and pattern of development in the Third World has varied greatly and will continue to do so. A few countries, mainly small ones in East Asia, already have many of the characteristics of the more=developed countries. Others, including some large ones, are likely to reach a similar stage by 2010. Others, however, including some of the largest and poorest ones, face problems which, on current trends, are likely to keep them far behind for several decades more, although by 2010 most of them will have achieved higher average living standards than they have at present.

> ### Third World issues: impact on Britain
>
> ■ Tougher competition in world markets from newly industrialising countries
>
> ■ Demand for more development aid to poorer countries
>
> ■ Need for financial and technical aid to Third World countries for environmental protection measures

Total gross domestic product of the Third World countries will by 2010 have grown considerably. Although it is still likely to constitute no more than one fifth of the world total, in absolute terms this will be equivalent to about three-quarters of the total GDP of all the OECD countries at present. Between them the countries of the Third World will comprise a very large market to supply or invest in, and some of them will also become significant sources of supply for industrial components and of competition in consumer goods in world markets.

The more-developed countries' policies for aid, trade, investment and debt remission will have an important bearing on the economic growth that can be achieved in many of the Third World countries, and hence on the extent to which they become expanding markets for the developed countries' exports.

The cooperation of the Third World countries will be essential for combating global warming, but they will not be willing or able to provide it without substantial financial and technical assistance from the more-developed countries. Future transfers motivated by self-interest on the part of the industrial 'North' are likely to be much greater than past ones motivated by altruism.

The ending of the Cold War, particularly if followed by concerted efforts to reduce international arms sales, could be a major gain for Third World countries, leading to more pressure and opportunity for reduction in their expenditure on armaments.

Extreme inequalities of income within and between countries, made more evident by urbanisation and modern communications and entertainment media, may be expected to lead to unrest and conflict in some countries. This in turn is likely to lead to growing pressure for the more-developed countries to provide more aid and receive more immigrants; or, failing that, at least to export more capital and import more goods in order to contribute to prosperity and stability in Third World countries.

China

China is in many ways part of the developing world, but merits consideration in a separate section because of the exceptional importance of future developments there and the exceptional uncertainty about what course they are most likely to take.

China is important to the rest of the world mainly on account of its size and of the future potential implicit in its size. Its population of 1.1 billion, more than one fifth of the world total, is much the largest of any country in the world, despite the efficacy of ruthlessly enforced family planning policies in bringing about a sharp drop in fertility rates. It is also the second largest country in land area and has very considerable mineral resources. It also has the largest army in the world and is held together by an authoritarian government with a militant ideology. Its ultimate potential is clearly considerable.

Anyone visiting Hong Kong cannot fail to be struck by its dynamism. A small place with no natural resources and a population of only 6 million has, by the energy and enterprise of its people, made itself into a significant force in the world economy. If the Chinese people in China were to operate with the same dynamism as the Chinese people next door in Hong Kong, the impact on the world would be considerable: for China has the population of 190 Hong Kongs, 18 West Germanys, 9 Japans or 4 United States. If they produced the same output per head as the Chinese in Hong Kong, the Chinese economy would be larger than the economies of the United States and the European Community combined, and growing at about twice the rate. It would presumably also be using up raw materials and energy at a corresponding rate, and generating a huge volume of 'greenhouse' gases. It might also be publishing similar numbers of books, performing similar numbers of symphony concerts and sending similar numbers of tourists round the world on package holidays. And it would also have the technology to be the world's strongest military power. In short, there are many world perspectives which would look radically different if this potential were realised.

It is therefore relevant to ask: why are the Chinese in China not making the same impact on the world as the Chinese in Hong Kong? And, of more practical importance, are they likely to do so in the future?

Past performance

The answer to the first question lies in China's history. The country is not only very large, it is also very old, with a culture stretching back for more than four thousand years. During most of that time its rulers saw it not merely as the largest country in the world but as the *only* country: beyond its borders lay a peripheral barbary of no particular significance. It is only in the present century that China has had much contact with the rest of the world, experiencing civil wars and foreign invasions in the first five decades, and communist government in the following four. Millennia of government through the imperial confucianist bureaucracy were superseded after 1948 by decades of government by the new communist bureaucracy, punctuated by the upheavals of the Great Leap Forward and the Cultural Revolution.

The centralised control and monolithic conformity which characterised both periods was not conducive to the enterprising kinds of economic behaviour shown in Hong Kong. As far as the outside world was concerned, China remained asleep.

About ten years ago Deng Xiaoping began to introduce a series of radical economic reforms which decentralised control, encouraged local initiatives and provided incentives. The result was the setting up of many new enterprises, some of them highly successful, the release of new energies, a quickening of economic activity, and some increase in prosperity. There was an opening up of trade and other links with the rest of the world; but also a widening of disparities in income and wealth, an increase in corruption and nepotism, and a rising rate of inflation.

The intention of the leadership had been the reverse of that in the Soviet Union: to introduce reforms to set up a more market-oriented *economic* system, while holding back from changes in the *political* system. However, as the economic changes gathered pace, the freer institutions and the freer ways of acting and thinking needed for them to work properly and, in particular, the liberal ideas imported from abroad by the foreign businessmen and technicians brought in to help, and by the students sent away to study, brought an increasingly relaxed political atmosphere. Expectations arose that, by degrees, the party was moving towards the introduction of political reforms, possibly on similar lines to those being introduced in the Soviet Union, in order to ensure the success of the new economic policies.

Thus up until the spring of 1989 it seemed very probable that the country was at last emerging from its isolation and bureaucracy and that new energies would be released. It would take time to build up, but within the span of the next two decades there was the real possibility of a new economic force emerging, much bigger than Hong Kong, bigger even than Japan, and later in the century, possibly bigger even than the United States. The world balance was potentially changing.

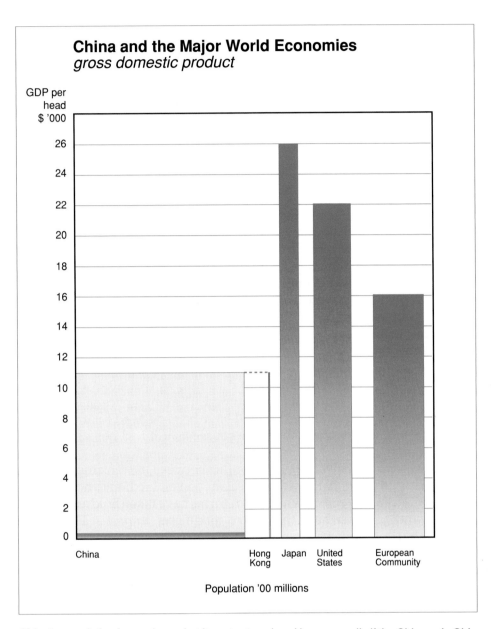

China and the Major World Economies
gross domestic product

GDP per head $ '000

Population '00 millions

China's population is very large, but its output per head is very small. If the Chinese in China were as productive as the Chinese in Hong Kong, the Chinese economy would be nearly as large as the United States, Japan and the European Community combined.

Future prospects

As it turned out the course of events was abruptly changed. The student demonstrations in May 1989 sought to accelerate the pace of political change at a rate the party was not yet prepared to accept; and the resulting crisis and crushing of the students in June led not only to the end of political reform but also to a halting of further economic change. It has also produced a situation where the future prospects are much more uncertain than in any other region of comparable importance. There are several, very different, possibilities.

One is that the current political repression will continue, and be intensified, and the economic reforms will be reversed, bringing the country back to a situation superficially like what it was before the reforms were introduced – but more insecure, because memories of ideas acquired abroad and of experiences in China in 1989 will not disappear, and will indeed be nurtured by the improved communications links which make it more difficult than before to isolate the country from the outside world and prevent people learning of the changes that have happened in other communist countries.

Another possibility is that the new ideas will be too strong to be repressed for long. They will lie dormant for a while, but will re-emerge when the ageing existing leadership dies out, so that after a while the previous course will gradually be resumed. The emergence of China as a major economic force in the world will have been delayed for a while, but will in the end follow much the same course as if it had not suffered the interruption.

A third possibility is that the conflict between the reformers and the old guard within the party will not easily be resolved, and nor will the conflict between the regions where the reforms have taken hold and proved popular and others where they have made less impact. There may therefore be continuing differences between factions, between regions, and in due course also between military commanders in different regions, leading to indecision, anarchy and, ultimately, civil war.

Implications

Any of these three courses of events (or others) is entirely possible, and experts disagree as to which is the more probable.

But the implications for the rest of the world are considerable: the first or the last of the three imply a China in a straitjacket or in turmoil, having little interest in, or effect on, the rest of the world; while the middle one implies a new force which will have a major impact on the world by 2010 and possibly an even greater one thereafter. The actual outcome may turn out to be somewhere among the three. It is a major question to which at present there is little basis for giving a confident answer.

0. Soviet Union & Eastern Europe

The Soviet Union has long been a country of intense interest to the countries of Western Europe: first, as the leading communist state; secondly, as one of the main protagonists in the Second World War; and thirdly, as an instigator of the Cold War. With the ending of the Cold War, the Soviet Union and the former 'satellite' countries of Eastern Europe have become a focus of urgent attention because of the political and economical changes they are undergoing.

Soviet background

During the three decades of Stalin's dictatorship the Soviet Union experienced severe internal repression in the course of which millions died; a war in which much of the country was occupied and millions more died; and, at the end of it, the extension of Soviet power, through satellite régimes, over most of Eastern Europe.

When Stalin died in 1953, some experts expected the régime to continue unchanged under a new dictator; others that it would rapidly change into something very different. In the event the outcome was something in between: the excesses of internal repression were reduced, and no subsequent leader achieved the previous degree of absolute power. But the basic monolithic, authoritarian structure of the system was maintained, albeit with increasing lethargy and declining conviction.

However, when Andropov, the former security chief, came to power in 1983 he surprised the world by initiating a number of reforms; and since Gorbachev came to power in 1985 the pace of change has been dramatic. Future prospects for both the Soviet Union and the countries of Eastern Europe already look very different from how they appeared only a few years ago – and also much more uncertain. The changes now in train are likely to have important military, political and economic implications for the rest of the world, and in particular for the countries of Western Europe.

The speed and vigour with which the recent changes have been introduced in the Soviet Union owe much to the charisma, vision and political skills of Mikhail Gorbachev, the General Secretary of the Communist Party and now also the President of the Soviet Union. However, the origin of the decision to undertake the changes, and to put him in power to carry them through, appears to go back to the perception by the leadership as a whole that:

- the economy was performing sluggishly and was particularly weak in the new technologies crucial to success in the future;

- this economic failure was already defeating hopes of higher living standards for the population and would in the future undermine Soviet military strength and call into question the Soviet Union's credibility as a superpower;

- It was therefore essential to make major changes so as to rejuvenate the system to enable it to compete effectively with the West and in the international economy as a whole.

Perestroika and glasnost

Unlike in China, where the attempt was made to introduce radical *economic* reforms without changing the *political* system, in the Soviet Union major *political* changes were considered to be essential for the success of the *economic* reforms. The stultifying conformity of the previous six decades is being abandoned in favour of *glasnost* (openness) intended to open up debate, stimulate new thinking, and bring both policies and policy makers under critical scrutiny. The rigidities of the previous political and economic structures are being subjected to *perestroika* (restructuring) with the aim of building a new institutional framework for the proposed changes.

Political changes

Political changes already undertaken include:

- opening up of the media to frank discussion, including criticism of individual and institutional failures;

- freedom of individuals and groups to express their views and to campaign for them through forming voluntary associations (which have been evolving into political parties);

- formal abandonment of the 'leading role' of the Communist Party of the Soviet Union;

- holding of real elections (the first in living memory) which have resulted in the removal from positions of power of many unpopular party leaders and the election to places in republican parliaments and on party committees of independent-minded reformers;

- reduction in the size of the party bureaucracy and removal from office of many corrupt, incompetent or reactionary officials;

- freedom of religion;

- proposals for devolution of more power to regional and local *soviets*, whose leaders will be elected, thus ensuring further transfer of power to more popular and, in many cases, reform-minded people;

- constitutional amendments to provide a legal procedure for secession of member republics from the union and for a new federal structure allowing far greater autonomy to the republics.

Economic changes

Economic changes already made include:

- adoption of fundamental reform plans intended to bring about a change to a more market-based economic system;

- reduction in the size and powers of the central planning organisation;

- greater financial autonomy for company managements, particularly on pricing and raising of capital, and the setting up of new organisations to provide finance, with a view to stimulating local enterprise;

- arrangements to encourage setting up of joint ventures with foreign companies with a view to importing western management expertise and, if possible, technology;

- heavy cuts in defence industries with a view to shifting much of their production to meeting civilian needs;

- agricultural reforms to encourage production from family plots and to stimulate small scale rural industries; and

- plans to phase out subsidies with a view to introducing economic realism in inefficient sectors and reducing the budget deficit.

Threat of reversal

In general, the *prospect* of political and economic reforms has received widespread public support; but the *performance* so far achieved has been another matter. The specific economic changes have been controversial, incomplete and delayed – in some cases blocked by party bureaucrats who do not approve of them anyway. The result is that the economy, instead of being rejuvenated, has been faltering, shortages of consumer goods have been worsening, and living standards have actually been falling; and the resulting disillusion and discontent have been given much more effective expression than would previously have been possible, thanks to the new conditions of *glasnost*.

If *perestroika* is failing to deliver the goods, does this mean that the conservatives will be able to exploit popular dissatisfaction and get the whole process halted, or even reversed? There are a number of reasons why it would be difficult for those opposed to the changes to reverse them.

- The changes have been introduced from the top by the party itself. To reverse them requires a decisive shift in the power balance in the party or a coup from outside to remove a government already in possession of the instruments of state power.

- With each month that passes, more reformers move into the positions of power and more of those opposed to the changes are moved out of them.

- Thanks to *glasnost*, and the holding of relatively free elections, people are aware of the extent of the unpopularity of the old leaders.

- Thanks to the growth of independent political movements, the reformers are not only more confident, they also have much more effective influence – they have won control of the government of the Russian republic which has half the total population of the Soviet Union and far more than half of its total economic resources.

◆ The suppression of reform would probably require not only ruthless determination but also considerable military force. However, the size of Soviet military forces is being rapidly reduced; and any use of military force to suppress popular movements would, as in China, have the effect of drying up the economic and technical help from the West which is seen as essential for restoring the economy.

◆ The old system is not only discredited: it is also, by degrees, being dismantled. It would be immensely difficult to restore the centralised authoritarian system, and the attempt to do so would bring even more upheaval and dislocation than is being caused by reform.

◆ The opponents of the changes lack unity, organisation, charismatic leadership or any set of coherent alternative policies to put in place of the present ones.

Moreover, even if there were a successful coup, the new leaders would be faced by the same underlying problems as faced the politburo when it put Gorbachev in power to deal with them; and the circumstances of the situation would in time be likely to force them to consider similar solutions. The reality is that the changes have already gone so far that there is now little possibility of a restoration of the previous system, and a coup would be more likely to delay further changes than to reverse those already made.

Difficulties with continuation

If a successful counter-reformation coup seems unlikely, it does not therefore follow that the reforms will go ahead without major upheavals. The difficulties in turning the economy round quickly are formidable – and made more so by the obstruction of disaffected officials who, if they lack the power to reverse the changes, are many of them still in positions where they have the power to impede their progress. There has been much dispute over the form and pace of the changes needed and even if, as looks probable, the advocates of speedier and more radical changes gain the upper hand, the economic restructuring will be difficult, will take time to bring results, and will be heavily dependent on the amount of aid received from the West – in competition with claims from countries in Eastern Europe, from the Third World and from the countries damaged by the conflict in the Gulf.

There are also other destabilising factors which are likely to prove important.

Population change

One of these factors is population change. In European Russia, as in most other industrial countries, fertility rates have dropped and the population is ageing and no longer increasing in total size. But in Soviet Central Asia, as in most Third World countries, fertility rates have remained high and the population is young and increasing in total size. Hence, if recent trends continue, by 2010 more than half of the population of the Soviet Union will be Asian, as will more than one third of the soldiers in the Red Army.

Separatist tensions

The Central Asian republics are among the poorest in the Soviet Union and although they have had the benefit of substantial investment in their development, some of the largest projects have been badly mismanaged, leading to large-scale environmental damage. The rapid rise in population has overloaded the public services in some areas and made it increasingly difficult to provide employment opportunities for everyone. There is thus the basis for economic tensions, with Moscow resenting the cost of the burden of providing support and the regions demanding more investment for development and more local control over the management of projects.

The Asian peoples in the Soviet Union comprise many different nations, with important linguistic and cultural differences from one another and from the Russians. The majority of the Asians are muslim and there has in recent years been an upsurge in fundamentalist activity, stimulated partly by radio broadcasts and literature from Iran and Afghanistan. This may provide a further cause of future tensions and heighten the desire to establish a separate identity through greater republican autonomy.

Further west, in Armenia, a revival of nationalist sentiment has led to a declaration of independence; and in Georgia the violent suppression by the military of a protest demonstration inflamed local feelings, turning a desire for regional autonomy into a demand for outright independence. In Moldavia (until 1939, Bessarabia, part of Romania) there have been riots and demands for independence. In the Baltic republics (before their annexation by Stalin in 1939, the independent states of Lithuania, Latvia and Estonia) there have been declarations of independence, leading to tense confrontations with the Soviet Union. Revival of nationalist feelings in the Ukraine (the second largest of the republics and once an independent state) has led to a declaration of sovereignty. Even in Byelorussia there have been stirrings of nationalism and calls for greater regional autonomy.

Finally, the Russian republic itself, which stretches from west of Moscow to beyond Vladivostok, has declared its sovereignty, saying it will not accept Soviet laws unless they are also passed by its own assembly.

Almost all of the 15 republics of the Soviet Union have already proclaimed their sovereignty or declared outright independence. Further, many regions and districts *within* the republics have claimed *their* independence. These smaller areas often represent minority ethnic or cultural groups within their republics. Thus there have been tensions, often erupting into violence, not only between the Soviet Union and its constituent republics, but also *between* one republic and another, and between different groups *within* some of the republics.

The mix of the Soviet Republics

	Population (millions)	Ethnic Russian (per cent)	Main Religion
Russia	145	82	Christian
Ukraine	51	21	Christian
Byelorussia	6	12	Christian
Estonia	2	28	Christian
Latvia	3	33	Christian
Lithuania	4	9	Christian
Moldavia	4	12	Christian
Georgia	5	7	Christian
Armenia	3	2	Christian
Azerbaijan	7	8	Muslim
Turkmenia	3	13	Muslim
Uzbekistan	19	11	Muslim
Tadzhikistan	5	10	Muslim
Kirghizia	4	26	Muslim
Kazakhstan	16	41	Muslim

Transformation of the Soviet Union

It is not yet clear what will be the outcome of this revival of nationalism. It is unlikely to be feasible to return to the repressive methods of Stalin. It is therefore probable that these pressures will lead in the next few years to a transformation of the Soviet Union, with the centrally-controlled empire, built up by the Czars and extended by Stalin, being replaced by voluntary, and hence much looser and more varied, forms of association in a new confederation.

The Baltic states are likely to insist on a return to full independence, although possibly maintaining close economic links with the Soviet Union. Moldavia, also, is likely to want full independence or reunion with Romania. Georgia and Armenia are likely to want full independence, but may feel the need to balance this against the advantages of economic links with the Soviet Union, while the Central Asian republics, much poorer and less developed, are even more economically dependent on the Soviet Union. It is likely that most of these republics will seek to get the best of both worlds with substantial local independence within a wider Soviet Confederation.

The Ukraine, with a population of more than 50 million, is clearly viable as a fully-independent state; but may nonetheless see advantages in federal links with the other two predominantly slav republics – Byelorussia and Russia itself.

Thus, depending on the relative strengths of nationalist feelings and perceived economic advantages, and also on the skills exerted in devising new political structures, the outcome by 2010 may be anything from a large, loosely-linked confederal union, shorn of some of its peripheral parts, but encompassing essentially the same area as now, to a smaller, tighter union made up of only the three slav republics, or even the Russian republic alone.

Even the latter extreme case would still leave Russia as a major power. The Russian republic, which extends across Siberia, has a population of more than 145 million, and considerable natural resources. And the new state would not have the economic burden of supporting less-developed republics, or the military burden of keeping order within and between them. It would retain the bulk of the Soviet Union's existing industry, technology and defence capability – including the arsenal of nuclear weapons. However, in contrast with the early postwar decades, it would no longer be a superpower comparable in global influence with the United States.

The transition from empire is unlikely to be achieved without protracted and serious friction. This is partly because it is being attempted with considerable haste, and partly because even the severance of the union into separate parts will not produce a tidy solution. The economies of the republics are fully integrated with one another and their populations are not homogeneous. Most of the republics have substantial ethnic Russian minorities and one in six of the inhabitants of the Russian republic is non-Russian. And in many of the republics there are also substantial non-Russian minorities. Hence, for most of the republics, full independence could produce serious economic problems, could make substantial numbers of ethnic Russians into second-class citizens, and could make problems also for other ethnic minorities. It is therefore likely that the upsurge of nationalist and separatist aspirations will be accompanied by economic dislocations and by ethnic clashes between republics and within them. These have already brought violence in Armenia, Azerbaijan and Turkestan. In the 1990s they could erupt into full-scale wars and force major migrations, with disruptive effects on neighbouring countries.

Other countries in Eastern Europe

Over the past four decades, most of the other countries in Eastern Europe have tended to be thought of in the West as 'the satellites', as though they were a single, monolithic bloc, whose main point of interest was their domination by the Soviet Union. They are, however, separate nations, distinct and different from one another, and conscious of it, and these differences are likely to re-emerge into greater prominence in the course of the next two decades.

The main common factor between most of them at present is that they are experiencing fundamental political and economic changes. Even in the matter of change, however, there are important differences between them.

Circumstances of change

Timing
In Yugoslavia the break came in 1948. In Poland and Hungary the process of political change started several years ago. In East Germany, Czechoslovakia, Bulgaria and Romania change came suddenly in the second half of 1989. In Albania it has yet to come.

Instigation
In Hungary and Bulgaria change was initiated by reformers within the Communist Party itself. In Poland it followed years of campaigning by the Solidarity movement. In East Germany and Czechoslovakia it was triggered by popular protest demonstrations. In Romania it came only after bloody riots and insurrection.

Extent
In East Germany, Czechoslovakia, Hungary and Poland fundamental political changes have already been made and fundamental economic changes are in progress. In Bulgaria and Romania the extent of political change achieved and of economic change intended are both more in doubt.

Future prospects

The countries of Eastern Europe also differ greatly in their prospects for the coming decades.

East Germany, having opted for reunification with West Germany, has been taken automatically into the European Community, and should by the late 1990s have a Western European economy – but not without dislocation and hardship in the years during which the transformation is being accomplished.

Czechoslovakia, Hungary and *Poland* are all committed to democratic political systems and are in the process of changing rapidly to more market-based economic systems. However all three of them, in particular Poland, have serious economic and environmental problems. The far-reaching changes being undertaken will involve many economic difficulties, and probably much unemployment and social distress. The next few years will be tough ones, although the difficulties may be eased by financial and technical help from the European Community and the United States.

Bulgaria and *Romania* have economies which are less developed. Their problems are more severe and the political and economic changes made so far are more limited. Both countries also have major unresolved problems with ethnic minorities. They probably face a period of economic difficulties and further political upheavals.

Yugoslavia has over a period achieved limited progress on the basis of limited economic and political reforms, but prospects are blighted by internal divisions between the richer north and the poorer south and between the six different nations which make up the country. The resurgence of traditional animosities may well cause the country to break apart, perhaps violently, in the 1990s.

Albania so far shows little outward sign of change. As with Romania, when change does come it will probably be sudden and violent.

Brezhnev and Sinatra

Most of the changes in Eastern Europe came with great suddenness. Is there a risk that they will be reversed – for example, if there is a change in the leadership in the Soviet Union?

The key factor underlying recent changes in Eastern Europe is the replacement of the 'Brezhnev doctrine', that the Soviet Union has the right to intervene to keep sympathetic communist parties in power in the countries in the Soviet bloc in Eastern Europe, with the 'Sinatra doctrine' that each of the countries has the right to 'do it my way'. Russian tanks came in to crush the attempted assertion of independence in Hungary in 1956 and the Prague Spring in 1968. There was little question of their being sent in to block the changes in 1989, and it has been the growing realisation of this that has enabled the changes to spread wider and proceed faster.

This change in Soviet policy came about for a number of cogent reasons.

♦ Using Soviet power to prop up increasingly unsuccessful and unpopular régimes in Eastern Europe was becoming a tiresome burden when the Soviet economy was itself in trouble and resources were needed for its rebuilding.

♦ Repression in Eastern Europe would lead to extreme tension with Western powers, alienate public opinion in the West and greatly reduce the chances of getting western support for economic restructuring or cooperation in arms reduction.

♦ Parallel changes in the other countries of Eastern Europe would complement the *glasnost* and *perestroika* in the

Soviet Union, while the maintenance of régimes hostile to change could pose a threat to the reforms in the Soviet Union if Eastern European leaders aligned themselves with anti-reform groups in Russia.

◆ And, finally, it is probable that the new leadership in Moscow had a genuinely less imperialist attitude towards its neighbours.

There are also a number of reasons why this change in Soviet policy is extremely unlikely to be reversed.

◆ The reasons that originally prompted the policy's adoption will still apply.

◆ Overturning any of the new, popularly-based, governments would require far more force than would have been needed merely for maintaining the old ones in power, or for restoring just one régime as in 1956 or 1968.

◆ Soon the Red Army will be far smaller, will no longer have bases within the newly-independent countries of Eastern Europe, and will no longer be able to count on the support of allies in the Warsaw Pact in any intervention.

While the changes in Eastern Europe have probably gone farther and faster than was expected, or intended, the Soviet Union no longer has the capability to reverse them, even if it wished to.

Implications

The late 1980s have been a period of profound change in the Soviet Union and further changes are likely in the 1990s. The programme of political and economic reforms is unlikely to be reversed, indeed, is more likely to be accelerated, but developments are likely to be turbulent and unpredictable.

Major difficulties are being experienced in trying to revitalise the moribund economic system and it will take a number of years before reforms produce substantial results. Meanwhile popular discontent with the slow pace of progress will put pressure on the Soviet Government to seek external economic and technical assistance and to achieve faster cuts in defence spending.

The probable transformation of the Soviet Union into a looser, confederal grouping, with some of the republics separating completely, together with the effective dissolution of the Warsaw Pact and together with continuing economic difficulties, will leave the Soviet Union much weaker militarily, although still a potent nuclear power.

The associated release of previously repressed nationalist and religious feelings in the context of the mixed ethnic composition of many of the republics, is likely to generate ethnic clashes, possibly leading to large-scale migrations and localised wars. These may bring much disruption and suffering, but are unlikely to involve countries in Western Europe directly.

The change to more market-based economic systems, combined with friendlier political relations, is likely to bring increased trade and investment links between Western and Eastern Europe. The extent of Western investment in the Soviet Union will depend greatly on how far the transition to a market-based economy and democratic federal system is accompanied by civil unrest and economic disorder among the republics. The many difficulties of the Eastern European economies imply that in the coming decade the advantages of economic exchanges are likely to be largely one-way, but in the first decade of the next century a more balanced, complementary relationship may well build up, with Western Europe offering more sophisticated products and services and more advanced technology and the Eastern European countries offering cheaper labour and more extensive mineral resources.

In short, the changes in the Soviet Union and Eastern Europe are sure to go on; but they will not all be good and they will not be predictable. There will be benefits, but also difficulties and risks, including the possibility of collapse into anarchy, fragmentation and strife. Western Europe is likely, on balance, to benefit substantially from the changes and will have, unlike hitherto, a significant influence on the outcome of events.

Western Europe

There is little doubt about the stability of the democratic institutions in the countries of Western Europe, or about the prospects for continuing development of their economies. Where there is considerable long-term uncertainty is about the future development of political and economic links *between* the countries of Western Europe and between them and the soon-to-become-democratic countries of Eastern Europe. Will the existing European Community (EC) develop by 2010 into a closer European Union, with a federal structure, making it in some ways more comparable with the United States? And are the existing 12 members of the European Community likely to be joined by others in Northern and Southern Europe? Or by countries until recently behind the Iron Curtain in Eastern Europe?

Background

After the Second World War the continental European countries were concerned to establish links that would make a future war impossible, and to replace prewar protectionism with a market like that of the United States so that they could combine their strength in a world dominated by the superpowers. They set up first the European Coal and Steel Community, then the general common market and European Community, with its innovative institutions looking after trade (both internal and external), agriculture and a range of other economic and social matters.

Initially there were six members – France, West Germany, Italy, the Netherlands, Belgium and Luxembourg. Britain stayed out, sceptical of the feasibility and desirability of a full customs union, and oriented more towards historic associations with the Commonwealth countries and the United States. Britain did, however, join with Sweden, Norway, Denmark, Austria, Switzerland and Portugal to form the European Free Trade Association (EFTA).

Later, when the common market and its associated institutions were seen to be working, and exclusion from them was seen to be a disadvantage, there was a change of policy in Britain. After an abortive attempt at entry in 1961-63 (blocked by de Gaulle), Britain finally joined in 1973, together with Ireland and Denmark, followed later by Spain, Portugal and Greece.

In the 1960s the original customs union was securely established, but further movement towards a fuller economic union was blocked by de Gaulle who believed in a Europe of separate nation states (with a leading role for France); in the 1970s there were the problems of the oil shocks and stagflation; and in the early 1980s further moves towards closer union were made difficult by the opposition to moves towards greater integration by Greece and Denmark and, in particular, in the early 1980s, by Britain, with its concerns about budget contributions.

Nevertheless, the Community continued to develop, with the pace accelerating in the late 1980s under the impetus of the Single European Act. Significant steps in 1970s and 1980s included:

- reform of the Common Agricultural Policy to reduce the problem of expensive food surpluses;

- special arrangements to alleviate anomalies in budget contributions and to increase the structural funds to help the new southern members;

- the establishment of the European Council of heads of state and government and, through the Single European Act, the greater use of majority voting;

- the introduction of direct election to, and a stronger legislative role for, the European Parliament and the launching of the programme to eliminate the proliferating non-tariff barriers still to trade.

Single market after 1992

In 1987 the Single European Act came into force. This aims to complete the transformation of the customs union into a genuine single market by providing for the abolition, by the end of 1992, of all the remaining non-tariff barriers to trade. Among the measures included are:

- dismantling of frontier controls and formalities;

- harmonisation or mutual recognition of national norms, standards and other technical regulations which have presented obstacles to trade;

- abolition of foreign exchange controls and provision for free movement of capital;

- ending of state aids (subsidies and tax breaks) which give unfair market advantages to the recipients;

- prohibition of national discrimination in public procurement;

- some harmonisation of VAT rates.

Provision has been made for qualified majority voting in some areas so that a proposal can be blocked by two major countries and one small one, but no one country can exercise a veto over a proposal that has the support of all the others.

Negotiations to give effect to these measures have proceeded rather better than expected. Many of the provisions are already in place; by the end of 1992 the great majority are expected to be agreed; and there is general confidence that the parts not completed by then will not be important enough to cause much concern and will be brought in satisfactorily in the following years.

The EC under the Single Market will have a combined gross domestic product roughly equal to that of the United States and about two-thirds greater than that of Japan, and a population about 30 per cent larger than the United States and nearly three times that of Japan. It is hoped that its creation, by removing barriers and other distortions, will make Europe better placed to compete with the United States and Japan.

It is difficult to measure exactly the effect that the Single Market will have on economic growth. In principle, the creation of a single market, through the removal of barriers and other distortions, should reduce costs and increase efficiency, investment and technological progress through the new opportunities for specialisation and scale and through sharpened competition.

For empirical evidence, the nearest comparable development available was the coming into force of the European Economic Community in 1958. In the following decade the rate of economic growth in the six members of the customs union was 5.2 per cent a year, which was greater than that of most other countries in Western Europe and North America. An investment boom followed the first move towards the customs union, and it seems fair to suggest that it owed much to the dynamic effects of the customs union project, without which the member states would hardly have maintained through that decade a growth rate only fractionally less than the 5.4 per cent that they achieved in 1953-58, when their growth was still boosted by the effects of post-war reconstruction.

The best available estimate of the likely economic effects of the Single Market is provided by the Cecchini Report[60] commissioned by the Commission of the European Community to assess the impact. The study provided a range of estimates, the centre points of which are summarised in rounded form below.

Estimated medium-term effects of Single Market on EC economy
(comparison with what would have happened otherwise)

	present policies	more expansionary policies
GDP	+5%	+7%
Prices	-6%	-4.5%
Employment	+2m	+5m
Budget balance	+2% of GDP	+⅓% of GDP
External balance	+1% of GDP	-¼% of GDP

If the medium term is taken to be five years, this amounts to an extra 1 per cent a year growth in gross domestic product. Spread over a ten year period it amounts to 0.5 per cent extra growth a year – equivalent to increasing by one fifth the average annual growth actually achieved in Britain since 1979.

Too much reliance should not be placed on the accuracy of estimates of this kind, since psychological factors are important, and some critics have argued that the gains in overall efficiency will be achieved at the cost of heavy job losses in countries such as Britain.[61] It is, however, reasonable to hope that the economic gains should be substantial.

Plans for closer union

It is possible that the completion of the Single Market will turn out to represent the furthest limit reached in the process of economic integration in Europe. This seems unlikely, however, since the preparations for the Single Market have served as a catalyst to further moves towards closer union in Western Europe and the recent dramatic changes in Eastern Europe have instilled a new sense of urgency.

In June 1988 the European Council of Heads of State commissioned the Delors report[62] to explore the means of achieving economic and monetary union. The report was unanimously agreed by the members of the committee, which included the governors of all the member states' central banks, including the Bank of England. The report set out a Stage 1 in which all member states would join the existing exchange rate mechanism; a Stage 2 in which institutions would be prepared; and a Stage 3 in which a single European currency would replace the member states' currencies or in which exchange rates would be finally fixed among the members, amounting to a common currency in all but name, with responsibility for its management entrusted to a European System of Central Banks. Provision would be made for control of the budget deficits of member states and for use of structural funds to help weaker members through a policy of 'social cohesion'.

At the Strasbourg meeting of the European Council in December 1989 it was agreed to:

- confirm the commitment to complete the Single Market by the end of 1992;

- use the December 1990 Council meeting to inaugurate negotiations for establishing monetary and economic union;

- endorse a Social Charter to provide rights and safeguards for employees;

- set up a European Bank for Reconstruction and Development to channel economic support into the new democracies in Eastern Europe.

Since then Britain has joined the European Exchange Rate Mechanism and the meeting of the European Council in Rome in October 1990 has set January 1993 as the target date for starting Stage 2, and January 1997 as the date to consider arrangements for moving on to Stage 3. Also, Germany and France have called for a commitment to move towards 'political union', although without going into detail as to what is meant by this; and the European Council agreed to convene a second inter-governmental conference to negotiate treaty amendments in this area.

If these plans go ahead, what is in prospect is that by the turn of the century there will be in place most of the elements of a common European monetary and economic policy, together with strengthened supranational institutions to operate them and a strengthened European Parliament to exercise democratic control over them. The changes are likely to include an increase in the Community budget from the nearly 1.5 per cent of gross domestic product planned for 1992 (if all items of expenditure are included) to something in the range of 2 – 3 per cent; and closer cooperation in external economic and foreign policy, and possibly in security also. This would produce a momentum which would make it likely that further moves would follow. In short, by 2010 the member countries would have gone a large part of the way to establishing a 'United States of Europe'.

Prospects of European Union

These moves towards closer union have attracted support in varying degrees from the governments of all the EC member countries except Britain. In most of the countries they have also attracted support from opposition parties, business and unions. They have also received the goodwill of the United States.

Given this weight of support, and notwithstanding the many difficulties that will lie along the way, the balance of probability would seem to be strongly in favour of the process towards closer union continuing – at any rate unless some very powerful force arises to block it.

Could Britain be that force? There was a time when de Gaulle could, and did, veto proposals for closer union. He was able to do so because he was determined to do so, because a European Community without France was unthinkable, and because West Germany, still recovering from the physical and psychological shocks of the war, made it the centre of its policy to go along with French wishes.

Now, however, the situation is very different. Germany is fully recovered, strong and confident, and also larger as a result of reunification. France is setting the pace towards monetary union, concerned that the newly-unified Germany could become too dominant unless integrated closely within such a European structure.

Before reunification West Germany was already the largest and economically strongest country in Western Europe, accounting for nearly one fifth of the population of the European Community and one quarter of its gross domestic product. However, the addition of East Germany will add only a little over one quarter to West Germany's population and a far smaller proportion to its gross domestic product. Moreover, the East German economy is very run-down and the country has many severe environmental, social and economic problems, so it is probable that for some years to come it will be a net liability, making West Germany not stronger but weaker than it would have been on its own. And even in the longer term it will not alter very much the strength and importance of Germany relative to the rest of the European Community. It therefore seems likely that French worries about the weight of Germany in the Community will prove to have been exaggerated.

Even so, combined French and German pressures towards some sort of a closer union constitute a powerful force against Britain, the only one of the 12 which has so far been strongly opposed; and in practice, Britain will not be in a position to block it. Britain would have the right to veto reform of the EC's institutions; but if economic and monetary union goes ahead, reform of the institutions is anyway likely to come sooner or later, particularly if further enlargement makes the institutions in their present form too difficult to operate.

Inner and outer Europe

Thus if the others wish to go ahead, as they appear determined to do, they can if necessary do so without the participation of Britain. The issue, then, is not whether Britain will block the others, but whether Britain will choose to go with them – or to stay apart.

If Britain decided not to go along with the others, it would probably be possible to maintain an association limited to the arrangements for the

Single Market. It is also possible that Britain could be joined by European Free Trade Association countries such as Austria, Switzerland, Sweden and Norway, but several of them have applied, or are considering applying, to join the Community themselves.

It seems probable that, in staying out of moves towards closer union, Britain would come to be seen as peripheral to European affairs: no longer included in the full institutional arrangements and benefits; no longer involved in key economic decisions; no longer a favoured site for European investments or the best base for European financial operations, a semi-detached, second-class member of the Community.

Perhaps the decisive factor will prove to be shifts in attitudes in Britain itself. Business has all along been predominantly in favour of closer links with Europe. Trade unions, previously doubtful, have recently become more sympathetic, impressed among other things by the benefits for workers from the Social Charter to balance the benefits for business from the Single Market. Public opinion in general in Britain (and also in Denmark) has all along been less enthusiastic about closer union in Europe than it has in the other ten countries. In recent years, however, there appears to have been a substantial shift in attitudes in Britain.

A Eurobarometer survey in 1987 found that 52 per cent of the British respondents were in favour of the evolution of the EC towards a United States of Europe, compared with 37 per cent who were against. They were evenly balanced as to whether they expected to use a European currency or elect a head of a European government by the year 2000. Twice as many were prepared to entrust a European government with responsibility in economics, foreign affairs and defence by the second decade of the coming century as were not. The results of the European elections in 1989 suggest that since the survey was made opinion may have become still more favourable towards European unification. Surveys also indicate that the younger generation is much more 'European' in outlook than the over-50s; this implies a progressive shift in attitudes over the period to 2010 in favour of closer European integration.

In view of these considerations the balance of probability would seem to be that, despite real doubts and difficulties, at some point in the 1990s Britain will decide to swallow its objections and join the movement towards economic and political union. The prospect, then, is that by 2010 there is likely to be a union, covering a wide range of economic and external policy areas, with a powerful supranational authority administering them, with the European Parliament jointly with the Council of Ministers exercising the main control over it – and with Britain a member.

Additional members of the Community

It is probable that by 2010 the European Community will have been joined by additional members, and that others again will have acquired various kinds of associate status.

New members in Western Europe

Austria, Norway, Sweden and Finland all have special trading arrangements with the EC, but some of them have been finding it irksome that, with the growing power and importance of the Community, in increasingly many ways they are in practice obliged to fall in with EC decisions, without having any say in them. This problem is likely to get worse with the provisions of the Single Market; and worse still if there are further moves towards closer union. The question is therefore increasingly being asked: should they reconsider their earlier decisions not to join the European Community?

All these countries are stable, secure, prosperous democracies, with relatively open and highly competitive economies. For the EC there would be few serious problems in accepting them into full membership. In the past the main objections in all of these countries (except Norway) have been not economic but political. Sweden has a long tradition of international neutrality and Finland and Austria have had neutrality forced upon them after the war and this effectively has prevented them from joining a grouping which was seen as by no means neutral in the Cold War.

Recently, however, Soviet attitudes to the EC, previously hostile, have become much more benign, it being seen as a source of support for the struggling economies of Eastern Europe and the USSR. And with the ending of the Cold War, Soviet policy on the neutrality of Finland and Austria has been greatly relaxed, and Swedish political anxieties about involvement with the Community have been reduced.

It is therefore likely that, during the coming decade, for these countries, the advantages of joining the EC will increase, the disadvantages of staying out will also increase, and the importance of preserving neutrality will diminish. Accordingly, Austria has already applied for membership, the other three may well do so quite soon, and by 2000 it is very probable that all four of them will have joined the Community.

Switzerland, although no less well-suited than the other four countries for membership in terms of its social, economic and political institutions, has a particular reluctance to join any international organisation, membership of which could be thought to prejudice its independence and neutrality; and this makes it less likely than the other four countries to join the Community before the turn of the century. However, the changes taking place in Europe may be expected to make it likely that Switzerland also will join in the early decades of the next century.

New members in Eastern Europe

The return of democracy and national independence and the move to more market-based economic systems make feasible the accession to the Community of new members in Eastern Europe. The development of associate membership is likely to precede any new accessions.

Czechoslovakia, Hungary and Poland tend to see themselves as part of *Central* as opposed to *Eastern* Europe, and are likely to seek ever closer links with Western Europe. They are already receiving substantial economic assistance. The considerable differences in their present economic and social structures would make difficult an early acceptance into full membership, particularly in the case of Poland. However, it is likely that a looser form of association will soon be renegotiated, and it is quite likely that well before 2010 they will have changed sufficiently for full membership to have been achieved. Czechoslovakia and Hungary in particular may well be in a position to join by the late 1990s.

Yugoslavia's internal difficulties make full membership in the 1990s very improbable, but by 2010 it is possible that internal conflicts will have been settled and democratic institutions established making membership feasible, either for Yugoslavia as a whole, or for a break-away Slovenia or Croatia.

Applications to join may also be expected from Bulgaria and Romania and (after political changes) Albania. Differences in levels of development and in economic and social structures make full membership for all three rather improbable by 2010, although forms of association, particularly economic and environmental links, are likely to develop in the 1990s.

There may at some stage be applications from the Baltic states, Ukraine or other republics in the Soviet Union. While by 2000 the Baltic states are likely to have achieved independence and may be seen as possible members if Poland and the Nordic countries have already joined the Community, the likelihood of other republics in the present Soviet Union getting full membership before 2010 looks more remote.

Other possible new members

Finally, there is a fair probability that Iceland will have joined the Community by 2010; and there are already requests for membership from Malta, Cyprus and Turkey, each of which gives rise to problems of various kinds. It seems likely that Malta and Cyprus will have joined by 2010, but the more difficult problems raised by Turkey suggest that some form of association is more likely.

Effects of new members

The increase in the membership of the Community from six to twelve between 1970 and 1990 had the effect of nearly doubling its population; at the same time the acquisition of the new members, combined with the continuing growth of the original members, meant that its total gross domestic product more than doubled. In 1990 the reunification of Germany brought the automatic incorporation of East Germany into the

The Expanding European Community

1970

1990

Members

West Germany
France
Italy
Netherlands
Belgium
Luxembourg

Members

Germany   Britain
France   Spain
Italy   +   Denmark
Netherlands   Greece
Belgium   Portugal
Luxembourg   Ireland

Population
'00 millions

Population
'00 millions

Gross Domestic Product
'000 bn ECUs at 1990 prices

Gross Domestic Product
'000 bn ECUs at 1990 prices

Between 1970 and 1990 the European Community's membership doubled, its area and population nearly doubled and its gross domestic product more than doubled.

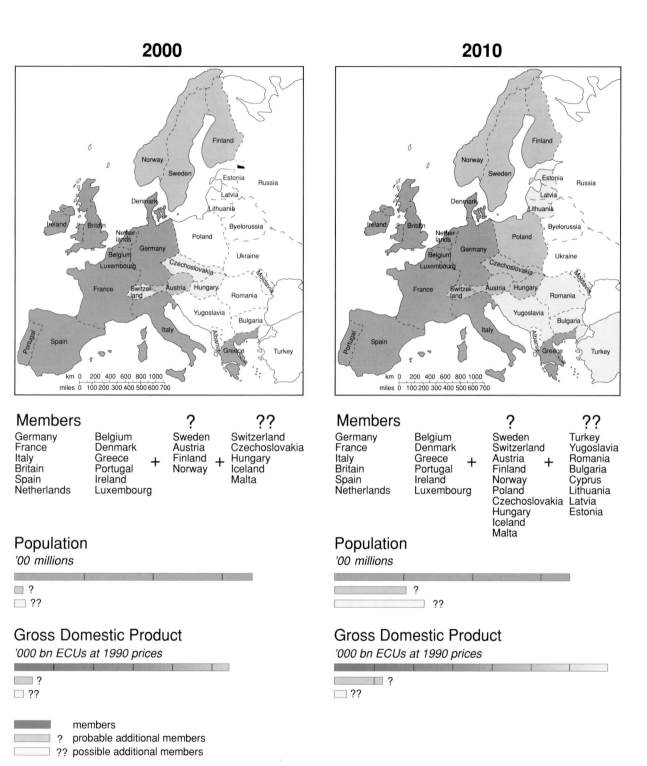

2000

Members

		?	**??**
Germany	Belgium	Sweden	Switzerland
France	Denmark	Austria	Czechoslovakia
Italy	Greece	Finland	Hungary
Britain	Portugal	Norway	Iceland
Spain	Ireland		Malta
Netherlands	Luxembourg		

Population
'00 millions

?

??

Gross Domestic Product
'000 bn ECUs at 1990 prices

?

??

2010

Members

		?	**??**
Germany	Belgium	Sweden	Turkey
France	Denmark	Switzerland	Yugoslavia
Italy	Greece	Austria	Romania
Britain	Portugal	Finland	Bulgaria
Spain	Ireland	Norway	Cyprus
Netherlands	Luxembourg	Poland	Lithuania
		Czechoslovakia	Latvia
		Hungary	Estonia
		Iceland	
		Malta	

Population
'00 millions

?

??

Gross Domestic Product
'000 bn ECUs at 1990 prices

?

??

members
? probable additional members
?? possible additional members

Between 1990 and 2010 its membership may double again; but if all ten of the most likely new members join, this will increase the Community's total population by less than one third, and its gross domestic product by less than half the increase expected in the economies of the existing members.

Community, adding a further 5 per cent to its total population and a smaller percentage to its total GDP.

It can be calculated that if the four most likely countries join the Community by 2000 they will add a further 7 per cent to its total population, and if the five next most likely countries join they will add a further 10 per cent. In terms of additional GDP the effect of the former group of countries would be to add about a further 14 per cent (less than half the increase expected from the growth of the existing members), while the next most likely five would add a further 7 per cent or so.

If by 2010 all the more probable countries joined the Community, its population would be increased by about 30 per cent above the 1990 level; and if all the possible ones joined as well the total increase in population would be about 70 per cent. The increase in total GDP, if all the former group joined, would be about 30 per cent above the 1990 level (less than half the increase from the growth of existing members), and the increase from the possible extra members would be a further 7 per cent or so.

These estimates are based on UN population forecasts (which may be slightly inaccurate) and the broad-brush assumption that GDP grows at an average rate of 2.5 per cent a year (which is much more likely to be wrong – but not by enough to change the broad conclusions).

The conclusion which emerges is that the difficulties in enlarging the membership of the Community will not be primarily to do with *size*:

- *Population*
  total population will be increased by only about 30 per cent by the addition of the more probable new members;

- *GDP*
  the prospective new members will bring a much smaller increase in the total size of the economy than that which is likely anyway from the growth of the existing members.

The main practical difficulties with enlarging the membership seem much more likely to be related to *other* aspects such as:

- *number of members*
  an increase in membership from 12 to 22-30 would tend to make the European Council and the Council of Ministers unwieldy and would require a restructuring of many of the Community's administrative arrangements;

- *institutions*
  an increase in membership from 12 to 22-30 would also multiply the number of different legal, political, administrative, and business systems which would need to be accommodated;

- *cultures*
  an increase in the number of languages used from 9 to 18-28, together with a widening of the range of other cultural differences, would involve further problems and increases in costs;

- *distance*
  Ankara is nearly three times as far from Brussels as Rome is, and Reykjavik is six times as far from Brussels as London is.

It therefore seems that, while size in itself is unlikely to preclude a substantial enlargement of the European Community in the next twenty years, the need for radical reform of its institutions will set limits to the number and diversity of new member countries which can be absorbed by 2010.

Implications

While there is inevitably much uncertainty about the exact form the future of Europe will take, the most likely outcome by 2010 is probably:

- movement by the existing 12 members of the European Community (including Britain) towards a much closer European Union, with supranational control over large areas of economic and social policy, with a much stronger European Parliament, but stopping short of full control of international relations and defence;

- addition to its membership, very probably; of the Nordic countries, Austria, Switzerland; and quite probably also of Czechoslovakia, Hungary, Poland, Cyprus, Malta and parts or all of Yugoslavia; with a looser form of association for a number of other countries in Eastern and Southern Europe.

The closer and wider union will have an economy comparable in size with that of the United States and larger than that of Japan or the Soviet Union. It should help provide increased competitiveness and fuller development of technology and hence the possibility of faster growth of productivity.

The Single Market, by removing possibility of protection by tariff and non-tariff barriers, and monetary union, by removing the possibility of exchange rate depreciation, will present problems for countries that are less competitive or become so through rates of inflation above the average. To avoid their being at risk of chronic deflation and unemployment, it is likely that mechanisms will need to be devised for rechannelling the surpluses of the economically stronger countries and providing regional support for the weaker ones.[63,64] Much more stringent environmental policies will also be needed to avoid further ecological degradation from economic growth, especially in Eastern Europe and the Mediterranean countries.

The much greater range of areas covered by decisions of the supranational institutions will erode national sovereignty, giving importance to the application of the principle of subsidiarity (devolving of decisions to the lowest level practicable) and to the strengthening of the effectiveness of the European Parliament, which will increasingly become a major forum for political debate.

Distinct separate national identities will not be in danger of being erased, and strong differences in language and culture will persist, but there will be some tendency towards cultural convergence and English will tend to become even more the leading language, with German probably supplanting French as the EC's 'second' language.

Not only in consumption of the goods in the shops, but in attitudes generally people in Britain will become far more 'European' by 2010. Transnational news and entertainment media, increased travel and much more frequent movements between countries for work and study will all tend to increase the feeling of being European as well as being British.

BRITAIN IN 2010

The previous nine chapters considered some of the main global changes, and developments in particular countries and regions, that are likely to influence Britain in the next two decades and to set the context within which policy makers in Britain will need to operate.

The next six chapters consider the future of Britain itself, the main focus of the report. They examine the likely developments, the links between them and the factors affecting them, with a view to arriving at an informed, consistent and objective view of the prospects ahead.

Chapter 12 considers projected changes in population and their implications for other areas; and Chapter 13 considers the future work force, changes in employment and the outlook for unemployment.

Chapter 14 examines developments in the environment – regional shifts, the countryside, towns and cities, shopping, housing, water, waste management, air pollution, transport, energy and global warming – and the interactions between them.

Chapter 15 reviews prospective advances in science and technology and assesses the extent to which they are likely to be used and the effects they may be expected to have.

Chapter 16 appraises the prospects for the economy in the light of the developments considered in the previous chapters and forecasts the likely future rate of growth and the form it will take.

Chapters 17 outlines the main social changes likely to develop over the next 20 years in Britain: the changes in individual consumption and in social provisions, in personal life-styles and behaviour patterns, and in community attitudes and values.

Chapter 18 illustrates some of the economic implications of alternative policy choices. Three scenarios outline the impact of some policy measures based on market-oriented, interventionist and environmentalist approaches.

BRITAIN in 2010

**P**opulation

12. **P**opulation

Since it is the aims and needs of people with which, fundamentally, we are concerned, and it is also people who provide the prime resource for fulfilling them, population is the natural starting point for any study of the longer-term future.

There are also a number of practical considerations that make population an appropriate area with which to start. First, population forecasts can be made to a large extent independently of developments in other areas, while their results have important implications for developments in other areas. Hence there are advantages in undertaking population forecasts first so that the results can be used in subsequent consideration of possible developments in other areas.

And second, population is an area in which data are relatively full and accurate and available in a form that enables forward projections to be made with a reasonable degree of confidence.

This is not to say that population forecasts are always reliable – on the contrary, some of the most carefully worked out ones have turned out to be substantially inaccurate – but merely that experience has shown that forecasts founded on demographic projections have more often been vindicated by events than those based on expected developments in other areas, such as breakthroughs in science or shifts in social patterns.[65]

There are four main elements in population forecasts: mortality rates and fertility rates, which together give the natural increase or decrease in the original population; and inward and outward migration flows, which together give the net migration rate. The natural increase or decrease in the original population, together with the net migration change, gives the total change in population. Each of these elements is affected by a number of different factors which can be considered separately.

In Britain the Office of Population Censuses and Surveys (OPCS) prepares national projections based on the latest available census in 1981, subsequent records of births and deaths, and a number of assumptions about future rates of mortality, fertility and migration.[66] It prepares a *principal* projection that is its best estimate of the most likely outcome and is therefore usually the most appropriate one to focus on for planning and forecasting purposes. It also prepares a number of *variant* projections based on higher and lower assumptions for the component elements. These are useful in providing an indication of the extent of the uncertainties present and showing the range within which future population changes may be expected to fall.

Mortality rates

In the *principal* OPCS projection it is assumed that mortality rates will 'improve' (ie people will be living longer) over the next 40 years, but not thereafter. Initially, it is assumed that rates of improvement similar to those that have been experienced recently will persist, but in later years the rate of improvement will diminish, halving for each successive ten year period. The overall improvement over the 20 years to 2010 ranges from about 15 per cent for infants and people in their late 60s and 70s to about 10 per cent for people in their late 30s. Quantitatively, the greatest impact is on the elderly population. Life expectancy at birth for men rises from 72.3 in 1990 to 74.3 in 2010, and life expectancy for women from 78.2 to 79.4.

The *variant* OPCS projections consist of a *slow variant* in which mortality improves at only half the rate in the *principal* projection and a *fast variant* in which it improves at one-and-a-half times the rate in the *principal* projection.

During the course of the present century average life expectancy at birth has increased by nearly one half. The main improvements have been in the younger age groups as a result of a dramatic cut in maternity and infant death rates and in far fewer deaths from diseases which previously were often fatal in the younger and middle age groups. For those aged 75, on the other hand, life expectancy has changed very little, and the tiny proportion of people surviving to the age of 100 has not increased at all. The difference in the overall figures is because far fewer infants and young people are dying prematurely and hence a higher proportion of people are living the full 'natural span' of 70 or 80 years – *not* because more old people are living on to an even greater age.[67]

Factors in past mortality rate changes

Part of the improvement in mortality rates which has taken place has been due to advances in medical science and improvements in medical services, particularly for childbirth; but a more important factor has probably been the general improvement in living conditions, particularly in sanitation, water, housing, heating and nutrition. World Health Organisation statistics[68] show that life expectancy of men aged 65 is substantially higher in Japan, Switzerland, Canada, Sweden and the United States than in Britain, suggesting there is the possibility of further improvement in Britain as living standards rise further in the future; on the other hand, life expectancy is also higher in Cuba, Greece and Spain, suggesting that overall levels of affluence are not the only factor involved.

Also, within Britain at present there are substantial differences in mortality ratios between different social classes (with different income levels). Mortality ratios in general rise in regular steps from social class I (professional) through to social class V (unskilled manual). For deaths from strokes they are two-and-a-half times as high in class V as in class I, and for deaths from lung cancer and from stomach ulcers four times as high.[69] This suggests there may be lower overall ratios in the future when people in the manual worker social classes enjoy higher standards of living as a result of increases in general national prosperity, or change their diets or reduce their smoking as a result of greater awareness of health risks.

However, it cannot be taken for granted that rising living standards in the future will necessarily lead to longer life expectancy. Higher living standards may also be associated with life-styles which bring more obesity, alcoholism, stress and lack of fresh air and exercise, tending to *reduce* life expectancy; on the other hand they may go with increased concern over healthy diet and more widespread adoption of régimes to maintain physical fitness. In the United States both kinds of development are being experienced simultaneously in different sections of the population.

All in all, the evidence of past trends suggests that it is reasonable to expect some further decline in mortality rates – but probably on a diminishing scale. The long decline in infant mortality rates has recently been tending to level off[70] (possibly because of worsening living conditions in the very poorest families despite the increase in general prosperity); the death rates in the middle age ranges are already low, making it difficult to achieve substantial further improvements; while in the highest age groups there is still no sign of people living beyond the 'natural span' after which life prospects appear still to be constrained, ultimately, by the limits of nature's 'program' for the species. As age increases, cells reproduce more slowly, bones become brittle, muscles get weaker, sight and hearing deteriorate, vital organs work less reliably, brains cease to work efficiently and the immune system loses its effectiveness.

Are there any new factors which may overrule these 'natural' limits and bring significantly greater life expectancy? Or others which may reverse the past trends and reduce it?

New factors in longevity

In 1975 in the United States Congress founded the National Institute on Aging,[71] with funding which has since increased to $200m a year, and there has been a considerable research effort by private sector companies, particularly in the United States and West Germany, to develop products and techniques to retard or arrest the process of ageing. Anti-ageing has become big business – a congressional study has estimated it to be worth as much as $3bn a year.[72] However. all this effort does not yet appear to have achieved any breakthroughs. Products have been put on the market which are claimed to reverse hair loss and skin wrinkling and others under development aim to prevent memory impairment, to control hypertension, to maintain the efficiency of the immune system and to provide replacements for worn out organs. Considerable claims have also been made for numerous dietary and exercise régimes. It seems likely that some of these developments may help keep people healthy, active and good looking for longer, but it is doubtful if any of them will make more than a very minor dent in the mortality statistics.

A more radical approach has been adopted by a number of companies in America which are offering their clients resurrection through cryonics – deep-freezing their bodies in liquid nitrogen in the hope that at some future time medical science will have found a way of reviving them. This is a very long-shot hope, since at present no-one has much idea of what techniques could be used for achieving the re-animation. So far only a few bodies and heads (which are cheaper to keep frozen) have been preserved in this way and their future, if they have a future, looks like being an extremely distant one.

Still more fundamentally, research is being undertaken with a view to understanding, and perhaps eventually modifying, the genetic agents which are believed to control the ageing process. This is probably the only area of research which, if successful, would offer the potential for radically extending the normal life-span – with the very considerable consequences this would imply. However, there is little reason to suppose that this research will lead to practical results for a very long time – if ever – and almost certainly it will not do so before 2010.

Thus there seems very little likelihood of any new factor emerging that will lead to a dramatic lengthening of life expectancy. Is there any risk of a new factor working the other way, leading to a *shortening* of life expectancy and reversing past trends?

AIDS

In the past there have been three major causes of sharp increases in mortality rates: wars, famines and epidemics. There seems little risk of Britain being involved in a major war in the course of the coming two decades (see Chapter 3); or of suffering from famine; or from epidemics of any of the traditional diseases. There is, however, a new threat in the form of Acquired Immune Deficiency Syndrome (AIDS). How serious is the threat? Is it of such a scale that it could upset previous mortality trends in Britain?

The condition, which is believed always to be fatal eventually, and for which at present there is neither vaccine nor cure, has already killed large numbers of people in several countries in Africa and is spreading to most other parts of the world. The World Health Organisation (WHO) reports a total of 263,000 cases of AIDS in 156 countries by mid-1990, but believes the true total is three times that and expects a total of about 6 million cases worldwide by the year 2000.[73]

In Britain the number of people suffering from AIDS, although rising, is still relatively small, but estimates of likely future numbers vary greatly and some are high – the OPCS has estimated that AIDS will kill 100,000 men in England and Wales by the year 2000 and 200,000 by 2030,[74] while the AIDS working party of the Institute of Actuaries has estimated that AIDS has doubled the risk of dying early for men in the 30-50 age range.[75] A more recent estimate by the Public Health Laboratory Service suggests that the number of deaths may turn out to be only about half that originally estimated.[76]

However, the reality is that at present estimates cannot be more than speculative. This is because the nature of the disease and the circumstances of infection (through blood and other body fluids, particularly in sex) are not well understood and, crucially, because there is an incubation period of about 8-12 years between infection and the appearance of the first symptoms of the disease itself.[77,78] Thus the new cases of AIDS today are people who were infected, typically, about ten years ago – and there is no accurate information available about the (possibly much greater) numbers infected since.

However, a major study of sexual behaviour[79] is being undertaken, and should improve understanding of the circumstances of transmission; and a broad programme of anonymous blood testing[80] is being carried out to provide data on the numbers who are HIV-positive (infected with the virus but not yet showing symptoms of the disease itself), and this should provide much firmer evidence of the numbers likely to suffer from AIDS in the coming ten years or so.

In Britain up to now the great majority of people with AIDS have been in three categories: haemophiliacs who were infected through being given contaminated blood;[81] drug abusers infected through the shared use of contaminated needles;[82,83] and active homosexuals who have up to now been much the largest category. Following changes in behaviour, there are signs that the incidence of infection among homosexuals has stopped rising and has probably started to fall.[84]

The main uncertainty is whether HIV infection is likely to spread widely – it may indeed already have done so – among the much larger heterosexual population. In some African countries the majority of those with AIDS are in the heterosexual population and in Britain the numbers of cases of AIDS acquired through heterosexual contacts has doubled in 12 months.[85] The numbers are still small, but are expected to reach nearly 1000 by 1992, and by 1994 it is expected that more new cases will be occurring in heterosexuals than in homosexuals or drug abusers.[86]

It is possible that when firm information becomes available of the extent of HIV infection it will turn out that the numbers are much smaller than some of the early estimates have suggested. It is also possible that, if the figures are large, they will lead to changes in sexual behaviour. Finally, it is possible that the long incubation period may mean that, for at least a proportion of those infected, effective treatments may have been developed before the time when symptoms of the disease itself appear. Leading pharmaceutical companies in a number of different countries are committing very considerable resources to AIDS research. One drug already in use appears to have some effect in delaying the onset of AIDS symptoms,[87] there are a large number of potential treatments on trial and under development,[88,89] and some scientists are now predicting that a vaccine could be ready by the end of the century.[90]

Thus there are a number of reasons for expecting that AIDS will probably not result in a sharp rise in mortality rates in Britain, but the absence of satisfactory evidence at present means that for the time being all estimates are highly speculative.

Fertility rates

In the years following the Second World War, birth rates rose sharply in Britain, as in most of the other countries in Western Europe, but subsequently they fell back to rates near, or below, the level needed to achieve replacement.

The OPCS *principal* projection assumes that in the coming two decades fertility rates in Britain will rise a little, but will remain just below replacement level. Average completed family size for women born in 1975 will reach 2.0 children, as opposed to the 2.1 needed to achieve replacement. This is a somewhat higher level than is predicted for women born in the early 1960s (1.95), but considerably below the level for women born in the early 1940s (2.38). The average age of motherhood for women born after 1965 is assumed to be 28 years, the same as for women born in the 1920s, but higher than for women born in the 1940s (26 years).

The *low variant* for fertility assumes a continuing fall in average family sizes to a level of 1.8 children for women born in 1980 or later, a level similar to that for women born at the beginning of the century. The *high variant* for fertility assumes an increase in average family size to 2.2 children for women born in 1970 or later, a level which is nevertheless lower than that for women born in the 1930s and having children in the early 1960s.

Whereas, except in time of war or disaster, mortality rates normally change only slowly, fertility rates, which are more a matter of individual choice, can change more suddenly as a result of changes in social attitudes and customs, particularly with regard to sex, marriage and family planning, and also in response to changes in opportunities in education and employment, in incomes and in general confidence about the future.

There is thus the possibility of fertility rates changing substantially in the space of a short period. Even quite large changes, however, will affect only the numbers in the youngest age groups and so will have only a limited effect on the size of the total population in 2010 – particularly if the changes occur in the later part of the period.

There is some possibility that future birth rates may fall a little as a result of improvements in family planning methods, or rise temporarily if new health risks are discovered which discourage the use of certain existing methods. There is also the distant possibility that techniques will be developed for choosing in advance the sex of babies, potentially leading to a disruption over the long term in the balance between the numbers of each sex.

Much more important, however, are likely to be social factors. For example, birth rates will tend to *fall* if more women give priority to their jobs and careers and have fewer children, later children or none at all; if housing shortages or high house prices or reduced child benefits or high unemployment make it more difficult to afford the costs of supporting children; or if increased preferences for expenditure on other things in order to get a higher material standard of living results in people deciding to keep their families smaller than otherwise.

On the other hand birth rates will tend to *rise* if, for example, tax and benefit changes (for example for child minders) make it easier financially for women to go out to work despite having young children; if fuller employment and shortages of juvenile labour result in more jobs for women, particularly part-time jobs, so that more women have the opportunity of employment while their children are young; or if increasing prosperity means that fewer families depend on earnings from the woman to maintain reasonable living standards.

The net effect of these and other social considerations is not easy to predict with confidence and there is thus the possibility that fertility rates will turn out to be substantially different from those assumed in the OPCS forecasts. In the absence, however, of any strong reasons for expecting particular alternative rates, the assumptions used in the OPCS forecasts would seem to be the best available basis to work on.

Migration

In recent years total immigration into Britain has been roughly balanced by emigration out of Britain and the net change in total population due to migration has in consequence been small. The OPCS assumes that over the next two decades there will be a slightly larger net movement out, averaging about 17,000 a year, resulting in a total decrease in population due to migration between 1990 and 2010 of about 350,000 – offsetting about one seventh of the natural increase of the existing population expected over the same period. In the course of the subsequent three decades it is assumed that the net outward migration will decline to zero.

Past migration

In the immediate postwar period there was some migration into Britain of people from continental Europe and, in the 1950s, 1960s and early 1970s, people from many parts of the world, in particular from the Caribbean countries, the Indian subcontinent, East Africa and Southern Europe, mostly coming in search of better employment opportunities. In the period

1974-1988 (the most recent 15 years for which figures are available) the inward movement has been mainly from the Indian subcontinent (59,000 net) and from the African Commonwealth countries (14,000 net)[91] but, with much tighter entry restrictions, the total numbers have been smaller than before and composed predominantly of dependants of earlier immigrants.[92]

In the 1974-78 period the largest net outflows were to Canada, Australia and New Zealand, but in the 1984-88 period movements in both directions were much smaller.[91]

The migration flows between Britain and the other countries of the European Community (mainly those in Southern Europe) greatly increased between 1974-78 and 1984-88, with a small net outflow in the earlier period changing to a small net inflow in the later one.[91]

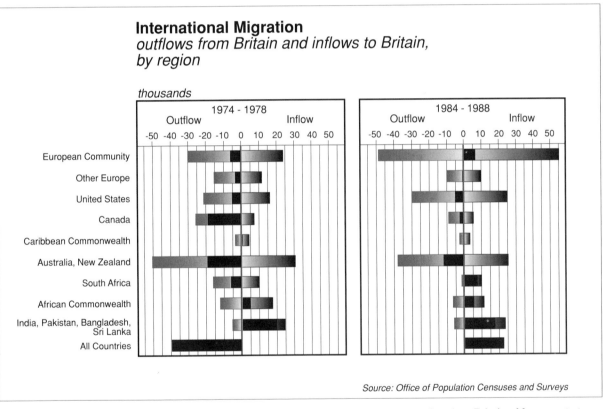

International Migration
*outflows from Britain and inflows to Britain,
by region*

Source: Office of Population Censuses and Surveys

Between 1974-1978 and 1984-1988 the net flow out of Britain has turned into a net flow into Britain. Movements to and from Canada and Australia have declined, and movements to and from the EC and the United States have increased.

Future inward migration

After 1992 the Single European Market will provide for mutual recognition of work qualifications. This will not necessarily lead to much increase in the numbers of people coming from the other European countries to live in Britain, because movement between the EC countries is already relatively unrestricted, and people considering leaving countries in

Southern Europe in search of better employment prospects may tend to prefer to go to other countries in Northern Europe if their living standards are higher, growth rates faster and unemployment levels lower than they are in Britain. However, the recent increase in net movements into Britain raises the possibility that people from some EC countries may in future choose to come to Britain in more substantial numbers.

The major political and economic changes taking place in the Soviet Union and Eastern Europe may be expected to lead to closer economic links between the European Community and some of the countries of Eastern Europe, but it seems likely that few of them will be joining as full members (with free movement rights) until some time in the 21st century (see Chapter 11). It therefore seems unlikely that large numbers of people will be coming to Britain from Eastern Europe in the period up to 2010. However, there will probably be substantial population movements in the USSR and pressures on EC states, especially Germany, from Soviet and Eastern European 'economic migrants' seeking better opportunities in Western Europe.

Developments in Hong Kong could lead to substantial numbers of people coming from there to Britain in the late 1990s. The scale of this movement will depend on developments in China, restrictions on entry to Britain and restrictions on entry to other countries. There is at present great uncertainty on each of these points, and although the OPCS assumptions do not seem to make allowance for much increase in inward migration from Hong Kong, there is the possibility of an increase on a considerable scale.

Finally, there is the possibility that economic and environmental or political problems in parts of the Third World (see Chapters 5 and 8) will lead to pressures on Britain to accept more people from them.

Future outward migration

Over a very long period there has been a flow of migration out of Britain to other countries thought to offer better opportunities, in particular to Canada, Australia and the United States. This may be expected to continue, especially if living standards in Britain are believed to be significantly less attractive than in these other countries.

With the Single Market there will be no formal barriers to prevent people from Britain migrating also to countries in Europe with higher living standards. However, even after the establishment of the Single Market there will still be institutional, cultural and professional obstacles to deter people seeking to move to professional, managerial and technical jobs in other countries. The relatively small number of British people who are fluent in foreign languages seems also likely to remain a barrier, although recent educational changes and growing links with other EC members should lead to a gradual rise in our skills in this area.

Type of migration

In some ways more important than the total size of migration is the characteristics of the migrants themselves. They tend to include disproportionate numbers of males in the younger, economically-active, age groups, so that inward movements tend to strengthen the productive capacity of the economy and outward movements to weaken it.

The migrants who came into Britain in the 1960s and 1970s were mainly manual workers from less prosperous countries who took low-paid jobs in sectors in which it had been difficult to attract enough local people – Caribbeans in health, transport and local authority services, Asians in clothing, textiles and retailing. Those moving out of Britain have tended to be those with higher-level manual skills in demand in other countries and, particularly, people with high-level professional qualifications sought after in countries like the United States – the 'brain drain'.

Future migration movements may be increasingly of people with above average skills and qualifications: managers and key technicians moving between countries for multinational companies, senior administrators, professional and business people coming in from Hong Kong; top academics and researchers going to North America and, possibly, some kinds of technician and skilled manual worker going to other countries in Europe.

Forecasts

Total population

The OPCS *principal* projection forecasts an increase in total population of 4.5 per cent (2.6 million) from 57.4 million in 1990 to 60.0 million in 2010. This is more than the increase of 3.3 per cent (1.8 million) in the previous 20 year period.

However, this greater total increase indicates not a return to a permanently faster rate of population growth, but a surge which will level off by the end of the period. Total UK population increased by only 0.2 per cent in the five year period 1975-80, but the rate of increase speeded up to 1.4 per cent in the five year period 1985-90. This faster rate of increase is expected to be maintained in the 1990-95 and 1995-2000 periods, but to fall back to 0.7 per cent in the 2005-2010 period. Moreover this slowing down is expected to be followed by a small decline in later periods.

A similar pattern of stabilising population levels is forecast in most other countries in Western Europe.[53,93]

The *high variant* forecast (obtained by combining the faster improvement in mortality assumptions with the higher fertility rate assumptions) suggests a total increase in population between 1990 and 2010 of 8.2 per cent (4.7 million); and the *low variant* (obtained by combining

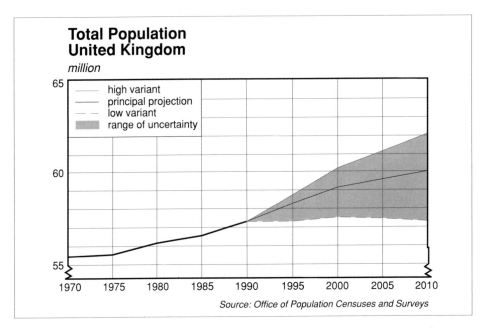

**Total Population
United Kingdom**

million

— high variant
— principal projection
– – low variant
▓ range of uncertainty

Source: Office of Population Censuses and Surveys

Between 1990 and 2010 the total population of the United Kingdom is forecast to increase by 2.6 million (4.5 per cent); however the range of uncertainty spreads from an increase of 4.7 million to no increase at all.

the slower improvement in mortality with the lower fertility assumptions) suggests no increase in population at all between 1990 and 2010.

Population structure

In some ways more important than the changes in total size of the population will be the changes in its structure. Only insignificant changes are forecast in the balance between the sexes – there will continue to be slightly more males than females in the younger age groups up to the mid forties, and slightly more females in the older age groups, with markedly more after the mid-1970s.

Between 1990 and 2010 the number of children under 15 is forecast to remain about the same (fewer infants in 2010 offset by more older children); and the number of teenagers (15-19), which has recently been falling sharply, is forecast to drop only a little further but then return to slightly above the present level by 2010.

More striking are the changes in the numbers of young adults. Between 1990 and 2010 the number in the 20-24 age group, already declining in the past five years, is expected to fall by 14 per cent (0.6 million), the number in the 25-29 age group by 23 per cent (1.1 million), and the number in the 30-34 age group by 17 per cent (0.7 million). Altogether, then, the total population aged 20-34, which rose by 2 million between 1970 and 1990, is expected to fall by nearly 2.4 million (nearly one fifth) between 1990 and 2010.

About half of this decline in the number of younger people of working age is forecast, however, to be offset by increases in the numbers in the older working age groups. There is also forecast to be an increase of 0.6 million people in the 60-64 age group.

The number of older people in the 65-79 age groups is not forecast to change greatly, but the number aged 80 or more is forecast to increase by 26 per cent (0.6 million) by 2010. This compares with increases of 20 per cent (1.1 million) in the 65-79 age groups and of 73 per cent (0.9 million) in the over 80s in the 1970-1990 period.

Altogether, the percentage of the total population under the age of 20 will be unchanged and the proportion over 60 will increase, with the result that the proportion of working age (20-59) is forecast to fall slightly from 53.4 per cent of the total in 1990 to 52.1 per cent in 2010.

Population forecasts to 2010

- Probable total increase of 2.6 million (4.6 per cent)

- Faster increase than in 1970-90

- No further fall in teenagers

- Fall of 2.4 million in young adults

- Higher average age in working population

- Little change in total aged 65-79

- 600,000 increase in over-80s

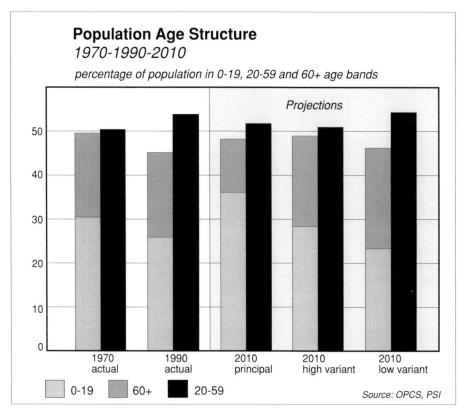

Population Age Structure
1970-1990-2010

percentage of population in 0-19, 20-59 and 60+ age bands

Projections

| 1970 actual | 1990 actual | 2010 principal | 2010 high variant | 2010 low variant |

0-19   60+   20-59

Source: OPCS, PSI

In 2010 the proportion of people under 20 is forecast to remain about the same, and the proportion over 60 is forecast to increase so that the proportion in the working age groups is lower than in 1990, but not as low as in 1970.

All the above changes are with the *principal* (most probable) forecasts. With the *high variant* there will be relatively more children and older people, leaving only 50.5 per cent of the population in the 20-59 age groups; and with the *low variant* the reverse, giving an increase to 54.3 per cent in the proportion of the population in the 20-59 age groups.

Implications

The total increase in population by 2010 expected in the OPCS *principal* forecast (2.6 million) is not large enough to be likely to give rise to serious social or economic problems, or to make the country feel noticeably more crowded than it does at present – although population movements within the country may lead to much faster population growth in some areas (see Chapter 14), with consequential pressures on housing, transport and infrastructure facilities, and on wages and prices.

The *low variant* forecast foresees *no change* in total population; and the *high variant* a faster rate of growth with a total increase in population between 1990 and 2010 of about 4 million. Even this latter increase would not, in itself, be likely to give rise to serious problems: although it would

Population forecasts: policy implications

- Fall in school rolls will not go on
- After 2000, fewer young adults wanting homes
- Big increase in over-65s comes after 2010, but pension issues become urgent well before 2010
- Increase in over-80s means more pressure on health and social care services

involve a rate of growth more than twice as great as that experienced in the past two decades, it would still be less than the increase accommodated in the two decades before them.

The expected changes in age structure are potentially more important in their implications. The dependency ratio (the non-working age population as a percentage of the working age population) is expected to worsen a little by 2010, but will still be more favourable than it was in 1970; and even with the *high* variant the dependency ratio is no worse than it was in 1970. However, it needs to be remembered that these comparisons are based on calculations in which the 'working age' range is treated as being the same at all dates. In reality, of course, the proportion of people in each age group who are actually seeking and available for work on the labour market varies over time in accordance with changes, for example, in the proportions of young people in education and training, the proportions of parents looking after children, and the proportions of older people in retirement, which in turn depend largely on the sizes of pensions and the ages at which people become eligible for them.

The numbers of children of different ages needing different types of education will, as in the past, fluctuate substantially, but probably not unmanageably. The increase in the number of school-age children expected will not be too great to be possible to handle; however, the important point is that it *will* be an *increase* – there is no prospect of a continuation of the sharp falls in school rolls which have made educational problems easier to cope with in the 1980s. And with the higher fertility assumptions in the *high* and *young variants* the numbers would of course be greater.

The sharp decline in the numbers of teenagers which has tightened the labour market in the past few years is not expected to go much further. However, even if the numbers in the age group stabilise, employers may still find increasing teenage recruitment problems if an increasing proportion stay on at school or go on to further or higher education or training – as will happen if policies are adopted to bring us more into line with practice in other leading industrial countries. One consequence of a further tightening of the supply of teenagers may be to push up juvenile wage rates; another may be increasing employment of women and creation of more part-time jobs.

The drop in the numbers of people in their 20s and early 30s implies fewer people in jobs but without family commitments and hence less purchasing power in the markets for young people's fashion goods and leisure activities; and also fewer people starting families and buying baby products.

The fall in numbers in the younger working age groups and the rise in numbers in the older working age groups will mean that the average age of the labour force is higher than in earlier periods, particularly if there is an increase in the proportions staying on in education and training.

The number of older people above the present pensionable age is forecast to increase, and would increase by more with the faster improvement in mortality rates in the *high* and *old variant* assumptions. If the age of eligibility for pensions were reduced the numbers drawing pensions would increase by a greater amount, and if the recent trend towards earlier retirement were to continue, the number of retired people would increase further still.

The increased number of old people may imply more people living on small incomes, with limited purchasing power directed mainly towards necessities. On the other hand, if pension levels improve in real terms, or more people have part-time semi-retirement jobs, there may be a growing market made up of people who have incomes quite high in relation to their family commitments, and who are fit and active and have the leisure to spend their discretionary income on various kinds of leisure activities.

The expected increase in very old people (aged 80 and over) is not very great in absolute numbers (about 550,000), but represents an increase of one quarter on the present numbers. With the *high* or the *old variant* the number would be more than 800,000, but even that would be less than the 900,000 increase already accommodated in the two decades since 1970. An important consideration with increases in the numbers of very old people is that a high proportion of them need medical and domiciliary care and consequently *any* increase in numbers implies additional burdens on health and social care services. In the past many of these very old people have been looked after by female relatives in the generation below. In 2010 it is expected that there will be more women than now in these age groups, but with changing attitudes to work and increasing employment opportunities it is likely that a higher proportion of them than now will be in jobs and a smaller proportion of them will be willing to undertake the care of elderly relatives. This implies the prospect of a further increase in pressures on publicly-provided care services.

Future migration patterns are very uncertain, and the net changes include a substantial proportion of people who migrate for a limited period and then later return home; but even if the numbers are small, the kinds of people involved may be of disproportionate economic importance. Potential inward migrants from Hong Kong are likely to be far more affluent, educated and commercially-skilled than most of the immigrants in the 1960s and 1970s; and inward migrants from Australia, Canada, India and the United States are likely to include a proportion of people with high-level professional skills. On the other hand, potential outward migrants to European countries are likely to include people with key industrial skills, and those to North America to include top research scientists, whose contribution to Britain's academic excellence and industrial competitiveness may be important.

BRITAIN in 2010

 # Employment

13. Employment

What are the long-term future prospects for employment? Is there likely to be a good match between the people wanting work and the jobs for them to do? Or are there likely to be too few suitable jobs for all the people wanting work – and hence unemployment? Or too few suitable people for all the job opportunities created by developments in the economy – and hence labour shortages and inflation?

The future of employment, and unemployment, is partly a matter of numbers – how the total number of people in the potential labour force compares with the total number of potential jobs; and it is partly a matter of characteristics – how well the potential workers and jobs are matched to each other in time, place, cost, skills and other characteristics. We consider first the potential total future labour force, and second the potential total future jobs; and then go on to consider how good a match there is likely to be between the characteristics of each and the possible implications for actual employment and unemployment over the period to 2010.

Potential labour force

The potential future labour force (that is, the total number of people in work or seeking work in the labour market) can best be estimated by taking the forecasts of the numbers of people of each sex in each age group expected in future years and estimating the percentages of them likely to be in jobs or seeking them (their activity rates).

For future population numbers the most suitable starting point is the *principal* forecasts of the OPCS discussed in the previous chapter. For the percentages of different age/sex groups likely to be economically active there are no forecasts available for Britain for as far ahead as 2010. The Department of Employment's forecasts[96] extend from 1990 to 2001 and even the Department's less ambitious forecasts to 1995 warned that 'figures for later years must be treated with greater caution'.

The reason for the scarcity of longer-term forecasts is that activity rates have changed greatly in the past, and are likely to change further in the future, in response to a variety of factors which are not easy to predict accurately for long periods ahead. Consequently, some of the predictions which have been made, for example those made for 1975-1995 for the European Commission,[97] have proved unreliable.

Accordingly, it has been necessary for PSI to prepare special forecasts through to 2010, and these must be regarded as tentative. Although separate activity rates have been prepared for each five-year age group of each sex, the assumptions adopted can most conveniently be explained in terms of four broad age/sex groups.

Men aged 25-59

This group is the least problematic of the four; activity rates have been very high over a long period, although there has been a gradual fall, particularly in the older part of this age group. It is assumed for the projection that 1990 activity rates in each of the five-year age groups will continue unchanged to 2010, but because the proportion of the total in the upper end of this age group (where activity rates are lower) is expected to increase a little, the effect is to lower slightly the overall activity rate for all men aged 25-59.

Women aged 25-59

Women's activity rates have been rising steadily since the war towards the point when the rate for childless women equals that for men. This rate was reached for women in their 20s during the 1970s and for women in their 30s in the 1980s, but rates are expected to continue rising for women in their 40s during the 1990s and for women in their 50s during the first decade of the next century.

The effect of these rising rates in the upper age groups and also of changes in the proportions of women with children in particular age groups, will be to increase the overall activity rate for all women aged 25-59.

It should be noted that these activity rates will be higher if stronger feminist attitudes result in more women being determined to pursue careers; or if improved child-care facilities, grants or tax allowances make it easier to go to work while children are young; or if employers provide improved opportunities for part-time or shift work, or crèches for employees.

Men and women aged 60 and over

The proportion of people continuing to work beyond the state pension age (at present 60 for women, 65 for men) has been falling over the entire postwar period. This appears to have been associated with the rise in the value of state pensions and in the value and coverage of occupational pensions and in the value of capital assets in people's possession. The fall has accelerated in recent years because of the serious deterioration in employment opportunities for older people and the use of early retirement to secure workforce reduction. This has also had a marked effect on the activity rate of men in the 60-64 age group (immediately before retirement age) which, after falling from 91 per cent in 1961 to 82 per cent in 1975, has since fallen even further to 55 per cent in 1990.

For the forecasts it has been assumed that for men in the 60-64 age group activity rates will continue at their present levels; but that for men and women above pension age activity rates will decline at an exponential rate until they reach 'saturation' levels which a Europe-wide study of labour market behaviour[99] suggests may be reached at 5 per cent for men aged 65 and over and for women aged 60-64, and 1 per cent for women aged 65 and over.

If the pension age for men is reduced below 65, for example in response to high recent levels of early retirement, or to bring it into line with the age for women, this may be expected to lead to activity rates lower than assumed for the forecasts. On the other hand, if the pension age is *raised*, because people are living longer and the increasing proportion of old people in the population is making the payment of pensions an increasing burden for people in the younger age groups, this may be expected to lead to activity rates higher than those assumed in the forecasts.

Young people aged 16-24

At present 75 per cent of people in the 16-19 age group and 81 per cent of those in the 20-24 age group are economically active, and only about 25 per cent and 5-6 per cent respectively are in full-time education or training. One possibility is that the low proportion in education and training will continue through to 2010. An alternative possibility is that measures will be taken to double the proportions of these age groups who are in full-time education or training by 2010 in order to bring the situation in Britain into line with what has been achieved in some of our main competitors already.[100]

For the main forecasts we have assumed no change in the proportions economically active in these age groups; but we have also, for comparison, made alternative calculations on the basis of a doubling in the proportions in full-time education and training.

Potential labour force in 2010

The assumptions used for the forecasts result in a drop in the overall activity rate (the percentage of the total population in a job or seeking one) from about 50 per cent in 1990 to about 49 per cent in 2010, but this is slightly more than offset by the rise in population over the two decades, with the result that the potential labour force is expected to increase by about 600,000 (about 2 per cent) between 1990 and 2010. On the alternative assumption of a doubling of the numbers in full-time education and training there would be a *decline* in the potential labour force of about 1 million (about 3.5 per cent).

The proportion of women in the potential labour force, which rose from 37 per cent in 1970 to 43 per cent in 1990, is not expected to continue rising further in the coming two decades.

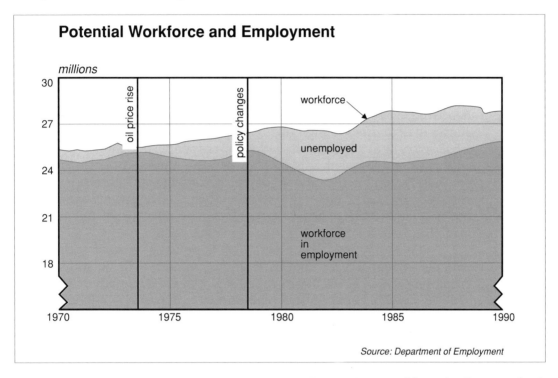

Potential Workforce and Employment

millions

Source: Department of Employment

In the mid-1970s the prospective workforce increased, but employment did not, leading to a rise in unemployment; in the early 1980s employment fell and unemployment rose sharply; in the late 1980s employment rose again, but not by enough to prevent continuing high unemployment.

The proportion of young people aged under 25 in the potential labour force is expected to drop from 21 per cent of the total in 1990 to 19 per cent in 2010, or only 15 per cent on the alternative assumption that the proportion in education and training is doubled. And the proportion of the labour force accounted for by people aged 60 and over is expected to fall from 5 per cent to 4 per cent, the increase in the size of the population in these age groups largely making up for the fall in their activity rates.

The proportion of the labour force which will be in the 25-59 age groups is expected to remain about the same, but with a lower proportion of them in the 25-34 age group and a higher proportion in their late 40s and 50s. This, together with the fall in the proportion of young people under 25, means that the average age of the people in the potential labour force will be older than at present.

Interactions between labour force and employment

It would be possible to estimate the total size of the potential future labour force by taking expected future population and the proportion of it expected to be wanting jobs (as described above); and to estimate the total size of potential employment likely to be generated by the economy (as described in Chapter 16); and to infer the size of future unemployment to be indicated by the difference between them.

However, such a comparison of the first-order figures would not be satisfactory, because neither of the two main variables, labour force and jobs, is independent of changes in the other. The availability of suitable jobs is one of the factors determining the proportion of people seeking jobs, and hence the size of the effective labour force. Analysis of labour market data shows that, in times of high unemployment, an increase in the number of jobs becoming available tends to draw more people into the labour market, so that unemployment falls by less than the number of extra jobs; and, conversely, a fall in the number of jobs becoming available tends to cause some people to drop out of the labour market, so that unemployment rises by less than the fall in the number of jobs. This effect needs to be allowed for in the forecasts.

It also happens that, when a job is potentially on offer, if no-one suitable is available to take it, then the vacancy will go unfilled and employment will be smaller, and unemployment greater, than otherwise. This mismatch between the requirements of particular jobs and the availability of suitable people may arise from a number of possible causes. For example: if the potential labour is too expensive in relation to the value of the prospective work; if the potential worker is at a different place from the potential job and will not or cannot move; or if the potential worker does not have the particular skills or other special qualities regarded as necessary for the job. These considerations also need to be allowed for in the forecasts.

Location

One possible cause of mismatch is if the new jobs becoming available are not in the same places as the old jobs becoming redundant. The greatest growth in employment is expected to be in the expanding new industries in the southern half of Britain and in the fastest growing parts of the service sector in London. The areas of declining old industries and highest unemployment, on the other hand, are in the North of England and in Wales, Scotland and Northern Ireland. There is thus the possibility of a locational mismatch unless either more of the new jobs are located in the areas with high unemployment or more of the people looking for jobs move into the South from other regions.

During most of the post-war period there were government measures designed to avoid regional imbalance by restricting new development in the more prosperous areas (for example through Industrial

Development Certificates and office planning controls) and encouraging location in the development areas (for example by regional grants, advance factories and help with office relocation). Research has shown[101] that when firms had a need to move or expand, these measures were important in steering much of the new employment to the areas with high unemployment.

In recent years, however, both the restrictions and the incentives have mostly been removed, and employment expansion has been stronger in the more prosperous parts of the South. At the same time, high house prices and rents in these areas, particularly London, have made it much more difficult than before for people to move into them from other parts of the country. As a result, in early 1990 unemployment has fallen to around 4-5 per cent in East Anglia, the South East and the South West, while still remaining about twice as high in Scotland and the North and about three times as high in Northern Ireland.

The effects of this imbalance have not yet been widely felt because, with high general levels of unemployment, there has until recently been *some* unemployment in all areas. However, if in the future the *general* level of unemployment falls further, it may be expected that there will still be high unemployment in some areas while there are full employment, labour shortages and unfilled vacancies in others. Past experience suggests that market forces are unlikely to do much to correct this until the imbalance has become severe.

For the purposes of the forecasts we assume that regional imbalances will have some effect in constraining the potential growth in total employment in the 1990s and that this is likely to lead to the reintroduction of regional employment policy measures, but not on the same scale as in the earlier post-war periods.

Labour costs and flexibility

Another factor which could constrain growth in employment is disparities between labour costs and labour productivity. Research has shown that in some economies (for example Austria and the Nordic countries), where central regulating and planning mechanisms have been established to achieve cooperation between government, business and trade unions, these have kept wage increases broadly within what can be afforded as a result of productivity increases; and in some other economies (for example Japan, Switzerland and the United States), with less unionisation and less government intervention, wages tend to be kept within the limits of what can be afforded through the operation of free market forces; but a third group of countries, including Britain, are in an intermediate position, without the regulation of the first group or the flexibility of the second group, with the result that wage increases frequently exceed productivity increases. In consequence, costs and prices tend to be pushed up, industry loses competitiveness, and employment growth is less than it would have been otherwise.

A further problem is lack of flexibility in responding to economic setbacks or shocks, so that when unemployment increases sharply it can take a long time to recover to previous levels.

In the past, attempts have been made to overcome these problems in Britain through the introduction of national incomes policies, but on each occasion so far they have, after a while, broken down. More recently, attempts have been made to restrain wage rises through the application of market pressures; but even when unemployment has been above 3 million, wage rates, and even more, earnings, continued to rise at inflationary rates. Hence, unless some way can be found of moderating wage increases, there is the likelihood of employment growth being less than it would have been otherwise.

These difficulties may be expected to become greater after 1992 when international competitive pressures become stronger with the Single European Market. They will also be more difficult to avoid now that joining the European Exchange Rate Mechanism has removed the possibility of allowing depreciation of the exchange rate to compensate for higher rates of inflation than in other countries.

Occupations and skills

Another important consideration affecting future employment is changes in occupations and skills. *Actual* employment will fall short of *potential* if there are not enough people with the skills or other qualities needed for the jobs which are potentially available. What, then, are the likely changes in occupations and in the skills needed for them? And how likely are they to be met?

Trends and prospects

Between 1951 and 1971, non-manual jobs rose from one quarter to nearly one third of total employment in Britain, and they have since increased further. There are signs of a tendency to convergence in all the advanced industrial economies towards a situation in which non-manual jobs account for between one third and one half of total employment.

Also, within non-manual employment, there has been a tendency for an increasing proportion of the total to be in the higher-level occupations – professional, scientific, technical, managerial, administrative and entrepreneurial. These latter are estimated to have increased their share of total male employment from 13 per cent in 1947 to 25 per cent in 1972 and about 32 per cent in 1986.[102,103] (On some definitions they already account for more than one half of all jobs.) At the same time, within the manual occupations, there has been a shift from the unskilled to the skilled occupations.

In some ways more important than the increases in numbers in the higher level occupations and the skilled manual ones has been the tendency towards increasing quality requirements at all levels, with a steady rise in both the formal qualifications and the general knowledge and abilities expected in most occupations.

The obverse of the rising skill expectations for employment has been the increasing vulnerability to *unemployment* of those without the required skills. The heavy unemployment in Britain in the late 1970s and 1980s has been predominantly of people in manual occupations.[104] Youth unemployment has been mainly among school leavers with low educational qualifications or none at all.[105] And, once unemployed, those with the least qualifications have been the ones with the most difficulty in getting back to work, while those with some qualifications have had much more success in persuading employers that they are employable and, in particular, are trainable for new kinds of work.

The most authoritative forecasts of occupational changes in the 1990s[106,107] suggest a strong continuing increase in the numbers in scientific, engineering, technical, managerial, entrepreneurial and other professional occupations; smaller increases in office and personal services and in skilled manual occupations; but continuing decline in the numbers of manual and low-skilled jobs.

This latter decline is expected to be slower than in the past two decades and to be the net outcome of two opposite trends. On the one hand there seems likely to be some further *increase* in some lower-skilled manual jobs, particularly in hotels and catering. This work is being done, increasingly, not by juveniles, but by older married women, frequently on a part-time basis. These women often have more experience and better qualifications than are strictly required for the jobs, thereby reducing training and supervision needs, and this has been leading to changes in work organisation and to improvements in pay.[108]

On the other hand, there is also expected to be a continuing and larger *decrease* in the number of males in manual occupations in manufacturing industry; and it is people in this category who have accounted for the bulk of unemployment, particularly of long-term unemployment, in the 1980s.

These forecasts of changes in occupations appear consistent with the changes forecast in employment in terms of economic sectors, which show the main expansion in business and miscellaneous services, which use a high proportion of people with high-level qualifications.

A further point is that the changes in employment structure which are expected imply substantial numbers of people moving from one sector to another, putting a premium on retrainability and general flexibility, which tend to go with higher standards of previous education and training.

The general prospect, then, is of strong and substantial upward movement towards occupations with higher-level skill requirements, with increased demand for scientists, engineers, managers, entrepreneurs and other professionals – and there are already signs of companies seeking to increase their recruitment of graduates for technical and managerial posts.[109] At the same time there is also increasing demand for a general upgrading of skills at intermediate and lower levels, with signs that companies are already expressing their interest in the form of larger pay offers to groups with specially sought after skills.[110]

There seems every likelihood that these existing trends will continue and be further stimulated by three factors likely to be of increasing importance in the next two decades: upward changes in consumer tastes, with greater emphasis on quality; the development of the Single European Market; and the wider use of new technologies.

Quality

Rising competition in industrial markets has led to an increasing emphasis on product and process quality among UK companies seeking to meet the challenges posed by low-cost competitors (as in the Far East) and high-quality producers (for instance, in Germany and Japan). Increasing affluence is already being reflected in changing tastes among consumers and this may be expected to continue over the next two decades. Consumer preferences in products are becoming more demanding, with increasing interest in quality, reliability and novelty, and this has led to greater emphasis on total quality in production processes, which in turn has led to increased concern with standards of work[111,112] and mounting difficulty for workers seeking to price themselves into jobs if they lack the required qualifications.[110]

In the service sector also there is a strong tendency to go up-market to provide higher quality service for more affluent consumers – for example, private motoring in place of public transport; washing machines in place of laundries; foreign holidays, often long-haul ones, in place of local holidays; convenience foods, take-aways and, increasingly, restaurant meals in place of home cooking.[113,114] In the construction industry too the movement has been up-market, with greater emphasis on central heating, double glazing, luxury kitchens and electrical, electronic and security systems, with consequential increases in special skills requirements.[106]

These market developments will put new demands on the skills of:

- *managers* to organise the production of more complex products at more consistently high quality levels, and to organise the delivery of higher quality and more sophisticated services;

- *entrepreneurs* to take advantage of new and perhaps rapidly changing market opportunities;

- ◆ *scientists and engineers* to develop new products in a climate of increasingly rapid obsolescence, to design for higher quality standards, and to devise and operate new high technology services;

- ◆ *professionals in other fields* to upgrade practice in a world of higher standards and increasing sophistication;

- ◆ *workers at other levels* to improve their performance to provide higher quality and improved standards of service.

Single European Market

The establishment of the Single European Market after 1992 and the closer economic integration of Europe subsequently may be expected to offer new opportunities for economies of scale in a wider market.[60] However, these benefits will accrue through increased trade and intensified competition leading to further industrial restructuring[115] – a process in which the more effective competitors will flourish and the less effective will not. The stakes will therefore be higher, with greater rewards for good performance and greater penalties for falling behind. This will bring stronger pressures to perform at levels equal to the best in Europe:

- ◆ *managers* to use the best practice in production, marketing and industrial relations to run larger, more complex businesses, with operations in different countries and using various languages;

- ◆ *scientists and engineers* to keep at the forefront of their fields to get most advantage from participation in the increasing number of international collaborative research and development projects between companies and public agencies;

- ◆ *professionals* in other fields to be able to seize new opportunities for international competition in service activities, particularly in the provision of high level financial, legal and business consultancy services;

- ◆ *workers* at other levels to achieve the productivity and quality standards of the best European competition.

There can be little doubt that the increased opportunities and risks arising from more effective intra-European competition will put a premium on improved skills at all levels.

New technologies

A third factor likely to raise the demand for skills is the increasing importance of new technologies, particularly information technology. In the early days of the 'microelectronics revolution' there were forecasts that it would bring not only widespread de-skilling[116,117,118] but outright loss of jobs in very large numbers – 50 million worldwide,[119] 2.5 million in France by 2000,[120] 40 per cent of all clerical jobs in West Germany by 1985,[121] 45 million jobs in the United States[122] and, in Britain, 5 million jobs by 2003[123] and a 90 per cent fall in employment in manufacturing by early in the next century.[124]

In the event, actual job losses have proved much smaller. Four major surveys covering the whole of manufacturing industry in Britain[125,126,127,128] have estimated the total loss of jobs as a direct result of use of microelectronics in products and production processes at about 15-20,000 a year between 1981 and 1983 and about 40-50,000 a year between 1983 and 1987 – the latter equivalent to about 2 jobs per factory per year. Parallel surveys revealed a similar position in West Germany and France.[129] Further analysis of the UK data[130] has shown that in the period 1985-87 the loss of jobs from all causes (as opposed to those directly associated with the use of microelectronics) was actually *less* in the plants using microelectronics than in the ones which were not, implying that the use of new technology was associated with stronger competitiveness and enhanced ability to maintain employment.

The main reason why the introduction of new technology has not resulted in major reductions in employment is that it has been used not so much to cut jobs or costs as to raise quality standards and output, both in industry[128,131,132] and in offices.[133,134] The result has been that in industry the number of unskilled manual jobs has been reduced, but the number of skilled manual and white collar jobs has been *increased*,[128] and there has been an increasing demand for people with new skills and with multiple skills.[130,135]

The largest survey ever undertaken in Britain on the effects of new technology in the workplace[136] showed emphatically that the overall effect has been to require more skills rather than less, in both manual occupations and office ones, and in the opinion of both managers and trade union shop stewards. Similarly, the introduction of new materials such as advanced polymers and composites has also resulted in new skills needs.[112]

While the need for increased skills in the general workforce with the introduction of new technology was not at first widely appreciated, the need for more specialist scientists and engineers was never in doubt. The scale of the need, however, has been greater than many expected. In four major surveys of manufacturing industry the shortage of specialists with technical expertise was shown not merely to be a common obstacle to the use of microelectronics technology, it was cited more often than all the other difficulties together.[128] It was the number one problem in plants of all sizes, in all industries, in all regions, with all types of application, and with widely differing experience of use, scales of application and degrees of sophistication.[137] Other surveys have shown it also to be the most important problem in West Germany,[138] France,[139] Sweden,[140] Denmark[141] and New Zealand.[142]

The key shortage in Britain has been of engineers with expertise in microelectronics. Between 1981 and 1987 the number of them in manufacturing industry trebled, but in each year the plants using the technology wanted on average one third more of them than they had already, with the result that over this period the number more wanted also trebled, despite the increase in their numbers.[125,126,127,128] Moreover, those wanting more of these engineers included new users and established ones; low-tech plants and high-tech ones; plants with few engineers, or none at all, and plants with large numbers of them already. And plants in France and West Germany, despite having more of these engineers than Britain, also wanted still more.[129]

There seems little doubt that the demand for more high-level technical expertise is not just a teething problem experienced by plants attempting to use the technology for the first time, but something that will continue to grow for many years to come as microelectronics and other new technologies are used more widely and with increasing sophistication across a growing range of industries and services.

The increasing use of information technology implies not only more specialists with high-level skills, but also a more general diffusion of IT skills among:

- *managers*, so that they can use it to help run their organisations more efficiently;[130]

- *entrepreneurs*, so that they can use the opportunities provided by the technology to get access to a range of information previously available only to large organisations and to use relatively small-scale, flexible production systems which can achieve economies previously available only to mass producers;

- *other professionals*, so that they can make use of IT systems in law, libraries, teaching, medicine, finance, insurance, retailing, stock control, selling, transport, administration and many other fields.

Those who use IT clearly do not need to acquire the same level of expertise as those who design the equipment and systems: indeed, much effort is put into making them as 'user friendly' as possible. Even so, there is little doubt that considerable extension of skills will be needed in the years ahead, not only to provide more experts, but also to ensure that a wide range of other people understand enough about IT and other new technologies to be able to use them to maximum effect.

Education and training

Thus it seems clear that current trends, reinforced by the effects of more up-market consumer tastes, stronger competition in the European Single Market, and growing use of new technologies, will lead to increasing demands for high-level skills in managers, entrepreneurs, scientists, engineers and other professionals; and also for higher standards of skill for the rest of the workforce. Indeed, the attainment of these improvements will be a necessary condition for getting the full increases in employment envisaged. Is it likely that these improvements will in fact be achieved?

Higher level qualifications

The need for higher qualifications in the future has to be seen in the context of the levels achieved at present and, in particular, how they compare with Britain's main international competitors.

Two recent reports[143,144] have drawn attention to weaknesses in the qualifications of UK managers, particularly in comparison with those of managers in competitor countries.[145] Recruitment to management is often from lower occupational backgrounds with limited educational qualifications,[146] and analysis of Labour Force Survey data[106] shows that in 1986 only 25 per cent of corporate managers and administrators had degree or equivalent qualifications and 25 per cent had no qualifications whatever.

With entrepreneurs ('manager/proprietors') qualifications are lower than among managers – only 10 per cent have a degree level qualification and about half have no qualification at all,[106] although recently there appears to have been increasing mutual interest between young graduates and small firms.[109]

In natural science graduates Britain compares more favourably with other countries, although their impact has been limited by the fact that a higher proportion of them than in most other countries work in the defence industries. However, the ending of the Cold War should mean that during the 1990s many of those currently engaged on defence work will come into civil markets.

The supply of students for engineering degree courses was regarded as deficient by the Butcher report in 1984[147] and the number of engineers with degrees or equivalent qualifications (relative to size) is lower in Britain than in France, Germany and the United States and only half that in Japan.[148]

Manufacturing industry has been trying to attract more graduates, but is being faced with increasing competition from commerce, which has doubled its graduate recruitment between 1979 and 1988, and now takes as many graduates as manufacturing. The legal profession has also doubled its intake of graduates and as many graduates now go on to further law study as to teacher training, compared with only one third as many who did this in 1979.[110]

General qualifications

Even more important than the supply of graduates is the level of education and training achieved by the rest of the population. The proportion of young people staying in education or continuing with full-time vocational training after the minimum school leaving age of 16 is about 50 per cent in Britain. This is less than in Spain, Italy and Germany and compares with more than 75 per cent in France, Belgium and Denmark, and more than 90 per cent in the Netherlands, Sweden, Canada, the United States and Japan.[149] In Britain 35 per cent stay on in full-time education and training through to the age of 18. This too is less than in Spain, Italy, Germany and France and compares with 75 per cent or more in the Netherlands, Belgium, Sweden, Canada, the United States and Japan.[149]

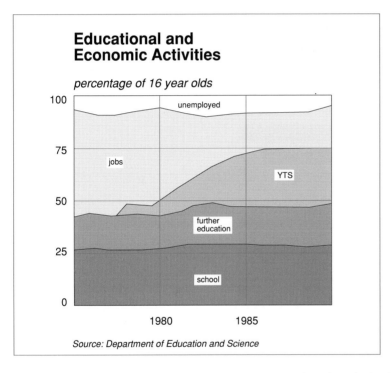

Educational and Economic Activities

percentage of 16 year olds

Source: Department of Education and Science

Less than half of 16 year olds stay in school or further education. In the 1980s fewer went into jobs, but unemployment did not increase because more went into the YTS.

About half of those who leave school at 16 in Britain go on to the Youth Training Scheme, but only 28 per cent of those joining the scheme so far have left with a recognised vocational qualification.[150] This is partly because of the low level of prior educational attainment of most of those joining the scheme – 41 per cent of young people leave school without even one A-C grade GCSE/O level.[151] Thus about one young person in three goes through the British system without acquiring any recognised educational or vocational qualification at 18-plus – a situation without parallel in any other advanced industrial country.

International comparative studies have shown that the uneven educational background and lack of a systematic national training scheme results in a general level of skill qualifications lower than in competitor countries[152,153] and provides a weaker base for subsequent further training or retraining.[154]

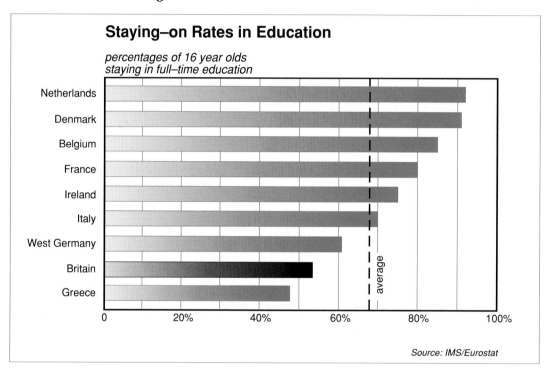

Staying–on Rates in Education

percentages of 16 year olds staying in full–time education

Source: IMS/Eurostat

Staying on rates in full-time education in Britain are well below the West European average.

Requirements and prospects

While there is no sure basis for a precise figure, it is probable that, in order to provide the skills needed for effective competition in a rapidly changing and increasingly competitive international economy, it will be necessary to contemplate something in the order of a doubling of the proportion in higher education by 2010, and also a doubling of the proportion staying on to 18 in full-time education or training.

The former objective has been acknowledged in the government's recently announced target of a doubling of the numbers in higher education within 25 years; and a consensus is building up about the need for major improvements in the education and training of the remainder of the population. However, no firm plans have yet been made and the problems involved are considerable, including:

- educating the extra educators and training the extra trainers;

+ providing resources for their salaries (in competition with commercial employers) and for buildings and equipment;

+ accepting the loss of output and tax revenue during the period that the additional students are in education and training;

+ improving motivation by making education courses more relevant, training more systematic, and employment more assured at the end of it, but conditional on achieving the required educational attainments;

+ removing the temptation of dead-end, unskilled, juvenile jobs at 16 by curbing juvenile wages, providing maintenance support for students and trainees and/or by raising the minimum age for leaving education or recognised training schemes.

In the past there has often been a gap between recognising needs and taking action to meet them – particularly when what is required involves expensive investment[155] with a pay-off only in the longer term. Accordingly, for the purposes of the main forecasts we have assumed that both the proportion in higher education and the proportion staying in full-time education and training to 18 remain unchanged. However, some of the implications of a substantial increase in the numbers on training schemes are outlined in Chapter 18.

Employment forecasts

The forecasts of future employment and unemployment are based on the labour force projections described in the first part of this chapter and the economic projections described in Chapter 16, with adjustments for the effects of the level of employment on the labour force, the impact of wage inflation, possible regional imbalances, and mismatches between skill requirements and availabilities.

It should be noted that the initial labour force and employment projections inevitably embody a number of elements of uncertainty and the subsequent process of iterative adjustments inevitably adds further ones. Consequently, the resulting forecasts should be seen as no more than approximations. The forecasts for unemployment, being the residual from two other much larger variables, each of them subject to uncertainties, should be regarded as particularly tentative.

Nevertheless, they probably constitute the best available indicators of the prospects ahead for Britain. The forecasts are that:

- ◆ the total workforce will grow over the period to 2010 by between 2 and 3 million;

- ◆ jobs will increase rather faster, by a total of 3 to 4 million;

- ◆ unemployment will fall, during the second half of the coming decade and during the following one, to somewhere in the region of 800,000 by 2010.

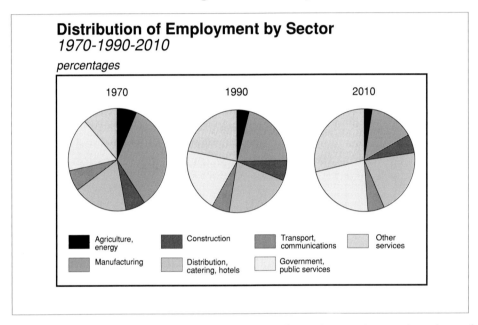

Distribution of Employment by Sector
1970-1990-2010

percentages

1970   1990   2010

Agriculture, energy

Manufacturing

Construction

Distribution, catering, hotels

Transport, communications

Government, public services

Other services

Between 1990 and 2010 there will be further declines in employment in manufacturing and agriculture (but increases in output due to higher productivity). The main increases in employment will be in business and professional services.

The number of young people aged 16-19 in the workforce will increase by about one tenth and the number aged 20-24 will fall by about one tenth (and the numbers in both of these groups would fall by 25-30 per cent on the alternative assumption of a doubling of the numbers in full-time education and training). The number of young adults aged 25-34 in the workforce will fall by around 15 per cent, and the number of older people over 65 in the workforce will fall by about a half, but numbers in the main working-age groups will increase substantially.

The main sectoral shift in employment will be from manufacturing and agriculture, employment in both of which will continue to decline absolutely, into parts of the service sector, in particular into business and professional services. Within manufacturing, there will be reductions in employment in almost all industries, but they will mostly be smaller than the reductions between 1970 and 1990, particularly in industries such as electronics and vehicles where large increases in output are expected (see Chapter 16).

Implications

The balance between those potentially at work and those potentially dependent on them, as indicated by the overall activity rate, is not expected to change greatly between 1990 and 2010, although it is likely to become more unfavourable in the following two decades.

However, the increasing numbers of elderly dependants, particularly the very old ones, may place burdens on the social services because a higher proportion than before of people in the generation following them are likely to be economically active and reluctant to give up jobs in order to provide informal care for elderly relatives.

The future dependency ratio is subject to a number of uncertainties and is particularly subject to the effects of government policies: on the school leaving age, on the number of places in higher education and vocational training, on the retirement age and conditions for state pensions, and on the provision of incentives in the form of tax allowances, cash benefits or facilities to encourage women with children to go out to work. Policy decisions in other areas, taken for other reasons, may therefore bring significant shifts in the dependency balance; but, by the same token, they may potentially also be used to offset any adverse shift in it.

The level of unemployment is expected to fall from between 1.5 and 2 million in the mid-1990s to somewhere in the region of 800,000 by 2010. However, even relatively small deviations from the forecast figures for future labour force or jobs would imply appreciably smaller or greater levels of unemployment. In considering changes in unemployment it must be remembered that the figures are affected by the many changes which have been made in the method of counting;[156] also that the figures do not bring out the flexibility possible in the system through changes in the amount of overtime, part-time and casual working. At present male workers in Britain work an average of about three hours a week (7 per cent) longer than the average for the European Community,[157] and trade union pressures to reduce hours, unless they are offset by increases in productivity, will tend to have an effect in some ways equivalent to reducing the numbers in the labour force.

The balance of advantage or disadvantage involved in regional policies is essentially a trade-off between, on the one hand, the costs of the measures themselves and of sub-optimal locations for some of the enterprises affected and, on the other hand, the wider economic and social benefits obtained from a more even distribution of activity and employment. It may be supposed that the balance will be more favourable to regional policies in times of strong economic growth and high employment than in times of depression and high unemployment.

Employment change: policy implications

- Need for more people in higher education, especially engineers and scientists

- Need for more people in education and training after 16

- Pressure for measures to bring wage inflation down to average European Community levels

- Pressure for measures to reduce regional imbalances in the labour market

The labour market characteristics which in the past have led to wage inflation are expected to continue to be an important factor limiting the growth of employment, particularly after entry into the European ERM has made exchange-rate depreciation difficult – unless ways can be found of making market forces more responsive, or forms of incomes policy more effective and acceptable.

While appropriate macroeconomic policies will continue to be relevant, it seems likely that deficiencies in high-level and general skills standards will become an increasingly important source of unemployment unless standards can be raised to levels more competitive with those achieved in competitor countries. However, this will require the investment of substantial public and private sector resources with pay-back over a fairly lengthy period.

The importance of higher skill levels for higher employment levels will be accentuated by up-market shifts in consumer tastes, stronger competition in the Single European Market and international markets, and the growing importance of IT and other new technologies.

The shift towards high-level occupations and the rapid decline in unskilled manual jobs, if accompanied by inadequate education and training, may lead to an increasing proportion of the population making little contribution to the economy, getting few of the fruits of growing affluence, and becoming increasingly alienated from the rest of society.

BRITAIN in 2010

 **Environment**

14. **E**nvironment

The environment shapes the quality of life. A healthy environment can widen horizons, enlarge opportunities, enrich life-styles and extend the scope for personal fulfilment; a poor environment can constrain, frustrate, threaten and corrupt, diminishing the possibilities available. The creation of a successful built environment, and the maintenance of the natural environment, are therefore goals of particular importance in any civilised society.

There are many ways in which the quality of the environment in Britain has improved in the course of the past two decades, for example with better housing, greater comfort, increased mobility and improved

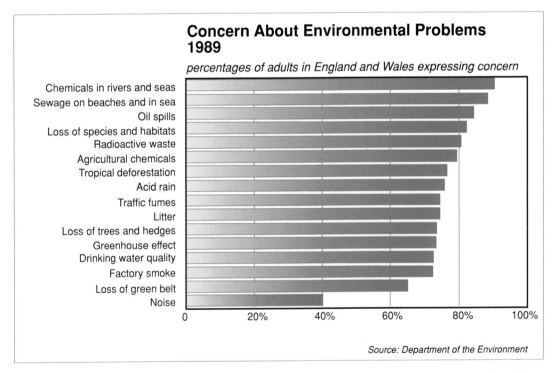

Concern About Environmental Problems 1989

percentages of adults in England and Wales expressing concern

Chemicals in rivers and seas
Sewage on beaches and in sea
Oil spills
Loss of species and habitats
Radioactive waste
Agricultural chemicals
Tropical deforestation
Acid rain
Traffic fumes
Litter
Loss of trees and hedges
Greenhouse effect
Drinking water quality
Factory smoke
Loss of green belt
Noise

0   20%   40%   60%   80%   100%

Source: Department of the Environment

There is widespread concern in Britain about most of the main environmental problems.

amenities. But there are also environmental problems that may give rise to increasing difficulties in the coming two decades: overcrowding and congestion in both towns and country areas, dilapidation of buildings and overloading of infrastructure, and threats to health and safety from pollution of air, water and land; and over everything hangs the long-term threat posed by global warming.

It is therefore important to examine recent and prospective developments in a number of different areas: the balance between different regions and between urban and rural areas; the transport facilities for movement between and within them; the attractions of the countryside and the amenities of the towns and cities; the supply of homes to live in and of water and energy; the management of waste and the prevention of pollution and of threats to health and safety; and the impact of possible responses to the threat of global warming. Developments in these areas are complex and interlocking and strongly influenced by government policies. Lead times are mostly long, and therefore the quality of the built and natural environment in Britain in 2010 will depend to a considerable extent on the policy decisions taken in the years immediately ahead.

Regional changes

England is a relatively small country, but there are important differences between regions that attract feelings of enthusiasm and dislike, and in Scotland, Wales and Ireland there are strong feelings of separate national identity. Yet there have been substantial movements between the regions of England and between the component countries of the United Kingdom, and also movements out of the older towns and conurbations into rural and semi-rural areas. Reasons for movement have been positive – free pursuit of a more attractive job or a more congenial home; and also negative – the pressures of unemployment and depressed living conditions. The consequences have been important, both for the regions individually and for the country as a whole, and are likely to continue to be so in the two decades ahead.

Population

Total population in Britain rose by about 1.8 million (3.3 per cent) between 1970 and 1990 and is expected to rise by about a further 2.5 million (4.5 per cent) between 1990 and 2010 (see Chapter 10). While these rates of total increase are not sufficiently large to give rise to major environmental problems, the changes in the regional distribution of population that have already taken place, and the further changes expected, are of potentially greater importance.

Office of Population Census and Surveys figures for the period 1971-1986[66] show increases in population of about 15 per cent in East

Projected Changes in Population
1985-2001

English counties percentage changes

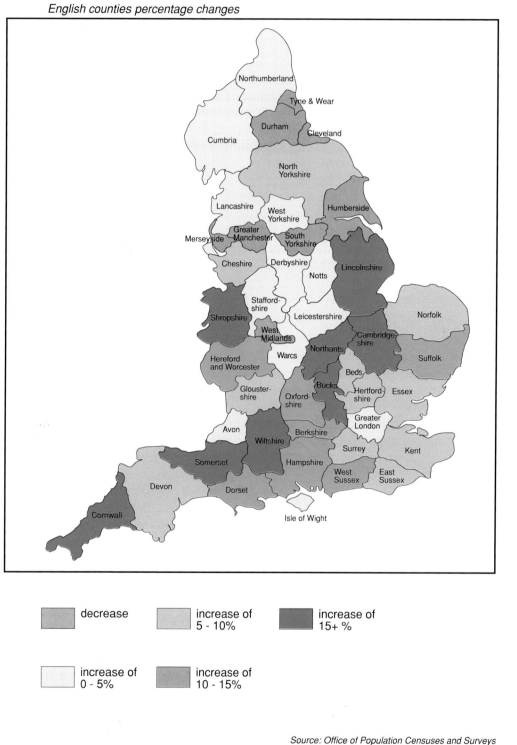

Source: Office of Population Censuses and Surveys

The fastest projected increases in population are neither in the North nor in the South East but in an arc of mainly rural counties from Suffolk to Dorset.

Anglia, 10 per cent in the South West, 9 per cent in the South East (excluding London) and 7 per cent in the East Midlands; only small changes in West Midlands, Wales and Yorkshire and Humberside; and *decreases* of 2 per cent in the North and 4 per cent in the North West. In London there was a *decrease* of 10 per cent between 1971 and 1981, but little change in the following five year period.

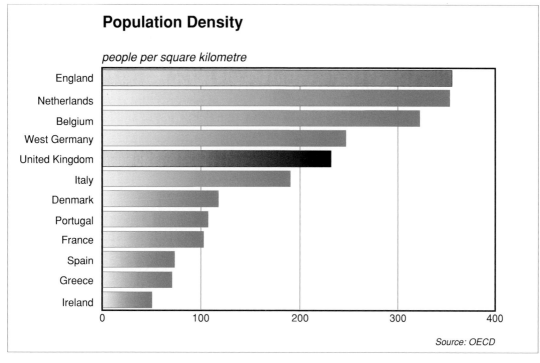

Population Density

people per square kilometre

Source: OECD

The United Kingdom as a whole is quite densely populated; England on its own is the most densely populated country in Western Europe.

For the following fifteen-year period, 1986 to 2001, projections made by FACT of the Department of the Environment[158] show a similar pattern, giving for the thirty years as a whole increases of 52 per cent in Cambridgeshire and 50 per cent in Buckinghamshire, more than 30 per cent in Cornwall, Northamptonshire, Somerset and Shropshire, and more than 20 per cent in Hereford and Worcestershire, Wiltshire, Suffolk, Lincolnshire, Hampshire, Norfolk and Oxfordshire; but *decreases* in Durham, Humberside, Cleveland and all of the metropolitan counties.

Other projections for the period 1985-2000 show a similar picture.[159] The pattern which emerges is that, if current trends continue, by the turn of the century:

+ the growth in population will be almost entirely in the South;

- within the South there will be movements out of London and the West Midlands to less densely populated parts of the region;

- population increases will be particularly rapid in the 'crescent' of areas immediately beyond the home counties and in the South West;

- population increases will be predominantly due to migration, as opposed to differential fertility or mortality rates.

However, the regional projections available extend only to the turn of the century and there are reasons for expecting that current trends may *not* continue unchanged right through to 2010.

Employment

The main cause of past and projected inter-regional movements of population is changes in employment. Regional analysis of changes in employment by Cambridge Econometrics[160] shows that in the 1970s employment increased in the South and the Midlands, but not in the North; in the early 1980s employment fell slightly in the South, but much more heavily in other parts of the country; while in the late 1980s employment increased strongly in the South, but much less elsewhere. In the 1990s employment is projected[160] to increase substantially in the South and Midlands, but not in other parts of the country where high rates of unemployment are expected to continue.

There are a number of factors behind these changes.

- *Decline of manufacturing*
  Total employment in manufacturing has been falling since the mid-1960s and fell particularly sharply (by nearly one quarter) between 1980 and 1985. This affected the North (where manufacturing accounts for a larger percentage of total employment) more severely than the South.

- *Changing structure of manufacturing*
  The old heavy industries (which are located mainly in the North) have been declining in employment, while the new light industries (located mainly in the South) have more often maintained their employment levels. The new industries do not need to be near coalfields or deep water ports and they have tended to prefer to be located near motorways, international airports, universities, sources of skilled labour and good housing and

recreational amenities, which have been more widespread in the South. This is particularly true of the electronics industry, the one sector in manufacturing in which employment is expected to grow strongly, which has expanded mainly in a crescent along the M4 and M11 motorways.

Expansion of service sector
The decline in manufacturing employment has been accompanied by an increase in parts of the service sector, and this has happened mainly in the more prosperous towns in the South and, most recently, in the expansion of financial services in the City of London.

The result of these changes has been a shift in employment from North to South and also away from London to the counties around it.[161,162] A study of 280 local labour market areas[163] found that the 35 most prosperous ones were *all* south of the Humber-Mersey line.[163]

Growing wealth and higher disposable incomes will act as a continued spur to the growth of the service sector and to a shift of economic activity from urban to rural areas, especially in the South East, where financial and business services have overtaken manufacturing as the main source of employment.[160] This growing service sector will want to locate in business parks, in towns with good road connections and in semi-rural surroundings, and new light industry will also often show a preference for single-floor manufacturing premises in semi-rural surroundings – half of all foreign companies moving to Britain since 1983 have chosen to set up in rural areas in the South.[160]

The forces pulling employment and population from North to South will be reinforced, after 1992, by the effects of the Single European Market which will intensify competition and, since Britain is on the periphery of Europe, will give a competitive advantage to the South East, the part closest to the centre of the market. The opening of the Channel Tunnel, with the proposed new network of high speed train links to many of the major centres of Europe, will intensify the advantage of the South East and make other parts of Britain seem even more peripheral to Europe as industrial or commercial locations. A key consideration is whether high speed, Berne gauge, rail links are extended past London to other parts of the country. If they are, this will effectively bring other regions closer to the continent and reduce their competitive disadvantage.

The economic forces which have been pulling jobs and people to the South East will not continue to do so indefinitely. During the 1990s increasing congestion and labour shortages will reduce the attraction of parts of the South for some industries, while housing shortages and high housing costs will continue to constrain the ability of people to move to the South from the North. This will tend to slow down the expansion in the South, while not preventing further decline and continuing high unemployment in the North. This lack of regional balance will prevent the

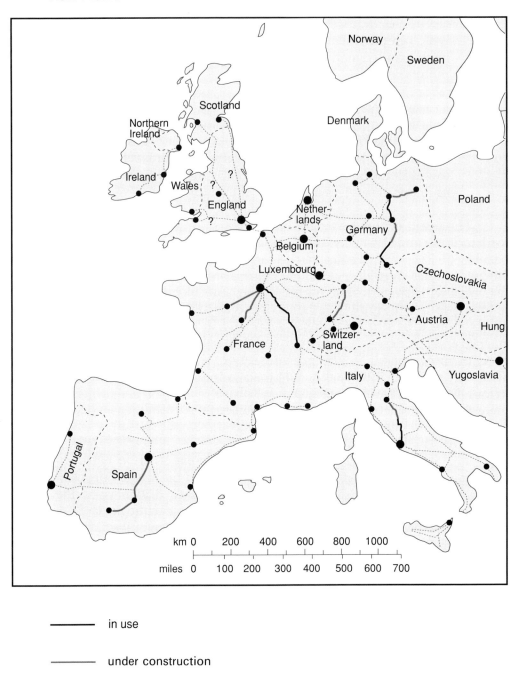

Europe's High-Speed Rail Plans

Norway
Sweden
Scotland
Denmark
Northern Ireland
Poland
Ireland
Wales
England
Nether-lands
Germany
Belgium
Luxembourg
Czechoslovakia
France
Austria
Switzer-land
Hung
Italy
Yugoslavia
Portugal
Spain

km 0   200   400   600   800   1000
miles 0   100   200   300   400   500   600   700

—— in use

—— under construction

·········· planned

Source: Community of European Railways

A network of several thousand miles of high-speed railway lines is planned to provide new links between the countri of Western Europe. In Britain the plans for the line from the Channel Tunnel to London have not yet been finalised a no decision has been taken on possible links with the rest of the country.

164

full use of national economic potential and constrain the rate of economic growth attainable. It is probable that it will lead to the reintroduction of regional policies designed to reduce the imbalance by bringing more employment to the North.

Retirement

In some parts of the country a further major factor in regional population movements has been retirement. Large parts of the past and projected future increases in population in counties such as Cornwall (36 per cent), Somerset (33 per cent), Wiltshire (30 per cent), Suffolk 28 per cent), West Sussex (26 per cent), Hampshire (25 per cent) and Devonshire (18 per cent) are due to people moving to these areas in search of a congenial environment for their retirement years. The same movement explains part of the decline in population in the conurbations, with a particularly high proportion coming from London where greater than average congestion has encouraged people to leave when no longer tied by their jobs, and higher than average incomes have given them the means of doing so. In recent years, however, the decrease in population in London from this cause has been offset by increased inward migration from areas of high unemployment and from overseas.

It may be expected that in the coming decades increasing affluence will result in more people seeking to move to southern coastal and inland areas for their retirement years. However, it may also be expected that rising population in these areas will make them more crowded and push up property prices, thereby to some extent reducing the attractiveness and feasibility of these movements.

Countryside

The idea of 'countryside' looms large in the national psyche in Britain, with notions of 'sceptred isle' and 'green and pleasant land' still widely cherished as part of an idealisation based on 'nostalgic visions and utopian dreams'.[165] However, the reality is that there have been important changes in the countryside, particularly in the past two decades, and these have been analysed by researchers[166] and recognised by people in general; in a survey in 1988[167] the view that the countryside had 'changed a lot' in the past twenty years was endorsed by 55 per cent of all respondents and by 75 per cent of those actually living in the country. The most conspicuous changes have been in population movements, social structure, agriculture and the growth of tourism and recreational activities.

Population movements

Over the past two decades the shift in population from North to South has been accompanied by an even more marked shift from large towns and cities to smaller towns and country areas. An analysis of household formation rates to the year 2000[158] suggests that population will continue to grow at much faster rates in rural areas than in urban ones. The fastest growing counties, on this analysis, with growth rates of 20-30 per cent, are expected to be Buckinghamshire, Cambridgeshire, Wiltshire, Hampshire and Northamptonshire. They contrast with Merseyside and Tyne and Wear which are expected not to grow at all.

Analysis of the rise in population between 1971 and 1986 in the 33 fastest growing rural areas[168] has shown that 97 per cent of the increase was due to migration, the majority of it from other regions. These changes in population have been the net results of opposing migration flows.

On the one hand there has been a small migration flow out of many rural areas of young people faced with rising house prices and falling employment in agriculture and seeking the employment and entertainment opportunities of the cities. On the other hand there has been a much larger inward flow of mainly older people moving out of the big towns and their suburbs. This latter movement has been largely of people leaving crowded towns in search of more peaceful areas for their retirement, and of people still in employment in the towns but willing to travel further to work in order to enjoy better living conditions by making new homes in country areas. Both developments have been made possible by greater affluence, enabling people to move to more congenial but more expensive homes and life-styles, by faster commuter train services, by a willingness to spend more time and money on travel, and by greater car ownership making it feasible to commute to work over greater distances.

In the next two decades it seems likely that further increases in affluence will result in more people wanting to move to rural areas. On the other hand, further overcrowding and rises in property prices in the more popular areas may tend to reduce their attractions, and changes expected in transport may put up the cost of long-distance commuting.

Social changes

The migration movements have been bringing changes not only in the size of the populations in many rural areas but also in their characteristics. In many places there had been small, close-knit, homogeneous communities, long established in the area, deeply rooted in the land and very traditional in their attitudes. The newcomers, in contrast, have tended to be diverse in their origins, attitudes and occupations, not working locally, and not interested in the land except for recreation. Some of the newcomers have their roots elsewhere, using their country homes as dormitories from which to commute to jobs, sometimes on a weekly basis, and sometimes a considerable distance away.

Perhaps more important than the other differences is that the newcomers tend to be older than the original inhabitants and to have much higher incomes. One consequence of this has been an ability to buy up houses coming on to the market and, in doing so, to push prices up to levels beyond the reach of young local first-time buyers.[169,170] In some areas this has resulted in serious housing problems for local people. A survey has revealed that the shortage of housing in rural areas is such that an estimated 376,000 households are in need of homes within the next five years.[171]

Another consequence of the newcomers' higher incomes has been their dependence on a car-borne life-style, going to towns for jobs, shopping and other services. This has tended to undermine the viability of country bus services, village shops, sub-post offices, schools, cottage hospitals, community halls and other local amenities; and hence indirectly to increase the pressures on some of the original inhabitants to move to the towns.[172] The dependence on high weekly car mileages also has the effect of making the new life-style vulnerable to any measures which may have to be taken to raise the cost of private motoring in response to the threat of global warming.

To the extent that migration from the towns continues, it may be expected that these social changes will go on and the composition of rural communities in many areas will become increasingly weighted towards people with urban links and upper income life-styles.

Agriculture

More than three-quarters of the total land area of Britain is farmed in one way or another, and agriculture is still the most important single activity in most country areas. However, since the war there have been many changes which in a number of ways have turned farming into an industry.

- New methods and equipment have greatly raised productivity – the number of full-time workers in agriculture is now only one quarter of the 1945 level.[173]

- Efficient use of the new methods and equipment has required larger units and more intensive farming – 56 per cent of total agricultural output comes from the 11 per cent of biggest farms.[173]

- The shift towards larger units has been further stimulated by the form taken by the EC Common Agricultural Policy (CAP) – 80 per cent of subsidised commodities are now produced by 20 per cent of farms.[174]

- Much marginal land has been brought into intensive agricultural use – since 1945 an estimated 33 per cent of upland grasslands and heath, 50 per cent of lowland bogs and ferns, 60 per cent of lowland heaths, 80 per cent of chalk/limestone grasslands and 95 per cent of lowland herb-rich grasslands.[173]

- New methods of intensive animal rearing and poultry and egg production have been widely adopted.

- Use of agricultural chemicals has increased 8-fold compared with pre-war levels.

- Improved strains and varieties of crops have been developed and livestock with more valuable characteristics have been bred.

These changes have resulted in a great increase in production; for example, since 1945 milk output has doubled, output of wheat has risen five times and of barley six times. These increases have helped improve food supplies, reduce imports and increase farmers' incomes. However, they have also brought, particularly in recent years, increasing concern about a range of different issues:

- the loss of hedgerows (one quarter of the total) and deciduous woodlands (one half of the total),[173] and the consequential reduction in wildlife habitats and change in the appearance of the countryside have brought protests from conservationist groups;

- public alarm over the treatment of battery hens, hormone-fed calves and other practices has led to a growth in sales of free-range eggs and the introduction of 'organic' meat;

- research into the health consequences of toxic pesticides and herbicides entering the human food chain has led to the withdrawal of some chemical products and given encouragement to organic farming and increased sales of organic produce in supermarket health food counters and chains of specialist shops;

- outbreaks of salmonella and other kinds of food poisoning have generated pressures for increased research into food safety and stricter control of production processes;

- concern over the contamination of drinking water supplies by pesticides, slurries and silage and the leaching of nitrates into aquifers as a result of over-use of fertilisers has brought numerous prosecutions and attracted the attention of the European Commission.

While each of these problems may lead, directly or indirectly, to some changes in future agricultural practice, it is probable that a far bigger impact will be made by the major changes underway and in prospect in agricultural support policies.

The European Community's CAP has been reformed with a view to eliminating the generation of costly 'mountains' of surplus foods. Lower support prices are likely to lead to reduced output levels, income levels and employment levels, and to the removal of land from intensive production.

Diversification policies will encourage farmers to go in for tourism, farm-based small industry and rural crafts; to plant deciduous woodland or other alternative, non-subsidised crops; to raise alternative livestock; or to develop land for non-farm uses such as golf courses or, in some cases, housing. The government's 'set aside' policy provides financial incentives to leave up to 20 per cent of land on each farm idle. Less intensive farming involves a decrease in inputs of fertilizer and pesticides, and thus a decrease in production, while leaving the same land area in farming.

Estimates of the net results of these changes are matters of debate, depending partly on yield forecasts, on biotechnological improvements in plant and animal breeding, and on the degree of extensification. Estimates of the amount of land going out of production by the year 2000 range from 700,000 to two million hectares, representing from 4 to 10 per cent of current agricultural land. Up to about 25 per cent of farmland may go out of production by 2010. This means about 20 per cent of the land area of Britain may be available for alternative uses. Some land will revert to lowland and upland grassland; and some will certainly be used for farm woodlands, both coniferous and deciduous, thus shifting forestry development towards new lowland areas. Much of the rest of the land going out of agricultural production may become available for other uses such as housing, recreation and tourism.

Tourism and recreation

Even before the recent changes in agricultural support policies, the use of country areas for tourism and recreation activities was increasing rapidly under the stimulus of rising incomes, greater leisure and more widespread car ownership. Many further developments are already planned.

The English Tourist Board foresees a 20 per cent increase in rural tourism by 1995[175] with 'visitors now an unbeatable source of income and jobs for rural communities', and with the newly appreciated health risks of sunbathing seen as possibly encouraging a resurgence of tourism in temperate areas. Grants will be available for many kinds of tourism, sport and recreation developments on marginal agricultural land or as on-farm diversification.[176,177]

Changes in the Countryside

- Less intensive farming practices

- Promotion of rural tourism and release of farmland for leisure, housing developments and forestry

- Continuing migration from cities to the country for commuting and retirement

- Increased tension between environmental concerns and development pressures

The rising demand for tourist accommodation has led to the conversion of many cottages for holiday lettings or second homes – in some villages in Cornwall more than half the housing stock is unoccupied for most of the year.[178] Planning applications for developments in or near the Lake District, Brecon Beacons, Pembrokeshire Coast and other national parks have reached what the chairman of the Council for National Parks has described as 'crisis proportions'.[179] Land in the vicinity of national parks is already under great pressure. For example, traffic on Lake District roads increased by 42 per cent over the decade to 1988, and similar growth is likely in the 1990s. Fourteen million people entered the Lake District in 1988, and Bank Holiday traffic jams outside Windermere now stretch six miles.[180]

There is also the possibility of developments on the land of the 234 National Nature Reserves[181] and on the half million acres of undeveloped land previously owned by the water authorities.[182] This includes 15 per cent of the Peak District National Park, 7 per cent of the Lake District, 5 per cent of Dartmoor and 4 per cent of the Brecon Beacons. The potential value of the land of the former Thames Water Authority alone is estimated at £1bn.

There is little doubt that increasing affluence and mobility between now and 2010 will lead to increasing demand for more use of rural land for tourism and recreational activities; and that with changes in agriculture, particularly 'set-aside', more rural land will potentially become available for development. At the same time there is also little doubt that the developments needed for accommodating additional tourism and recreation are liable to affect the character of the areas in which they are placed – in particular, their visual appearance.

The rural environment of Britain is strongly marked by the consequences of many centuries of human activities (in its 'natural', pre-human condition most of the land area was covered in deciduous forest); but apart from a few areas of genuine wildness, the beauty and charm of the English countryside is widely felt to be in its gentle, peaceful mixture of little fields, hedges, streams, trees and hills. Hence its appeal is reduced when agricultural development brings very large, bare fields, or ugly farm-sheds; or when tourism and recreation development brings buildings, roads, vehicles and lots of other people. Accordingly, there are intrinsic difficulties in developing the rural environment without damaging it; in making it accessible to more people without eroding the special qualities they have come to it to enjoy.

Certainly, in the course of the next two decades there will be increasing demand for development for tourism and recreational uses, and increasing difficulty in meeting it without inflicting damage on the quality of the environment. In the more popular areas it is likely that preservation of their special characteristics will require restrictions not only on development but also on access. In the United States, even for an area as large as the Yellowstone National Park, it has been found necessary to encourage use of public transport and to limit private car numbers by restricting entry to those with permits issued in advance. Such 'rationing' of popular sites which are vulnerable to tourist pressures is likely to become increasingly prevalent in Britain.

Towns and cities

All the conurbations in Britain and many of the large towns, particularly in the North, have declined in the course of the past two decades. Each has had unique features and London, in particular, has been different in a number of ways, experiencing some of the problems on a larger scale, but recently undergoing a revival largely associated with the growth of financial and other services in the City. Most of the larger towns and cities, however, have experienced patterns of development with important characteristics in common.

Industry

In most large towns there used to be a significant amount of industry, both small workshops and large factories, in the inner areas near the centre. Most of these have now gone because of:

- old, multi-storey buildings unsuited to modern methods of production;

- cramped sites which restrict loading, unloading and parking and make expansion of buildings impossible;

- congested streets which impede collections and deliveries and access by employees;

- restrictions on activities considered environmentally undesirable;

- high labour costs;

- high rates, rents and property values.

Typically, a firm which had been managing despite increasing difficulties would decide to leave when expanding prospects made more space essential, or when a sudden jump in rent or rates made site costs prohibitively expensive, or when an offer from a property developer was worth more than the total value of the business.

Initially, a firm would tend to think of moving as short a distance as possible down the radial road away from the town centre, with a view to keeping its existing labour force; later, or immediately if no site nearby was available, it would probably move further out to the suburbs, or to a smaller town outside or, if pressed, to a development area. In recent years the trend has increasingly been to seek a new site right outside the town, often on a purpose-built industrial estate or science park, offering modern, single-storey buildings; space for loading, unloading and parking; space for expansion; a pleasant working environment; moderate rents and rates; quick access to trunk roads and motorways for goods; and easy access to residential areas for staff (by car but not, usually, by public transport).

Offices

There have been similar developments with offices in or near city centres. Rising rents, rates and property values, cramped buildings, lack of parking space, and commuting difficulties due to increasing congestion, have combined to encourage smaller organisations to move out to cheaper and more agreeable locations in the suburbs, or small towns nearby, or (occasionally) to landscaped sites in a more rural environment.

The same factors have also encouraged larger organisations to move out completely or, more commonly, to move out to somewhere cheaper the routine, back-office operations involving large numbers of staff and large areas of space, while keeping at the centre a nucleus of senior staff with key functions.

However, with offices, unlike manufacturing industry, the general expansion in employment has tended to mean (particularly in London) that the movement of some offices *out* has sometimes been offset by others coming *in* because of a perceived need, for operational or prestige reasons, to have a presence in the centre, despite the high costs and inconvenience.

Residential areas

The movement of industry and offices out of the inner areas of cities has been parallelled by a movement out of people. At the end of the war much of the property in inner city areas was cramped, sub-standard, dilapidated or destroyed, and those who had the opportunity to do so tended to move out to better quality housing in the suburbs or in the New Towns; while those already further out tended to move on in search of a still better environment in outer suburbs or adjacent towns or country areas. Later, when local industries closed down or moved out, more people left the inner areas in search of jobs. There was a similar move when other local employment opportunities ended, as in London, with the closure of the docks and the produce markets.

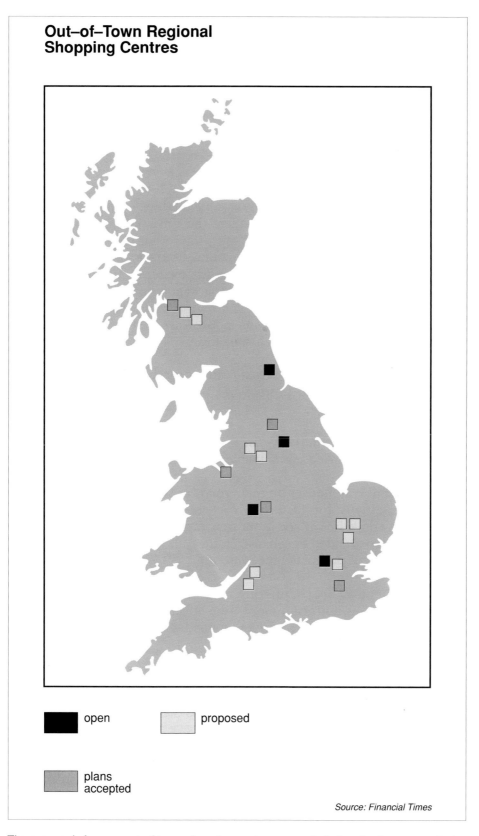

Out–of–Town Regional Shopping Centres

open   proposed

plans accepted

Source: Financial Times

The proposals for new out-of-town shopping centres currently in the pipeline are equivalent to more than two fifths of total existing town centre retailing provision.

Consequently, over a period, some of those inner areas have become characterised by derelict property, diminished population, limited local employment, high rates of unemployment, low average incomes and various kinds of social problem. Others, particularly in London, have become home for immigrants from overseas, or been 'gentrified' by professional people seeking the advantages of residence close to their jobs in the city centre.

Shops

Since the war there have been many significant developments in retailing: abolition of Resale Price Maintenance; the growth of self-service and supermarkets; the decline of local shops; the recent recovery with Asian family businesses offering extended opening hours; and the ascendency of large groups in some product areas – for example, five retailers now account for almost three-quarters of all packaged grocery sales.

More recent developments are potentially more important, however, in that they may have a profound effect on the whole development pattern of cities. They include:

- shopping complexes in city centres (or suburban centres) offering covered-in areas and a wide range of shops in a compact space;

- large supermarkets ('hypermarkets') at the edges of towns offering the convenience of on-site parking;[183]

- retail warehouses on main roads at the edges of towns, originally for furniture, carpets and bulky electrical goods, with car access for easy carrying away, but often now extended to sell also clothes, shoes, toys and other kinds of product at the same site;[184,185]

- dispersed shops, offering easy car access to fast food, banking, entertainment and specialist shops at the roadside near the town instead of in the crowded shopping streets inside it;

- retail parks, consisting of clusters of retail warehouses and dispersed shops, laid out so that shoppers can move easily from one to another by car,[186,187] accounting for 79 per cent of out-of-town floorspace in 1988;

- regional shopping centres (or 'shopping cities') serving a wide catchment area with large numbers of shops in a single, covered site, together, usually, with a range of leisure, recreational and catering services.[188]

It is in out-of-town retailing that the main growth is envisaged in the next decade or two. The most important characteristics of the new kinds of development are that they rely predominantly on the private car for access and many are sited near motorways; and offer not only shops and high street services but also a range of leisure attractions designed to give 'a good day out for the whole family'. The major centres are large, aimed at population catchment areas of half a million or more. Most proposals have planned floorspace of over half a million square feet each (more than three times that of an average town centre scheme). One of the largest ones, Meadowhall in Sheffield, has 1.2m square feet of retail floorspace (equivalent to one quarter of total national new floorspace each year in the 1970s) and parking for up to 12,000 cars, and is intended to attract 25 million shopping visits a year from the 2.2 million population within half an hour's driving distance and the 9 million within driving distance of an hour.[189]

The total increase in out-of-town floorspace has been large and rising fast. Until 1980 it averaged about 5m sq.ft. a year. Since then it has averaged more than 10m sq. ft. a year, rising to about 23m in 1989 and an estimated 30m in 1990.[190] The total capacity of the proposals currently in the pipeline is equivalent to more than two-fifths of total existing town centre retailing provision.[191] Not all will be built, but with a recovery of the property market in the mid-1990s and in the absence of planning control to the contrary, up to ten regional centres could be added during the 1990s. The scale of out-of-town developments is sufficient to pose a threat to existing central area centres. For example, new retail warehouse developments in Avon have a floorspace greater than the centres of Bristol, Bath and all the other towns in the county combined.[190]

But it is not just the highly visible and politically controversial regional centres which are indicators of the direction of development in the 1990s. Rather it is the *cumulative* effect of retail dispersion of all sorts, combined with the dispersion of housing, employment and leisure. Although the level of regional mega-centre proposals is dropping off, retail warehousing may more than fill the gap. For example, the new 1.15m. sq. ft. regional centre at Thurrock on the M25 is adjacent to a retail warehouse park of 20 superstores, cinemas and 3 drive-in restaurants.

North American experience

One indication of possible prospects ahead is provided by North America, where these kinds of development started much earlier, with the opening of the first out-of-town shopping centre in Kansas in 1926, and have subsequently proceeded much further. An extreme example is the city of Houston, Texas, where high rates of car ownership and the relative absence of planning controls has led to a completely dispersed pattern of development. Out-of-town shopping complexes have attracted to them catering, entertainment and recreation facilities and office developments, with the result that the original city centre is no longer a place of particular significance, since its functions have been spread over a number of different suburban centres.

Within North America a number of serious drawbacks have been found with this dispersed pattern of development.

- ◆ It severely damages retailing in the old city centre. In Detroit there is no longer a single department store in the city centre. In Memphis the city centre now accounts for only 3.5 per cent of total city retail sales.[192] In Dallas the city centre's share of total city sales fell from 31 per cent in 1970 to 3 per cent in 1985. In a total of 59 US Metropolitan Areas studied, central area sales fell from 35 per cent of the total in 1948 to 8 per cent in 1972.

- ◆ It displaces offices from the old city centre. In 1987 the 'newer' cities of Houston, Dallas and Atlanta had only about 27 per cent of their offices still in the city centre, compared with 67 per cent and 85 per cent respectively in the 'older' cities of New York and New Orleans.

- ◆ It deprives the city centre of other amenities such as restaurants, hotels, cinemas, banks and libraries when other services follow the shops to the new suburban centres.

- ◆ It depresses central area business and residential property values, creating a dead hole at the heart of the city.

- ◆ It removes prospering commercial developments to outside the city limits so that they no longer provide tax revenues to support city services.

- ◆ It cannot easily be served by public transport and the consequent increases in total car mileage can lead to all-round, all-day traffic congestion.

In the face of these disadvantages some American cities (Boston, Baltimore, Cleveland, Dayton, Providence) have built new city-centre shopping complexes, imitating those out of town. However these tend to 'suck in' property values off surrounding streets and can lead to a very 'down-market' city centre, outside the covered malls.

European experience

In most of the countries of continental Europe, on the other hand, a very different pattern of development has emerged. In most continental

European cities space is more constricted than in North American cities, car ownership is lower, public transport services are stronger and planning controls are tighter. The American car-based, dispersed pattern of development has therefore tended to look less attractive or feasible.

Consequently, most other countries in Western Europe have all along discouraged out-of-town shopping developments, regarding them as incompatible with the continuing vitality of existing city centres. The main exceptions used to be France and West Germany, both of which allowed a number of major out-of-town developments in the 1960s. More recently, however, they too have taken firm measures to restrict them through legislation, in France in 1973 and in West Germany in 1968, 1977 and 1986.[193]

For most major European cities (eg Stockholm, Amsterdam, Munich) an approach has been adopted which is fundamentally different from the American. Instead of developing new out-of-town complexes, the emphasis has been placed on positive measures to strengthen existing city centres by:

- building new shopping and leisure complexes on city centre sites;

- creating pedestrian precincts;

- upgrading existing shopping streets by covering them over to make weather-proof arcades;

- improving access with better public transport into and within the central shopping areas;

- restricting access and parking of private cars.

The last item – restriction of car access – is often feared by retailers as likely to lead to a ruinous decline in business. Continental experience has been the reverse. Retail turnover has *increased* when streets are pedestrianised and exceptionally *high* turnover levels are experienced in Munich which has a largely pedestrianised city centre, exceptionally *low* car parking provision and an excellent public transport system.[193]

In Britain, urban policy in the 1980s has swung in the opposite direction from that in continental Europe, with more sympathy than before for proposals for out-of-town developments, but also combined with a wish to maintain the health of existing city centres. It is not at present clear whether future policies will follow the pattern set by much of North America or that of continental Europe, and Britain is probably at the end of the phase when it could hope to realise what are mutually incompatible objectives.

Since urban development is an area in which lead times are long, the decisions taken in the next few years will to a large extent determine the shape of urban Britain in 2010. In particular, the decisions taken on proposals for major out-of-town shopping complexes will be one of the key factors affecting the future of Britain's cities.

London

London has a number of unique advantages arising from its greater size; but it also experiences a number of urban problems in a particularly acute form. Since 1982 London has boomed as a business centre. Employment, which fell steadily from the 1960s as industries closed, is now rising in the financial and professional services sectors. The London Planning Advisory Committee forecasts a net continued growth, mainly in service employment, of 1.8 per cent a year until 2001, adding about 14,000 jobs each year to London within the context of a continuing shift from industry to services.[194]

However, factors which reflect the very success of London as a world city (high land prices, high rents, high wages, intensive use of infrastructure) are also beginning to impose constraints on its operation and management. There appears to be a serious deterioration of its physical infrastructure: the public transport system is old and overcrowded; its sewers are crumbling; and it is reputed to be the dirtiest capital city in Northern Europe.[195,196] There is no level of government which seems able or willing to cope in a systematic way with the cumulative problems of urban management, such as transport congestion.

High housing prices in London will make it increasingly difficult to recruit employees in public transport, health services and education, and for local government throughout the 1990s. Skill shortages in the private sector will result in a continual increase in the disparity between public and private sector wages, and this will affect the ability of public agencies to deliver essential services.

There is evidence that the London commercial boom will ease, not so much because of any fundamental change in the nature of financial and business services, but because of the costs of congestion and the high cost of land for commercial activities and housing. But the beneficiaries of London congestion are less likely to be the North or Scotland than East Anglia, the South West and the East Midlands, which will increase their employment by about 25 per cent by the year 2000.

Other cities

In the 1990s, growth in the service industry, outside the London area, is likely to be in Swindon, Bristol or Cambridge rather than in Liverpool, Manchester or Newcastle. A recent study suggests that as much as 85 per cent of new job creation is in the South and Midlands;[197] for example, between June 1986 and June 1988 the number in work rose by 11.6 per cent in East Anglia but by only 0.9 per cent in Humberside while it actually *declined* by 0.1 per cent in Scotland. Reinforcing these trends is the growing attraction of villages and countryside as residential locations, fuelled by increased mobility from rising car ownership, and the attraction of smaller, non-industrial market towns in the North as well as the South.

Some former industrial cities are enjoying revivals, mainly retailing-led, but these may be in danger from the dispersal of retailing and leisure activities and from slow growth in consumer spending in the North and North East.[160] The North American experience suggests that the dispersal of retailing will weaken city centres, although the evidence from the first big out-of-town centre in Britain, at Gateshead near Newcastle, is inconclusive at this stage.

In the context of limited growth in the North, the potential for renewal of former industrial cities will vary. The decline in household size due in part to divorce, and the growth of two income households, suggests the possibility of further gentrification of traditional inner city housing areas in the 1990s. Many of these neighbourhoods are occupied by home owners from ethnic minorities who may prefer to move to the suburbs. But the inner city of Victorian housing is not the inner city of derelict industrial land, and their futures will need to be assessed separately. Overall, the degree of renewal that can be expected in the 1990s hinges on a number of factors.

- The availability and marketability of 'levers' which can raise people's perceptions of the potential attractiveness of an area and thus investor confidence and private investment. Waterside redevelopment (ocean, river, canal, dockland) and science parks were the levers of the 1980s; options for the 1990s and beyond include rapid transit, heritage architecture, arts-based tourism and other leisure-oriented Developments.

- Institutional arrangements which forge a partnership between public and private sectors and allow initial public investments to draw in private investment at a suitable rate.

- Mechanisms for packaging derelict land and raising investor confidence in a larger area or even a city as a whole, rather than attempts to attract investment on a piecemeal or site-by-site basis.

- Urban environmental improvements and major urban renewal schemes which tie together residential, leisure and retailing developments on a single site.

Suburbs

The already apparent problems of city centre congestion will be more than matched in the 1990s by dispersed congestion in suburbs and some lowland countryside, especially in the South East. The Department of Transport forecasts that outer London traffic volume will grow at twice the rate of that of inner London, at about 2 per cent per year or 22 per cent during the 1990s. The continued growth of traffic, the trend for the separation of top management and back-office functions in companies, and a dispersal of offices and housing into suburban and semi-rural locations will contribute to the condition of dispersed traffic congestion which at its worst is called 'gridlock'. Such congestion is already beginning to be experienced in outer London and its hinterland, and the growth of cross-suburb commuting and a continuing trend towards longer-distance commuting from home to work will exacerbate the situation. Britain is particularly sensitive to gridlock because it has one of the highest densities of vehicles per road mile in the world. Both dispersed land uses and growing congestion reduce the capacity of bus and rail transport to address the problem.

The cumulative effects of urban pressures, combined with the release of land from agriculture, are likely to lead to the spread of low-density suburbanisation into rural areas, with a scattering of housing, businesses and leisure facilities such as golf courses and motor sports centres. This tendency may be checked, however, if green belt policies are strengthened or if development is channelled into new country towns.

Housing

People's homes determine how they can live in many important ways, and hence the availability and suitability of housing is an aspect of the environment which is of particularly close concern.

Housing stock

The high rate of new housebuilding in the 1960s fell back by 18 per cent in the 1970s, and in the 1980s has fallen by a further 30 per cent. But while the rate of new house construction in recent years has been little more than half the rate in the 1960s, the reduction in the rate of loss from slum clearance and other causes has meant that the rate of *net* gain in the housing stock in recent years has been only about one fifth below the rate in the 1960s. Altogether, over the past two decades, the net gain in the housing stock has amounted to more than 4 million dwellings, an increase of about one fifth.[198]

The English House Condition Survey[199] showed that the number of dwellings unfit for human habitation fell by more than one half between 1971 and 1986. Also the General Household Survey[200] showed that

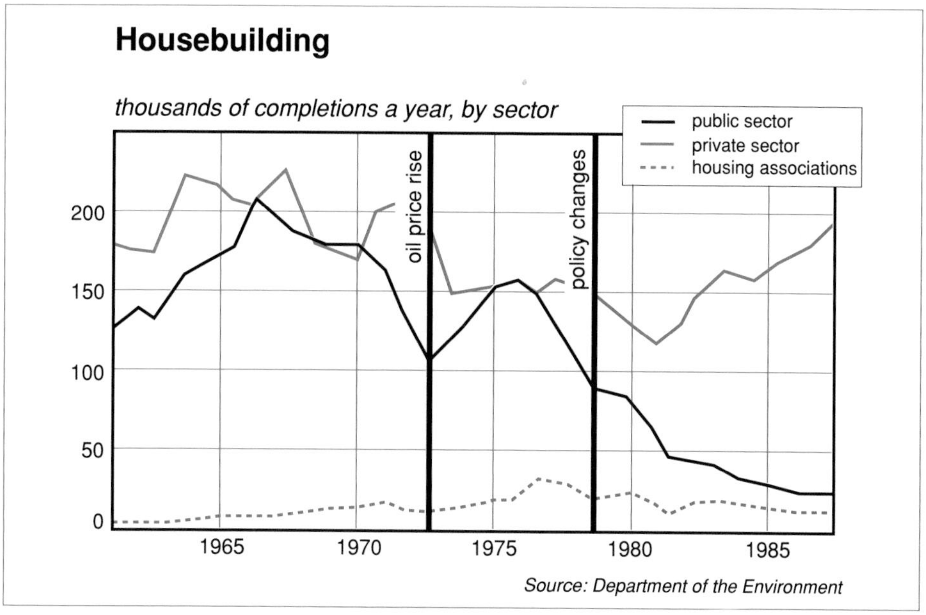
Housebuilding
thousands of completions a year, by sector
public sector
private sector
housing associations
oil price rise
policy changes
200
150
100
50
0
1965
1970
1975
1980
1985
Source: Department of the Environment

Private sector housebuilding has been increasing, but the virtual ending of housebuilding by local councils, together with sales of council houses to tenants, has greatly reduced the stock of housing available at 'social' rents.

between 1976 and 1988 the proportion of dwellings without the use of a bath or shower fell from 12 per cent to 2 per cent, and the proportion below standard for bedrooms fell from 9 per cent to 3 per cent. Over the same period the proportion without central heating fell from 65 per cent to 28 per cent.

However the survey also showed that the number of dwellings (about 5 per cent of the total) which were in serious disrepair or unfit for habitation did not drop over the period, and a recent study[197] suggests that there are currently 0.75 million council houses and 2.75 million private houses in poor condition, with nearly 1 million of the latter 'unsuitable for human habitation'. The total backlog of disrepair amounts to about £50bn. Current legislation and investment is unlikely to provide for more than a holding operation, and substantial additional investment in housing will be needed if this situation is to be corrected by 2010.

Housing needs

Projections of household formation[198] suggest that the rate of new formation is likely to decline as a result of demographic and social changes; and the characteristics of households, and hence of their housing needs, will also change.

The proportion of one person households, which rose from 12 per cent in 1961 to 22 per cent in 1981, is expected to continue rising to 31 per

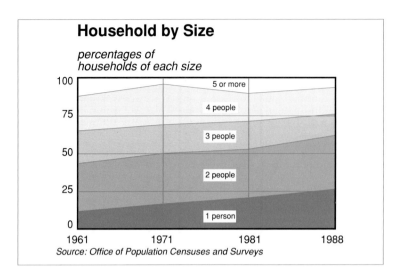

The proportion of one-person households has been rising steeply and average household size has been falling. However, in the 1990s when the 'baby boom' generation start their families there are likely to be more larger households.

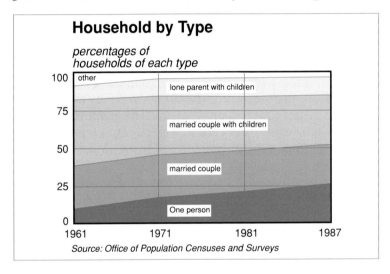

cent in 2001. In the 1970s the increase was mainly due to more women above pension age living alone, but in the 1980s the main increase has been of men of working age. At the same time the proportion of large households of five or more people has halved from 14 per cent in 1971 to 7 per cent in 1988, and the number of married couples with dependent children has fallen from 35 per cent of all households in 1971 to 28 per cent in 1987.[198] However, the number of larger households is likely to rise again in the 1990s as the 'baby boom' generation bring up their families. It will then decline again after the turn of the century.[201]

These changes in the size and type of households imply changes in the mix of housing that will be required.

Housing finance

The effective demand for housing will be much affected also by the continuing rise in incomes which is expected and by forms of tenure, house prices and government policies.

Owner occupation has been rising ever since the war and, stimulated by the new right of tenants to buy their council houses, the proportion of owner-occupied households rose from 49 per cent in 1971 to 69 per cent in 1987, and is likely to rise further.[198]

However, the Duke of Edinburgh's enquiry suggested that by 2000 about one quarter of households will still require rented accommodation – some of them single people wanting temporary accommodation or mobility for employment or educational reasons, and others people who cannot afford owner occupation and need 'social' (ie subsidised) rented housing. However, 1.5 million rented homes (one fifth of the total) have disappeared since 1978, the majority because of council house sales and reduced council building, and the numbers accepted as homeless has doubled over the same period, many of them put up in bed and breakfast hotels which, in London, cost nearly twice as much as the cost of providing accommodation in council dwellings.[202]

House prices, stimulated in the 1980s by the increased availability of mortgages on favourable terms, have tended to rise more rapidly than inflation, particularly in London and the more prosperous parts of the South. The high prices in some areas are a factor likely to check the increase in numbers able to contemplate buying houses.

Housing, and housing finance in particular, is an area in which the course taken by future developments will be particularly heavily influenced by government policies – on mortgage tax relief, on interest rates, on local government finance, on council house building, on council house sales, on tenants' and landlords' rights, and on town and country planning. Accordingly, long-term forecasts are subject to an exceptional degree of uncertainty.

Housing location

A total increase of about 1.3 million households is forecast by 2001,[203] and further increases are likely subsequently. Many of the extra homes for them will be wanted in the already crowded South East. It will be possible to build some of them on sites within existing urban areas; but there will not be enough sites for all of them, so some will presumably need to be built elsewhere. This will raise difficult issues: about whether they should be on former agricultural land peripheral to existing towns, thereby encroaching on green belts; or near existing small towns, thus changing them substantially in character; or in villages and open countryside, changing the character of rural areas. Here too, policy decisions will be the decisive factor in what is done.

Water and waste

Supplies of clean, safe water are a basic requirement for a wholesome environment; likewise, safe and efficient disposal of waste products. In both areas there has been much progress over many decades, but in recent years a number of problems have given rise to concern.

Water

In the 1970s the European Commission set standards for drinking water purity which came into effect in 1985. However, in November 1988 the Secretary of State for the Environment
reported that about 200 UK drinking water supplies 'regularly exceed one or other of the limits set by the EC drinking water directive'. In November 1988 a study claimed that a total of 298 drinking supplies were contaminated.[204] Altogether, about 4 million people in Britain drink water which breaches EC limits at one time or another.[205] In January 1989 the environment minister responsible for water estimated that it will take until 1995 to comply with all the most important European standards for drinking water.[206] While at least one expert has expressed the view that the EC standards are unnecessarily stringent,[207] there has been widespread concern about the consistency of standards, and a number of government measures have been introduced with a view to improving the situation. There are four main sources of contamination: nitrates, toxic chemicals, hydrocarbons and lead.

Nitrates
The problem with nitrates is that they leach through the soil under fields to the water table where they contaminate the sources of water used for about one third of total supplies.[208] They also run into rivers, lakes or coastal seas where they encourage eutrophication, a process in which the growth of algae is stimulated, oxygen depleted and fish life threatened (and beaches made unattractive to holidaymakers). This process has eliminated fish life in many lakes in North America and is reported to be giving problems in some rivers and lakes in Britain.[209]

The nitrate gets into the soil partly through natural processes, but the main cause of the recent increases is believed to be the use of nitrogen fertilisers in quantities greater than can be absorbed by the crops, the excess soaking into the soil or getting washed into rivers.[210] The secretary of the Agriculture and Food Research Council, who chaired a Royal Society group on nitrate pollution, has estimated that the excess fertiliser wasted this way each year is probably worth £100 million – a sum equal to the entire annual budget of the research council.[211]

A further cause of nitrate pollution is from animal slurry on farms, which is up to 100 times more damaging than untreated sewage, and from the liquor from silage, which is 200 times more damaging. A report by the

Water Authorities Association and the Ministry of Agriculture[212] records that in 1988 there were 4,141 reported cases of farm pollution of rivers, leading to 148 prosecutions.

Because treatment plant to remove the nitrates from drinking water is expensive, the main thrust of policy measures has been to encourage farming methods which are less likely to lead to release of nitrates. A major problem is that the nitrates take many years to leach down to the water table, so that even if all further release of nitrates were to stop, the quantities released in earlier years would still be entering the water supply for a long time to come. A study published by the Department of the Environment[213] warns that in three of the ten catchment areas studied, water will exceed EC nitrate limits for at least another 50 years.

Toxic chemicals
The second source of contamination is from toxic chemicals: careless use of pesticides (for example in sheep dips); herbicides (widely used for weed control); and spills of industrial solvents – all of which can leach into the water supply and present risks.[214]

Hydrocarbons
The third risk is from hydrocarbons shed from coal tar linings in water mains, which are thought to contain carcinogens similar to those in cigarette smoke. The problem here is the cost of removing the linings. The former Thames Water Authority, which has 15,000 miles of this type of pipe, has said it would cost £1 billion to reline them all,[215] and it is estimated that there are about 125,000 miles of pipe in the country as a whole, implying a total cost which could be as high as £8 billion.

Lead
The final risk is from lead in domestic water pipes, mainly in older houses. These too will be expensive to replace.

There is much controversy about the seriousness of these problems and about the best way to deal with them; but it seems likely that any complete solution will be expensive and, in the case of leaching of nitrates, unlikely to be fully effective by 2010.

Liquid waste

In general, in recent years the record of pollution control in rivers and dumping in seas around Britain has been one of steady improvement, assisted by agreements on reductions arrived at in a series of international conferences.

The main area of contention in the past has been over the disposal of sewage. Britain, alone of North Sea countries, discharges untreated sewage from many coastal towns directly into the sea, resulting in one in three of Britain's bathing beaches failing to meet EC cleanliness standards; and it also dumps one third of its treated sewage sludge into the North Sea.

In the past there has been much controversy over the environmental soundness of both practices and, in deference to objections, a programme was started to extend sewage outfall pipes further out to sea at a cost of £1.4bn. In March 1990, however, previous policies were reversed with the announcement that dumping of sludge will be ended by 1998, and the sewage discharged into coastal waters from long pipe outfalls will all be treated first by 2000.[216] The cost of the extra treatment plant, landfills and incineration facilities to make these changes possible is estimated to be about £1.7bn, to be covered, it seems, by an extra 6 per cent on the bills of water consumers. At an international conference in March 1990,[217] agreement was reached on reductions in estuary discharges and sea dumping of a number of other pollutants and there are grounds for confidence that by 2010 the seas around Britain will be cleaner and safer than now. The main potential threats remaining will be from nuclear waste (if sea dumping of surplus naval reactors is undertaken) and from oil spillages as a result of tanker accidents.

Solid waste

The arrangements for disposal of toxic and hazardous solid waste has been causing increasing concern in recent years. The head of the Hazardous Waste Inspectorate resigned after submitting three annual reports, 'all three equally critical', and complaining of not having been given the powers and resources necessary for doing the job.[218] The parliamentary Environment Select Committee has published a highly critical report.[219] And its chairman has asserted that Britain has come perilously close to suffering a disaster from its 'appalling' waste disposal system.[220]

The grounds for their concern are that there are about 5000 waste disposal sites, about 550 of them licensed to dispose of hazardous waste. Some of them are near inhabited houses. Until recently, there were only six inspectors to supervise them, standards of control were uneven, and information about their contents and condition was limited.

While it is hard to know what degree of risk there may have been in past arrangements, it would seem highly probable that, with the increased level of environmental awareness, arrangements for effective control of these sites will be in operation long before 2010.

Transport

Personal mobility is one of the most keenly sought after goals for most people, who want to be able to travel to get to more attractive jobs, to better shops, to places of recreation and entertainment, to visit friends and relatives and, in some cases, to do so from more congenial homes in

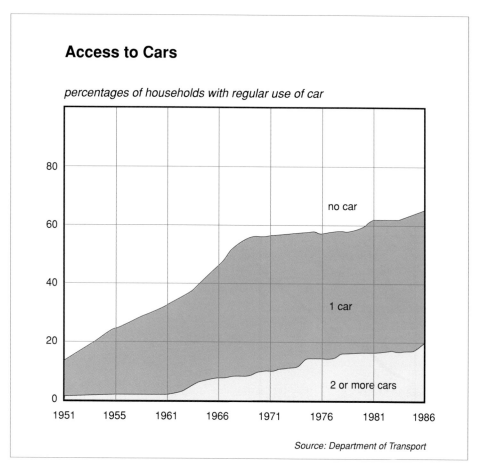

Access to Cars

percentages of households with regular use of car

no car

1 car

2 or more cars

80

60

40

20

0

1951   1955   1961   1966   1971   1976   1981   1986

Source: Department of Transport

In 1951 six households in seven had no car; now only one household in three has no car, and one household in five has two or more cars.

peaceful rural areas. They have sought this mobility increasingly through the use of the motor car, which has been a great liberator for many in the past, but which is likely to give rise to increasing problems over the next twenty years.

Past growth in traffic

Between 1970 and 1990 total annual car mileage has more than doubled, growing at about three times the rate of bus and coach mileage and about double the rate of heavy goods vehicle mileage.[221] In the course of two decades the total number of cars has increased by three quarters and so also has the average annual car mileage per person.[221] Two households in three now have cars and one in five has more than one car.[222] On average, people now travel more than 6,000 miles a year by car, more than twelve times as far as they travel by rail or by bus and coach and more than one hundred times as far as on internal air services.[221] Cars account for more

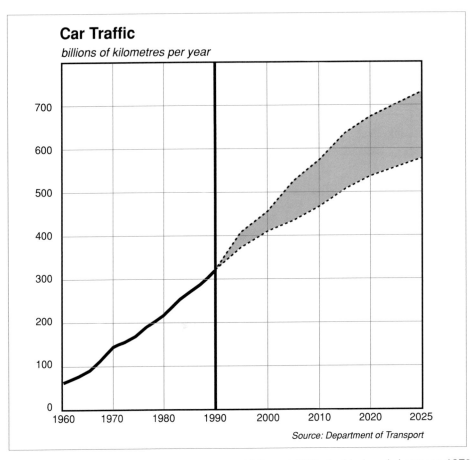

Car Traffic

billions of kilometres per year

Source: Department of Transport

Cars are popular. Car traffic doubled between 1960 and 1970, doubled again between 1970 and 1990, and is forecast by the Department of Transport to grow by a further 45-76 per cent by 2010. However, these forecasts do not take account of the possible impact of measures to reduce global warming.

than five-sixths of all household expenditure on transport, and more than one eighth of total household expenditure.[223]

If personal transport in Britain has been increasingly dominated by the car, it is because it can offer unrivalled advantages to the user: fast, clean, warm, dry, comfortable, effortless transport from door to door, independent of timetable constraints, and able to carry other passengers, shopping and luggage. It has enabled people to commute more distantly, work more efficiently, shop more conveniently and enjoy wider opportunities for social, recreational and holiday travel. In short, for many people the motor car revolution has brought a significant, and welcome, change in life-styles.

Government forecasts of future traffic

In view of the evident popularity of the motor car, it is hardly surprising that its use is predicted to go on rising in the years ahead. The Department of Transport has prepared a number of forecasts of the growth in car traffic to 2010, with separate upper and lower estimates based on alternative assumptions of future growth of the economy. These forecasts have been rising in recent years from an increase of 17-34 per cent predicted in 1985,[224] to an increase of 45-76 per cent on 1989 levels in the most recent forecast in 1990.[221]

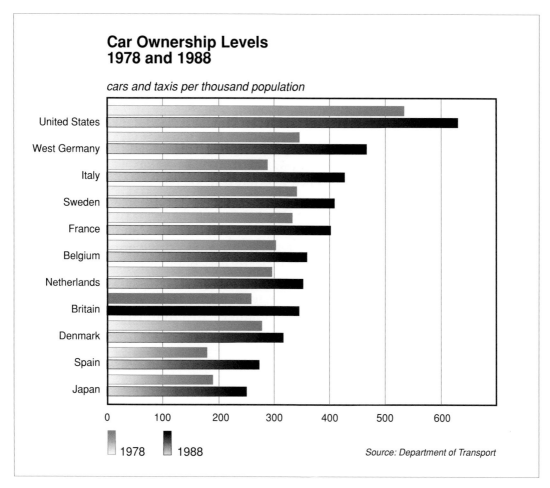

Car Ownership Levels 1978 and 1988

cars and taxis per thousand population

□ 1978   ■ 1988

Source: Department of Transport

Despite the great increase in the proportion of households with cars, car ownership in Britain is not yet as high as in some of the other, more prosperous, countries in Western Europe, and is barely half as high as in the United States.

The most recent forecast, that by 2010 car traffic will increase by between one half and three quarters, is not incompatible with past trends. The lower figure requires only a moderate rate of economic growth (which seems likely); while the upper figure implies a rise in traffic much faster than the rate of economic growth (which is what has happened in recent periods). The underlying assumption is that increases in incomes will continue to bring more than proportionate increases in traffic.

Certainly, there are reasons for supposing that potential demand is not yet saturated. Households in the lowest income quarter, and those headed by unskilled manual workers, are twice as likely as the average to be without a car, implying that the proportion of car-owning families may increase further with increases in lower incomes and a smaller proportion of people with unskilled manual jobs.[223] At the other end of the range, the rise in households with two or more cars has been faster than the rise in total traffic, and the proportion of households with two or more cars is more than twice the average in households in the highest income quarter, and in those headed by managers and professional people, implying that car numbers may go up further as more people reach these income levels and join these occupation groups.[223] Moreover, present levels of car ownership per head are higher in other countries with higher income levels, such as France, Germany, Italy, Switzerland, Norway and Sweden, and three-quarters higher in the United States,[221] implying that higher income levels in the future in Britain will bring higher levels of car ownership here also.

Thus past trends suggest strong enthusiasm for the car, and overseas experience suggests there may be some way to go before saturation levels are reached in Britain. In the past, once people have had the income, they have wanted to buy a car; and if they already had one, once they had more income, they have wanted a second one or a third one, or cars which are larger, faster or of superior quality; and if they have had the opportunity, they have tended to want to drive greater distances in them. In the sense that the car is clearly very popular, and pent-up demand for it may still be great, it is reasonable to expect past trends of traffic growth to continue – barring major changes in circumstances.

However, such major changes in circumstances now seem increasingly probable as a result of environmental problems and the responses likely to be made to them.

Traffic congestion problems

In London, more than one million people come in to the central area each morning to work, and go back home again each evening; and others come in to visit shops and offices during the day, and for entertainment in the evenings. Some come by car and the consequent traffic congestion has long been unpleasant and expensive and now extends right through the day. Average traffic speeds in the central area are now down to 12 miles per hour – only 3 miles per hour faster than in 1912 and only 4 miles per hour faster than was achieved with horses and carriages in 1890.[225,226]

Over the past four decades many measures have been tried in the hope that they would deal with the problem: road widening, fly-overs and new roads; one-way systems, synchronised traffic lights and traffic management schemes of other kinds; staggered working hours; provision of off-street parking and restrictions on on-street parking and deliveries; more police, traffic wardens, wheel-clamping, towing away and tougher penalties for offences; and a number of measures of other kinds.

Most of the measures have succeeded partially, for a while; but all of them have failed completely, in the end. This is because once particular measures bring faster traffic flows in an area, this tends to generate more traffic up to the point where traffic congestion is back to the previous level. Consequently, despite all the measures which have been adopted over the past four decades, central London traffic speeds have been getting *slower*, and ambulances and fire engines are taking twice as long to reach the scenes of major incidents as they were a decade ago.[227] And there are similar, if less serious, problems in other cities.

Alternative policies for congestion

In the light of these intractable difficulties, there are three different policy approaches which have been suggested.

No change

The first is simply to continue with variations on the piece-meal mix of policies used over the past four decades. This would not necessarily lead to a complete seize-up because, as congestion gets worse, it tends to choke off additional would-be car users; but nor would it be likely to lead to lasting gains since, on past experience, local improvements suck in extra traffic until the previous level of congestion is restored. The most likely outcome, therefore, would be a continuation of congestion at levels not very different from those experienced in the past: probably sufferable, just about, but an approach unlikely to be pursued indefinitely if alternative options look more attractive.

North American approach

The second alternative, the 'Los Angeles solution', is to adopt a more full-blooded approach: build enough new roads to accommodate all the motorists wishing to use them. However, London is less spacious than Los Angeles or Houston. At present, only one commuter in seven comes into central London by car.[228] To enable the other six to do so would require creating seven times the present access and parking capacity, demolishing a large part of the inner area for new roads and flattening the whole of the centre to provide parking space.

Even in Los Angeles the solutions of the 1950s and 1960s are no longer found to be very satisfactory, and in the 1970s and 1980s the car-centred approach has been modified. In essence it has become: if you cannot get all of the cars into the main city centre, then allow development to be dispersed over a number of peripheral centres which they *can* get into.

This approach has been giving rise to problems, even in sprawling cities such as Los Angeles and Houston. Traffic has grown to such an extent that the effect of the dispersion of development has been to spread the congestion more widely, so that instead of a jammed-up city centre area there is now a 'gridlock' of traffic jams spread over a very wide area. There have been similar problems in other American cities with a dispersed pattern of development.

In Britain, population densities are much greater than in California and Texas, particularly around the main conurbations, and there is not plenty of free space in which to site new urban development and road systems. Construction costs would therefore be higher, environmental damage greater and local opposition stronger. And the risk that it would end merely in creating a more dispersed pattern of congestion seems correspondingly greater.

In this regard, the experience of the M25 London orbital motorway is not encouraging. It was designed to relieve congestion on the periphery of London and constructed at a cost of £1bn. Yet within three years of its opening in 1986 most sections were already carrying traffic greater than the upper limit forecast for 2001, and plans were under consideration for widening it at the cost of a further £1bn.[228] This suggests that in the areas immediately outside the main conurbations there is such a pent-up demand for road space that even very large and expensive construction programmes could not be relied upon to remove congestion.

Circumstances in crowded Britain would be much less favourable for a dispersed pattern of development than in many American cities and, even in North America, 'Los Angeles solution' is increasingly becoming the subject of criticism.

Continental European approach

The third possible approach is the one that has been adopted by most of the major cities in Western Europe and, more recently, by an increasing number in North America also. In essence it is to give up trying to get every prospective driver into the city centre by car, and concentrate instead on getting them there more satisfactorily by other means. The measures used have included some or all of the following:

- high quality metro and commuter rail systems, with park-and-drive facilities for longer distance commuters (new or radically upgraded metro systems in Paris, Munich and Stockholm, also in Toronto, Washington, San Francisco and Osaka);

- faster and more frequent bus services with priority traffic lanes for buses, taxis, minibuses and shared cars (in use also in many American cities) and priority at intersections;

- separated lanes and other forms of encouragement for cyclists (27 per cent of commuter journeys in the Netherlands are made by bicycle, compared with 4 per cent in London;[229] 5,000 free bikes have been made available to commuters in Copenhagen);[230]

♦ improved central area provision for pedestrians, with traffic-free zones, covered-over shopping streets and, prospectively, special free central-area travel systems;

♦ reduced off-street parking capacity in the centre and reduced on-street parking to improve the capacity of access routes (100,000 street parking places are being abolished in Paris);[231]

♦ tougher enforcement of traffic regulations, particularly bus lanes and parking restrictions;

♦ charging for use of road space in the most congested central areas, using electronic systems which do not interfere with traffic flows (a charging system is already in use in Singapore for several years; and one is in trial use in Hong Kong; a system is in operation in Oslo; there are plans for Stockholm based on phone-card type discs; and studies by EC aiming to ensure compatibility between disc systems of different member countries).

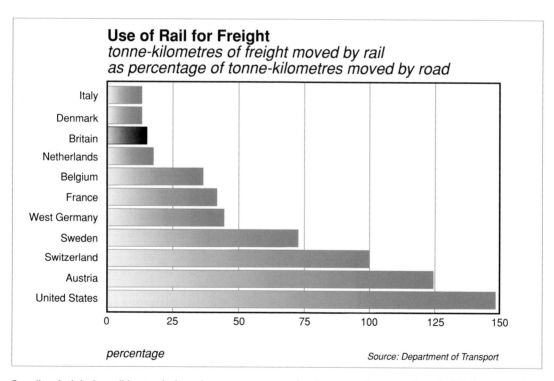

Use of Rail for Freight
tonne-kilometres of freight moved by rail
as percentage of tonne-kilometres moved by road

percentage

Source: Department of Transport

Sending freight by rail instead of road saves energy and reduces road congestion. In Britain seven times as much freight is sent by road as by rail. In France, Belgium and Germany the proportion sent by rail instead of by road is more than twice as great as in Britain; in Sweden, Switzerland and Austria more than seven times as great; and in the United States more than ten times as great.

These measures to deal with city centre congestion have been complemented in residential areas by measures for traffic calming and improved facilities for pedestrians and cyclists; and for longer journeys, by measures to reduce motorway congestion by shifting more of the traffic from road and air to rail. A high speed rail network is planned to link the main centres of Western Europe and relieve the congestion in Europe's crowded air lanes and airports,[232,233] and already in France and Germany the railways carry more than double the percentage of national freight that is carried by rail in Britain.[221]

Recent policy measures in Britain – traffic management schemes, road construction schemes, planning approval for out-of-town shopping complexes, new underground lines – include elements from all three approaches, and it is not at present clear which way the emphasis of policy will move in the short term. In the longer term, however, it seems likely that the first approach will prove unsatisfactory, the second one not practicable in British conditions, and the third approach increasingly adopted – although the considerable investment needed and the long lead times involved imply that, whatever is done, congestion is likely to get worse before it gets better.

Thus the solution of the problems of congestion is likely to require reduced reliance on the private car, at least in city centres. There are also a number of other environmental considerations which seem likely to check the increase in car use over the medium and long term.

Safety

The number of deaths per year from road accidents fell by 32 per cent between 1967 and 1987, despite the near doubling of vehicle mileage over the same period.[221] The reduction has been attributed mainly to the introduction of the annual MoT test, drink-driving tests and compulsory seat-belts. Road deaths, both per thousand population and per thousand vehicle miles, are now the lowest in Western Europe by far.[234]

Even so, a total of more than 5,000 people are killed on the roads each year, and a further 60,000 are seriously injured. It has been calculated that about 220,000 people alive today will die as a result of a road accident.[235] More than one person in every thousand will be killed by 2010 and one in every hundred seriously injured.

Death rates per passenger mile in cars are still far higher than in trains and buses, and rates for cyclists are ten times as high as for cars, and for motor cyclists 23 times as high.[221]

Hence it seems likely that there will be continuing emphasis on improving road safety. Among the more probable measures are:

- lower alcohol driving limits and random enforcement checks;

- lower speed limits and electronic enforcement systems;

- improved provision for cyclists (including children, most of whom have bicycles but few of whom are free to use them on the roads);

- better arrangements for pedestrian safety (including elderly people, many of whom are infirm and do not have access to cars).

Costs

The demand for motoring, as for other things, is affected by the level of the costs incurred and how these compare with the costs of other means of travel and other kinds of expenditure. It seems likely that in the course of the next two decades the cost of private motoring will be affected by a number of factors, the net effect of which is likely to make them higher, particularly in relation to other modes of transport.

Car prices

The cost of new cars is likely to be *increased* by £300-£500 by the requirement to fit catalytic converters from 1992, and possibly later by the need to fit equipment for greater safety or more efficient traffic control. Car prices in Britain will be *reduced* if the special car tax is abolished as part of a process of tax harmonisation for the Single European Market. On the other hand they might ultimately be *increased* again if Dutch and German suggestions are adopted for higher car taxes on environmental grounds.

Taxes on car ownership and fuel

If the annual road fund licence is abolished it will *reduce* the cost of owning a car, but if it is shifted to the tax on petrol it will *increase* the cost of running a car – no change overall, but a shift in favour of those who do low mileages at low speeds in small cars against those who do the opposite. Petrol costs could go much *higher* still if taxes are introduced to reduce emissions of greenhouse gases.

Parking

Parking in central areas is likely to become *more expensive* if full economic rates are charged – for example, the market value of a parking space in central London is estimated to be £15-£25 a day.

Driving

Driving in central areas will become much more expensive if road pricing is introduced. For example, the charge proposed for driving in central Stockholm is about £75 a month.

Company cars

The special tax treatment of company cars in Britain is hardly likely to survive two decades of fiscal harmonisation in the Single European Market. The number of people with company cars has been rising steadily and company cars now account for over half of all new car registrations in Britain,[221] compared with less than 10 per cent in France and West Germany. The tax on company car users has greatly increased over the past few years, but company cars still offer considerable financial advantages to users – calculated to be the equivalent of extra pay of around £7,500 a year for a Cavalier 1600 and much more for the larger cars provided for senior executives.[236] The effect can be that of a subsidy on congestion: for example for an inner London journey from Notting Hill Gate to Battersea and back it makes the direct cost to the driver of a company car (paying only for petrol) about 60p, compared with £3.40 by tube and bus.[235] For the company car user, almost any inner city journey will be much cheaper by car than by public transport, as well as quicker and more comfortable. If the reduction of this specially favourable tax treatment, already begun, is continued until it is removed altogether, the effect will be to *increase greatly* the cost of driving for people with company cars.

The demand for private motoring is also likely to be affected by the relative cost and quality of alternative public transport, which in turn will depend on the level of public subsidy. At present in most countries in Western Europe government subsidies for railways are higher than in Britain[237] and subsidies on municipal transport in major cities are much higher. In consequence, fares in London are the most expensive in Europe, with an average 10 km journey costing at least twice as much as in any other capital city in Europe.

Growing environmental pressures in the course of the next two decades may push Britain towards the policies in use on the continent.

Air pollution

In an opinion survey in Britain for the Department of Environment more than 70 per cent of respondents expressed concern about traffic exhaust fumes, and similar anxieties have been felt in most other advanced industrial countries. This has led to international agreements for restricting vehicle exhaust emissions (see Chapter 5).

In Britain vehicle emissions of lead (which can cause brain damage) have already been much reduced as a result of legislation to cut by two-thirds the maximum lead content of petrol and of voluntary switching, encouraged by a tax differential, to lead-free petrol.

Future changes will concentrate on other exhaust emissions: carbon monoxide (which is toxic in confined spaces), hydrocarbons (which can be carcinogenic), and nitrogen oxide and sulphur dioxide (which cause smog and ozone depletion, irritate eyes and respiratory organs, corrode stonework and kill trees and plants through defoliation – 'acid rain'). In Britain road transport is estimated to account for 85 per cent of total carbon monoxide emissions, 28 per cent of hydrocarbons and 45 per cent of nitrogen oxide.[18]

Restrictions on emissions, first introduced in the United States in 1963, have since followed in many other countries. In 1989 the European Commission agreed regulations which will impose the full US standards for new cars sold in Europe after July 1992.[238] These standards can in practice be met only by fitting cars with catalytic converters to break down the exhaust gases into less harmful products.

The new standards are more stringent than those originally proposed and there is some possibility that eventually the standards will be made tougher still. Los Angeles, which already has the tightest emissions standards in the United States, intends, as interim measures, to enforce compulsory car sharing by commuters and a legal limit on the number of cars each family can own; followed, by 2010, by a complete ban on all petrol driven cars, permitting only the use of methanol powered or electric vehicles.[239]

> ## *Policies to cut air pollution*
>
> - Fitting costly flue gas scrubbers to large power stations
>
> - Burning imported, low-sulphur coal
>
> - Promoting energy conservation and efficiency
>
> - Constructing new gas-fired power stations
>
> - Using catalytic converters, lead-free petrol and new engine designs in vehicles

While the catalytic converters are expected to be effective in cutting nitrogen oxide and sulphur dioxide emissions by 70 per cent, they do have disadvantages. They add to costs, reduce performance and increase petrol consumption. They also bring an increase in emissions of carbon dioxide, the principal gas involved in global warming, and release nitrous oxide, which is also a greenhouse gas.[240]

Greenhouse gases

There is now confirmation from a panel of the world's leading scientists in this field[30] that emissions of carbon dioxide and other greenhouse gases are causing global warming which will eventually have very serious environmental consequences worldwide (see Chapter 5). Consequently, it is likely that there will fairly soon be international agreement on targets for limiting emission levels of carbon dioxide and other greenhouse gases.

Since road vehicles are estimated to account for 16 per cent of total carbon dioxide emissions in Britain,[18] any policies for reducing them are likely to include measures to reduce emissions from cars by encouraging people to use them less (and also to make more use of public transport). These measures may take the form of restriction or prohibition of particular kinds of use. More probably, the main emphasis will be on higher petrol taxes (or possibly the issue of tradable permits), leaving market forces to determine who makes which adjustments in the form of lower mileages, slower speeds, smaller vehicles or use of more energy-efficient engines.

It is likely that early targets will be lenient and tax increases moderate – and the impact on car-use patterns correspondingly marginal. However, in later years, as the evidence of the consequences of global warming becomes clearer, emissions targets are likely to be tightened and tax rates increased to meet them. Because the demand for petrol, at least in the short term, is extremely inelastic, the tax increases might have to be very high indeed in order to bring about the required reduction in emissions.

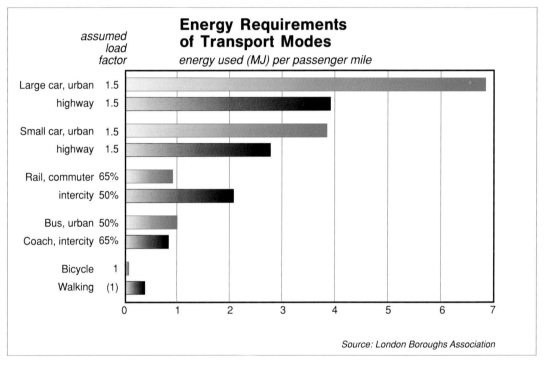

Energy Requirements of Transport Modes
energy used (MJ) per passenger mile

	assumed load factor
Large car, urban	1.5
highway	1.5
Small car, urban	1.5
highway	1.5
Rail, commuter	65%
intercity	50%
Bus, urban	50%
Coach, intercity	65%
Bicycle	1
Walking	(1)

Source: London Boroughs Association

Cars are convenient, but they use more energy than other modes of transport. For a town journey even a small car uses four times as much energy per passenger mile as a bus or train. Cycling and walking use no fossil fuel energy at all.

Future car use

Future levels of car use are inevitably a matter of considerable uncertainty. Past trends have been strongly upwards, but future developments seem likely to be mainly of kinds which will tend to reduce use. Among the latter possibilities are more expensive parking, road pricing in congested areas, dearer petrol, less favourable tax treatment, lower speed limits, tougher alcohol limits, better provision for cyclists and pedestrians and improved standards and lower charges for public transport services. The extent to which changes actually happen and affect car use will depend largely on decisions in transport policy, and also in urban planning and social policy.

In the longer term, much the most important new factor is likely to be global warming. It is looking increasingly probable that it will lead to major policy changes in many areas, almost all of them more likely to reduce car use than to increase it, with some of them specifically aimed at reducing greenhouse gas emissions by cars. It is likely that emissions will be reduced substantially by further improvements in engine efficiency in the coming years and, eventually, engines will be developed which run on alternative, non-fossil, fuels. Meanwhile, however, the main contribution, will have to come from cuts in car mileage.

The most probable outcome, therefore, is that by 2010 car use in city centres and for long-distance commuting will be much reduced; but use for driving to stations, local shopping and some social and recreational activities will remain attractive, if much more expensive than hitherto. Thus cars will probably continue to be much loved by their owners, but the steady rise in numbers and mileage is unlikely to continue for much longer.

Energy

Adequate supplies of energy are essential in any advanced society, but they need to be provided in ways which do not inflict unacceptable damage on the environment.

Forecast demand

Energy consumption in Britain grew quickly in the early postwar period, more slowly in the late 1960s and early 1970s. The slow growth since then has been checked by falls in consumption after each of the oil price shocks in the 1970s, with the result that current consumption is still below the peak level reached in 1973.[241] These changes were not widely foreseen and many forecasts of future demand proved to be far too high.

In its proof of evidence for the Sizewell 'B' public enquiry the Department of Energy made forecasts of total UK energy consumption in 2010 and cautiously gave a wide spread of figures, 308-515 million tonnes of coal equivalent – anything from a decrease of 10 per cent to an increase of 50 per cent on the estimated 1990 level and a mid-range increase of about 20 per cent.

A more recent forecast,[242] understood to have been prepared for the International Panel on Climate Change, is for 438 million tonnes in 2005 and 517 million tonnes in 2020, suggesting an increase of about 35-40 per cent between 1990 and 2010. This latter forecast (which does not take into account possible changes due to environmental considerations) looks high in relation to the increase of less than 5 per cent between 1970 and 1990.

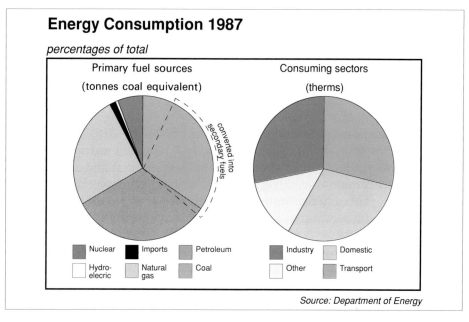

Energy Consumption 1987

percentages of total

Primary fuel sources
(tonnes coal equivalent)

converted into secondary fuels

Consuming sectors
(therms)

Nuclear	Imports	Petroleum	Industry	Domestic
Hydro-elecric	Natural gas	Coal	Other	Transport

Source: Department of Energy

About one third of primary energy in Britain is from coal (mostly used for conversion into electricity), another third from petroleum (mostly for transport), and a quarter from natural gas (much of it for heating and cooking).   Only 6 per cent is nuclear.

Available supply

However, even an increase as large as this would seem unlikely to pose major problems in terms of availability of supplies. Reserves of North Sea oil and gas are continually being revised upwards as new discoveries are made and recovery techniques improve, and world reserves of petroleum are considerable, although located in part in countries with unstable governments. UK coal reserves are sufficient for more than a century of consumption at current rates and world reserves of coal are much higher still, some of them located in places where sources are abundant and cheap.

Thus, while world reserves are being depleted and must obviously run out eventually, there is no risk of this happening for a long time to come; and while prices may well go up and at times of crisis supplies may be reduced, there is little reason to doubt that supplies of oil, gas and coal will be available to meet, if necessary, the increased levels of consumption forecast for 2010; and these fuels account for 90 per cent of Britain's primary energy consumption now and are expected still to be doing so in the government's forecasts for 2010.

If there is going to be a problem in Britain with energy by 2010, it will be not because of depletion of resources but because of other environmental problems, of which the two most important are air pollution and global warming from greenhouse gases.

Air pollution

The Clean Air Acts of 1956 and 1968, by reducing emissions of smoke, were successful in reducing winter fog and doubling the average hours of January sunshine.

The current problem, however, is emissions not of smoke but of gases which cause acid rain, which damages trees, crops and buildings. The scale of the damage has become serious in Britain, and also in other European countries, and because the acid rain is blown by winds across national frontiers, the problem has become the subject of international negotiations which have led to agreements on targets for reductions in the emissions of nitrogen oxide and sulphur dioxide, the two gases which cause the main damage (see Chapter 5).

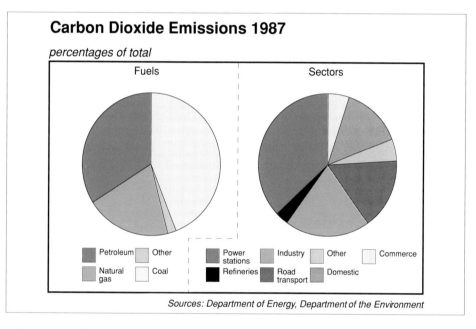

Carbon Dioxide Emissions 1987

percentages of total

Sources: Department of Energy, Department of the Environment

44 per cent of carbon dioxide emissions in Britain are from coal and 34 per cent from petroleum. The sectors mainly responsible are power stations (37 per cent of the total), industry (20 per cent), road transport (16 per cent) and domestic (14 per cent).

The emissions of the gases are mainly from industrial processes, vehicles and power stations. Industrial emissions have been reduced already. Emissions from cars will be much reduced by the fitting of catalytic converters to the exhausts of new cars after 1992. The emissions from power stations present more difficult problems since the equipment to clean flue gases is extremely expensive, especially when retrofitted to existing stations. Britain was planning to invest £2bn in a retrofitting programme for some of its largest power stations[18] and in Germany the government is spending £6bn on a retrofitting programme.

More recently, however, it appears to have been decided to reduce the scale of the retrofitting programme and to seek to achieve the same objectives more cheaply by making greater use of imported low-sulphur coal and by introducing new power stations fuelled by natural gas, the combustion of which emits less of the gases which form acid rain – and also less of the carbon dioxide which causes global warming. Attention is also being given to the possibility of new techniques which involve cleaner burning of coal.[243]

Thus it seems that there are a number of ways in which the acid rain problem will be dealt with, but all are expensive and likely to involve higher prices for energy users.

Greenhouse gases

A much greater problem is that posed by the gases whose emission is implicated in global warming. An intergovernmental panel of the world's leading scientists has recently reported that the phenomenon is indeed being experienced and that, in the absence of adequate counter-measures, the long-term effects will be grave[30] (see Chapter 5). In the face of these risks it now seems likely that in a few years' time international agreement will be reached on targets for cuts in emissions of the greenhouse gases, in particular of carbon dioxide which is produced by the combustion of fossil fuels. Accordingly, any assessment of Britain in 2010 needs to take account of the growing probability that provision will have to be made for a considerable reduction in carbon dioxide emissions.

Fossil fuel power stations

Concern over greenhouse gases is likely to encourage construction of combined cycle gas power stations which emit much less carbon dioxide than conventional coal fired ones, and which are relatively quick and cheap to construct and flexible in operation. There may also be new interest in combined heat and power units in urban locations which can help reduce emissions by generating power partly by burning waste materials. However, the main attention is likely to be focused on nuclear power, renewables and enery efficiency.

Nuclear power

Nuclear power stations produce no greenhouse (or acid rain) gases at all and on the face of it the most obvious way to reduce emissions will be to increase the proportion of power generated by nuclear stations – at present about 17 per cent in Britain compared with 33 per cent in West Germany, 46 per cent in Sweden and 70 per cent in France.[244]

However, nuclear energy involves difficulties of other kinds. There are formidable problems in the disposal of high level nuclear waste and in the decommissioning of power stations at the end of their lives, and there are deep public anxieties, accentuated by the incidents at Chernobyl and Three Mile Island, about the possibility of major accidents. France's chief inspector for nuclear safety has recently estimated there is at least a 1 in 20 chance of a serious nuclear accident in France in the course of the next 20 years.[245] Largely as a result of these concerns the nuclear power construction programmes have been halted in nearly all the countries in the western world and plans have been adopted for reducing dependence on nuclear power or phasing it out altogether in several of them.

In Britain there is the further drawback that nuclear power has in practice been far more expensive than electricity from conventional stations[246] and the differential would be likely to widen further if nuclear stations were used for more than the base load. In consequence, prospective private sector investors have expressed reluctance to invest in the existing nuclear stations which they tend to see as liabilities rather than as assets. It is largely because of these high cost levels that there are no firm plans at present to build any more nuclear power stations in Britain beyond the ones that are already under construction.

Finally there is the consideration that at present nuclear power accounts for only about 8 per cent of primary energy world wide and about 7 per cent in Britain.[247] With the very high capital costs and long lead times involved in the construction of nuclear power stations, it is hard to see how they could make much more than a marginal additional contribution to the solution or containment of the global warming problem by 2010.

Renewables

Another possibility for reducing emissions of greenhouse gases from the burning of fossil fuels in power stations is to make more use of some of the renewable sources of energy.

Hydroelectric

There is some further scope in Britain but the best sites are already being exploited, capital costs are high, lead times are long and most of the potential additional schemes involve some unavoidable damage to the local environment.

Tidal

Britain has some of the best natural sites in the world, capable of generating substantial amounts of power. Some of them are likely to be developed when the need to phase out fossil fuel energy sources becomes more pressing but, as with hydroelectric power, capital costs are high, lead times are long and local ecological damage is probable.

Wind

Wind is one of the few new forms of power that is already of proven economic viability in suitable locations, with commercial wind farms already in operation in California and Denmark. There are suitable sites in Britain, but the need to avoid populated or scenic areas limits the potential scope, and power supplies would vary with weather conditions.

Wave power

This is a field in which Britain had a world lead until research on it was stopped several years ago on the grounds that costs would be too high – although it has since transpired that wave power is in fact less expensive than nuclear energy (248). Work has continued in Norway and Japan and Britain's coastal waters offer potential for becoming a major source of power eventually. However, considerable further research and development will be needed to test systems and bring down costs.

Geothermal

There are a few possible sites, but at present they do not seem likely to offer large-scale power prospects (although there is the possibility of importing larger amounts of geothermal power by undersea electric cable from Iceland).

Solar

In Britain's climate the main scope is probably for small-scale, mostly domestic, applications.

Biomass (wood, organic wastes)

Here too there is useful scope, but probably only on a small scale over the period to 2010.

A common factor with most of the renewables, as with other new technologies at an early stage of development, is that unit cost levels are likely to come down substantially with further research and development; however, the resources committed to them so far have been trivial compared with the scale of investment in nuclear power.

Estimates of costs depend critically on the precise accounting conventions used, but it is probable that several forms of renewable energy are already cheaper than nuclear; and their economics relative to fossil fuels will be transformed when, in response to the threat of global warming, the latter are made subject to special taxes. The contribution they are making to UK energy needs by 2010 will depend largely on the scale of the investment made in them in the intervening years.

Energy conservation and economy

The key consideration with both nuclear power and renewables is that, whatever their other merits, they cannot be expected by 2010 to make more than a marginal contribution to the solution of the global warming problem. At present levels of consumption they account, together, for only about 10 per cent of primary energy in Britain and about 22 per cent of electric power.[241] Even if they were used to generate nearly *all* the electric power in Britain (which is all they *can* be used for) it would reduce the generation of greenhouse gases in Britain by only about one quarter. The remaining three-quarters of present greenhouse gas emissions are accounted for mainly by the use of petroleum in vehicles and aircraft and industrial processes; of gas in space heating and industrial processes; and of coal in industrial heating processes. It is in these areas that the greater part of any major reductions in emissions will have to be found.

Many savings in energy use have been made already following the jump in energy costs in the 1970s, and greater savings still have been made in Japan and the Nordic countries. There is no doubt that in Britain considerable scope remains in many areas for reducing energy needs or for using it more efficiently, for example in industrial machinery and heat-using processes; in insulation of domestic, commercial and industrial buildings; in regulation and control of space heating, cooling and ventilation systems; in use of less energy-intensive materials and processes; in vehicle design and engines, such as the economical lean-burn engines currently under development; in use of trains and buses instead of cars, and of telecommunications links instead of physical transport of documents and people.

Substantial savings could be made without need for the use of new, untried technologies. For example, it has been estimated that use of the best available technology currently marketed in commercial lighting, industrial motors and domestic refrigerators and freezers would cut total electricity consumption by 11 per cent.[249] If the UK building stock was uprated to the proposed new UK building regulations insulation standard it would cut total UK carbon dioxide emissions by 5 per cent; and if raised to the standard of the Danish building regulations it would cut them by 7 per cent.[249]

Many of the ways in which there is scope for using energy more economically involve investments which can show a good rate of return and are worth doing in any case; and many of the investments in energy *saving* offer a better payback than the alternative of investments in additional power *generation*.

The 1989 report of the House of Commons Energy Committee on the Energy Implications of the Greenhouse Effect found:[251]

> The most striking feature of our Enquiry has been the extent to which improvements in energy efficiency – across all sectors of the economy – are almost universally seen as the most obvious and most effective response to the problem of

global warming. Energy efficiency investments offer multiple attractions: many are inherently economically attractive at present energy prices, whilst others are relatively low cost; they are environmentally benign, and they are capable of speedy introduction, thereby ensuring an early reduction in carbon dioxide emissions... The EC commission are similarly persuaded...

Similarly, in the United States, the Environmental Protection Agency reported:[250]

In contrast to the common notion that limiting global warming would require great sacrifices we find that many of the policy options that are available for reducing greenhouse gas emissions appear already to be attractive in many respects.

Thus, if the global situation turns out to require a major reduction in greenhouse gases, the main contribution will have to come from improved energy conservation and efficiency in use. This will involve changes in many areas and will need education, research and incentives – in particular very large increases in the effective price of energy. However, experience after the oil shocks of the 1970s suggests that even quite large savings can probably be accommodated without undue damage to the economy or intolerable disturbance to individual life-styles.

Implications

There are a number of new factors which are likely to result in changes in the environment in the coming two decades taking a course somewhat different from developments in the past two. Among the more important are:

- increasing public concern, shown in opinion polls and voting in the European elections, to improve the quality of the environment and reduce threats to it, generating much greater pressure than before for active intervention;

- the Single European Market, the Channel Tunnel and the developing new European rail network reinforcing the pull to the South East and intensifying the re-emerging problems of regional imbalance;

- the proposals for giant new 'shopping cities' which, if they go ahead, will radically change shopping and traffic patterns and undermine existing city centres;

- new agricultural policies which will tend to reverse past changes in rural land use and generate pressures for new kinds of development;

- EC directives and wider international agreements imposing standards/quotas/prohibitions aimed at protecting or improving the common environment; and, probably much the most important,

- The grave long-term threat posed by global warming and the need for an effective response.

The various elements in the environment are to a large extent interdependent and the interactions between them are numerous and complex. For example, regional changes in employment can bring movements of population; changes in housing needs and prices; changes in transport and infrastructure requirements; congestion; labour shortages; wage inflation and checks to national economic growth. Changes in agricultural practices can increase productivity; reduce employment; cause migration from country areas to towns; contaminate drinking water; and damage seaside tourism and coastal fisheries. The adoption of measures to reduce carbon dioxide emissions can affect choices on methods of power generation; industrial production processes; heating, ventilation, insulation and lighting of buildings; design of towns and city centres; modes of transport; and much else besides.

The extent of the interactions means that environmental problems are not a number of discrete and separate issues but different aspects of a single problem of the need for *sustainable* exploitation of resources throughout the economy.

In many areas the most important factors affecting the course of developments are the policy measures of the government itself, for example:

- *transport*
  policies on road building, traffic management, bus and cycle lanes, provision for pedestrians, road pricing, parking restrictions, company cars, petrol tax, public transport, shopping centre developments, office developments, regional balance;

- *housing*
  policies on planning appeals, security of tenure, rights of purchase, interest rates, mortgage tax relief, rent support, council building, housing associations;

- *country areas*
  policies on agricultural support, use of chemicals,

support for rural bus services and amenities, planning appeals;

- *pollution*
  policies on research, monitoring, education, regulation, taxation, prohibition, inspection, prosecution, investment in cleaner, safer, more environmentally friendly processes and equipment; and

- *global warming*
  policy measures affecting a wide range of areas will be essential if a major response is required.

Since the issues are interdependent, the policies for addressing them need to take account of this. If policies for each area are conceived in isolation they are likely to be of reduced effectiveness, or even in conflict with each other. A single issue with many dimensions requires an integrated strategy applied consistently across the whole range of policy areas involved.

Some of the possible measures are cheap and easy to implement; but some involve major investment in, for example, new high speed, Berne gauge rail links, underground lines and light railways; electronic traffic control and charging systems; upgrading of shopping areas; refurbishment of ageing housing stock; renewal of water mains; installation of sewage treatment plant; extension of toxic waste treatment facilities; provision of safe storage for nuclear waste; retrofitting of flue gas cleaning equipment in power stations; insulation of buildings; development of commercially viable renewable energy sources; development of more energy-efficient industrial processes; development of more energy-efficient vehicle engines and, eventually, of alternative power sources for vehicles.

Some of these investments are likely to be very expensive, requiring a significant part of the proceeds of future economic growth to be 'spent' on them. This makes it important to get the priorities right between them: hence the need for a single, integrated approach to policy on the built and natural environment.

It also raises other questions. Who is to undertake and manage the investments? What will they cost? And who is to pay for them? Some, such as improving insulation, are likely quickly to pay for themselves and to be worth doing anyway. Others, such as road-pricing equipment, can easily be made self-financing. But with others, such as expensive pollution-reduction equipment, there will be the questions: is it feasible to make the polluter pay? Is it fair to make the consumer pay? Or should it be a charge on the community as a whole? And where the costs are large the world of clear-cut absolutes will inevitably give way to the world of shifting trade-offs. The question will be not how can we get total success in particular areas regardless of cost, but how much more are we prepared to pay to get a given improvement in environmental quality.

A further important consideration is that for many of the possible investments (for example, new underground railways, development of renewable energy sources) the lead times are long. Early decisions will be needed if the benefits are to be felt by 2010.

If the threat of global warming makes it imperative, first, to check the increase in emissions of greenhouse gases, and later to reduce them, this will certainly prove to be much the most important and difficult environmental problem in the next two decades, with consequences felt in a great many different aspects of personal, commercial and industrial life.

The policy measures for reducing the emissions are likely to include initially a range of information services, incentives, penalties and regulatory arrangements. Since in Britain, as in other democracies, governments normally seek to avoid painful measures if they are able to, at first they are likely to be at rates which do not hurt much – in many cases encouraging people to do things which it would have made sense to do anyway.

However, if the short- and medium-term measures prove to be insufficient and more drastic ones are needed, a number of daunting questions are likely to arise on how best to manage the necessary changes. Take, for example, the key area of suppliers of fossil fuel energy: in the past their efforts have been concentrated on improving their competitive efficiency so as to increase their sales and market share. But in a greenhouse world the paramount need will be to *reduce* consumption. Will the marketing managers be instructed to seek *falling* sales with a view to *reducing* their market share? Should they offer *lower* tariffs to *small* users, and special incentives to encourage customers to buy *less*? What form can competition usefully take?

The logic of global warming would seem to imply that many approaches that have worked well in the familiar world may need to be stood on their heads in the greenhouse world where conservation, not expansion, is the yardstick of success. There will be need for new, hard thinking in the 1990s if the necessary changes are to be managed efficiently in the next century.

BRITAIN in 2010

Science
and Technology

5. **S**cience & Technology

During the second half of this century scientific knowledge has been expanding at a very rapid rate, and there have been equally dramatic advances in the technologies for putting it to practical use. The developments of the past two decades have made a major impact; will those of the next two make a greater one? In assessing this it is important to distinguish between the *potential* of the various developments in prospect, and the extent to which the potential is in practice likely to be *realised*. Probable and possible developments in a number of important fields are outlined in the section below; and the extent to which they are likely to result in widespread applications is considered in subsequent sections.

Developments in information technologies

Information technology (IT) is a cluster of technologies encompassing the storage, processing and transmission of data. It includes microelectronics, computer hardware and software, and telecommunications.

Major technical breakthroughs giving extensive scope for useful applications have brought rapid expansion in the past two decades and are likely to bring further rapid expansion in the next two. By 2010 the IT and electronics industry is likely to be the largest in the manufacturing sector and information handling is likely to be the largest area of economic activity.[251,252]

Microelectronics

The development of the transistor to replace the thermionic valve brought great gains in size, reliability and cost (and hence in applications) in the 1950s; and the development of microelectronics technology based on forming integrated circuits on wafers of silicon has brought even greater gains in the late 1970s and 1980s.

Advances in microchip technology have doubled the power of chips every two years. For example, in 1979, Intel's 8088, the chip which powered many of the early microcomputers, had 29,000 transistors; its 1989 successor, the i486, has 1.2 million; and by the year 2000 Intel expects processor chips to carry more than 50 million transistors. Similarly with memory chips, the capacity of Toshiba's chips has increased from 0.25 megabits (million bits of information) in 1985 to 4 megabits in 1989, with 16 megabit chips planned to be in production in 1992.[253]

A number of important developments offer potential for further rapid development in chip performance.

- X-ray and electron beam technologies offer the possibility of reducing the scale of components below 0.5 microns (considered to be the practical limit with the optical lithography used at present) to perhaps as little as 0.1 microns – albeit at high cost.

- Gallium arsenide will be used to provide much more power than is possible with silicon, but high costs and technical difficulties mean that these chips are likely to be used only for the largest and most powerful computers and in special applications.[254]

- The effectiveness of silicon chips is increased by use of RISC (Reduced Instruction Set Computer) chips which are designed to make more economical use of a chip's capacity, as opposed to increasing its power.[255]

- The practical effectiveness of chips is also increased by use of ASIC (Application Specific Integrated Circuit) chips which can be tailor-made, without undue cost, to the specific needs of a particular application.[256,257]

- Transputer chips, which contain their own processors and memories, increase the speed of large computers by making it easier to undertake lengthy computing operations in parallel.[258,259,260]

- Techniques to enable wafers containing more than 200 separate microchips to function as a single memory chip are likely soon to make 200 megabit memories possible.[261,262]

- Self-testing chips are being developed which will remove the need for expensive testing of complex chips on the assembly line.[263]

 • Work is in progress on much faster chips using opto-electronic (light operated) switches.[264]

 • Chips which are much faster still (as much as a hundred times as fast as silicon ones) may eventually become possible using superconducting materials.[265,266]

 • Still more radically, research is proceeding on 'molecular electronics' which aims to produce ultra-small circuits ('biochips') based on organic materials.[267]

While the last three of these technologies are unlikely to produce commercial applications before 2010, there is no doubt that *incremental* developments in other areas will continue to be rapid and important.

Computer hardware

The spectacular improvements in chip performance have made possible corresponding improvements in computer performance. Today's microcomputers provide the power of yesterday's mainframes, with greater reliability, in much smaller space and at a tiny fraction of the cost – and are accordingly sold in much greater quantities. At the same time the speed of the most powerful machines has steadily increased. For example, a particularly complex problem, analysing three dimensional supersonic airflows past a wing, which would have taken many years to solve with the most powerful computers available in the late 1940s, needed only two days with the most powerful machine in 1969, 4 hours in 1976, 1 hour in 1985 and an estimated 20 minutes with the latest machine currently under development.[268]

There is no doubt that further developments in chips and in computer design will bring continued improvements in performance, and there will also be further improvements in data storage – for example, a recently launched 'digital paper' storage medium is claimed to be much cheaper than magnetic disks and also much more compact, with a single 2400 ft reel holding as much information as 1000 compact disks.[269] Storage of data on optical compact disks and in memory chips is likely to gain significantly in importance in the medium and long term. Improvements in optical disk storage and in flat display screen technology should lead to the emergence of 'electronic books' as a powerful medium by the late 1990s – for instance, for reference books and catalogues.

Computers will therefore continue to get more powerful, with ever greater compactness and portability for the power available in personal computers. Some of them will combine several functions in one machine (for example, fax, phone, sound, and video as well as computer applications). They will also continue to get cheaper in relation to what they can do. Hence they will go on being sold in ever increasing numbers for an ever wider range of uses.

At the same time the speed of the largest computers is likely to be further increased by the use of new designs of chips and parallel processing and, just possibly, towards 2010, with computers using non-linear optical systems, or 'neural' systems modelled on the way the human brain works.[256,270,271,272] These very powerful (and very expensive) machines will have applications in areas demanding very high capacity, such as aircraft design, scientific modelling and visualisation of data, artificial intelligence, image processing and weather forecasting; and also, of special importance for a world threatened with global warming, for modelling atmospheric and ocean circulation processes and for analysing climate change.

Software

Computer software has developed much more slowly than hardware, largely because writing programs requires large inputs of specialist skills and tends to be slow and expensive. These considerations are likely to remain a major constraint on the speed of diffusion of IT into new areas of application in organisations and households, although increasing efforts are being made to circumvent the problem by creating new software 'tools' to raise productivity in developing systems.

Progress is likely in some special applications, such as the development of expert systems, to make specialist knowledge more widely accessible in areas such as medicine, the law and product and process fault diagnosis, maintenance and repair.

The main emphasis of future development is likely to be on the improvement of the software 'interface' with users, with the aim of making systems easier for people to use without extensive training; for example by developing new methods of receiving instructions and displaying information; and perhaps by making more use in software systems of 'fuzzy logic' which works more like the human mind.[273,274]

Particular efforts will continue to go into research on voice recognition with a view to developing machines which can respond to oral instructions (a voice-activated word processor with a 30,000 word vocabulary has recently been announced);[275,276] into machine translation to enable documents to be translated automatically and conversations conducted between people speaking different languages; and into sensors and vision systems to enable robotic devices to recognise patterns and operate in a more human way.

All these latter developments involve very difficult technical problems; for many years they have been heralded as 'coming shortly'; but so far they have not arrived; and it seems they are unlikely to do so, except in primitive forms with limited applications, in the course of the next two decades. The computer which 'thinks' like a human being, also long predicted as imminent, will certainly not be around until long after 2010, if ever; and a machine which has feelings, personality and a will of its own, like the computer HAL in the film *2001*, is likely to remain in the realm of science fiction.

Telecommunications

Links between computers, whether adjacent or at long distance, have in the past been limited by lack of compatibility between machines of different makes, but progress has been made on refining the International Standards Organisation's proposals for Open Systems Interconnection (OSI). They will take a long time to implement but, well before 2010, 'Open Systems' technical standards should make it possible to link up computers and other equipment of all the leading makes and exchange data between them.

At present the main channels of long-distance communication are radio and television transmissions for general information and entertainment and the public telephone networks for personal and business communications. The public telephone network is in the course of being converted to digital operation which, by the end of the century, will provide an Integrated Services Digital Network (ISDN) which will offer improved facilities for transmission of computer data, fax, text and pictures as well as for telephone calls.

Over the period to 2010 existing telecommunications systems will be supplemented by:

- improved data compression techniques to enable the existing copper cable (narrowband) telephone networks to have increased capacity in order, for example, to be able to carry videophone services, enhanced data transmission services and better definition television pictures;

- fibre optic cable (broadband) to give virtually unlimited capacity to the ISDN network, enabling it to carry many television channels, high-quality pictures and sound, colour fax, and interactive links for video-conferencing, tele-shopping or tele-working;

- direct broadcasting by satellite (DBS) to provide additional television channels and, potentially, also the other services possible with broadband cable;

- microwave video distribution systems (MVDS) for additional television channels over short distances;

- cellular radio to allow mobile access to the public telephone network, for example from private vehicles;

zone phones to allow small cordless phones to be carried by people for use anywhere within close reach of a base station.

In all of these technologies research and development is making rapid progress; in most areas new products and systems are already in use on a limited scale. They vary in the services they can provide and in their costs to suppliers and users. Some can be used in combination (for example, fibre optic cable for trunk transmission with MVDS for local distribution to individual subscribers); and different users may be served by different systems. At present the choice between links is being left largely to market forces, with a key role played by the government in setting the terms of competition. It is not at all clear which of the competing systems will have most success, but it does seem probable that by 2010 the majority of homes and businesses will have telecommunications links of one sort or another capable of carrying a much wider range of services than at present.[277]

Developments in other technologies

While the information technologies will continue to be the most widely pervasive ones in industry and in households, there will be important developments in other new technologies, with the most significant changes and take-up of applications likely to occur from the late 1990s.

Biotechnology

Biotechnology is a cluster of technologies based on developments in microbiology, genetics, biochemistry and fermentation technology. It encompasses recombinant DNA technology (genetic engineering), artificial cell fusion, enzyme technology and processing technologies. A number of important developments are likely in the course of the coming two decades. Given the technical complexity of many parts of this field, the public anxieties it arouses, and the regulatory and legal constraints on the introduction of new products, it is likely that biotechnological innovations will not have significant economic impacts until after 2000.

- Medical developments include new protein therapies (for example interferons), new vaccines and diagnostic test kits (for example for AIDS) and new methods of drug delivery; and in the longer term there is the possibility of widespread use of gene therapy (involving alterations to genes in non-reproductive cells) for treating genetically-related diseases such as cancers.

* In agriculture biotechnology is already being used for pest control and in animal health care and growth hormones; and in the longer term there is the possibility of genetic engineering of plants and animals to increase yields, accelerate growth and improve resistance to disease. There is also the potential for developing new techniques which will reduce farmers' reliance on large inputs of chemical fertilisers.

* In chemical production enzymes may be widely used as catalysts in place of compounds containing heavy metal pollutants such as tin and mercury.

* Microbial methods have been developed for oil and copper extraction and there is scope for their use in breaking down household and industrial wastes, for obtaining gas from landfill sites and for cleaning oil spills.

* Genetic profiling is already in use for criminal identification and there are many potential applications for knowledge gained from work on the sequencing of the human genome (the genetic 'map') which should be complete by around 2010.

* There are also many current and potential applications in the food and drink processing industry, for example, in development of new preservatives and artificial flavours.

New materials

Continuing work on the development of new materials promises to lead to applications of ceramics, plastics and alloys with important advantages over traditional materials.[112]

* New ceramics have properties of lightness, hardness, stiffness, compression strength, thermal stability, electrical resistance and corrosion resistance which make them potentially suitable for use in high performance engines, heavy-duty insulators and aerospace applications.[278]

* New engineering plastics and polymers, reinforced by carbon fibres, have combinations of properties which can be of value in vehicles, aerospace, sports equipment and various kinds of industrial applications.

♦ New alloys and special steels also offer important potential advantages in a wide range of industrial applications.

♦ New kinds of laminated wood, three times as strong as ordinary timber, may provide an alternative to steel and concrete as a building material.[279]

♦ New materials are being developed for use in liquid crystal displays and for opto-electronics applications.

♦ The Japanese are working on the development of 'functionally gradient' materials which change their composition (for example from metal to plastic) between one surface and the other. These could have important applications in the aerospace industry.[280]

♦ New forms of engineering involving manipulation of matter at the molecular and atomic level are being researched and may lead to the development of many new and improved materials over the longer term.

Superconductors

Superconducting substances allow the flow of electricity to take place without resistance. Until recently superconductivity could not be harnessed economically, except in a few special applications, because of the extremely high cost of cooling the substances involved to the very low temperatures required for the phenomenon to take place. Recently, the discovery of ceramics which display the phenomenon at much higher temperatures has started a race to find materials which superconduct at near room temperature or with relatively low-cost cooling systems. If this succeeds (which is unlikely for many years) there could be scope for very important applications in:

♦ high density electrical storage to reduce power plant capacity needs;

♦ power transmission with no energy loss;

♦ power generating plants half the size of existing ones;

♦ magnetic levitation for high speed trains (a 375 kph prototype is already working in Japan);[281]

◆ very fast semiconductors for computers – possibly the earliest practical use because for this application cooling costs are likely to be less of a problem.

Environmental science and pollution control

This broad area of science and technology is certain to gain steadily in importance in both basic research and in technical development. As governments and industries seek to counter threats posed by environmental degradation, so they will need to be able to base remedial and preventive policies on far better basic scientific understanding of ecosystems and their interactions with man-made substances.

Multidisciplinary fundamental research will remain an urgent priority for understanding the complexities of climate change and stresses on ecosystems caused by global warming and other environmental threats such as chemical pollution of rivers and seas. International research efforts should give fairly clear-cut answers about the scale of the greenhouse effect by 2000, with more detail about regional and local effects of likely climate changes. However, it is clear that many uncertainties will remain beyond the turn of the century, and that sustained research efforts will still be needed, along with close interaction between scientists, engineers and policymakers.

The key challenge in pollution control will be developing process technologies for manufacturing industry which are as clean and economical with energy and resources as possible. Minimising waste, recycling and high energy efficiency are all targets which pose major challenges to industrial countries but which also open up significant opportunities for companies able to meet them and to produce and market 'green' technologies. The potential world market for environmentally benign products and technologies has been estimated at £100-150 billion a year, and the demand will increase as environmental regulations are steadily tightened over the next two decades in industrialised countries in response to international agreements on emission control. British companies will be subject to more stringent domestic regulations and to European Community standards for environmental protection.

Major research and development efforts will be needed to find substitutes for CFC chemicals used in refrigeration and other industrial processes which damage the ozone layer and contribute considerably to global warming. Current substitutes under development may also prove to have harmful side-effects and it is likely that more radical changes in process and product design will be needed over the next twenty years in order to eliminate the threats posed by CFCs and related substances. Transfer of new technology and expertise to developing countries will be essential in order to prevent a major increase in CFC emissions as countries such as India and China step up their production of refrigerators and other kinds of equipment which use the chemicals.

New technologies for the disposal of toxic waste will be needed as conventional methods such as landfill, sea dumping and incineration become more restricted and subject to public protest in the future. Biotechnology could produce novel techniques for breaking down wastes – certain microbial methods are already used for breaking down chemical wastes.

Energy

There are a number of important new technologies for generation of energy which will figure in policy debate in the coming years as industrialised countries look for reductions in use of fossil fuels:

- fast breeder reactors (using plutonium instead of uranium);

- nuclear fusion reactors, offering the possibility of unlimited, relatively clean nuclear power (almost certainly not before the middle of the next century);

- new, more efficient fossil fuel power generation systems (for example, combined cycle gas and combined heat and power);

- new designs of nuclear fission reactor which are safer and more efficient than current ones;

- technologies for exploiting renewable sources of energy: waves, tides, wind, biomass, geothermal energy and solar radiation;

- technologies to conserve energy, for example through improving efficiency of insulation, lighting, electric motors and vehicle engines.

General issues

Three general points stand out about the enormous variety of developments which can be expected to 2010.

Convergence

We can expect continuing *convergence* between scientific disciplines and technologies: advances in understanding, the development of new products and processes, and the education and training of scientists and engineers will take place increasingly in multidisciplinary contexts. There will be significant cross-fertilisation between areas of technology: IT will play a major role in research and development, allowing modelling of complex phenomena, rapid processing of calculations, new ways of storing data and presenting information. Advances in computer power will be crucial in the progress of research in areas such as climate change and engineering design. Biotechnological techniques will overlap with new materials research to develop new composite materials based on organic substances. New materials will be of importance in the development of microelectronic devices and new energy technologies. The increasing overlap between disciplines and technologies will call for greater flexibility in education and training systems for scientists and engineers.

Rapidity

The pace of technological development and growth of scientific knowledge worldwide will continue to be extremely rapid, placing major demands on the ability of individuals and organisations to assimilate new ideas and skills. Again, there are considerable challenges here for education and training systems: how best can provision be made for updating of knowledge and skills, as the effective lifetime of bodies of knowledge in many fields is reduced to only a few years?

Constraints

There will, despite the pace of discovery and innovation, be important constraints on scientific and technical activities, which will to varying degrees restrict the rate at which new products and processes diffuse in the wider economy and society, and which will increase the complexity of some of the issues facing decision makers in science and technology. Some of the main factors relevant here are considered in the next section.

Factors in adoption

There are many new technologies under development which have the *potential* for applications of major importance; but will the potential in fact be realised? It is tempting to suppose that the inventions of today will be used in every home, office and factory in the country tomorrow, and the assumption that technical advances will very quickly come into general use is one of the most common sources of error in long-term forecasting.[65] For example, eleven years ago, one of the best-known of the many books on the microchip revolution[282] predicted, 'not as sci-fi but as sci-fact', that by now we would have videos instead of books, educational machines in place of teachers, expert systems for professional advice, voice recognition and reproduction on bathroom scales and other household equipment, word processors which make no mistakes, a marked reduction in commuter travel to offices and a 20 hour working week.

In practice, the diffusion of new technologies is likely to be affected both by a number of general considerations tending to slow it down and also by the specific circumstances of science and technology in Britain.

General constraints

In practice new technologies are rarely adopted rapidly and widely by organisations and individuals because there are a number of considerations which tend to slow things down at each of the stages they must pass through on the way from invention to general adoption.

Scale

Once the idea has been tested and found to work, it must be further developed to the point where it works satisfactorily not only in the laboratory with a small test tube sample or a scaled-down prototype, but also in conditions of commercial scale production. This can involve many years of expensive development work if the technical difficulties are great, as with voice and pattern recognition systems, optical computing, magnetic levitation trains or computer classification of finger prints. It can keep commercial use perpetually over the horizon if difficulties are particularly extreme, as with nuclear fusion, superconductivity in electric power, bio-computers or robots for doing housework.

Utility

The innovation must do something useful, for which there is a market, and do it better than available alternatives – including further developments of existing products and methods. This requirement has blighted the prospects of a succession of new technology developments which, despite their technical feasibility and, in some cases, brilliance, have so far failed to offer a better way of meeting a perceived need: electronic diaries (paper ones are smaller and more convenient to use); video newspapers (printed ones are easier to scan and have up to a hundred times as much information to a page); domestic prestel (other information sources are quicker and easier to use); electric cars (limited range and speed).

Cost

The innovation must also be cheaper than what it is to replace, or at any rate be affordable and give better value for money. A further drawback with electronic diaries, video newspapers and electric cars is that, in addition to their performance inadequacies, they all cost markedly more than their existing alternatives. Personal computers, word processors, electronic calculators and watches, colour television, video recorders, video games, all achieved success only when their prices were brought down to affordable and competitive levels. Price is a key factor in business and public acceptance of products, and the development of large markets for many new and emerging technologies will depend to a large extent on how quickly they become cost-competitive with existing ones. A major influence in many cases will be environmental regulation affecting the cost of conventional products and processes.

Infrastructure

Appropriate supporting infrastructure must also be available for diffusion of innovations. This is particularly crucial with new telecommunications technologies and IT-based services such as tele-shopping. If Britain were to construct a national broadband telecommunications network over the next decade, then many new services and products could find a large market by 2010. In the likely absence of a 'national grid' for new IT services, the development of broadband systems will probably be gradual and localised, with correspondingly limited growth in markets for particular products and tele-services which require broadband capacity. Similarly, new forms of environmentally friendlier vehicle will succeed only if the service station network caters for them by offering new fuels, or recharging facilities for electric cars.

Another important infrastructural factor is the existence of national and international technical standards; incompatibility between rival technologies in IT generally will tend to continue to restrict certain markets and inhibit diffusion of new products and services.

Other requirements

Some new developments must pass further hurdles such as:

- meeting official standards requirements (particularly with products where safety is a consideration);

- undergoing stringently controlled field trials before gaining official approval (as with new pharmaceuticals and with the release of genetically-modified organisms into the environment);

- overcoming unfavourable public attitudes or legal difficulties (as with nuclear power stations, hydroelectric projects, new drugs and crops derived from use of genetic engineering);

- overcoming institutional problems (opposition in parent companies, sponsoring organisations, regulatory bodies);

- securing patent protection (particularly complex in new areas of biotechnology: can genetically engineered organisms be patented?);

◆ securing finance for development work, tooling up for production, setting up arrangements for promotion and distribution.

Time to diffuse

Even when a promising new product or process has been put on the market, its general diffusion will take time while potential users:

◆ get to know of its existence;

◆ become persuaded of its merits (and advantages relative to existing methods or equipment and other new options);

◆ wait until existing equipment or systems wear out or become obsolete, or until additional equipment or systems are required for expansion or for meeting new needs;

◆ check on compatibility with existing/remaining equipment or systems;

◆ work out their requirements and raise finance for purchase;

◆ train or recruit staff to operate new equipment or systems;

◆ place orders, take delivery, install and get systems running effectively, and, most difficult, make organisational changes in order to exploit the new opportunities offered by a technology.

Going through these stages and meeting these requirements can often be a lengthy process, with many years elapsing between initial technical advance, commercial-scale production and general adoption. It is accordingly probable that the majority of the innovations that will prove to be important in 2010 are already known about *now*. Breakthroughs are possible in many fields over the next twenty years, but are unlikely to result in large-scale applications affecting industry or everyday life before 2010. So the period to 2010 is likely to be dominated by the refinement of existing new technologies, with leading companies making the most sophisticated and rapid use of innovations, while the mass of organisations gradually adopt proven products and processes as they catch up with current practice by the advanced users of IT and other technologies.

Attitudes and actions in Britain

Given that there are a number of general considerations that tend to result in there being a substantial lapse of time before innovations in science and technology become widely adopted, are there any special factors that make Britain better placed, or worse, than other countries for getting new technologies adopted quickly?

General public attitudes to science and technology in Britain appear on the whole to be favourable. In a recent opinion poll of a cross-section of the population, 44 per cent thought that, overall, science and technology do more good than harm, against 9 per cent who thought the opposite; 74 per cent agreed with the proposition that many of the world's problems can be solved by scientific research, against 16 per cent who disagreed; and 72 per cent agreed with the proposition that national prosperity depends on science and technology, against 17 per cent who disagreed.[283] This apparent enthusiasm for science and technology in Britain has been reflected in high take-up rates for personal computers, video recorders and other new technology-based consumer goods.

Moreover, the British have an international reputation not only as consumers of new technologies but also as inventors of them. A few years ago a study by MITI (Japan's Ministry of International Trade and Industry) found that no less than 55 per cent of all the commercially important innovations made in the world since the war originated in Britain. Britain has produced many Nobel prize winners in the natural sciences and there have been many areas of technical innovation pioneered in Britain: for example, radar, jet engines, penicillin, hovercraft, transistors, supersonic airliners, wave power, fibre optics, programmable logic arrays, transputers, self-diagnosing chips. Yet in most of these the technological lead and effective commercial exploitation subsequently passed to other countries, and the perception is widespread, alike in public opinion polls,[283] in surveys of industrialists[285,286,287,288] and in expert studies[289,290,291,292,293,294,295,296,297] that Britain is falling behind other advanced industrial countries in the commercial exploitation of technology.

This perception is borne out in trade figures. One study[297] showed that between 1980 and 1986 Britain increased its share of world trade in only two of the ten fastest growing categories; another study[289] showed that between 1976 and 1986 the sales of British electronics companies rose by only 2.6 per cent compared with an average of 4.4 per cent for European companies as a whole, 6.6 per cent for American ones, 7.6 per cent for Japanese ones and 21.6 per cent for Korean ones.

A factor in this may be the level of expenditure on research and development (R&D). Between 1967 and 1985, R&D, as a percentage of total output, increased in Japan, the United States and Western Europe as a whole, but not in Britain; and likewise with the part of R&D that was financed by industry.[298] In consequence, in 1985, R&D expenditure in Britain was lower than in Japan, the United States and West Germany, although not lower than in Western Europe as a whole.

Industrial R & D as a Proportion of Industrial Output

	Total			Industry-financed		
	1967	1975	1985	1967	1975	1985
Japan	0.92	1.28	2.11	0.90	1.26	2.07
United States	2.35	1.84	2.32	1.15	1.18	1.54
W. Europe*	1.27	1.35	1.81	0.92	1.00	1.37
Britain	*2.01*	*1.72*	*2.01*	*1.34*	*1.08*	*1.32*
France	1.36	1.36	1.78	0.75	0.87	1.24
Germany	1.31	1.65	2.42	1.07	1.30	1.99

* Eight EC states plus Sweden
Source: OECD[298]

The UK's civil industrial R&D effort is concentrated in high-tech sectors, with particular strengths in chemicals, pharmaceuticals and telecommunications. In these sectors international competitiveness is generally high, although there will be no secure competitive leads over the coming decades; but in medium- and low-technology sectors the level of R&D investment has been markedly lower than in other advanced countries.

In Britain about half of R&D is devoted to defence. If defence R&D is excluded, the absolute level of R&D spending in Britain in 1987 was less than that in West Germany, France and Italy[299] and far less than that in the United States and Japan. The percentage of R&D expenditure which goes to defence is far higher in Britain than in most other European countries, and this means that far smaller proportions are available for other areas such as universities, industry and energy R&D.[300]

Government Funding of R & D
percentages of total

	Britain	Germany	France	Italy	Netherlands
Defence	*48.4*	12.7	34.2	7.0	2.8
Universities	*16.5*	29.9	12.0	30.3	40.7
Industry	*9.0*	15.6	10.7	22.4	17.6
Energy	*3.7*	8.8	6.7	10.1	4.0
Other	*22.4*	33.0	36.4	36.5	34.9
TOTAL	*100.0*	100.0	100.0	100.0	100.0

Source: EC Statistical Office[300]

The ending of the Cold War will lead to a shift in resources away from defence, and this will pose considerable challenges to British firms in electronics and aerospace whose innovative efforts have been focused mainly on defence R&D. It is likely that there will be continuing pressure on governments throughout the 1990s to increase the level of R&D expenditure on environmental research, pollution control technology and renewable energy technologies, and to divert resources accordingly from defence R&D

Another important factor that could constrain the use made of science and technology in Britain is the shortage in many fields of people with key skills. A report to the Advisory Board for the Research Councils (ABRC)[301] says that funding for scientific research in Britain is well below that in West Germany and France, and warns that

> unless action is taken very soon, there will be a critical shortage of suitably qualified and trained researchers in the 1990s.

A report of the Select Committee on Science and Technology[302] also warns that

> a shortage of skilled staff [will be] a certainty unless remedial action is taken soon.

Both reports point out that low salaries in science and technology in Britain are causing qualified graduates to move to better paid areas, such as finance. There are also persistent problems in attracting students to study engineering, in bringing more women into scientific and engineering careers, and in finding and retaining teachers of science and mathematics. Demographic changes will exacerbate these problems in the 1990s. There has also been criticism of the levels of investment in other key parts of the science and technology base in Britain – for example, in new equipment for university laboratories.

Thus there are reasons for believing that, while public opinion in Britain is on the whole sympathetic to science and technology, and the level of inventiveness appears to be high, the record in commercial exploitation has been disappointing, and current circumstances do not encourage optimism that in the future the speed of technology diffusion will be faster than in the past, or than in other advanced countries. The key issues over the next twenty years are likely to be familiar ones: the supply of qualified people in science and engineering, the readiness of UK industry to invest more in R&D, and government's commitment to maintaining and enhancing the science base and promoting diffusion of new technologies.

Applications of science and technology

While in any country it normally takes time for new technologies to become widely adopted, and in Britain circumstances do not appear to be particularly favourable for early commercial exploitation, it nonetheless seems probable, in view of the many important developments becoming available, that in the two decades to 2010 many new technology applications will be adopted. What general factors are likely to encourage diffusion? And what is the impact of new technologies likely to be on particular areas of potential application?

Factors favouring take-up

Factors which will promote diffusion of the 'core' technologies (IT, biotechnology and new materials) are:

- their applicability across a wide range of economic sectors: IT in particular has already spread very widely in all sectors and there is considerable scope for the diffusion of more products and services;

- they show continuing price/performance improvements (this is especially true of computer hardware);

- they can reduce labour costs in production; they can reduce capital requirements in many ways; they can improve production quality; and IT can assist in achieving greatly increased flexibility in production and organisation;

- new generations of managers, engineers and service providers will have had much more exposure to IT systems in their education and training than their predecessors; so they should take learned habits into working life and find it easier to make use of new IT products and services than the current generation of senior managers has done;

- all three core technologies have major environmental advantages. They can contribute to waste reduction and energy efficiency and to pollution control in many ways.

Perhaps it is the *environmental* aspects which will prove to be the most important of the factors favouring diffusion of the new technologies, particularly in relation to IT. Thus far there has been little sign of the great shift towards tele-working, tele-shopping, tele-learning and the 'intelligent home' prophesied by many of the forecasters of the late 1970s and early 1980s, although much of the technology needed is available. It may be that even with greatly improved software and telecommunications networks there will only be gradual take-up of tele-services and tele-working unless there is a compelling 'push' towards them by some 'external' factor.

The threat posed by global warming, bringing the need to change behaviour in order to reduce emissions of greenhouse gases, could provide such a push for the widespread take-up of forms of tele-working, new tele-services and 'intelligent' energy management systems in factories, homes and offices, as well as for the development of clean and energy-efficient transport technologies and adoption of new energy-efficient heating and lighting systems. The following sections briefly consider the likely effects of science and technology in different areas of application.

Agriculture

There will be further use of IT in agriculture (for farm management and sensing, for instance),[303] particularly where factory methods of farming are used, but the new technologies likely to be most important are in biotechnology. From the late 1990s there is likely to be increasing use of new biological pesticides and fungicides, of new vaccines and animal health care products, of hormones to get faster livestock growth, and of genetic engineering to produce new varieties of plants (for instance, with greater resistance to drought or disease) and livestock with more commercially valuable combinations of characteristics.[304,305]

Increasing public concern over food safety, animal welfare, ecological balance and the ethical issues involved in genetic engineering are likely to lead to tighter controls on the use of some new techniques and to an expansion of demand for organic produce. Public anxieties and regulatory changes are likely to mean that acceptance and application of biotechnological processes and products will be gradual. The overall effect is hard to forecast: new developments in IT and biotechnology are likely to be taken up by, and to reinforce the position of, large farming businesses; and they could exacerbate the problems of agricultural surpluses and add to pressures on the EC Common Agricultural Policy.[306,307,308] At the same time there will probably be a growing minority of organic producers rejecting hi-tech intensive agricultural practices, although some biotechnological developments could be seen as 'green', since there is the potential for new techniques to allow a major reduction in the use of chemical fertilisers.

Manufacturing

The use of microelectronics in manufacturing is one of the few areas in which diffusion of a new technology has been systematically charted in a series of major surveys.[125,126,127,128] These show that the use of microelectronics in products and processes by manufacturing industry increased in a single decade from under 5 per cent of all factories in Britain in 1977 to 63 per cent in 1987 – a much wider extent of diffusion than for other new technologies such as new materials, fibre optics or biotechnology.

During the period covered by the surveys there were also increases in the proportions using particular kinds of automation: computer aided design (CAD), robotics, automated storage and transport, quality control and inspection systems, computer integrated manufacturing systems (CIM) and flexible manufacturing systems (FMS). The surveys also found that the use of these technologies were considered by the users to be worthwhile and profitable.[112,128,132]

During the next two decades there is no doubt that there will be further increases in both the extent and sophistication of microelectronics applications in both products and production processes, with use becoming more general than before in the smaller establishments and the lower technology industries.

Use of New Technologies in Manufacturing
percentages of factories in Britain

	1977	1981	1983	1985	1987
Microelectronics	4	21	39	53	63
New materials					11
Fibre optics			2		6
Biotechnology			1		3

Source: PSI[125,126,127,128]

The effect will be, not merely to increase productivity and reduce costs, but also to increase options for decentralisation, faster response, shorter product life cycles and greater flexibility of operation more generally,[311] but at the cost of high dependence on IT systems and hence a new vulnerability to failures of hardware or software.

While the use of IT systems will grow, there will continue to be factors impeding adoption, in particular, lack of technical expertise, which has been shown to be the most widespread problem in all kinds of factory, in all sizes and sectors, and with all kinds of application. And while the degree of automation will increase, so also will the need for people with special skills to design, make, install, operate and maintain the increasingly sophisticated new equipment. Organisations will need to change considerably as the level of their IT sophistication grows, in order to make the best use of the technology and the abilities of the people using it, and this is also a major constraint on the speed with which manufacturers will move towards more integration of computer systems.[251]

The use of new materials will become increasingly important in some industries. In particular, there will be a steady rise in use of plastics and composites in vehicles and aircraft, and by the turn of the century engines will increasingly be made from composites and advanced ceramics.

As with microelectronics, the use of new materials has spread more slowly to smaller factories, and the pace of increase in use in the future is likely to continue to be impeded by lack of awareness, existing investments in metal-based products and production techniques, improvements in conventional materials and methods and, in particular, by shortages of people with the new specialist skills required.[112]

Use of biotechnology in production processes will also increase, particularly in the first decade of the new century, with the most important applications being in the food, drinks, pharmaceuticals and agricultural chemicals industries.[309,310]

Finally, while use of new technologies will undoubtedly be very important, it must be remembered that manufacturing will also be greatly affected by developments in other fields: for example in management techniques, with just-in-time (JIT) production methods, total quality control systems and improved human relations policies aiming to make more use of available and potential skills to secure more positive contributions from the whole workforce.[311]

Business organisation

In the past two decades there has been increasingly widespread introduction into offices of IT equipment and systems – copiers, personal computers, work stations, word processors, desk top publishing, electronic mail, fax, laptop computers, automated telephone exchanges and cellular phones. The rapid increase in use has been stimulated by the fall in costs and the increase in performance, versatility and reliability of the equipment and systems available.

The further advances expected in semiconductors, computers and telecommunications are certain to bring further increases in performance and reductions in cost which, together with improved compatibility through the adoption of OSI standards, may confidently be predicted to lead to considerable further increases in the take-up of office automation.[251,312,313,314,315]

There will be continuing growth in the use of word processors, spreadsheets, databases, document storage and retrieval systems and networking of computer systems. The Single Market in the EC will stimulate the use of electronic data exchange in many areas between organisations. As companies face more competitive and complex markets and put more of their knowledge and data into IT systems, so there will be increasing opportunities for the use of IT as an aid to decision making, operational control and servicing customers, and in increasing speed of response to changing market circumstances.

However, growth in the integration of systems and the use of tele-services is likely to be affected in the medium term by the following factors:

- relatively high costs of integrating systems and making associated organisational changes;

- the speed of development of international standards in tele-services, networks and new computer systems;

◆ the rate of development of ISDN services and broadband business tele-services;

◆ the level of awareness of technologies, especially among smaller companies;[312]

◆ the problem of keeping abreast of new technological developments which could open up opportunities for the organisation. How can organisations update their knowledge and maintain and enhance their ability to use new technical possibilities for business advantage? IT systems may be part of the solution, but in many cases they may become part of the problem, allowing access to unmanageable volumes of information. Many organisations will find that they need expert information managers who can filter out essential information from the mass of databases, tele-services and networks which are becoming available alongside the already vast numbers of printed information sources.

Given these constraining factors, there is likely to be gradual take-up of more sophisticated IT systems for business among the mass of organisations, while a relatively small number of leading users of IT continue to be foremost in introducing innovations and in integrating their systems into complex networks.

The 'paperless office' beloved of many forecasters has not yet arrived and, if anything, IT has helped to generate even *more* use of paper by organisations. However, there is the potential for using less paper as electronic document storage, retrieval and display systems improve; and environmental concerns over paper manufacture and waste paper disposal may prove to be an important factor in encouraging recycling and greater economy in the use of paper, which could in turn stimulate take-up of electronic systems in offices.

Financial services and retailing

The financial sector is already one of the most 'IT-intensive' in Britain, and considerable further investment in IT-based systems is planned, not only in banking, but also in insurance, estate agency and in financial, tax and legal services. Still greater use is likely of IT systems such as electronic data exchange, document storage and retrieval, and expert systems. There will also be heavy further investment by retailers in computer-based systems for sales monitoring and stock management, and for faster check-out systems making use of bar code scanners.

Probably the most important developments from the consumer's point of view will be the use of EFT/POS (Electronic Funds Transfer at the Point of Sale) to make shopping and other payments quicker and easier for retailers and their customers and cheaper to handle for the banks;[316,317,318] and the use of smart cards (credit card size pieces of plastic with microchips embedded in them) or laser cards (working on the same principle as the compact disk).

In Paris the use of smart cards in place of coins in phone boxes has reduced the proportion out of service to 3 per cent.[319] Much more powerful cards are being developed which have the potential for handling a wide range of financial transactions and also for holding a variety of personal, household, professional and business information – a sort of filofax on a credit card, which can also be used for identification, payments and other kinds of transactions.

While cash will remain the most convenient form of money for most small payments, the use of smart cards is likely to become widespread during the first decade of the next century. Before then, however, it will be necessary to overcome a number of difficulties, including the adoption of national and international standards for compatibility; to make arrangements to protect personal and commercial privacy and prevent counterfeiting and other kinds of fraud; to gain the support of prospective users; and to undertake considerable investment in the machines for handling the cards.[320,321,322]

Home banking services are likely to increase gradually as the ISDN network develops, but their importance will be limited, first, by their inability to receive or deliver cash and, later, by the increasing use of smart cards.[323]

Home shopping services are already technically feasible and have been the subject of a number of trials. However, results so far suggest that they are unlikely to be used on any great scale (particularly if there is no broadband cable network), because as yet they are costly, cumbersome and not very attractive to use for most kinds of shopping. Although services are likely to become much more sophisticated as software and visual display systems improve, there are significant costs and problems in the low-tech end of the operation – ie, delivery.[324] However, they may offer scope in special applications, for example for meeting the needs of those who are handicapped or house-bound, and their use may become more widespread towards 2010 if measures to reduce global warming lead to major reductions in the use of cars for shopping.

Public services

There will be considerable scope for IT-based systems in public services,[252] both for general administration and for special applications, for example:

- health: for storage of patients' records; in expert systems to help in diagnosis; in data analysis for epidemiology and drugs monitoring; and in various kinds of high-tech surgery and treatment; and in devices to aid the handicapped.[325,326,327,328,329] IT and biotechnological innovations are likely to combine in the form of self-diagnosis and monitoring kits for home use. Take-up of such 'D-I-Y' developments will be promoted by the need to contain health service costs and devote a rising share of resources to the needs of the growing elderly population over the next twenty years;

+ social care: for client records and for client information on eligibility for benefits and availability of services;[330]

+ education and training: as a teaching aid, especially in distance learning applications. There is considerable scope for the development of 'multimedia' computer systems for education and training, combining video, text, sound and conventional computer applications.

While wider use will be encouraged by the higher performance and lower costs of equipment and systems, it will be constrained by:

+ the probable lack of a nationwide broadband cable network for direct access by individuals and organisations to databases and other services;

+ the need for the establishment of standards in new areas of IT such as multimedia systems;

+ the need for secure IT systems to protect confidentiality;

+ the 'culture' of many in social work, which has tended to be somewhat suspicious of new technology,[331] although new entrants to the profession over the period will be increasingly familiar with IT;

+ the lack of specialist technical skills among practitioners and the scarcity of suitable user-friendly software;

+ budgetary constraints on many public services.

Domestic

Homes are likely to be equipped with increasingly many microelectronically controlled products, but by 2010 it will still probably be only a minority of affluent enthusiasts who go to the trouble and expense of installing fully-integrated home systems for entertainment, security and control of appliances.[332] Robots to do the housework will probably remain an unrealised dream, since the unpredictable circumstances of most homes make them one of the most difficult of all environments to program for safe and efficient operation of robots.

Many, perhaps most, homes are likely to be equipped by 2010 with substantially extended information and entertainment facilities, particularly if a national broadband network is installed over the period. From the mid-1990s enhanced definition television will be available, and by 2000 there may be a sizeable market for high definition television (HDTV) if costs have been brought down – it is already in use in Japan, but costs more than £2,000 a set – and if consumers want even better picture quality than conventional and enhanced systems will offer. There is, then, likely to be a much wider choice of land-based and satellite channels, with better-quality pictures and sound, but not necessarily any improvement in the quality of the programme content.

In theory, IT systems offer increased scope for working from home.[332] In practice, the opportunities have not been taken up on any substantial scale so far – out of about 700,000 people working from home, only about 80,000 seem to be 'new technology homeworkers'. It seems unlikely that in the absence of powerful incentives over the next two decades computer-based home working will attract more than a small proportion of the workforce, because of the loss of social contacts involved, the impairment of career prospects, the strains on domestic life and the unsuitability of most jobs for doing from a distance.[251,333] The balance of advantage could change if environmental concerns lead to a significant reduction in private car use, without an offsetting improvement in public transport services; but even then tele-working will probably still be feasible and attractive for only a minority of the workforce. Overall, gathering environmental pressures and increases in the scope of the telecommunications system will probably lead to a gradual rise in tele-working. One possible development is the adoption of home working for part of the week, and the setting up of 'halfway house' telework centres in localities from which employees can communicate with their organisations.

Environment, energy and transport

The take-up of technologies for waste recycling, pollution monitoring, energy efficiency and emission control will be promoted by legislation from British governments and from the European Community, by rising energy costs and by consumer pressures. Organisational changes designed to reduce energy consumption may well accompany the spread of environmentally friendlier technologies: subsidised shared transport for employees, reduced working weeks, flexi-time, increased tele-working. Clearly there will be a steady growth in market opportunities for the UK environmental technology industry, for consultancy and for training providers, as environmental pressures lead to changes throughout the economy.

Environmental concerns are likely to give a stimulus to new technology applications in transport – new high-speed train links, new materials in vehicle engines and bodies, microelectronics-based systems for improving engine efficiency, and IT-based systems for navigation, traffic control and road pricing.[335]

However, widespread use of electric cars is unlikely until there are radical improvements in battery performance, and large-scale production will probably develop only after 2000, so they will cost substantially more than conventional cars at first. The development of new fuels for vehicles is being stimulated by environmental concerns. Ethanol and methanol fuels and hybrid diesel/electric engines may be in limited use by the early 2000s. Hydrogen-powered vehicles would produce no toxic fumes or carbon dioxide, but are unlikely to be available before 2010. Legislative pressure over vehicle exhaust emissions is likely to be the main factor stimulating innovation by the motor industry: the tougher the regulations on emissions the more rapid will be the development of new fuel cell technologies and more efficient electric cars.

It is important to note that there are no ready 'technical fixes' for the problems posed by vehicle pollution. The most significant changes are likely to be increased use of public transport systems (mainly based on *current* technologies), increased reliance on walking and cycling, and reductions in car use.

Environmental concerns will also give a strong stimulus to development of techniques for energy conservation and efficiency (many of which are already economic and in limited use) and to development of alternative sources of renewable energy. The economics of these are likely to be improved (and hence their use increased) by development work to reduce their costs and by the increased costs of fossil fuels following the probable introduction of carbon taxes by the turn of the century.

Space

Developments in rockets and satellite systems are likely to lead to further unmanned exploration of outer space, use of space stations for scientific research, increased use of satellites for monitoring of environmental changes, and a great increase in satellite communications. However, so long as the cost of lifting materials into space is very high, the prospect of factories in space remains remote. The position could be changed by the development of re-usable spaceplanes to lift materials into orbit, or carry passengers on intercontinental flights, as is envisaged in the British HOTOL design, but the probable development costs are so large that they are unlikely to be in use until the first decade of the next century at the very earliest.

Manned space flight is likely to be constrained by the enormous costs and diversion of resources to other areas of more pressing concern (such as environmental research and protection measures); and by the growing problem of orbital debris, which by 2010 may pose a major threat to spacecraft.

Crime, legal and ethical issues

In this area the applications for new technologies are double-edged. The increasing use of IT is opening up whole new areas of crime in computer fraud (illicit switching of funds), computer hacking (breaking into personal and corporate systems to destroy data, disrupt operations or acquire confidential information) and counterfeiting and misuse of plastic cards. IT is also providing new tools for the operations of organised criminal groups.[336,337,338] At the same time new technologies will also be providing new means for combating crime, for example, surveillance devices, improved police computer record systems and radio links, DNA fingerprinting and electronic tagging.[339,340] There will also be new possibilities for miscarriages of justice and infringements of civil liberties.[251,252]

Copyright and patent law are likely to experience continuing controversy and confusion due to the proliferation of 'cloned' software and hardware systems, the ease of copying digital data (software, compact disks, etc) and the problems of intellectual property rights arising from the creation of genetically engineered micro-organisms, plants and animals: can and should genetically-modified creatures be patented? Who will 'own' genetic information obtained from research programmes such as the human genome project? These various problems are likely to assume increasing importance in the decades ahead: technical, legal and administrative solutions will need to be found and regulatory régimes frequently reviewed to take account of technological changes.

There are many areas where developments in new technology and science are likely to pose serious ethical and social problems. For example:

- anxieties over excessive isolation of people from community life because of the hi-tech attractions of new IT-based home entertainment systems. There may be a revival of the debates and moral panics of previous years over the cultural consequences of television, and concern that new home IT technologies may intensify the long-standing trends in industrial societies towards ever greater individualism and 'atomisation';

- ethical issues raised by new medical techniques and breakthroughs in biological knowledge: for instance, problems such as stigma and discrimination posed by new possibilities for genetic screening of individuals for inherited diseases; the use of foetal tissue in treating neurological disorders; the ethics of pre-embryo research and the donation of human eggs; and the ethical issues associated with new possibilities for organ transplants and synthetic organs;

- dilemmas over the admissibility of euthanasia and of using new medical technologies for prolonging life are likely to become more acute as the numbers of the very elderly increase and medical techniques improve;

- the growing vulnerability of an increasingly 'wired' society to human error in the design and operation of complex electronic systems, to computer sabotage, to terrorism and to electrical supply failures;

- the possible revival of a significant minority 'counter culture' hostile to science and technology if there is no checking of the current threats to the global environment. The emergence of extremist 'animal rights' groups may be a sign of worse to come. If the global environmental situation deteriorates over the next decade it is conceivable that 'eco-terrorist' actions by minority groups against companies and laboratories will become a significant threat.

Although there is no evidence of growing hostility among the general public to science and technology overall, it is likely that there will be increasing suspicion over many new developments in areas basic to everyday life – health and safety, reproduction, old age, privacy, food safety – where fundamental fears may be raised by innovations and where scandals and accidents, not necessarily in Britain, will have a serious impact on public opinion. Individuals and pressure groups are very likely to become less tolerant of 'self-policing' by experts in areas with potentially harmful implications for the environment, public health and safety.

Implications

The cluster of information technologies are of unique importance because of the spectacularly rapid pace of innovation, the exceptionally broad range of possible areas of application, and the dramatic lowering of costs which has made it possible for opportunities to be given practical realisation much sooner and more widely than with previous new technologies. There are also increasingly important developments in new materials and biotechnology; these too are key enabling technologies, making possible changes in many different areas. Finally, there are also developments of great importance in a number of other areas of science and technology such as energy, transport, the environment and medicine.

Effective use of established and new technologies is becoming an increasingly important factor in future expansion of the economy and improvement of living standards, and past experience in Britain has tended to be disappointing in that public approval of science and an exceptional record of innovativeness has not usually borne the hoped for fruit in terms of successful commercial exploitation.

The new core technologies (IT, biotechnology and new materials) are becoming increasingly interdependent and their successful exploitation appears to be highly dependent on government policies, in four areas in particular.

First, exploitation is associated with effective R&D. British industry has tended to invest less of its profits in R&D than industry in competitor countries, and government support, some claim, is not as great or as effectively deployed as in competitor countries. In particular, half of government R&D funding goes to defence (far more than in other European countries), where its value is more open to question with the ending of the Cold War, and this leaves less available for other areas. A key challenge for the coming two decades for governments and industry in the UK will be to find ways of promoting more investment in technological innovation, more effective technology transfer into industry, and more emphasis on growth areas such as environmental protection technology rather than on defence R&D.

Secondly, specialist skills are a key factor in all the new technologies, and weaknesses in our education and training arrangements in relation to science and technology raise problems which can be solved only through measures by government in partnership with industry and the education system.

Thirdly, in some areas government regulation and intervention is a key factor in the successful exploitation of opportunities opened up by technological change. This is particularly evident in telecommunications, where adoption of standards is crucial and where introduction costs to reach viable levels of operation are high. For example, the technical and economic factors involved in the choice between new systems based on fibre optic cable, DBS and MVDS are not straightforward. It may not be necessary to intervene actively to get one of them off the ground (as the French did with the electronic information service Minitel), and it may not turn out to be desirable to end up relying predominantly on any one of the alternative systems. However, there is the danger that too passive a reliance on market forces in the development of new telecommunications infrastructures may end with expensively wasteful duplication and provide too weak a base for *any* of the alternatives to build up quickly to a viable level.

Finally, there will be a growing role for public policy in promoting debate on the numerous legal and ethical issues which will be raised by new and emerging technologies over the next twenty years, in framing regulations in response to new developments, and in incorporating coverage of these issues in scientific and engineering education in schools and higher education.

BRITAIN in 2010

 **T**he Economy

6. **T**he Economy

Developments in the economy must be at the centre of any view of the future of Britain, for it is the economy that provides the means for meeting future needs, both of individuals and of+1.3% society as a whole. Bearing in mind the changes expected in population, labour force and skills, in the physical environment and infrastructure, in science and technology, and also the developments expected in the rest of the world, in particular the globalisation of the economy and the moves towards closer economic union in Europe, what rate of economic development is it realistic to expect?

Past rates of growth

The traditional measure of economic growth, gross domestic product (GDP), has been attracting increasing criticism for not taking account of important environmental considerations relevant to the goal of sustainable development. For example, it does not take account of the many costs and benefits which are not traded on the market; it does not take account of the disbenefits of constraints on consumer choice; and it does not take account of how welfare may be affected by the distribution of benefits between individuals and communities. However, until new, more comprehensive, measures are available, gross domestic product remains the most convenient and widely-accepted measure of general economic growth.

On this measure, over the past two decades the output of the economy has risen by about a half; over the past three decades it has nearly doubled.[341,342] However, a simple extrapolation of these past rates of change would be an unreliable guide to the future, since the past three decades include three periods of markedly differing characteristics.

In the first period, 1960 to 1973, there were substantial fluctuations between individual years, but over the period as a whole GDP grew by an average of 2.9 per cent a year, a rate similar to that achieved in the decade before.[341]

In 1973, the dramatic increase in world oil prices brought about by OPEC, the oil exporters' cartel, disrupted the economies of the industrial

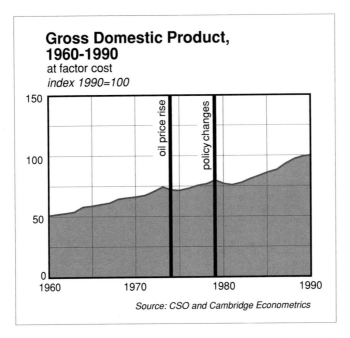

Gross Domestic Product, 1960-1990
at factor cost
index 1990=100

Source: CSO and Cambridge Econometrics

Gross domestic product (the standard measure of economic growth) rose by an average annual rate of:

2.9 per cent in 1960-1973;
1.3 per cent in 1973-1979 (in the depressed period after the oil price rise shock); and
2.1 per cent in 1979-1990 (with new economic policies).

countries, leading to much slower rates of economic growth in most of them. Consequently, in the following six years between 1973 and 1979, the British economy grew by an average of only about 1.3 per cent a year – less than half the previous rate.

Within this period, there was a sharp contrast between the first two years, when GDP actually *fell* by 1.5 and 1.9 per cent in the aftermath of the oil shock, and the remaining four years during which it rose by an average of 2.8 per cent – about the same rate as in the previous period.

Average Annual Rates of Change in Gross Domestic Product

1960-1973	+2.9%
1973-1975	-1.7%
1975-1979	+2.8%
1979-1981	-2.1%
1981-1986	+3.0%
1986-1988	+4.7%
1988-1990	+2.1%

In 1979 there was a further rise in world oil prices and a change of government that brought radical changes in economic policy in Britain. In the following eleven years, 1979-1990, economic growth has averaged

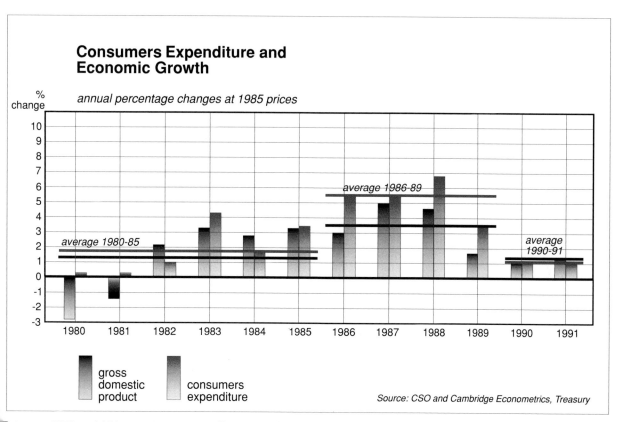

Consumers Expenditure and Economic Growth

annual percentage changes at 1985 prices

Source: CSO and Cambridge Econometrics, Treasury

Between 1979 and 1985 consumers' exenditure rose slightly faster than gross domestic product; in 1986-1988 GDP rose faster, but consumer's expenditure rose faster still; but this could not be sustained, and in 1989-1991 both GDP and consumers' expenditure have been rising more slowly again.

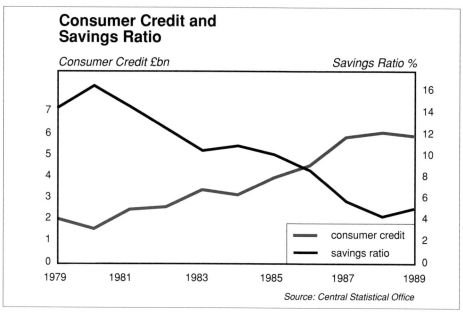

Consumer Credit and Savings Ratio

Consumer Credit £bn *Savings Ratio %*

Source: Central Statistical Office

Higher consumers' expenditure in the 1980s has been financed partly by credit (consumer credit trebled between 1979 and 1989) and partly by dissaving (the savings ratio dropped by more than a half between 1979 and 1989.)

243

about 2.2 per cent a year – about half way between the slower growth rate in the post oil shock period and the faster growth rate in the period before.

During this period also, the overall average conceals significant differences between different years. In the first two years GDP *fell* by 2.8 per cent and 1.4 per cent, even more sharply than at the start of the previous period; in the following five years it increased by an average of 3.0 per cent, about the same rate as in the previous periods; in the next two years it increased much more rapidly, by an average of 4.7 per cent a year; but in the final two years of the period the rate of increase has fallen back to 2.7 per cent in 1989 and probably about 1.5 per cent in 1990. The Treasury has forecast growth of only 1 per cent in 1991[343] and most forecasters expect only a fairly modest rate of growth in 1992 also.

Thus it seems that the very rapid growth achieved in 1987 and 1988 was not sustainable and is being followed by four years of much more modest growth. It would accordingly appear wiser to take neither the exceptionally rapid growth of 1987 and 1988, nor the much slower growth of 1990 and 1991, as indicators of future long-term growth prospects; but instead to consider the changes in performance over longer periods of years and some of the factors underlying them.

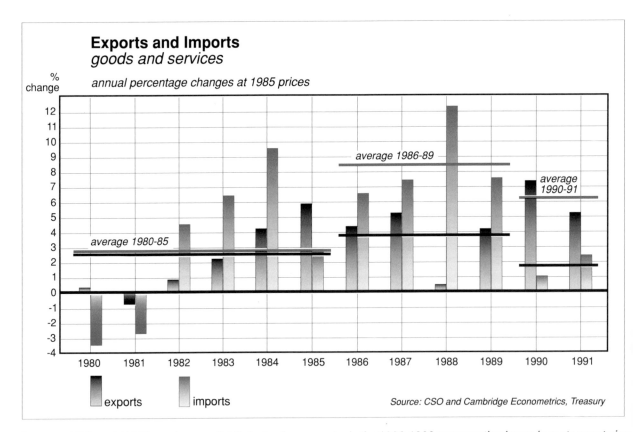

Exports and Imports
goods and services

% change   *annual percentage changes at 1985 prices*

average 1986-89

average 1980-85

average 1990-91

exports   imports

Source: CSO and Cambridge Econometrics, Treasury

Between 1979 and 1985 imports rose slightly faster than exports; in the 1986-1988 consumption boom imports rose twice as fast as exports; this led to overseas payments deficits and the need for slower growth to slow down the growth of imports in 1990 and 1991.

Factors in growth

There are a number of factors that have influenced the rate of economic growth achieved in the past two decades and which may have an influence on the rate achieved over the coming two decades.

Structural changes

As in most other mature economies, there has been a major shift in Britain from manufacturing to the service sector. Between 1970 and 1990, the rate of growth in gross output in the service sector has been more than four times as fast as that in manufacturing; and because service sector activities tend to be more labour intensive, total employment in services has increased by more than one third while employment in manufacturing has fallen by more than one third. As a result of these changes, the service sector now accounts for a larger share of total output than does manufacturing, and employment in it is more than three times as great as in manufacturing. No doubt a large part of future growth will also be in the service sector.

The fact that much of the service sector is engaged in activities that are not internationally tradeable means that there can be scope for expanding them, and thereby increasing total output and reducing unemployment, without at the same time also increasing deficits in overseas payments; but by the same token, expansion of these activities cannot help in *reducing* overseas deficits.

Inflation

Over much of the postwar period inflation has been at rates higher than have been desired, and higher also than in some of our main trade competitors, such as Germany, Japan and the United States. A major factor in this has been the structure of the labour market which has tended to result in money wage rates rising faster than productivity (see Chapter 13). Higher rates of inflation than in other countries have undermined our international competitiveness and led to depreciation of the exchange rate relative to countries with lower rates of inflation – and this in turn has brought more inflation through the effects of having to pay higher prices, in terms of sterling, for imports.

Membership of the European Exchange Rate Mechanism will in future limit the scope for exchange rate depreciation; and if full currency union is established later on this will remove the possibility of exchange rate depreciation altogether. The effect of joining the ERM will therefore be to *force* a convergence in inflation rates. This will mean lower inflation in Britain but (as in France in the 1980s) at the expense of slower economic growth and higher unemployment in the years of adjustment – unless there is a radical departure from past practices in the labour market. And as the

ERM has been joined at a relatively high parity for sterling, the latitude will be relatively small and the adjustment will need to be relatively sharp.

Supply-side changes

In the past decade a number of changes have been made with the intention of making the market work more efficiently, with fewer regulations, rigidities or distortions and, in particular, with more flexibility in the labour market. Some of the benefits of this are likely to be mainly psychological, encouraging greater confidence or more enterprise, and some are likely to be mainly qualitative – in both cases the benefits, even if substantial, will tend to be elusive and difficult to quantify.

In due course, however, any benefits should show in a form which can be measured – for example in higher exports. One area where they should be in early evidence is in improved figures for labour productivity. Interpretation of the figures for productivity is complicated by changes in the structure of the economy and the composition of the labour force and by the possible importance of other factors such as investment in new plant, introduction of new technology and adoption of new management techniques such as Just-in-Time systems. Consequently there has been much controversy over whether or not there have been significant improvements in productivity and, if so, what they have been caused by and whether they are likely to continue.

Some analysts[344,345] attribute valuable improvements in productivity to changes that have been made in the labour market; but some argue that the improvements have not been very great,[346,347] or that much of the productivity gain can be explained in other ways, or that much of the improvement is attributable to the heavy labour-shedding undertaken in the early 1980s in order to put an end to overmanning, and is therefore a once-for-all gain that cannot be continued.[347] There are several reasons why it would be imprudent to set too much store on the productivity figures as indicators of faster economic growth in the coming years.

First, the rise in productivity in manufacturing, 4.2 per cent a year between 1979 and 1988, although much higher than the 1.1 per cent average in 1973-1979, was not markedly better than the longer-term average of 3.7 per cent in 1951-1973.[347]

Second, while the main improvement in productivity has been in manufacturing, productivity in most parts of the service sector has been rising much more slowly, and some of the people whose departure raised the productivity figures in manufacturing have since become unemployed. Hence, *for the economy as a whole*, labour productivity rose by only 2.8 per cent a year in 1979-1988. While this was a modest improvement on the 2.2 per cent a year gain in 1973-1979, it was substantially *less* than the earlier long-term average of 3.6 per cent in 1951-1973.[347]

And third, productivity improvements are important mainly insofar as they lead to improvements in primary indicators such as output and exports. It is changes in these primary indicators that are more likely to give a reliable guide to the prospects for growth in the future.

Balance of overseas payments

Over most of the postwar period the balance of payments has been an important, often the most important, constraint on the pace of economic growth. Faster growth has tended to suck in more imports and divert exports to the home market, and this in turn has led to payments deficits, pressure on sterling, and a need to resort to more deflationary policies in order to curb imports and limit the size of the deficit and the extent of exchange-rate depreciation. Several econometric studies have suggested that this constraint is still present;[348,349,350] and the size of the current overseas deficit suggests that until it is greatly reduced it is likely to be a major constraint on the rate of economic growth attainable.

Accordingly, it is relevant to consider in turn the prospects for the three main constituents in the current overseas balance: manufactures, oil and invisibles.

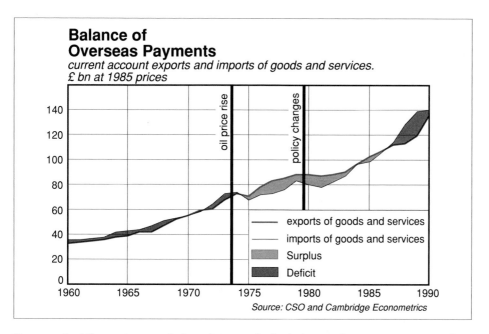

Over much of the postwar period weaknesses in the balance of overseas payments have been a constraint on economic growth.
In the late 1970s and early 1980s there were payments surpluses, but in the late 1980s there have been large deficits.

Manufactures

Manufacturing industry needs to be competitive internationally so that it can hold its home market against imports from abroad and sell its exports in the markets of the world.

International performance comparisons

The Organisation for Economic Cooperation and Development (OECD) has prepared figures that compare the performance of the British economy with that of the other leading industrial countries in the 'Group of Seven' in three periods: 1961-1973, 1973-1979 and 1979-1988.[351] These show that in all three periods the growth of the British economy as a whole was slower than that of the other countries, and that the growth in manufacturing was particularly weak.

In the first of the three periods the growth of manufacturing output in Britain was much slower than in any of the other countries in the group and was less than half the average for the group as a whole. In the second period, with the disruption following the 1973-74 oil shock, manufacturing output rose much more slowly in the other countries; but in Britain it actually *fell*. And in the most recent period, when manufacturing output was still rising only fairly slowly (by an average of 2.4 per cent a year) in the other countries, in Britain it rose by only 0.8 per cent a year – one third of the average rate of increase for the group as a whole, a relative performance actually *worse* than in the first period.

Manufacturing production and investment

Are there signs that British industry, whatever its *past* performance, has in recent years become stronger and is likely to improve its performance in the future?

In Britain the growth in total industrial production (including the energy industries) has been uneven, and with manufacturing itself the growth has been even more so. In the first period (1960-1979) manufacturing production rose unsteadily but substantially; but after the oil shock it fell and by 1979 had failed to get back to the level reached in 1973; and after 1979 it fell further and did not get back up to the 1973 level until 1988.[352,353] During the 1979-1989 period as a whole manufacturing production averaged 4 per cent less than the average level achieved in the previous period and 8 per cent below the peak level of 1973.

If manufacturing production has been rising only slowly, is it because weaker units have been shaken out in the recessions in the early 1970s and early 1980s, and the survivors can now be expected to perform more strongly in the future?

Probably the best single indicator of potential future competitiveness is the level of investment undertaken to make industry

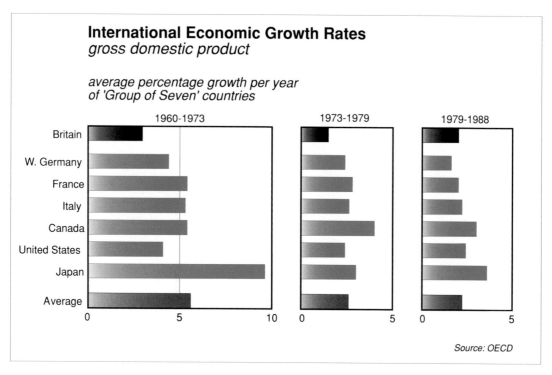

Economic circumstances have differed greatly in the three periods 1960-1973, 1973-1979 and 1979-1988; but in all three of them economic growth in Britain was well below the average of the 'group of seven' countries.

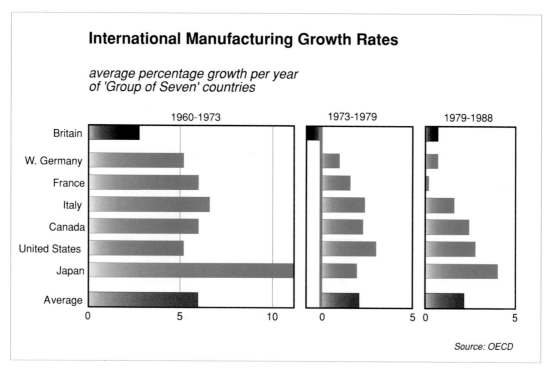

In rates of growth in manufacturing output Britain has also been behind the other countries of the 'group of seven' in all three periods – but by a bigger margin.

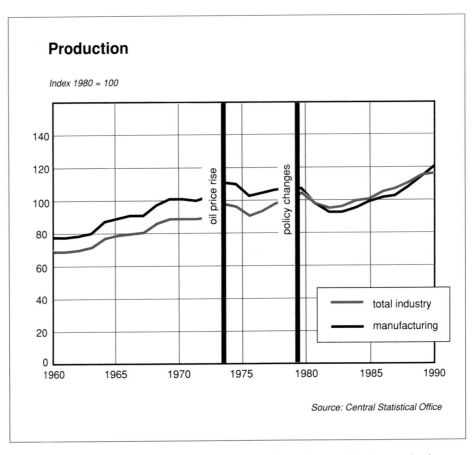

Production

Index 1980 = 100

Source: Central Statistical Office

Total industrial production in Britain has risen unevenly, and manufacturing production even more so. It fell after the 1973 oil shock, and again after 1979, before recovering in the later 1980s. During the 1979-1989 period as a whole manufacturing production has averaged 8 per cent below the earlier peak level of 1973.

Investment in manufacturing has been even more erratic than production. In the early 1980s gross investment fell to 40 per cent below the 1970 peak and it has only recently recovered to the level reached 20 years ago. In some years net investment has been negative.

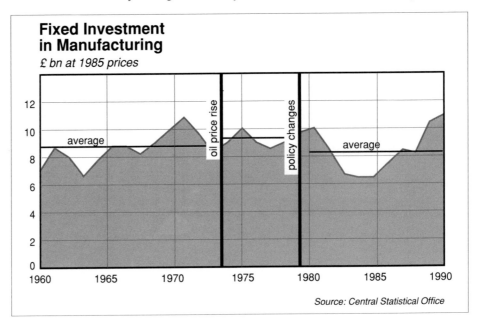

Fixed Investment in Manufacturing

£ bn at 1985 prices

Source: Central Statistical Office

more modern and efficient. In the first of the three periods gross fixed investment in manufacturing rose to a peak in 1970, but then fell back. In the second period, it dropped, following the oil shock, but then recovered, averaging about 7 per cent above the average of the previous period. In the most recent period it fell sharply to a trough 40 per cent below the 1970 peak and it is only recently that it has recovered to the level reached twenty years ago. Altogether, over the ten years 1980-1989 as a whole, gross fixed investment in manufacturing has averaged 13 per cent below the 1974-1979 level and 6 per cent below even the 1960-1973 level.[341,353]

These figures, it should be noted are for *gross* investment; the figures for *net* investment (the increase after allowance for depreciation of earlier investment) have actually been negative for much of the 1980s. The average for the nine years 1980-1988 was about – £0.4bn a year.[341]

The figures are slightly improved if allowance is made for leasing (not included in the CSO's tables for investment in manufacturing industry), and it must be remembered that changes in industrial structure have involved greater declines in the more capital-intensive basic industries. And of course the *quantity* of physical investment is not the only factor in potential improvements in efficiency; the *quality* of investment (about which quantified evidence is scanty) is also important, as is also the investment in *training* (about which the evidence is not encouraging – see Chapter 13).

Even so, the figures for investment do suggest that British manufacturing industry as a whole is unlikely to have been getting much stronger, and may even have been getting weaker, in a period when many of our competitors have been investing heavily to improve the efficiency of their industries. It seems unlikely that it is now much better equipped than it was before to meet the tougher competition to be expected in the Single European Market.

Imports and exports of manufactures

The real test of competitiveness is actual performance – how successful has our industry been in the markets of the world? Are there signs of the improved performance needed to achieve export-led economic expansion in the future, in which international competition is sure to become more intense?

While there are important differences between sectors (and even more between sub-sectors) the overall picture is not encouraging. Between 1973 and 1979 there was some increase in export ratios (the proportion of manufacturers' sales sold to export markets), but a similar increase in import penetration (the proportion of UK domestic markets captured by imports). Between 1979 and 1989 the increase in import penetration (from 26.9 per cent to 36.7 per cent) was *twice as fast* as the increase in the export ratio (from 25.1 per cent to 30.0 per cent).[353,354] On this test, competitiveness has been getting, not better, but significantly *worse*.

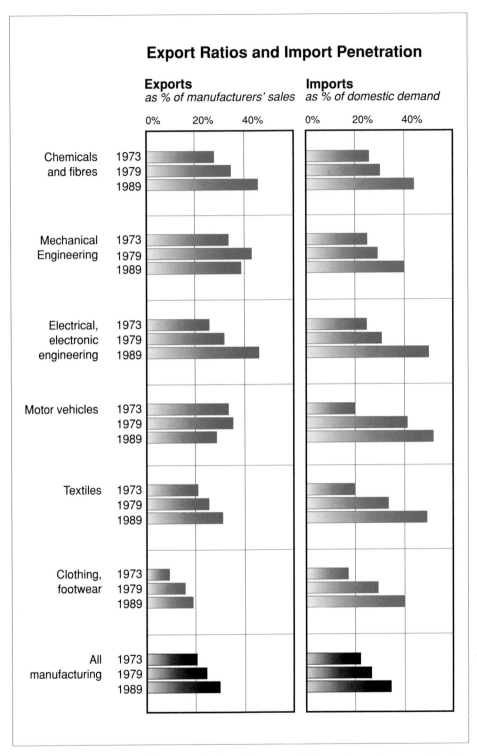

Export Ratios and Import Penetration

Exports
as % of manufacturers' sales

Imports
as % of domestic demand

One measure of competitiveness is the difference between import penetration (the percentage of the home market taken by imports) and export ratios (the proportion of sales to export markets). In 1979-1989 import penetration increased twice as fast as export ratios.

Another measure of competitiveness is share in total exports of manufactures of the main manufacturing countries. Britain's share has been falling over a long period: from 16.5 per cent in 1960 to 9.4 per cent in 1973, 9.1 per cent in 1979 and 7.6 per cent in 1986.[2] Since then it has recovered to 8.3 per cent in 1988 (half way back to the 1979 share), but it is too early to know whether this indicates a permanent recovery in performance, or whether, like previous improvements in 1975, 1977 and 1980, it will prove to be merely a short-lived interruption of the long, downward, trend.

If these changes are translated into total trade in manufactures, between 1970 and 1989 the volume of imports of manufactures has risen three times as fast as the volume of exports of manufactures; while the volume of imports of *finished* manufactures (ie excluding the semi-manufactures used by industry) has risen more than five times as fast as the volume of exports of finished manufactures.[353,354]

This tendency is not new – it was already in evidence long before 1970. What is discouraging is that the divergence has been proceeding at much the same rate in the most recent period as in the previous ones. Thus the evidence is starkly clear that, at least at prevailing exchange rates, British manufacturing industry in general is still *not* improving its performance internationally.

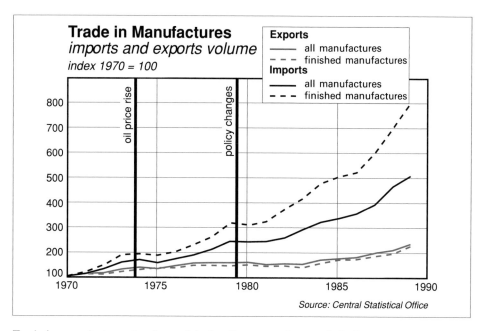

Trade in manufactures has been deteriorating over a long period. Between 1970 and 1989 the volume of imports of manufactures has risen three times as fast as the volume of exports of manufactures; and the volume of imports of finished manufactures has risen five times as fast as the volume of exports of finished manufactures.

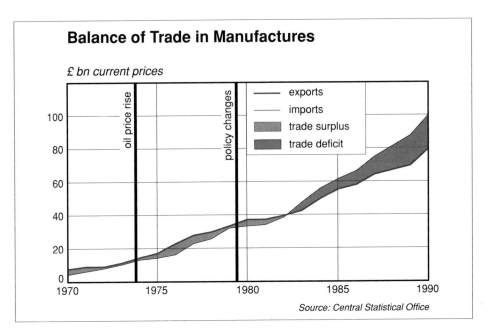

Balance of Trade in Manufactures

£ bn current prices

Source: Central Statistical Office

The balance of trade in manufactures, which up until 1981 had been in surplus, has since turned into deficits of increasing size – £5bn in 1985, £10bn in 1987 and £19bn in 1989.

Oil

The second major component of the overseas balance is oil, where the position has been changed dramatically by the increases in world oil prices in 1973 and 1979 and their subsequent decline in 1985, and by the coming on-stream of oil production from the North Sea, and its subsequent decline.

Before 1973 oil imports cost a little over £1bn a year, about 10 per cent of total imports; and oil exports were negligible. The quadrupling of oil prices in 1973 pushed up the cost of oil imports to more than £4bn in 1974, and more still in subsequent years, adding greatly to Britain's economic difficulties.

However, during the 1970s North Sea oil began to come on-stream and benefited from the further oil price rises in the late 1970s. In consequence, the oil deficit, which had risen to more than £4bn in 1976, turned into a small surplus in 1980 and a larger surplus in subsequent years, leading to a peak surplus of nearly £8bn in 1985. In the three years 1983-1985 oil earnings averaged more than £14bn a year, accounting for nearly one fifth of total exports, and the net oil surplus averaged more than £7bn a year.[353,354]

After 1985, however, the price of oil fell sharply and North Sea production declined a little, with the result that by 1989 oil export earnings were down to one third of the peak level and, although import costs fell too, the oil surplus almost disappeared.

In future years North Sea oil production will tend to fall as reserves from existing fields are depleted, but this may be in part offset by the discovery and exploitation of new fields, particularly if there is the stimulus of higher prices. The decline in production is, therefore, likely to be a gradual one. World oil prices will not stay at the high levels reached at the peak of the Gulf crisis. In the longer term they may well tend to move upwards; but there is also the possibility they will fall if world oil consumption declines as a result of measures to reduce emissions of greenhouse gases. The combined effects of changes in production, consumption and prices are hard to foresee; however, there is very little likelihood that oil will ever again provide the very large net surpluses achieved in the early 1980s.

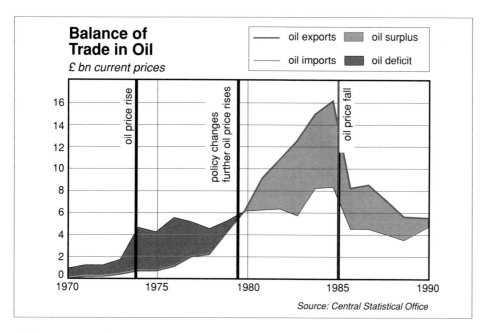

Balance of Trade in Oil
£ bn current prices

oil exports — oil surplus
oil imports — oil deficit

Source: Central Statistical Office

Oil imports cost about £1.2bn a year in the early 1970s. The 1973 price rises put up their cost to more than £5bn. More price rises in 1979 pushed the cost of imports up further, but meanwhile rising North Sea oil production brought in export earnings of £14bn a year in 1983-1985. Finally, with lower prices and falling production, the oil surplus had almost disappeared by the end of the 1980s.

Invisibles

The third major component of the overseas balance is invisibles, made up of three categories: services; interest, profits and dividends; and transfers.

Net earnings from services (tourism, shipping, airlines, insurance, banking and financial services, etc) doubled between 1982 and 1985, largely due to increased earnings from financial services and tourism, but earnings fell half-way back to the 1982 levels in 1988 and 1989.

Earnings from financial and business services have been rising strongly during the 1980s, but further expansion may be more difficult in the 1990s in the face of keener competition from other financial centres such as Frankfurt and Paris. (They would also be adversely affected if Britain were to remain outside the proposed European Monetary Union.) Earnings from shipping have been dropping with the run-down of the merchant fleet. Earnings from tourism are much affected, like physical trade, by relative exchange rates, and the poorer performance recently reflects the encouragement given by a strong pound to Britons to take holidays abroad and to foreigners not to take holidays in Britain. In the longer term it is far from clear whether earnings from tourist visits by foreigners to Britain will grow faster or slower than outgoings from overseas holidays by Britons; or how, with both, the trend towards longer-haul journeys would be affected over the long term by higher aviation fuel prices as a result of measures to reduce greenhouse gas emissions.

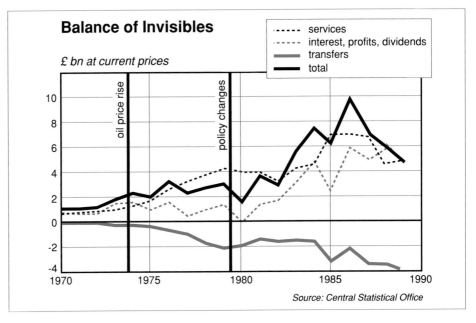

In the early 1980s invisible earnings from dividends and interest on overseas assets and from tourism, insurance and other services, rose strongly; but in the late 1980s they had fallen back again.

Net earnings from interest, profits and dividends rose from nothing in 1980 to nearly £5bn in 1985 following the removal of controls on capital movements. The size of overseas assets is now very considerable and earnings from them may be expected to remain high for many years to come, although possibly offset to some degree by increasing payments on foreign assets in Britain if the recent upsurge in inward investment to Britain continues.

The third category, government transfers, has been a negative item of growing size during the 1970s and 1980s. To a large extent these transfers reflect EC payments, and may be expected to increase as a result of the changes planned in the Community.

Information on invisible earnings is much more limited than that for physical trade and the official figures are subject to frequent and sharp revisions; and the net figures for total invisible earnings, being the result of the balances between inflows and outflows of many different kinds of item, are apt to fluctuate somewhat erratically, making predictions of future changes particularly difficult. Over a long period net earnings have been positive, with the surplus rising from £2.9bn in 1979 to a peak of £9.4bn in 1986. In 1989, however, the net surplus fell to half that amount and future prospects are uncertain.[352,353,354]

The overseas balance

The combined effects of changes in the three main components has had important consequences for the overseas balance of payments on current account as a whole. Up until 1982 the balance of non-oil trade (largely manufactures) alternated between surpluses and deficits of moderate size; but from 1983 a deficit of unprecedented size has emerged. Expenditure on oil imports rose sharply after the rise in world oil prices in 1973. Rising production from North Sea oil meant that oil exports exceeded imports for the first time in 1980; and further increases in production combined with further price rises to turn a net oil deficit of £4.7bn in 1976 into a net oil surplus of £7.8bn in 1985. However a fall in oil prices, and some decline in production, caused the net oil surplus to diminish to less than £1bn by 1989. Finally, net earnings from invisibles, tending upwards in the 1970s, increased sharply between 1982 and 1986, but have since fallen back again.

The combined effect on the overseas balance was as follows. During the 1970s the expenditure on oil imports and the deficits on non-oil trade were largely offset by net surpluses on invisibles, containing the deficit in the poorer years and preserving a small surplus in the better ones.

In the early 1980s the build-up of oil earnings, and later of invisibles also, was more than large enough to offset the substantial deterioration in non-oil trade, giving large surpluses in the overseas balance.

In the later 1980s, however, the disappearance of the oil surplus and the reduction in the surplus on invisibles, combined with a considerable further deterioration in non-oil trade, have resulted in overseas deficits of record size.

The massive oil surplus is unlikely to return. The future of invisibles is highly uncertain: higher earnings are most desirable but may be difficult to achieve. And the deficit on non-oil trade has become very large and is likely to be difficult to reverse.

The scale of the problem is formidable. While the size of our overseas assets means that there is no necessity to turn the situation round immediately, the basic weakness in the overseas payments situation means that it is likely to be a constraint on faster economic growth for a number of years to come.

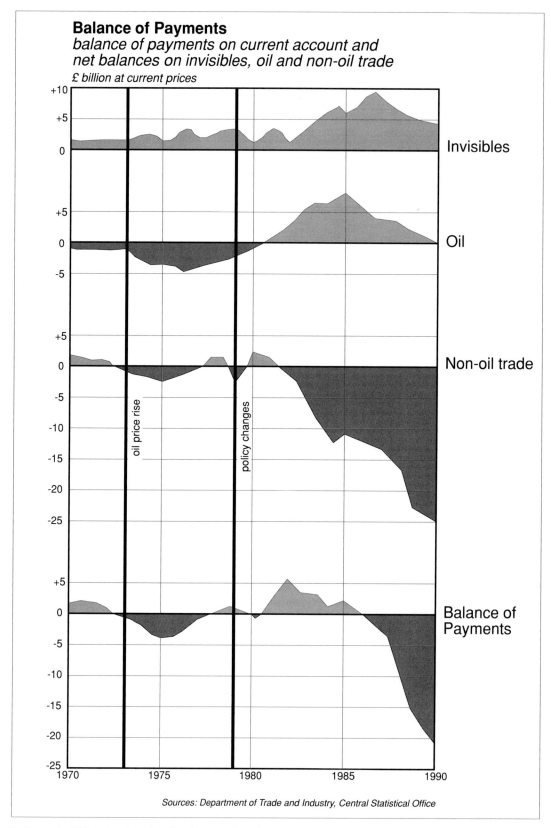

Balance of Payments
*balance of payments on current account and
net balances on invisibles, oil and non-oil trade*
£ billion at current prices

Invisibles

Oil

Non-oil trade

Balance of
Payments

oil price rise

policy changes

Sources: Department of Trade and Industry, Central Statistical Office

In the early 1980s the deterioration in non-oil trade was more than offset by high earnings from North Sea oil and from invisibles. In the late 1980s, the oil surplus had almost disappeared, earnings from invisibles have declined, and a further deterioration in non-oil trade had led to a very large deficit in the balance of overseas payments.

Basis of forecasts

Examination of past economic performance suggests that underlying weaknesses in the British economy have not yet been overcome, and gives little reason for expecting sharp discontinuities, with dramatically faster rates of economic growth in the future than have been achieved in the past. At the same time, the unevenness in past rates of growth makes any simple extrapolation from past trends an unreliable guide to the future: the rate of growth predicted will depend crucially on which period is chosen as the base for the extrapolation.

Accordingly, forecasts for economic growth to 2010 have been based on projections from the Cambridge Econometrics model which is one of the largest and most disaggregated of the models for the UK economy. (Brief particulars of it are given in the accompanying panel.) The model takes account of observed past relationships between the component elements of the economy and incorporates specific values for each year for more than 60 economic variables, such as interest rates, exchange rates, tax rates, government expenditure and economic performance in other countries.

The assumptions made for the projections broadly reflect the main expected developments described in earlier chapters. Some developments are very policy-dependent and for the main projections the assumptions about future government policies are those considered to be the most probable. Alternative scenarios, designed to illustrate some of the effects of three different overall policy approaches are outlined in Chapter 18.

Among the more important economic assumptions made for the purpose of the projections are that:

♦ base interest rates will be brought down to an average of 10 per cent over the period from 1991 to 2010;

♦ North Sea oil and gas production will fall between 1990 and 2010, but this will be offset by higher prices; and

♦ world industrial production will continue rising, with Japan growing much faster than the OECD average in the first decade, but slowing down to nearer the average in the second decade to 2010.

It must be remembered that even the best econometric models are subject to a number of important limitations and uncertainties, and actual rates of growth may well turn out to be faster, or slower, than those in the forecasts. However, it must be stressed that the overall rate of growth forecast is believed to be fully in line with the analysis of past performance and with the various future developments expected; and the use of the model has the advantage of enabling the overall forecast to be disaggregated between economic categories, sectors, consumer product groups and so on in a way that is internally consistent.

The Cambridge Econometrics Projections

Projections for the economy to 2010 have been prepared by Cambridge Econometrics. The organisation was founded in 1978 to provide regular economic and industrial forecasts on a commercial basis. In addition to its own staff it has access to the academic resources of the Department of Applied Economics at Cambridge University.

Cambridge Econometrics publishes two reports a year which provide the most detailed economic and industrial forecasts available for the UK. The projections, which hitherto have gone to the year 2000, have now been extended to the year 2010 with a view to their use in the *Britain in 2010* study.

This report gives the projections to 2010 in outline form only. A much fuller account of the projections, including detailed breakdowns by economic sector and figures for individual years, are given in the Cambridge Econometrics' twice-yearly reports, which also give a fuller explanation of the forecasts and of the assumptions made for the projections. Copies of these reports can be obtained from

Cambridge Econometrics
21 St. Andrew's Street
Cambridge CB2 3AX.

The Cambridge Econometrics model

The projections are based on version 8 of the Cambridge Multisectoral Dynamic Model (MDM8) which is distinguished from other UK econometric models by its degree of disaggregation. With over 5,000 variables, it is the largest model of the UK economy available and, in addition to forecasts for macroeconomic aggregates such as Gross Domestic Product, it also provides forecasts for 43 different industries, 45 investment sectors and 68 categories of consumers' expenditure.

The model is designed to analyse and forecast changes in economic structure. To do this, it disaggregates industries, commodities and consumer and government expenditures, as well as foreign trade and investment; and the detailed variables are linked together in an accounting framework to ensure consistency and correct accounting balances in the model's projections and forecasts.

The model is a combination of orthodox time-series econometric relationships and cross-section input-output relationships. It forms aggregate demand in a Keynesian manner, with a consumption function and investment equations. The supply side comes in through the export and import equations, in which capacity utilisation affects trade performance as well as a set of projections for the paths of industry-level productivity growth.

A comprehensive account of the methodology used in the model is given in the book, *The Cambridge Multisectoral Dynamic Model*, edited by Terry Barker and William Peterson and published in 1988 by the Cambridge University Press (507 pages).

Forecasts of growth to 2010

The projections provide forecasts of likely growth between 1990 and 2010 both for gross domestic product as a whole and for its various component parts.[355]

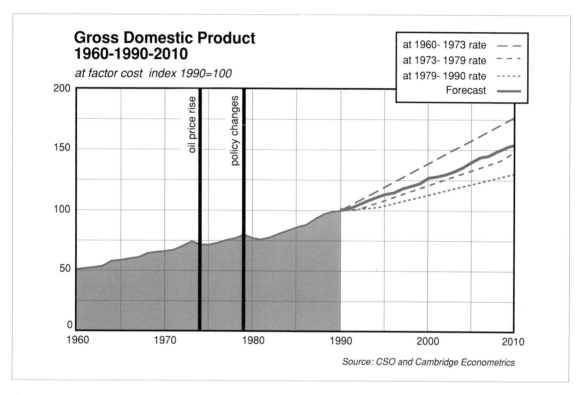

Gross Domestic Product 1960-1990-2010

at factor cost index 1990=100

at 1960- 1973 rate	— —
at 1973- 1979 rate	⁻ ⁻ ⁻
at 1979- 1990 rate	·····
Forecast	▬▬

Source: CSO and Cambridge Econometrics

Between 1990 and 2010 gross domestic product is forecast to increase by an average of about 2.3 per cent a year – marginally faster than in 1979-1990 – bringing a total increase of slightly more than a half.

Gross domestic product

On the combination of assumptions adopted, total GDP is projected to grow by an average of about 2.3 per cent a year in the twenty years to 2010. This is marginally faster than in the 1979-90 period, and substantially faster than in the 1973-79 period after the shock of the rises in oil prices, but it is considerable slower than was achieved in the earlier 1960-73 period.

It is forecast that by 2010 total GDP will be slightly more than *one half* greater than in 1990, compared with an increase of only about *one third* if output grew at the same rate as in the 1974-79 period, or an increase of about *three-quarters* if it grew at the faster rate of the 1960-73 period.

Changes in components of GDP

It is forecast that between 1990 and 2010 consumers' expenditure will grow more slowly than GDP (the reverse of 1970-90); government consumption will grow rather more slowly than GDP (as opposed to *much* more slowly in 1970-90); and gross fixed investment will grow more quickly than GDP. Partly because of the establishment of the Single European Market, both exports and imports are forecast to grow much more quickly than GDP, but exports substantially more than imports (the reverse of the pattern in 1970-90).

Changes in components of Gross Domestic Product
£bn at 1985 market prices

	1970	1970-1990	1990*	1990-2010**	2010**
Consumers' expenditure	156	+118 (+76%)	274	+127 (+46%)	401
Government consumption	56	+22 (+39%)	78	+36 (+46%)	114
Fixed investment	52	+26 (+50%)	78	+50 (+64%)	128
+ Exports	57	+70 (+123%)	127	+154 (+121%)	281
- Imports	57	+82 (+144%)	139	+134 (+96%)	273
Gross domestic product	266	+152 (+57%)	418	+233 (+56%)	651

* Estimate
** Projection

Sectoral changes

In the two decades to 2010 the output of all the main sectors is forecast to increase (in terms of constant prices), but some more rapidly than others. Manufacturing's share of the total, which declined from 41 per cent in 1970 to 34 per cent in 1990 is forecast to recover to 37 per cent in 2010, reflecting in part higher export sales with more favourable exchange rates.

The share of non-government services, which doubled between 1970 and 1990, is forecast to continue to increase, but less rapidly, from 17 per cent of the total in 1990 to 21 per cent in 2010, and the share of transport and communications is also expected to grow a little. Other sectors, while growing absolutely, are forecast to account for reduced shares of the total.

Within the manufacturing sector the most spectacular increase is expected again to be in the electronics industry, the output of which rose from £6bn (in terms of 1985 prices) in 1970 to about £20bn in 1990 and is forecast to rise further to more than £50bn by 2010, when it will be the largest of all the manufacturing industries in terms of value of gross output.

Other disproportionate increases in output are forecast in vehicles, paper and printing, and rubber and plastics.

Outside manufacturing, the most marked increases in value of output are forecast in communications, banking, insurance and business services.

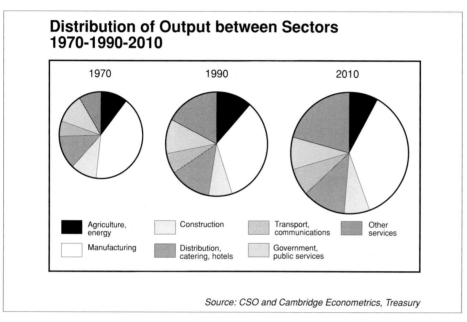

Distribution of Output between Sectors 1970-1990-2010

Source: CSO and Cambridge Econometrics, Treasury

Between 1990 and 2010 output is forecast to increase in all sectors; but agriculture, distribution and government services will account for a reduced proportion of the total, and manufacturing, communications and other services for an increased proportion.

Imports and exports

Exports of goods and services, which grew by an average of 3.4 per cent a year between 1979 and 1990, are projected to grow by an average of about 5 per cent a year in the five years to 1995 and by an average of about 3.5-4 per cent a year in the remainder of the period to 2010. Imports, on the other hand, which grew by an average of 4.8 per cent a year between 1979 and 1990, are projected to increase by an average of only about 3.5-4 per cent a year in the 1990s, and by an average of about 3-3.5 per cent a year in the period 2000-2010.

As a result of these differential rates of increase the deficit in the overseas balance is projected to be eliminated around the turn of the century. Subsequently both exports and imports will be growing at a rate much faster than GDP, with the result that over the two decades 1990 to 2010 exports will increase their share of GDP from 30 per cent to 43 per cent and imports from 33 per cent to 42 per cent.

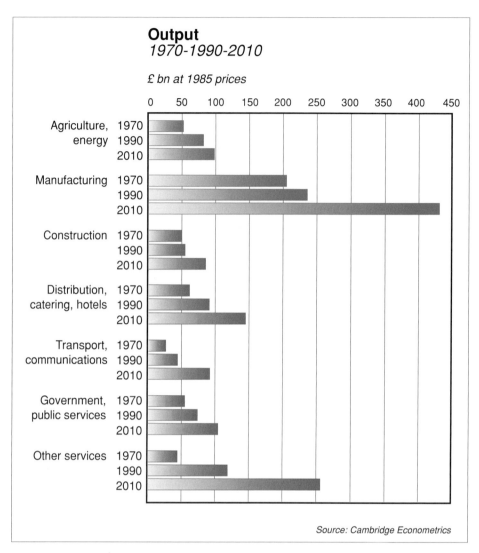

Output
1970-1990-2010

£ bn at 1985 prices

Source: Cambridge Econometrics

Growth in output is forecast to be strongest over the next twenty years in manufacturing and in private sector services.

Investment

The increase in the level of investment has varied greatly in the past, from an increase of more than 3 per cent a year (slightly more than the rate of increase in GDP) in the 1960-73 period, to almost no increase at all in the 1974-79 period, to about 1.5 per cent a year (in line with GDP) in 1980-85, and finally an average increase of about 9 per cent a year (far more than the increase in GDP) in the 1987-89 period.

Investment is projected to increase at an average of about 2.5 per cent a year (slightly faster than the rate of increase of GDP) over the two decades to 2010.

Most of the fixed investment in the future, as in the past, will be in the private sector; but with much investment needed for the renewal of

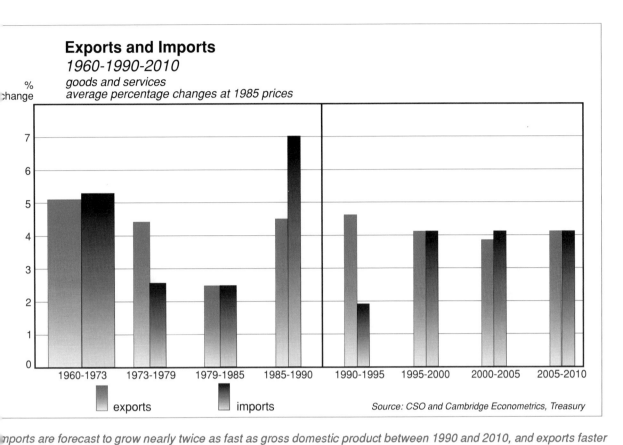

Exports and Imports
1960-1990-2010
goods and services
average percentage changes at 1985 prices

exports   imports   *Source: CSO and Cambridge Econometrics, Treasury*

imports are forecast to grow nearly twice as fast as gross domestic product between 1990 and 2010, and exports faster still to pay for the imports and clear the overseas payments deficit. Imports' share of gross domestic product, which rose from 21 per cent in1970 to 33 per cent in 1990, is forecast to rise further to 42 per cent in 2010.

infrastructure, it is expected that there will be increases in some categories of government investment also, particularly between 2000 and 2010.

Government consumption

In the 1980-85 period increases in government consumption were kept below the rate of increase in GDP, and in the 1986-89 period they were held down to about one quarter of the rate of increase in GDP. In the next ten years it is expected that public desires for improved services will lead to a somewhat faster increase in government spending on current consumption, and in the remainder of the period to 2010 it is expected that government consumption will rise more or less in line with GDP.

Consumers' expenditure

Consumers' expenditure grew roughly in line with GDP in the 1960-73 and 1974-79 periods, but rather faster than GDP in the 1980-85 period and

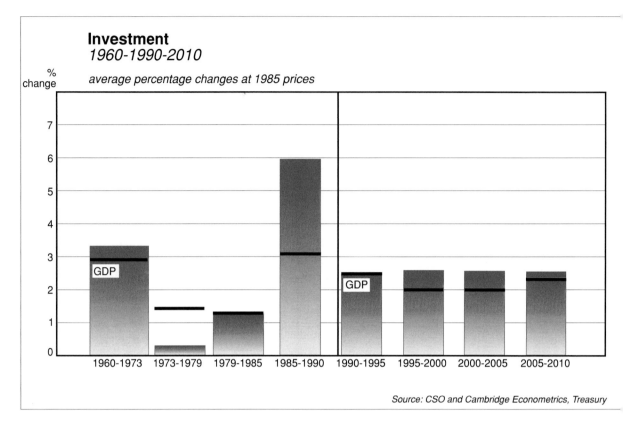

Investment
1960-1990-2010

%
change   *average percentage changes at 1985 prices*

Source: CSO and Cambridge Econometrics, Treasury

Investment, which was rising at a much faster rate than gross domestic product in the late 1980s, is forecast to rise on, slightly faster than GDP in the period to 2010.

one-and-a-half times as fast as GDP in the 1986-89 period. However, this latter rate of increase was not sustainable, and in the next two decades consumers' expenditure is projected to grow at an average rate of just under 2 per cent a year, slightly more slowly than GDP, in order to make room for higher exports, more investment and more government expenditure. Despite this slower rate of increase, total consumers' expenditure is forecast to increase by a total of *nearly one half* by 2010. The ways in which this increased expenditure is forecast to be spent are considered in Chapter 17.

Implications

There is no reason to believe that there has yet been a significant change in the strength of the British economy, and it is therefore unrealistic to expect economic growth to be markedly more rapid in the next two decades than in the past two.

The 'post-industrial society', in which services and, in particular, information processing are the keys to wealth creation, is unlikely to emerge over the period. Certainly, the manufacturing sector is much smaller than the service sector and employment in it will continue to decline as a result of rising productivity. However, the value of its output will *rise* and its importance will be vital. For we can no longer rely on large net earnings from North Sea oil or invisibles, and increased exports of manufactures will therefore be essential to pay for the imports expected by 2010 to grow to the equivalent of more than 40 per cent of GDP.

Hence manufacturing, which has, in general, been getting less competitive internationally, will need to be strengthened. Key factors in this will be higher investment, particularly in R&D, and improvements in technology transfer and in education and training. If assumptions in the forecasts are exceeded, the economy should grow faster.

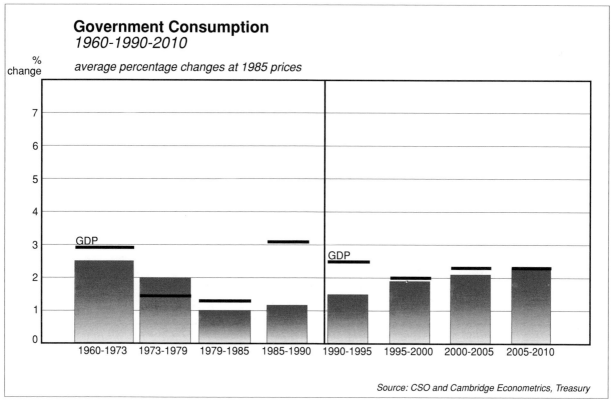

Government Consumption
1960-1990-2010

% change   *average percentage changes at 1985 prices*

Source: CSO and Cambridge Econometrics, Treasury

Government consumption was held down to less than half the rate of growth of gross domestic product in the late 1980s, but is forecast to recover to around the same rate as GDP in the course of the 1990s.

Even if, on the assumptions used for the projections, the pace of economic growth is not greatly different in the next two decades from what it was in the previous two, the cumulative effects will still be considerable, with total output increasing by about one half. This will make possible significant increases in consumers' expenditure and changes in life-styles. These are considered in the next chapter.

There are two major considerations not allowed for in the forecasts that may affect the outcome. One is the *ending of the Cold War*. The projections are based on the cautious assumption that defence expenditure remains at the current level in real terms (ie that it does not rise in line with economic growth). By 2010 this may be expected to bring savings of somewhere in the region of £10bn a year.

If it proves feasible to make real *reductions* in defence expenditure, then further large savings will be possible. If, for example, defence expenditure is reduced to *half* the current level, the total saving of around £20bn a year will be of the same order of magnitude as the *total* level of government expenditure today on health and education. The long-term impact on other areas could therefore be considerable, although it must be remembered that there will of course be time-lags and problems of various kinds in shifting resources to new uses.

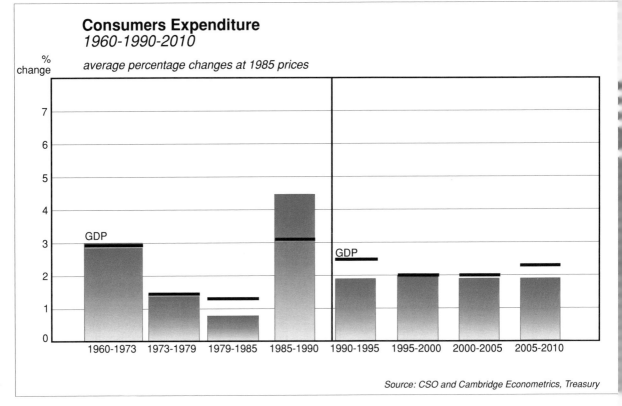

Consumers Expenditure
1960-1990-2010

% change

average percentage changes at 1985 prices

Source: CSO and Cambridge Econometrics, Treasury

Consumers' expenditure was allowed to rise substantially faster than gross domestic product in the 1979-1990 period. In the period to 2010 it is forecast to rise at a rate slightly below that of GDP.

The other major development for which no allowance has been made in the main projections is *global warming*. If targets are set for substantial reductions in emissions of greenhouse gases and new measures such as carbon taxes are introduced (as now seems likely in the course of the next decade) this will not necessarily require a serious slowing down in the pace of economic growth, as measured by GDP, but it *will* require major changes, not only in the energy sector itself, but also throughout the economy, particularly in transport and the more energy-intensive industrial activities. Some of the possible implications of this are outlined in Chapter 18.

BRITAIN in 2010

Life in

Britain in 2010

17. **L**ife in Britain in 2010

How will Britain change over the next 20 years? How will people live and what kind of society will we have by 2010? What changes will there be in how we work and the ways we spend our leisure time; in our homes and in the wider environment in which we live; in what we eat and how we dress; in family relationships and social life; in health and social care; in the underlying attitudes and values of society?

There are many factors affecting changes in each of these areas, and most of them are subject to major uncertainties. Nevertheless, it is possible to make forecasts reliable enough to provide a useful picture of what it is realistic to expect.

The following section describes the various different kinds of indicator used to get a view of likely future developments; and the section after it sets out the general context of life in Britain in 2010 that has emerged from the analysis in earlier chapters on population, employment, the environment, science and technology and the economy. The remaining sections set out what these imply for different aspects of life in Britain in 2010: work, incomes, homes, food and clothes, leisure and recreation, health and social care, families and friends, attitudes and values.

Indicators of future developments

The forecasts for life in Britain in 2010 are drawn partly from inferences from a number of different kinds of indicator.

Trends

In some areas past trends have been used to provide a first indication of possible future developments, subject to allowance for changes in the factors that have given rise to the past trends and for new factors that may change them in the future.

Predictive models

A more sophisticated approach is the use of mathematical models that produce projections for the future on the basis of measured relationships between relevant variables in past periods and stated assumptions about future variations. The Cambridge Econometrics model of the economy, one of the leaders in its field, is used to provide macroeconomic forecasts, including projections of consumers' expenditure. Independent forecasts for the economy, including consumers' spending on different categories of products and services, were prepared by PSI and taken into the Cambridge model so that, by an iterative process, agreed figures were arrived at which are consistent with the economic forecasts in other areas.

Attitudes

Opinion polls, surveys and other studies of current attitudes and changes in attitudes have been drawn on where they provide useful indications of likely future developments: sometimes the aspiration of today becomes the actuality of tomorrow.

Social example

More than a century ago, in the United States, de Tocqueville observed that what the few do today the many will do tomorrow; and subsequently in many other countries also it has been found that the life-styles and attitudes of the better-off groups in a society in one period can often be a good indicator of what will become the norm for the majority of the population when they become similarly well-off later.

International example

Similar phenomena are also often in evidence on an international scale, with many of the consumption patterns and other characteristics shown by people in the most economically advanced countries being replicated subsequently by people in other countries when their economies reach a similar level of development. However, there are important differences between the most economically advanced countries: in some areas the United States may give useful indications of what to expect in Britain in twenty years' time; in others Sweden or Germany may be a better guide.

Policies

In some areas outcomes are heavily influenced by government policy decisions. The aim has been to base the findings in this chapter on the policies considered most likely to be adopted, and in Chapter 18 to consider three different scenarios designed to illustrate some of the consequences of adopting different policy approaches.

Context

While these general indicators can provide some useful insights into what life could be like in 2010, this needs to be seen in the context of the analysis of probable developments in particular areas (outlined in previous chapters) which provide a structure within which changes in individual behaviour and social patterns will take place.

International context

The international developments over the next two decades which are most important in their effects on Britain are likely to be:

- the changes in the Soviet Union and Eastern Europe, which are bringing the Cold War to an end, reducing international tensions and releasing for other purposes many of the resources previously devoted to defence;

- the threat of global warming, which is likely to give rise to increasing concern and to changes in the pattern of economic development in response internationally agreed targets;

- the continuing integration of the world economy, which will mean that economic development in Britain is increasingly linked to that of other countries;

- closer economic union in Western Europe, which will involve integration of the British economy, closer political links and some convergence of environmental and social policies.

Population

Population projections, although subject to uncertainty, are more reliable than most other forecasts and have important implications in many other areas. The main demographic changes expected by 2010 are:

- total population is forecast to increase by about 2.6 million (4.5 per cent), compared with about 1.8 million in the previous two decades;

- the total change will not in itself be large enough to make much difference, but there is likely to be increased crowding in some areas due to population movements from North to South and from the conurbations to country areas;

- the total number of children in 2010 is expected to be about the same as now, but with fewer infants and more older children;

- the recent fall in the number of teenagers (15-19) will not continue much further, and by 2010 numbers are likely to have recovered to slightly above the present level;

- the number of young adults (20-34) will fall by about 2.4 million (one sixth), but this will be offset by greater numbers in the older working age groups;

- the number of people aged 65-79 will not change greatly, but the number over 80 will increase by about 600,000;

- the population in 2010 will reflect the results of two decades with more inward migration from European Community countries in Southern Europe and/or outward migration of skilled workers and professional people to countries in Northern Europe. There is also the prospect of inward migration from Hong Kong.

Employment

Changes in employment are more uncertain and more dependent on government policies. The main changes expected are:

- the number of young people (aged 16-24) in the workforce will not change greatly if the proportion staying in education or training to the age of 18 remains the same; but if the proportion is doubled (as it probably needs to be), the number of young people in the labour force will fall by 25-30 per cent;

- the number of young adults aged 25-34 in the workforce will fall by around 15 per cent, and the number of older people aged over 65 in the workforce will fall by about a half; but numbers in the main working age groups will increase substantially;

- changes in attitudes, in age structure and in numbers with small children will bring more women into the labour market, but the increase is likely to be smaller than in the two decades 1970-90;

- economic growth is expected to generate an increase in total potential jobs slightly greater than the expected increase in the prospective workforce, implying a fall in the level of unemployment to below 1 million. However, there is considerable uncertainty about this, with the outcome depending largely on macroeconomic and regional policies, policies for education and training, the age for pension entitlements and the competitiveness of the economy;

- employment in manufacturing and agriculture is expected to continue to decline, but this will be slightly more than offset by increases in the service sector;

- there will continue to be a strong increase in professional jobs and in jobs needing high skill levels, particularly in relation to new technologies, and a decline in employment opportunities for unskilled manual labour;

- there will be a continuing tendency for employment to move from North to South, and for manufacturing to move from urban sites to suburban ones, but both tendencies may be moderated by regional and environmental policies aimed at reducing congestion and housing pressures in the South East;

- there is likely to be increased movement, both temporary and permanent, of British people to jobs in continental Europe and of continental Europeans to jobs in Britain.

Environment

Concerns about environmental problems, and government actions in response to them, will bring important changes by 2010.

- The introduction of the Single European Market will give added impetus to the movement south of employment and people, increasing the congestion problems of the Greater London area. The opening of the Channel

Tunnel and associated high speed train links on the continent will accentuate this unless complemented by the extension of high speed links beyond London to other parts of Britain.

♦ The movement of population out of the conurbations, changes in agriculture, rising car ownership and increases in open air recreational activities will combine to put increasing pressures on the countryside.

♦ Giant new out-of-town shopping and leisure complexes, if plans go ahead, will pose major problems for existing city centres; for this reason the balance of probability is that policies will aim instead for rejuvenated city centres served by improved public transport systems such as light rail networks.

♦ Worsening traffic congestion and air pollution in cities has already led to compulsory fitting of catalytic converters to exhausts of all new cars from 1993, and is likely to lead also to higher taxes on large cars and company cars, more restricted parking, charges for use of central area roads, greater priority for buses, mini-buses, shared cars and cycles, and other measures designed to check the rise in use of private cars in cities.

♦ Greatly increased investment in public transport is likely by 2010 to show results in the form of improved facilities, particularly in better rail access to city centres.

♦ Substantial house building is likely in order to make good deficiencies in the housing stock (more than 3 million houses are in poor condition, one third of them classed as 'unsuitable for human habitation'); to provide for higher standards; and to meet the needs of the additional 2 million households expected by 2010.

♦ The proportion of homes owned by their occupants, which rose from 49 per cent in 1971 to 69 per cent in 1987, is likely to rise further, but it is expected that about one quarter of all households will continue to need rented accommodation.

♦ Commitments to improve the purity of drinking water supplies and to end sea dumping of untreated sewage will require heavy investment over the two decades, the costs of which are likely to be met, in the main, by higher charges to householders.

- Commitments to reduce air pollution will involve a combination of fitting expensive cleaning plant to coal-fired power stations, using cleaner but costlier types of coal, and investing in new combined cycle gas-fired power stations, also to be financed by higher charges to consumers.

- Concern with air pollution and emissions of greenhouse gases is likely to stimulate more active development of renewable sources of power, probably also involving higher costs, at least initially; and there will be much more investment in energy conservation measures by industry, the public sector and households, some of which will result in lower costs.

- The threat of global warming is likely to bring increasingly tough action from the late 1990s to cut emissions of greenhouse gases, and by 2010 the measures imposed (such as carbon taxes) are likely to lead to *very* high prices for electricity, petrol, gas and heating oil, possibly coupled with other measures to restrict more directly the use of private cars and of energy for space heating.

Science and technology

Further progress in science and technology, particularly in the information technologies, will find a steadily widening range of applications.

- Continued rapid advances in semiconductor power and computer performance, combined with falling hardware costs, will further extend the use of IT-based equipment and systems in factory and office automation and a wide range of other applications in banking, shopping, transport, health, social care, education and training, and other areas.

- Parallel advances in telecommunications will bring greatly improved business links and the possibility of a wider range of entertainment and other services being brought into the home.

- Advances in biotechnology are likely to make possible improvements in food and drink processing, drugs and agricultural chemicals; while from the late 1990s genetic engineering will bring improved varieties of plants and livestock in agriculture and new ways of treating genetically-related diseases.

+ Further use of microelectronics and, increasingly, of new materials, will make possible major improvements in a wide variety of industrial and consumer products.

+ Environmental concerns will promote increased use of new technologies throughout industry. Moreover, they may stimulate increased take-up of IT in industry, in offices and in the home: for instance, tele-working and tele-shopping could be promoted by measures aimed at increasing the cost of private transport.

The economy

There is no sign that any fundamental strengthening of the economy has yet been achieved in Britain and there are a number of indications of continuing weakness. Even so, an average growth rate of about 2.3 per cent a year is forecast – marginally more than the 2.2 per cent average in 1979-90, and substantially more than the 1.4 per cent average in 1973-79, but still well below the 2.9 per cent average achieved in 1960-73. By 2010 the cumulative effects of two decades of economic development will be considerable.

+ Gross domestic product (the measure of total growth) will be slightly more than half as great again as now.

+ Total investment will be nearly two-thirds greater.

+ Total current spending by the government will be greater by nearly one half.

+ Exports will need to rise to more than double the present level in order to match the expected increase in imports, which by 2010 will be equivalent to more than 40 per cent of gross domestic product and two-thirds of total consumers' expenditure.

+ Total consumers' expenditure is expected to increase by nearly one half. The percentage increase will be less than two-thirds as great as in the previous two decades, but the absolute size of the increase will be slightly greater.

These various changes set a context from which many inferences can be drawn in order to provide a picture of what life may be like in Britain in 2010.

Work

Perhaps the most important thing about work in 2010 is that there will still be plenty of it. The forecast is that in two decades' time there will be between 3 and 4 million more jobs than now. The vision of an automated economy, with almost all the work done by intelligent machines, and the main human problem being what to do with all the extra leisure, will not come true. This is because, even in manufacturing, the overall job displacement due to the use of new technology has been relatively small so far and is likely to remain so in the future; and in many of the activities in the service sector the scope for automation is much more limited.

In theory the productivity increases achieved by using new technology and other means, which are forecast to bring an *increase* in output of more than 50 per cent by 2010, could instead be used to produce the *same* output and allow more *leisure* – say, a 3½ day week, or an extra 15 weeks a year in holidays, or retirement at 50. In practice, however, this is most unlikely to happen. In the past much the greater part of the yield from higher productivity has been used to get increased output and higher consumption rather than less work and more leisure; and this has been the experience, not only in Britain, but also in other industrialised countries, including countries that have reached living standards substantially higher than ours. So, barring a near catastrophic change in environmental circumstances, or a fundamental change in attitudes, it seems unlikely that there will be a marked shift in favour of leisure in the future.

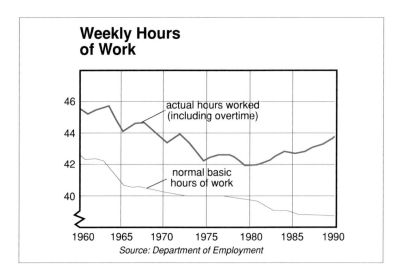

Weekly Hours of Work

actual hours worked (including overtime)

normal basic hours of work

Source: Department of Employment

Hours of work are likely to continue to become shorter, and holidays longer - but only gradually so. As in previous periods, it is likely that the bulk of the fruits of rising productivity will be taken in pay rather than leisure.

However, it *is* likely that there will be *some* reduction in the time spent on paid work. Over a long period, in Britain and in other countries, there has been a tendency for weekly hours of work to get shorter, for annual holidays to get longer, and for retirement to get earlier. For example, it has been estimated that between 1961 and 1983 the average time per day spent in paid work by everyone in Britain over 14 (excluding the unemployed) fell by about 13 per cent;[356] between 1961 and 1988 average normal basic hours of work per week for manual workers fell from 43 to 39;[357] and over the same period paid annual holiday entitlements rose on average from two weeks to four.[357]

International Labour Office figures show a similar gradual decline in weekly hours of work in other industrial countries. In 1987 average hours of work per week for male workers in the European Community countries as a whole were about 3 hours fewer than in Britain.[358] In some of the richer countries the difference was greater – 4 hours fewer in France and Italy, 5 in Belgium, 6 in Denmark and 7 in the Netherlands.

However, the decline in hours of work for men has been largely offset by an increase in the proportion of women in jobs; and the decline in basic hours of work in manual jobs has been largely offset by the longer hours commonly worked by many of the people in professional, scientific and managerial jobs and the increasing proportion of people in these occupations.

Thus some fall in basic weekly hours of work is likely to accompany greater future prosperity in Britain, but this may be offset by the longer hours worked in many higher level occupations and the increasing proportions of people in them. There is also likely to be some increase in annual holidays, which at present are shorter in Britain than in richer countries such as France and West Germany. A lowering of the existing national insurance pension ages is unlikely, however, since demographic changes will anyway pose problems for financing pensions at the present starting ages; but there may well be widespread departure from the present norm of complete retirement at a fixed age in favour of more flexible arrangements, with some people taking part-pension at earlier ages and continuing for a period with part-time or casual work, sometimes in a new occupation.

More important than changes in the *amount* of work in 2010 will be changes in the *kinds* of work that are done. There will be a continuing decline in unskilled manual jobs and a continuing increase in non-manual jobs, particularly in higher level professional, scientific, technical, managerial, administrative and entrepreneurial occupations. Across the whole range of jobs there is likely to be a steady rise in the formal qualifications required and in the general knowledge and abilities expected. There will be an increasing premium on training and retraining (and on the educational background to benefit from them) so as to acquire higher levels of skills, multiple skills, and successions of skills in the course of a career involving different kinds of work and rapidly changing methods.

New technologies, particularly information technologies, while not abolishing work, will certainly continue to change it. Professionals and executives will have access to much greater quantities of information and will need to be able to use it to best effect; office workers will need to be able to operate increasingly sophisticated equipment and systems; and factory workers will need to be able to supervise and control increasingly automated production processes. The ability to use computer-based systems (but not necessarily to design, make or repair them, or write programs for them) will become an essential requirement for an increasing proportion of jobs – and hence the lack of these skills may become a significant cause of unemployment.

New technologies will not only demand new skills, they will also change working conditions and job satisfaction – on the whole, for the better. A succession of surveys has shown that, in general, new technology has been favourably received by the workers directly affected by it,[128,132,134,136] and part of the reason is that managers and workers agree that in general it has not only required more skill, but has also brought more responsibility and variety.[134,136] Similarly in the future, the jobs using new technology will mostly be less than idyllic, but they will tend to have advantages in being quieter, cleaner, safer and less physically onerous than the jobs they replace, while offering the potential of greater job satisfaction through more interest and challenge and more dispersed control and responsibility.

Computer-based systems and telecommunications links will also open up increased possibilities for tele-working – operating a console from the living room or the garden and avoiding the cost, time, stress (and greenhouse gas emissions) involved in commuting journeys. There is a limited amount of tele-working already and some further increases are likely in the future – mainly from the kinds of people who work this way already, particularly computer professionals who are also mothers with young children.

However, many high-tech tele-workers at present appear to suffer isolation, stress and impairment of career progress, and take up tele-working more from necessity than preference. The balance of advantage may change in the future if commuting journeys become more difficult or expensive because environmental concerns have led to restrictions on private car use. Tele-working may then become more common, at least for part of the working week. However, social considerations and convenience are likely to limit the spread of tele-working, even in the jobs where it is in principle practicable; there is no question of it ever becoming the norm, even by 2010, whatever the advances in technology, for the simple reason that the great majority of jobs will continue to be of kinds that could not conceivably be done at a distance.

Another important way in which work is likely to change by 2010 is in the human relations involved. In industry, new management techniques, such as Just-in-Time and Total Quality Control systems require more active, intelligent and motivated participation by the whole work force, as do also some of the new IT systems, and many of the new methods used in service-sector activities. This is likely to lead to top-down hierarchic systems being superseded in an increasing number of organisations by a more participatory, collaborative, consensus style of industrial relations management, such as is already practised in many

Japanese companies and in a number of high-tech companies in the United States.[359] For many people, therefore, work in 2010 is likely to entail more positive involvement than it does today.

Two other developments likely to continue are the increases in sub-contracting and in self-employment. The total number of people self-employed rose from 2 million in 1971 to over 3 million in 1990, and the number self-employed in 2010 is likely to be substantially greater still.

Incomes

Gross domestic product is forecast to grow over the next two decades at roughly the same rate as in the past decade, and personal incomes may therefore be expected to grow broadly in line with it – but at a somewhat slower rate than in recent years because of the need to devote more of GDP to exports and investment.

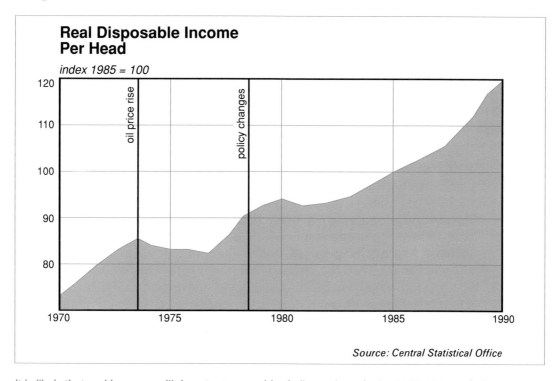

Real Disposable Income Per Head

index 1985 = 100

Source: Central Statistical Office

It is likely that real incomes will rise at rates roughly similar to those in the 1979-1990 period.

Earnings

Wages and salaries accounted for about three-quarters of all household income in most years between 1960 and 1975, but their share has since fallen to 62 per cent in 1988, and this gradual downward tendency seems likely to continue.[360] Similarly, there is likely to be a continuation of the slow rise in the proportion of total household income accounted for by self-employment (up from 5.5 per cent in 1980 to 10.4 per cent in 1988); and in the rise in the share of private pensions (up from 2.6 per cent in 1980 to 4.4 per cent in 1988); and in the imputed income from rent-free occupancy of property as a result of further increases in owner occupancy. Finally, the proportion of income from social security payments, which rose from 8 per cent in 1965 to a peak of 15 per cent in 1983 as a result of high unemployment, may be expected to continue to be affected greatly by changes in the level of unemployment.

Less likely to be sustained, however, is the recent trend in the distribution of earnings. In the 1970s the spread of earnings was fairly steady, with the bottom decile of earnings about 60-65 per cent of the median and the top decile of earnings about 140-150 per cent of the median; but in the 1980s the spread has widened markedly – the bottom decile of earnings has fallen from 66 per cent of the median in 1979 to 59 per cent of the median in 1989, and the top decile has risen from 157 per cent of the median in 1979 to 180 per cent of the median in 1989.[361]

It can be calculated that, if these trends were continued for a further two decades, by 2010 the bottom decile would have fallen to only about 46 per cent of the median and the top decile would have risen to about 237 per cent of the median. Thus the top decile, which was 2.4 times as great as the bottom decile in 1979 and 3.1 times as great in 1989 would have become more than 5 times as great in 2010.

A doubling of the gap between the top decile and the bottom decile of earnings in the space of 30 years would be more likely to be acceptable if it were seen as a necessary condition for securing much faster economic growth, and if the achievement of this faster growth made possible a rapid rise in the lowest tenth of earnings despite its falling share of the total. However, in the past decade the widening spread in earnings has *not* been associated with any dramatic improvement in economic performance; and it can be calculated that, if the trends of the past decade were continued for the next two decades, by 2010 median earnings would increase by about a half, and the top decile would nearly double, but the bottom decile would increase by only 17 per cent; and if economic growth turned out to be slower than forecast, the lowest tenth might get no increase at all.

Traditionally in Britain taxes have been related to ability to pay, and social benefits have been related to people's needs. Their combined effect is therefore to moderate the spread between high and low incomes. While the net overall effect of the tax and benefits system is still 'progressive' in this sense, it has been made less so than previously by the cumulative effects of a number of changes: the shift from direct taxes to VAT; the reduction in the upper rates of income tax; the introduction of the flat-rate community charge; and the linking of many social benefits to the cost of living index, so that they do not go up, as before, in line with earnings.

The full combined effect of these changes on the distribution of net disposable incomes over the past decade is not known because an analysis of the data covering the full range of incomes has not yet been made. However, figures already published by the Department of Social Security show that between 1979 and 1987: the average of all incomes increased by 23 per cent; the average of the upper half of incomes increased by 40.9 per

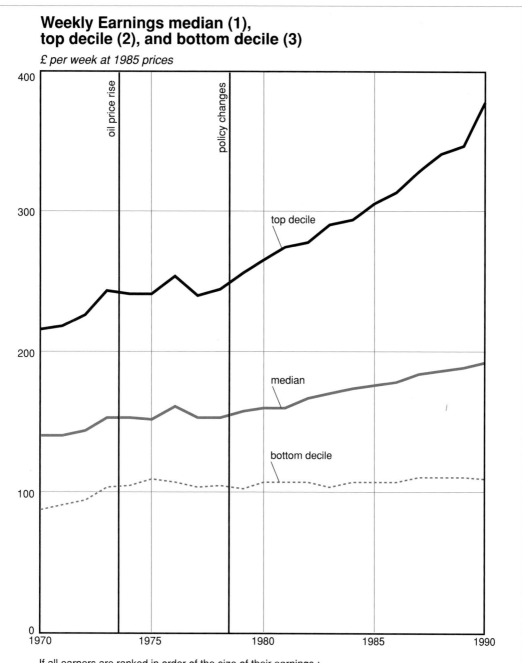

**Weekly Earnings median (1),
top decile (2), and bottom decile (3)**

£ per week at 1985 prices

oil price rise

policy changes

top decile

median

bottom decile

1970   1975   1980   1985   1990

If all earners are ranked in order of the size of their earnings :

1. the median earnings are those of the middle earner (the one
    with equal numbers of earners earning less and earning more)

2. the top decile is the one ranked 10% below the top one
    (i.e. 10% of earners are earning more and 90% of earners are earning less)

3. the bottom decile is the one ranked 10% above the bottom one
    (i.e. 10% of earners are earning less and 90% of earners are earning more)

Source: Department of Energy

*Between 1990 and 2010 gross domestic product is forecast to increase by an average of about 2.3 per cent a
year – marginally faster than in 1979-1990 – bringing a total increase of slightly more than a half.*

cent; the average of the lower half of incomes increased by 5.3 per cent; and the increase of the fifth percentile* was 0.1 per cent.[362]

One consequence of this is that, despite the substantial *rise* in average prosperity between 1979 and 1987, the percentage of adults with incomes (after housing costs) below half the average doubled (from 9.4 per cent of the total to 19.4 per cent), and the proportion of children in households with incomes below half the national average also doubled (from 12.2 per cent to 25.7 per cent).[362] There have also been other signs of increasing poverty in some of the poorest groups in the population – worsening nutrition standards, the rise in the number of homeless families,[202] and the visible increase in the numbers begging in the streets and sleeping rough.

It can be calculated that, if these trends in differential income increases continued for the next two decades, by 2010 average incomes would be 2.25 times 1979 levels; the upper half of incomes would be 3.75 times 1979 levels; the lower half of incomes would be one quarter above 1979 levels; and the fifth percentile* would have an increase of less than half of 1 per cent.

It would seem reasonable to expect that a continuation of such a widening gap in incomes would lead to more widespread poverty, increasing social tensions and movements of public opinion in favour of a less unequal distribution of incomes; and, while it is possible for elections to be won on quite different issues or with the support of the better-off majority without regard to the less favoured minority, it would seem improbable that these 1980s trends will continue through the next two decades, and more likely that they will be moderated, halted, or perhaps to some degree reversed.

Social benefits

The changes in the pattern of earnings have important implications for the future of social benefits. The Beveridge proposals for social security formulated during the last war envisaged a universal system of benefits to cover the main categories of need, such as old age and unemployment, supplemented by special arrangements, subject to evidence of need, for the small minority of people who might fall through the net by not being included in one of the general categories.

During the 1970s, however, increasing numbers of people became dependent on the means-tested benefits because the universal ones were not high enough to meet their needs; and in the 1980s it became policy to reduce the cost of the universal benefits by linking them to the index of retail prices instead of the index of earnings, thereby freezing their value in real terms and preventing them from rising with the general increase in

---

* If all earners are ranked in the order of the size of their earnings, the *fifth percentile* is the one ranked 5 per cent above the bottom one.

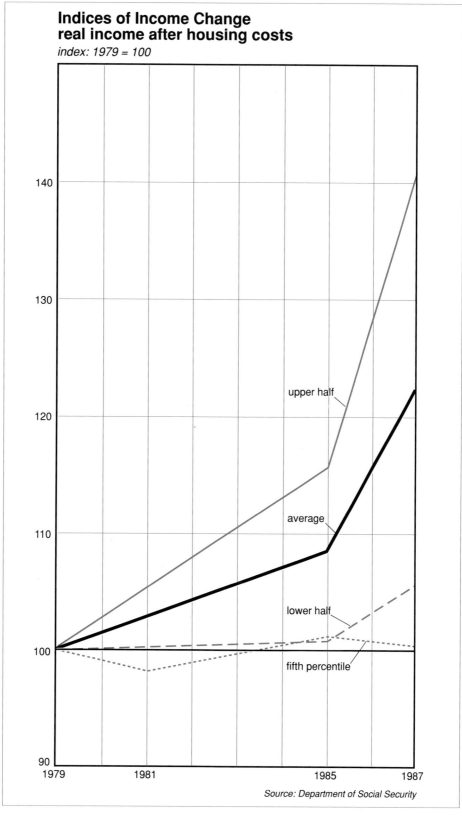

**Indices of Income Change
real income after housing costs**

index: 1979 = 100

upper half

average

lower half

fifth percentile

140

130

120

110

100

90

1979   1981   1985   1987

Source: Department of Social Security

Between 1979 and 1987 income increases were:
upper half of incomes   +40.9 per cent
average of all incomes   +23.1 per cent
lower half of incomes   +5.3 per cent
fifth percentile   +0.1 per cent

It seems improbable that a distribution in which the upper half increase their incomes seven times as fast as the lower half, and the poorest get no increase at all, will be capable of being maintained for a further two decades.

incomes. Instead, greater reliance has been placed on the range of benefits available only on application and subject to evidence of need, the aim being to economise on the £55bn or more being spent each year on social security and to 'target' the money on those in greatest need.

This approach has given rise to a number of problems. First, because of the stigma and difficulties involved in making claims, take-up of the means-tested benefits has been incomplete: for example, in 1985 only 48 per cent of those eligible for Family Income Support actually claimed it, compared with virtually 100 per cent take-up for child benefit and retirement pensions.[363] Second, levels of benefit have had to be kept low in order to keep them below wage levels, so as to leave people with an incentive to seek paid employment. And third, despite this, the scaling down and withdrawal of benefits in response to earnings means that those who take up jobs can face loss of benefit equivalent to more than 90 per cent of their marginal earnings, a rate of 'tax' on earnings far higher than was faced by people on very high incomes before the removal of the highest rates of income tax.

In consequence, many people have been caught in a 'poverty trap' from which it is difficult to escape into significantly higher standards, and they therefore tend to stay in a more or less permanent state of dependency and to place a continuing burden on the social security funds.

If the trend towards a wider spread of earnings were to continue, the relative fall in the level of earnings at the bottom would present an increasingly insoluble dilemma: either benefits would have to be set at levels so low that those living on them would not only be in relative poverty, in the sense of being unable to share in the same kind of life as the rest of the community, but would in many cases suffer severe hardship, with risks to the physical health of children and elderly people; or else benefits would rise into the range of lower earnings, in which case many people would no longer derive any financial benefit from getting a job, or from saving, and there would be an increasingly large underclass of people permanently trapped in long-term dependency.

The various difficulties in relying on a policy of 'targeted' means-tested benefits, in particular, the incompatibility with the aim of getting people out of a 'dependency culture', suggest that in the coming two decades there may well be some reversion to the use of universal benefits, rising with average earnings – in particular, child benefit, which can help cover the costs of bringing up children without at the same time reducing work incentives for their parents.

Some shift of emphasis back to universal benefits would put Britain more into line with other European Community countries such as France, Germany and Italy. It would also involve substantially higher insurance contributions or taxes.

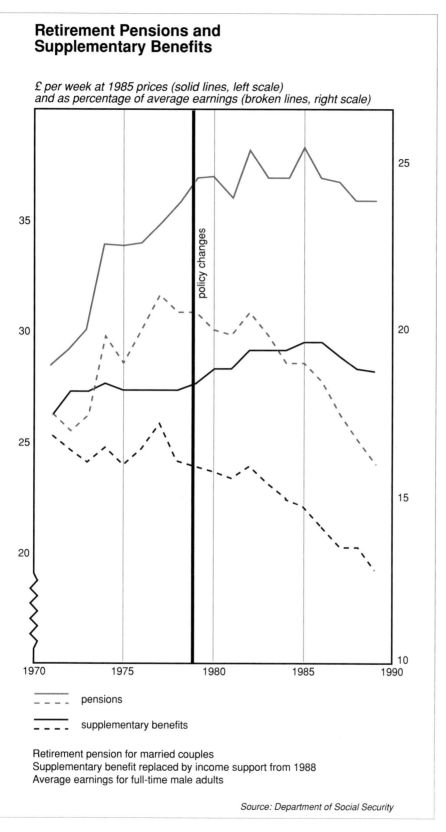

Retirement Pensions and Supplementary Benefits

*£ per week at 1985 prices (solid lines, left scale)
and as percentage of average earnings (broken lines, right scale)*

policy changes

| | pensions |
| | supplementary benefits |

Retirement pension for married couples
Supplementary benefit replaced by income support from 1988
Average earnings for full-time male adults

Source: Department of Social Security

In the 1970s supplementary benefits tended to rise roughly in line with national average earnings, and pensions by rather more than average earnings. After 1979 both were tied to the cost of living index (ie frozen in real terms) and since then they have fallen increasingly behind the rise in average incomes.

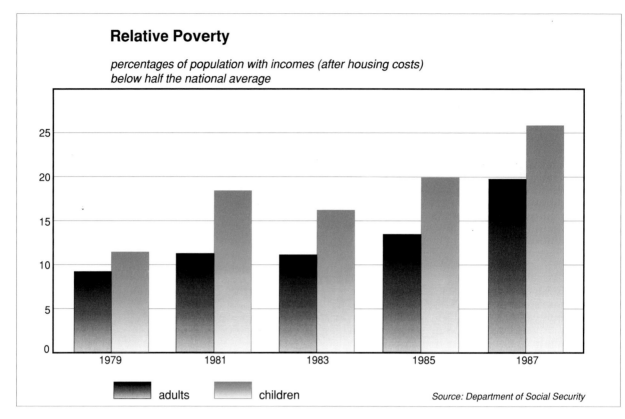

Relative Poverty

percentages of population with incomes (after housing costs) below half the national average

adults   children

Source: Department of Social Security

Between 1979 and 1987 the number of adults living in poverty has doubled, and so has the number of children. One quarter of all children are now in households with incomes below half the national average.

Pensions

The largest number of incomes after wages and salaries, and the largest category of expenditure in social security, is retirement pensions. There are a number of considerations which may bring changes in them by 2010:

- the number of people aged over 60 will increase by about 1.3 million (11 per cent) by 2010;

- the number of people at work will increase by a similar percentage if the numbers over 16 in full-time education and training remain unchanged;

- however, the number of people at work will increase by far less if the proportions staying on in education or training after 16 double (as they need to);

◆ in the decades after 2010 the ratio of workers to prospective pensioners will worsen substantially;

◆ this implies that, at some stage, either pension levels will have to fall relative to earnings, or the age of entitlement will have to be raised, or the contributions of those at work will have to be increased.

For whatever is done in the way of changes between public and private provision, or between funded schemes and pay-as-you-go ones, at any one time there is only a given total of goods and services being produced by those at work, and hence an increase in the number of pensioners relative to the number of people at work implies a decrease in the level of each retirement pension, unless measures are taken to get higher contributions from those at work or to reduce the number of prospective pensioners by raising the age, or changing the conditions, of eligibility.

In response to this problem a number of changes have been made in national insurance pensions, which between 1961 and 1979 rose by rather more than average earnings, but which have subsequently been raised only in line with prices, with the result that between 1979 and 1989 their real value was frozen and their relative value dropped from 20.4 per cent of average earnings to 16.2 per cent. At the same time occupational pensions and individual pensions with insurance companies have been encouraged. These will eventually provide pensions which will go up roughly in line with individual earnings, but which will have been funded by contributions which have also gone up in line with earnings.

If these changes were to persist over the next two decades, the effect would be to make the basic pension much lower, relative to earnings and to private pensions, to increase the proportion of people dependent on supplementary income support, and to undermine incentives for individual saving or insurance.

Accordingly, it seems likely that in the coming two decades further changes will be made, designed to ensure that everyone shares in rising national prosperity when he or she retires. This will imply some increase in contributions from those still at work and/or an *increase*, not a decrease, in the age of entitlement to a full pension – possibly a phased increase to 70 for both women and men – to reflect the fact that people are now living longer and staying fit and healthy for longer also.

It is possible that a new, more varied and flexible, pattern will be developed, with some people working on to 70 and then retiring on a full pension *higher* relative to previous earnings than they would get at 60 or 65 now, while others may choose to take *partial* retirement at an earlier age, supplementing a *lower* level of pension with earnings from continuing casual or part-time employment, possibly with a different employer, in a new occupation, or on a self-employed basis. No doubt there will be much to be learned from countries such as Sweden which already have more flexible schemes.

Homes

Although the rate of new housebuilding declined during the past two decades, housing standards in Britain have been improving: for example, between 1971 and 1987 the proportion of dwellings without sole use of a bath or shower fell from 12 per cent to 2 per cent; the proportion without sole use of an inside toilet from 15 per cent to 2 per cent; and the proportion without central heating from 65 per cent to 28 per cent.[199] There is no reason to doubt that standards will continue to improve over the period to 2010.

Throughout the postwar period housing has received substantial government support in the form, for example, of tax reliefs, grants and rent subsidies. However, in the past decade council house tenants have had rent increases, owner-occupiers have had higher mortgage interest rates, and have seen the value of tax reliefs eroded by inflation, while there have also been increases in payments on rates and community charges. In consequence, these costs have been rising faster than the general rate of inflation.[364]

Despite these rising costs, many people have attached a high priority to having bigger, better and, in some cases, second homes and have been ready to spend more of their rising incomes to get them. They have also been spending more on maintenance, repairs and insurance, and spending on do-it-yourself goods has trebled in real terms since 1970. These preferences seem likely to continue over the next two decades.

In consequence, housing's share of total consumers' expenditure, which increased from 12 per cent of the total in 1970 to 15 per cent in 1990, is forecast to rise further to 18 per cent of the total in 2010.

With energy for heating, lighting and power, which accounts at present for a further 3.5 per cent of total consumers' expenditure (over 13 per cent in the households with the lowest tenth of incomes), the main change over the past three decades has been the drop in spending on coal from £4.1bn in 1960 to only £0.7bn in 1990 (in terms of 1985 prices), with a corresponding increase in use of gas. While the increase in consumption has been small in volume, the gain in terms of comfort, convenience and clean air has been considerable. Over the next two decades, apart from a further drop in the use of coal, with an offsetting increase in gas, little further change in domestic energy consumption is expected – although this forecast may need substantial modification if the policy response to global warming brings much higher prices for energy and more investment in effective insulation of homes.

Over the past two decades the insides of people's homes have been improved through substantial spending on furniture, furnishings and floor coverings and this is forecast to continue over the next two decades. More spectacular has been the increase in major domestic appliances, spending on which more than trebled in real terms between 1970 and 1990. Spending on them is forecast to go on rising, although not quite so rapidly, to reach more than £9bn a year (in terms of 1985 prices) by 2010.

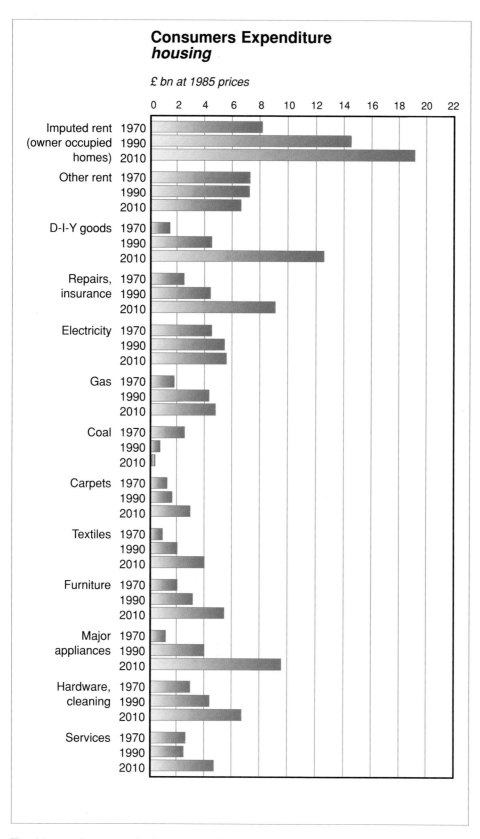

Consumers Expenditure
housing

£ bn at 1985 prices

The biggest increases in home spending are forecast to be on do-it-yourself goods, appliances, insurance and mortgages.

Most households in Britain already have refrigerators, freezers, washing machines and vacuum cleaners. Only a minority have microwave ovens, tumble driers, dishwashers or kitchen waste units, and there is likely to be some increase in ownership of these. There is also the possibility that new kinds of appliances will be developed and come into widespread use in the early years of the next century. It seems more likely, however, that higher spending on major domestic appliances will take the form mostly of going up-market into larger, higher performance or better quality models of existing types of appliance.

The outside appearance of people's homes is likely to change less than the inside. Buildings tend to have a long life and at least five out of every six houses and flats that people will be living in 2010 have been built already; and most of the new ones will use current designs and materials.

More visually striking than changes in residential neighbourhoods are likely to be changes in shopping areas. There will be a number of major new out-of-town shopping complexes, occupying large new sites and offering not only a wide range of shops but also a variety of leisure amenities and other services designed to turn shopping into a recreational experience for the whole family. If there are many of them, they are likely to undermine the viability of existing shopping areas, giving city centres a run-down, abandoned feel. More probably, however, the number of new out-of-town complexes will be restricted on grounds of over-dependence on access by car and the emphasis will be placed on improving existing city centres. This is likely to take the form of better access by public transport, greatly enlarged pedestrian precincts, streets glassed over to provide weather-proof shopping malls and, where sites can be made available, the construction of new shopping complexes in city centres.

Food and clothing

There are limits to how much people can eat and drink and consequently, as incomes go up, food and drink tend to account for a diminishing proportion of people's total spending. There is also a tendency, as people become more affluent, to move up-market to more expensive foods and drinks; and in recent years there has been increasing concern to adopt healthier diets (which tend to include more of the dearer kinds of foods), more interest in organically-grown produce (also more expensive), and greater inclination to use manufactured convenience foods (possibly less healthy but also more expensive). However, these considerations, which seem likely to apply over the period to 2010, have not in the past been sufficient to cause spending on food and drink to rise in line with incomes, and seem unlikely to do so in the future. Consequently, total spending on food, drink and tobacco fell from about 33 per cent of total consumers' expenditure in 1970 to 21 per cent in 1990, and is forecast to fall further to 13 per cent in 2010.

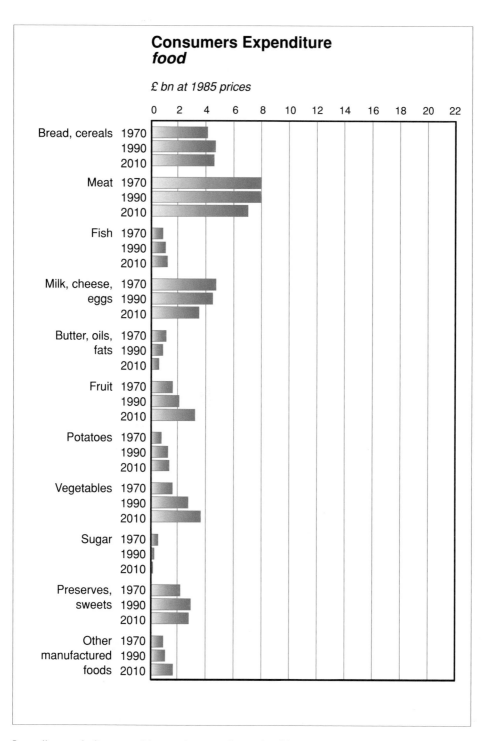

Consumers Expenditure
food

£ bn at 1985 prices

Spending on fruit, vegetables and convenience food is forecast to increase; but spending on meat, dairy products and sugar is forecast to decrease.

The changes in consumption have not been uniform across different kinds of food and drink. People have been consuming less milk, cheese, eggs, butter, oils, fats and sugar, and are forecast to consume less still of all of these in the future. On the other hand, they have been eating more potatoes, vegetables and fruit, and further increases in consumption of fruit and vegetables are forecast in the future. People are also expected to be eating more manufactured foods in 2010; in particular there is likely to be a continuing increase in consumption of convenience foods such as pre-prepared deep-frozen meals.

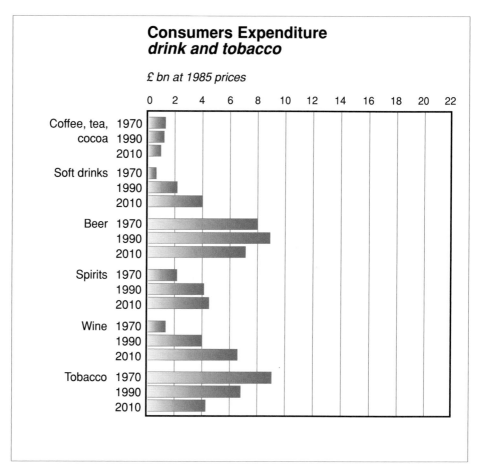

Consumers Expenditure
drink and tobacco

£ bn at 1985 prices

Consumption of wine and soft drinks is forecast to go on increasing, but consumption of beer to decline a little and of tobacco to fall by about a third.

In recent years people have been drinking more coffee but less tea. Consumption of the two together has fallen slightly over the past two decades and is forecast to fall rather more in the next two decades. Consumption of soft drinks, on the other hand, more than trebled between 1970 and 1990 and is forecast to rise by a further three-quarters by 2010.

Compared with 1970, people are now drinking slightly less beer but nearly twice as much spirits and more than three times as much wine – the result partly of changes in price differentials and partly of changes in tastes. By 2010 beer consumption is forecast to fall further, by about one fifth, but wine consumption is forecast to increase, by about two-thirds, mainly as a result of changes in tastes and lower duties in the Single European Market.

With greater awareness of the health hazards, consumption of cigarettes and tobacco fell sharply between 1970 and 1990 and is forecast to fall even more sharply in the period to 2010.

With clothing there is clearly greater scope for increases in consumption than there is with food, particularly when, with higher income levels, it becomes less a purchase of necessity and more one of fashion. In the course of the past two decades, stimulated by higher incomes (particularly, discretionary incomes of more fashion-oriented young people) and declining relative prices, consumption of men's clothes and of boots and shoes has nearly doubled and consumption of women's clothes has more than doubled.

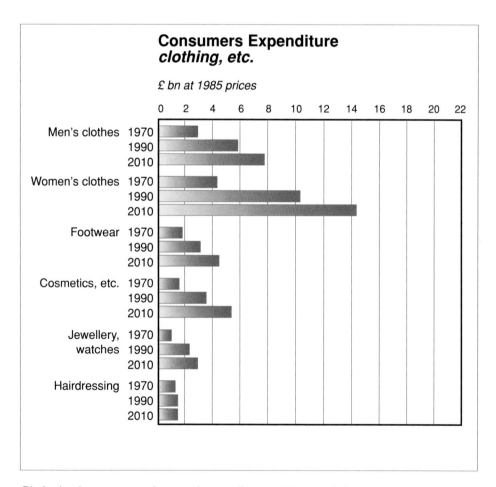

Big further increases are forecast in spending on clothes and shoes.

By 2010 it is expected that there will be some further fall in relative prices, but more of the teenagers are likely to be in school or full-time training (and so have less money to spend) and there will be fewer single people in their 20s with money to spend on fashion goods. Consequently, consumption of clothes and shoes is forecast to go on rising, but less rapidly, to about two-fifths more than the present level by 2010.

Between 1970 and 1990 spending on cosmetics and toilet articles and on jewellery and watches more than doubled (in real terms), but, for the same reasons as with clothes, a slower rate of increase is forecast to 2010. Increased use of hairdressers has been checked in the past two decades by the difficulty of keeping down costs in this very labour-intensive service, and similar considerations are likely to inhibit increased use in the next two decades.

Leisure and recreation

In Britain much the greater part of leisure time is spent in the home, and much the greater part of that, more than in all other domestic leisure activities combined, is spent watching television and listening to radio. On average people (aged 4 and over) watch television for 25 hours a week – people over 65 for 37 hours and even children of 4-15 for 20 hours – and in addition people listen to the radio for an average of 9 hours a week.[365] This is far more than in most other countries, a phenomenon variously attributed to the excellence of the television and radio programmes in Britain or to the lack of interest of the British in more physically or intellectually demanding activities.

In addition, half the households in the country have a video recorder, and hire between them more than 7 million video cassette tapes a week.[366] Listening to records or tapes is also one of the most popular domestic activities[200] and in 1988 sales of tape cassettes exceeded 80 million, of long-playing records, 50 million and of compact discs, 29 million[367] The total audience for opera on television rose in 1988 to 11 million.[368]

Over the past two decades sales of television sets and other audio/visual equipment have increased eight-fold to more than £4bn a year, while spending on licence fees, and on hire and repair charges, has reached £3bn; and spending on tapes, discs and other recreational goods has reached nearly £5bn.

In the course of the next two decades there will be an increase in the number of television and radio channels and the introduction of enhanced definition TV and large-screen high-definition television. These and other innovations may be expected to bring further increases in equipment sales, but are not likely to increase the number of hours a week spent on these pastimes.

Outside the home, there has been an increase in outings to tourist attractions of various kinds, a decline in attendance at most spectator sports (particularly football, though it remains much the most popular one), but an increase in participation in active recreations, such as walking and swimming, and in sport – spending on sports goods trebled between 1970 and 1990.[200,341,369]

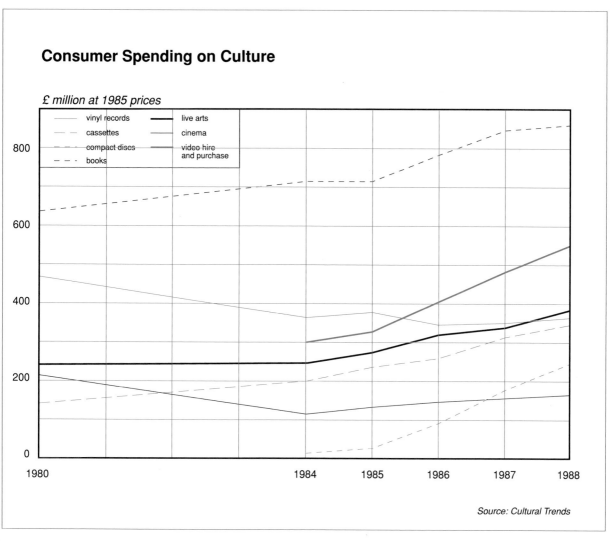

Consumer Spending on Culture

£ million at 1985 prices

Legend:
- vinyl records
- cassettes
- compact discs
- books
- live arts
- cinema
- video hire and purchase

Years: 1980, 1984, 1985, 1986, 1987, 1988

Source: Cultural Trends

Since 1980 spending on the live arts has increased by a half and on books by a third, but the strongest increases have been on videos, cassettes and compact disks.

However, the most common recreational activity is going out for a drink and the next most common one is going out for a meal. The biggest increases over the past two decades, in terms of what people spend on them, have been in eating out and holidays. Between 1970 and 1990 spending on meals out and holiday accommodation increased by more than 70 per cent and spending on travel abroad by more than 250 per cent – the two together accounting for about £28bn of consumers' expenditure

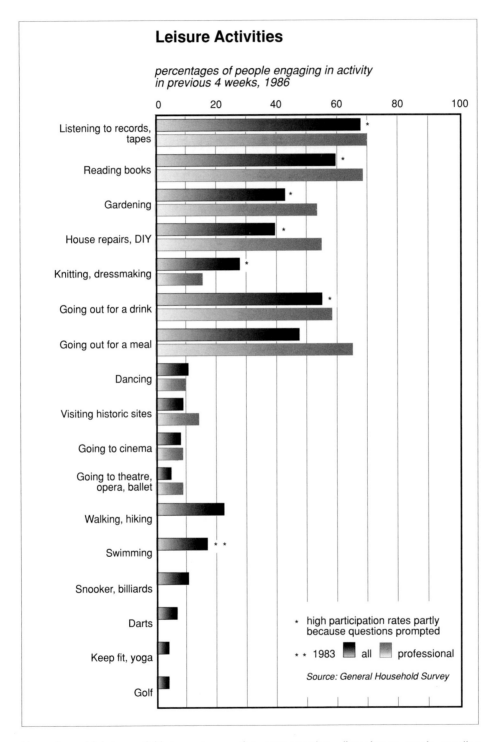

Leisure Activities

percentages of people engaging in activity in previous 4 weeks, 1986

Listening to records, tapes
Reading books
Gardening
House repairs, DIY
Knitting, dressmaking
Going out for a drink
Going out for a meal
Dancing
Visiting historic sites
Going to cinema
Going to theatre, opera, ballet
Walking, hiking
Swimming
Snooker, billiards
Darts
Keep fit, yoga
Golf

* high participation rates partly because questions prompted

** 1983   all   professional

Source: General Household Survey

Home-based leisure activities are among the most popular – listening to music, reading, gardening, do-it-yourself and watching television – also going out for a meal or a drink.

in 1990.[341] While these figures from the national income accounts include also meals in works canteens and travel by business people, it seems likely that the social and holiday part of them is greater than the spending on all other kinds of recreational activity combined.

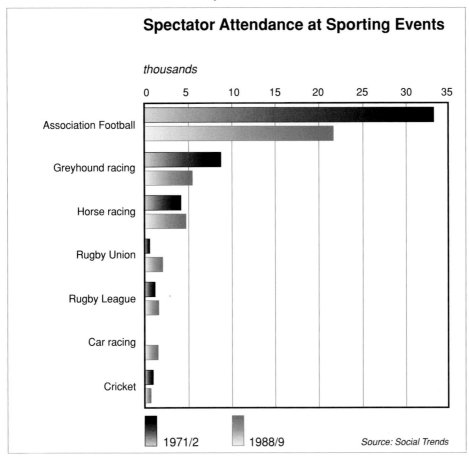

Spectator Attendance at Sporting Events

thousands

1971/2   1988/9   *Source: Social Trends*

Attendance at spectator sports has tended to decline over the past two decades. Attendance at football has fallen by a third, but it is still by far the most popular spectator sport.

There are three considerations that need to be borne in mind when interpreting what these changes in patterns of leisure may imply for the future. The first is that people in the higher-level occupations, although they tend to work longer and have less leisure time, paradoxically also tend to be more active in what they do outside working hours. The higher people's occupational status, their educational level and their income, the greater the number and variety of their leisure activities. They do more of almost everything from walking in the country to dining out in restaurants, from going to the theatre to visiting art galleries. In particular, they participate much more in active sports, including sailing, golf, tennis and squash. Higher-status occupations are associated with higher education, which predisposes people towards certain activities, and with higher incomes with which to indulge them.

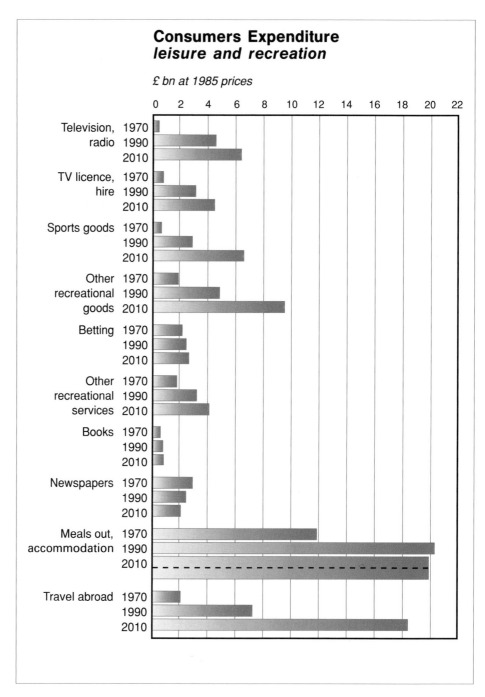

Consumers Expenditure
leisure and recreation

£ bn at 1985 prices

Still higher spending is forecast on television and sports and recreational goods, but these will be dwarfed by the massive increases in spending on meals out, hotels and foreign travel.

It may be supposed that, as more people will be in these occupations by 2010, more people are likely to acquire the interests and life-styles currently associated with them. There may thus be a disproportionate growth in the leisure activities particularly favoured by these groups, such as reading books, gardening and do-it-yourself hobbies; and, outside the home, going to concerts, theatres and art galleries, playing tennis and golf, dining out in restaurants and going on holidays abroad.

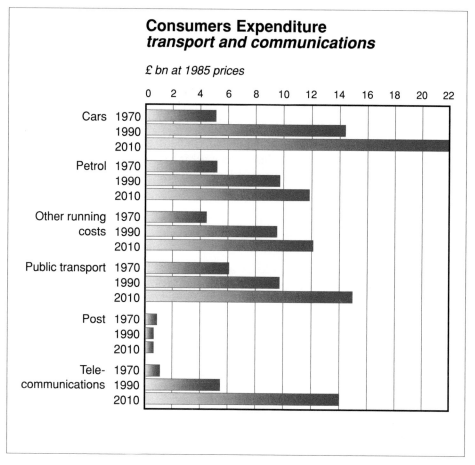

Consumers Expenditure
transport and communications

£ bn at 1985 prices

Considerable further increases in spending on cars is forecast; also on public transport and on telecommunications.

A second consideration is that demographic changes will mean that in 2010 there will be fewer people in their 20s, which will tend to check the growth of activities particularly favoured by younger people, such as dancing, and also the sports which require particular fitness, such as football and squash.

On the other hand, there will be more people in their 50s and 60s, on average probably fitter than people in these age groups today, with higher incomes, and possibly some of them in part-retirement, giving them more leisure time than when in full-time work but more income than when living wholly on a pension. This may give a stimulus to activities requiring a mix of time, money and fitness, such as sailing, golf and foreign travel.

The third consideration is that many of the recreational activities outside the home depend on access by car, and their popularity has been stimulated by the great increase in car ownership and use over the past two decades during which spending on motoring more than doubled, reaching more than £33bn (12 per cent of total consumers' expenditure) by 1990.[341] However, it is likely that in the coming two decades traffic congestion will get worse and the cost of private motoring will increase, and this will slow down the increase in car use. The effect may be to make access to some of these car-based activities more difficult and expensive and inhibit the expansion in them which would otherwise have occurred.

It is also possible that the response to the threat of global warming will include measures which make both air transport and private car use radically more expensive (see Chapter 18), thereby giving a stimulus to less energy-intensive leisure activities – ones which are home-based or can be reached on foot, by bicycle or by public transport.

Health and social care

Life expectancy at birth increased by about 3 years between 1951 and 1971, and by another 2.5 years between 1971 and 1985, and is expected by the

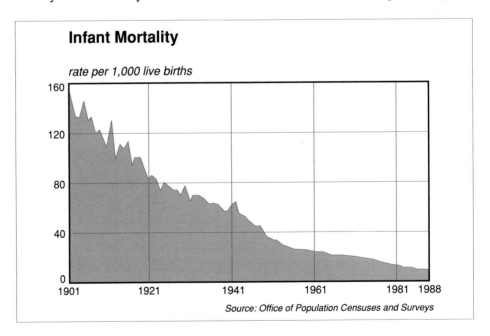

Infant mortality is now a tiny fraction of what it used to be, but rates are lower still in some other countries.

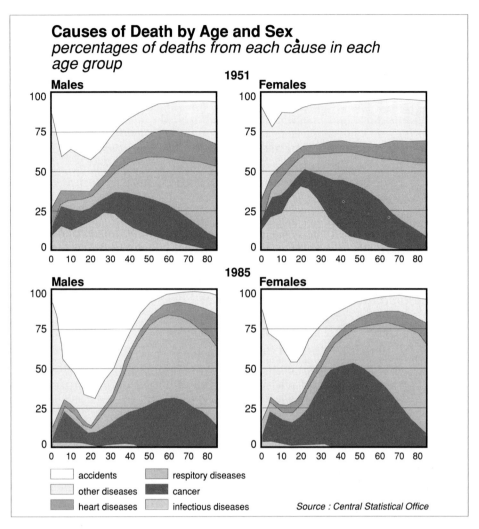

Causes of Death by Age and Sex
percentages of deaths from each cause in each age group

1951

Males / Females

1985

Males / Females

accidents
other diseases
heart diseases
respitory diseases
cancer
infectious diseases

Source : Central Statistical Office

Medicine has virtually eliminated the infectious diseases which used to kill many younger people, but cancer and heart disease are still big killers in later life.

Office of Population Censuses and Surveys to increase by a further 3 years by 2010. What does this imply in terms of better in 2010?

Past improvements in life expectancy have been achieved partly by improved nutrition, sanitation and general living conditions, and partly by improved medical care – in particular by reductions in the infant mortality rate (which has been cut by roughly one half every two decades in this century),[370] and by the virtual elimination of the infectious diseases which used to kill many people in early life.[371] As a result, accidents and violence have become the main cause of death up to about the age of 30.

The diseases which now kill the most people before old age are cancer and heart disease (and more recently AIDS). The incidence of these is strongly affected by personal behaviour, and it may well be that the abandonment of smoking and the adoption of healthier diets, safer sex, regular exercise and less stressful life styles will reduce their impact. But even if they do, there will remain many health conditions requiring treatment and care. There are a number of important developments in prospect in surgery, drugs, genetics and diagnostics.

Surgery

- Fibre-optics will be used to enable tubes to be passed into the body to remove gallstones and kidney stones, to remove obstructions in the bile duct, and to remove enlarged prostate glands.

- Lasers are already used in eye surgery, in the removal of skin blemishes and to clear airways blocked by lung cancer; possible future applications will be to treat lesions in the womb (as an alternative to hysterectomy) and to clear blocked coronary arteries (as an alternative to open coronary bypass surgery).

- Lithotripters are already being used to destroy kidney stones with high energy shockwaves (enabling patients to be discharged within 24 hours) and may in the future be used also for removing gallstones.

Drugs

A review published by the Association of the British Pharmaceutical Industry in 1988 claimed that a therapeutic revolution equivalent to that which occurred in the 1930s and 1940s is in prospect:

> a combination of... curative anti-cancer medicines, products to prevent the onset of Alzheimer's disease, malaria vaccines and effective anti-virals capable of controlling, if not curing, HIV infection could alter significantly the future course of human history.[372]

While claims for new drugs need to be treated with caution until they are fully tested, the drugs under development referred to include:

- targeted anti-cancer drugs which use monoclonal antibodies to attach to cancer cells before releasing the drug, thereby enabling treatment to be undertaken without serious side effects;

- drugs to treat Alzheimer's disease and other forms of dementia in old age;

- drugs for the prevention and treatment of heart disease;

- drugs for treatment or alleviation of psychiatric illnesses, including schizophrenia, anxiety and depression.

Genetic screening

The elucidation of the structure of DNA has led to 'a revolution in the biological sciences comparable to that in physics earlier this century'.[373]

One of the main applications of this new understanding to date has been to identify disorders in genes responsible for specific inherited diseases such as cystic fibrosis and sickle cell anaemia, in order to make possible pre-natal screening and diagnosis, with the possibility of abortion. Eventually, an understanding should be acquired of the genetic contribution to common illnesses such as heart disease, cancer and psychiatric disorders. Over the long term, gene therapy may become widely used in the treatment of inherited diseases, allowing modification of genes in non-reproductive cells.

Diagnostic services

Improvements in diagnostic techniques under development include:

- use of monoclonal antibodies and biosensors for diagnostic kits which can be used in hospital wards, outpatient clinics, GPs' surgeries, and even bought over the counter for use by patients in their own homes – already in use for pregnancy and fertility testing, and likely to be extended in the future for other purposes;

- computed tomography (CT) scanners, magnetic resonance imaging and positron emission tomography which allow a wider range of investigations to be undertaken than is possible with conventional X-rays – for example images of the brain and nervous tissue for investigating illnesses such as multiple sclerosis;

- computerisation of X-ray images, so that the picture can be made available instantly to a doctor in another part of the hospital (for example in outpatients), or in a different hospital or a GP's surgery.

Availability

Some of these new techniques are likely to *save* costs; but others will *add* to costs. Will they be affordable? They are not the only factor in costs. Much of the health service is involved in looking after chronic patients who need long-term, low-tech, labour-intensive care, offering little scope for economies. And demographic changes will not be helpful: in 2010 there will be half a million more people aged over 85; and people aged 85 and over cost the health service on average more than 13 times as much as people aged 5-64.[374] It has been estimated that the increased number of people over 85 will cost the health service an extra £400m a year by 2000, and more in later years,[375] although, if old people are fitter and healthier in 2010 than old people are now, it may be that the increase in medical attention needed will turn out to be less great than expected. Meanwhile, there have already been staff shortages, ward and theatre closures and long waiting lists for non-urgent treatments.

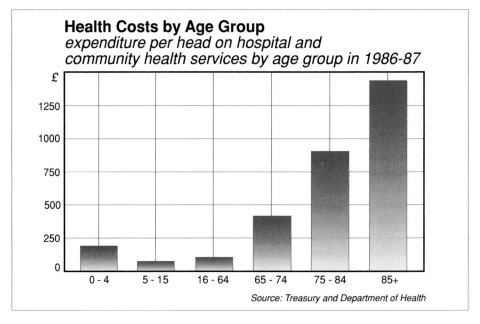

Health Costs by Age Group
expenditure per head on hospital and community health services by age group in 1986-87

Source: Treasury and Department of Health

People's health care gets more expensive as they get older. People over 85 cost the Health Service more than 13 times as much as people aged 5-64 – and the number of people over 85 will be 50 per cent greater in 2010.

Much has been done to try to improve efficiency and keep costs down in the health service. Between 1960 and 1985 the average length of stay of hospital in-patients in acute beds has been cut from 16.2 days to 7.7 days;[376] between 1964 and 1985 the number of patients treated per available bed has been doubled; and since 1970 the number of day cases has more than doubled.

Major changes in organisation are currently planned, but it will be a long time before their effects are known. However, a recent OECD study has shown that we spend a smaller proportion of GDP on health care in

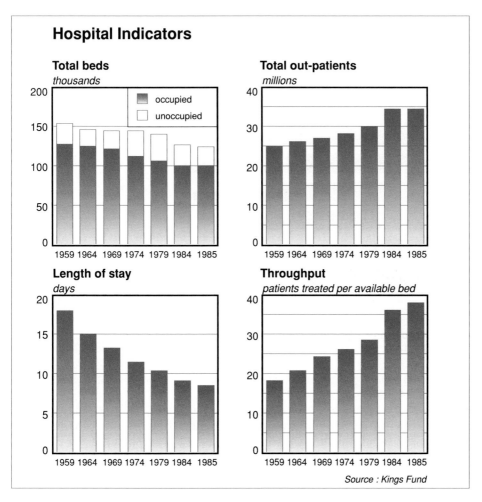

Hospital Indicators

More out-patients means fewer beds, and shorter stays mean faster throughput. Both save costs. But new drugs and high-tech equipment are often very expensive.

Britain than in any other major country[377] and, given the demographic shifts and the high costs of some of the new techniques, it is likely that in 2010 health care will be taking a larger share of national resources than now.

Social care

In terms of numbers, a greater problem than the people needing medical or nursing care will be those who have become too frail to look after themselves unaided and need care and support of one kind or another. The proportion of people needing this sort of care rises sharply with age, and by 2010 there will be half a million more people aged over 80. How will they be looked after?

Traditionally, for the great majority in need of it, this care and support has been provided by relatives, friends and neighbours, in

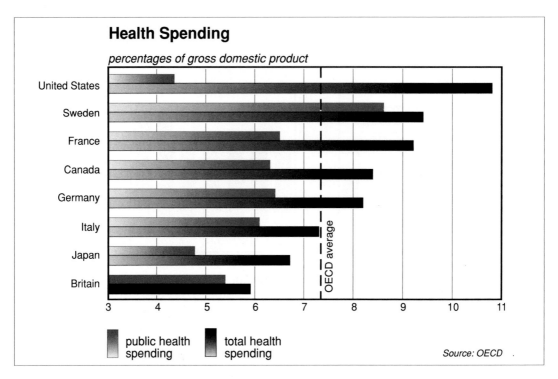

Health Spending

percentages of gross domestic product

In Britain both public health spending and total health spending (as a percentage of GDP) are below the levels in most other OECD countries.

particular by spouses and daughters. However, with rising rates of divorce, fewer people will have spouses when they become old; and with more women seeking and getting jobs, fewer old people will have children who are able and willing to devote themselves to looking after ageing parents. Thus there will be more old people needing looking after, but probably fewer people available to provide this care on an informal family basis.

It is likely that in 2010 people will not only be living longer, but also staying fit for longer so that they will not need care until a later age than they do now; and it must be remembered that an increase in the number of people over 80 even greater than the increase in prospect in the next two decades has already been accommodated in the previous two decades. Even so, the greater number of very old people may be expected to put further pressures on the nation's residential care facilities; and it is likely that, in the interests both of economy for the providers and of independence for the users, increasing emphasis will be placed on helping people remain in their own homes, by providing more help for informal carers and by improving services like home helps and meals-on-wheels.

An important contribution is likely to be made by the kinds of technical advance which have eased the burdens of housework over the past two decades – central heating, easy-care clothes, washing machines, vacuum cleaners, refrigerators, freezers, microwave ovens – and which will increasingly be used to make daily life easier for elderly people and their carers. There may also be new services intended specifically for old people, such as tele-shopping facilities and deliveries of deep-frozen convenience foods for easy heating in microwave ovens. New technology will also be used in security systems and alarms for summoning help in emergencies and in an increasingly wide range of devices to bring greater opportunities and independence to people with physical handicaps.

Family and social life

The nuclear family is still the basic social unit, but its characteristics have been changing and seem likely to change further by 2010.

Marriage is still a very popular institution and the marriage rate in Britain is the highest (along with Portugal) in the European Community.[358] However, the divorce rate has risen six-fold since 1961,[378] and it too is now one of the highest in the Community, second only to Denmark.[358] It has been calculated on the basis of marriages and divorces up to 1980 that about one in three of the 1979-80 marriages will end in divorce,[379] and more recent calculations suggest that for 1987 marriages the ratio has risen to four out of ten.[380] However, most divorced people remarry, and the proportion of all marriages in which one or both partners was previously divorced has risen from 9 per cent in 1961 to 33 per cent in 1988.[381]

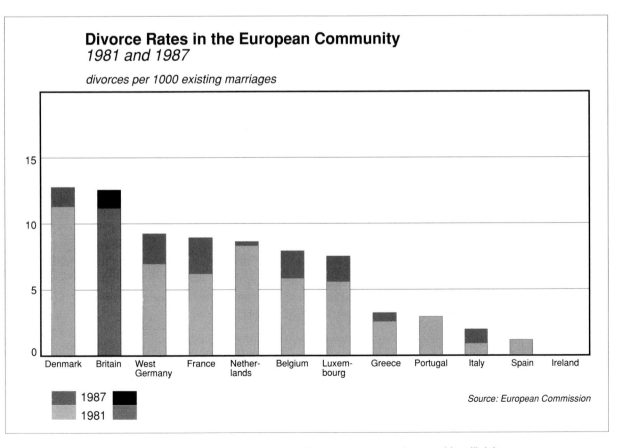

Divorce Rates in the European Community
1981 and 1987

divorces per 1000 existing marriages

1987
1981

Source: European Commission

Britain's divorce rate is almost the highest in the European Community – and is still rising.

The increase in divorce is partly explained by the greater ease of obtaining one following the 1969 Divorce Reform Act. However, it is also a consequence of fundamental changes in marriage relationships which have made divorce seem necessary to some couples. A 'symmetrical' marriage pattern has been developing, based on partnership in the home, on both partners working and on shared leisure. This kind of marriage is more demanding, and hence more vulnerable, than a traditional marriage with a rigid division of labour and with largely separate social networks.

Cohabitation without (or, frequently, in advance of) marrying has also been increasing – the proportion of 25-49 year old women cohabiting rose from 2.2 per cent in 1979 to 6.3 per cent in 1988; while for younger women aged 18-24 the proportion rose from 4.5 per cent to 12.4 per cent.[382] These figures show only those *currently* cohabiting. A recent survey has shown that about one third of couples married for five years or more, and no less than one half of those who had been married for less than five years, had lived together before marriage.[383] The increase in cohabiting is partly a reflection of more permissive attitudes to pre-marital sex, improved efficiency of contraception and the increasing economic independence of women.

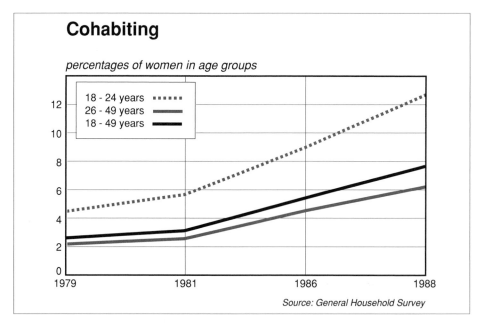

The percentage of women cohabiting has trebled since 1979. About half the couples now married for five years or less had lived together before marriage.

If these trends were to continue, by 2010 the majority of couples would cohabit before getting married and the majority of marriages would end in divorce, followed by remarriage. Certainly, some further increase in both cohabiting and divorce seems likely, but the rate of increase in both will probably slow down considerably.

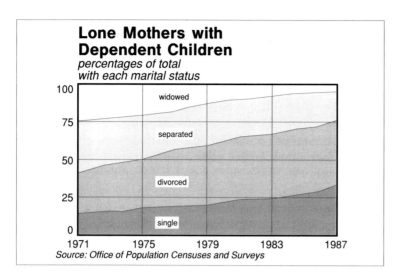

The number of lone-parent families with dependent children has increased from 8 per cent of the total in 1971 to 14 per cent in 1987. 29 per cent of them are single and 63 per cent separated or divorced

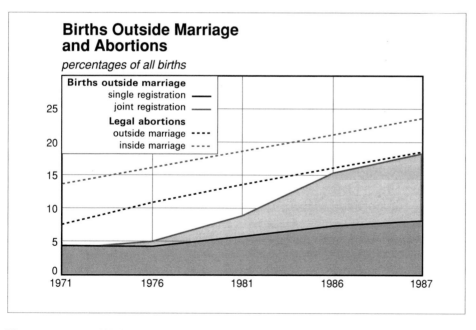

The percentage of births outside marriage has trebled since 1971, and abortions have also risen – there are now two abortions to every three births outside marriage. If recent trends continued, all births would be outside marriage well before 2010.

Increased divorce and cohabitation have led to an increase in the number of lone-parent families with dependent children from 8 per cent of the total in 1971 to nearly 14 per cent in 1987.[381] The proportion of lone mothers with dependent children who are divorced or separated has increased from 53 per cent of the total in 1971 to 63 per cent in 1987, and the proportion who are single has increased from 16 per cent to 29 per cent.[381]

The proportion of births outside marriage, which in the 1950s was around 5 per cent, rose to 7.6 per cent in 1971 and has recently risen more sharply to 25 per cent in 1988 – with a parallel increase of two abortions for every three births outside marriage.[381] If the 1981-88 trend were continued, *all* births would be outside marriage well before 2010.

However, such a continued increase is highly improbable and it would anyway be a mistake to see the increases in births outside marriage and in lone-parent families as indicators of reckless irresponsibility and breakdown in child care arrangements. Seventy per cent of the births outside marriage (accounting for the bulk of the increase) have been registered by both parents, implying a sense of continuing joint responsibility; and with 71 per cent of these the mother and father gave the same address, implying that at least half the children born outside marriage had parents who were living together in a potentially stable union.[381]

Similarly, lone parenthood is most commonly a temporary condition following separation or divorce, followed later by remarriage and renewal of two-parent status.

All this represents a fundamental change in attitudes to marriage and the family. Marriage, or partnership outside marriage, is regarded less as a lifetime commitment than as a more flexible arrangement, which may be succeeded by another partnership. The changes make for more instability in partnerships than in the past, more anxiety, and much unhappiness for some people, particularly the children of estranged parents. But it does not necessarily mean that marriage has become less valued or less important to people. It is partly because people expect *more* from marriage, which is more equal and based on more shared activities, that they are more often disappointed and decide to break up and maybe try again.

With more single-parent families, fewer very large families, more young single people leaving their parents' home to live alone or with contemporary friends, and with more old people living alone or with spouses, between 1961 and 1988 the proportion of single-person households rose from 12 per cent of the total to 26 per cent, the proportion of large households with five or more people dropped from 16 per cent to 7 per cent, and the average household size declined from 3.1 to 2.5.[381] This trend to smaller average household size may be interrupted in the next few years when women of the 'baby boom' generation start their families, but in the longer term the trend towards smaller household size seems likely to continue. Some further fall in household size seems likely by 2010, implying that the number of dwellings will need to be increased by more than the expected increase in total population.

While the nuclear family of two people, with or without dependent children, will continue to be the norm in 2010, extended families will also continue to be important. In the 1950s a common pattern in urban areas was for two generations to live close together, with members, most often mother and married daughter, meeting each other almost daily for companionship and mutual aid.[384] About one household in eight still conforms to this pattern, more commonly in settled communities than in mobile ones, in the North than in the South, and in working-class families rather than in middle-class ones.

However, the emerging pattern is of the *dispersed extended family*. This is also based on ties between parents and married children, but living further apart, usually within an hour's drive of each other, meeting once or twice a month, telephoning often between visits, and providing company and help in day-to-day things and in times of crisis. This pattern, more common among middle-class families in the South-East, has already spread to cover about half the population and may be expected to become the predominant one over the next 20 years.[385,386]

While relatives will continue to play an important part in most people's lives, friends and neighbours will play an increasing role.[387] Most people in Britain know their neighbours and have friendly relationships with them, finding them useful sources of support, advice and companionship; and this is likely to continue. At the same time, middle-class patterns of friendship are spreading and seem likely to become the norm: large numbers of friends, geographically dispersed, loose-knit networks (relatively few of the friends know each other), with couples mostly having other couples as friends.

One characteristic of both dispersed extended families and friendship networks is that they depend heavily on the use of the family car. If private motoring becomes more difficult and expensive because of policy responses to global warming it will put some strains on this life style.

Social attitudes

Sometimes the best indicators of the developments of tomorrow are the attitudes of today. For the way that people perceive and feel about things and, in particular, changes in their aims and aspirations, can give insights into the kind of future they *want*, which in turn can be a major factor in shaping the future which actually happens.

There have been many surveys and opinion polls seeking to gauge the attitudes of people in Britain. Some of their findings are ambiguous - sometimes people will assent to two apparently incompatible propositions at once, and sometimes they will say one thing when what they intend is something other. Even so, such polls can often give clues to what is in store in the future.

Sex and permissiveness

Underlying the changes in marriage, divorce and cohabitation are changes in attitudes to sex. In some ways attitudes appear to have become less permissive than in the 1960s. The Social Attitudes Survey in 1987[388] found that 60 per cent of people thought that AIDS would cause more deaths in the next five years than any other single disease, 66 per cent thought that official warnings about AIDS should say that some sexual practices are morally wrong, and 74 per cent thought that homosexual relationships were always or mostly wrong (compared with 62 per cent in 1983). On the other hand, the proportion disapproving of pre-marital sex fell slightly to 25 per cent (compared with 28 per cent in 1983), the proportion favouring women being allowed abortion on demand rose to 54 per cent (compared with 37 per cent in 1983), and the proportion thinking the portrayal of sex in films and magazines had gone too far fell to 56 per cent (compared with 66 per cent in 1979).

Position of women

Surveys in 1983 and 1987 showed little increase in the proportion of household tasks done jointly or mainly by the man. In both surveys all the household tasks considered, except for household repairs and disciplining children, were done mainly by the woman, and only marginally less so even in homes where both partners had a full-time job. However, some possibility of gradual changes over the next 20 years was suggested by the fact that, of those married already, a much higher proportion of them thought they *should* be done jointly; while of those not yet married, an even higher proportion took this view.[389]

A survey in 1988[390] found that a majority of both men and women now see many jobs traditionally regarded as the preserve of one sex as being equally suitable for either. Three-quarters of the respondents in the survey said they supported the legislation against discrimination on grounds of sex at work, yet 54 per cent believed job opportunities to be worse for women, 66 per cent regarded women's pay as worse then men's (for comparable work), and 81 per cent reckoned women were less likely to be promoted than men – a conclusion found also in a number of other studies.[391,392,393] In general these results suggest a continuing shift in attitudes, towards greater participation and equal opportunity in work for women.

In the 1988 survey,[390] 89 per cent of respondents regarded being an MP as a job equally suitable for both men and women, and in the 1987 general election a record 41 women were elected, but the percentage of the total was still lower than in any other country in Western Europe except France and Greece.[394] This situation seems unlikely to change rapidly; but it is probable that the gradual increase in the number of women in prominent positions in public life will continue.

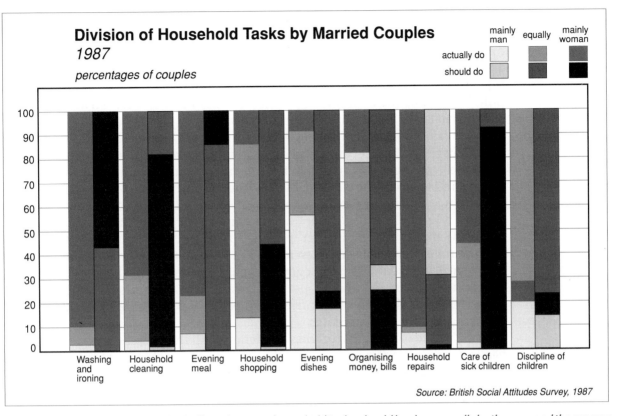

Division of Household Tasks by Married Couples

1987

percentages of couples

Source: British Social Attitudes Survey, 1987

An increasing proportion of couples believe that most household tasks should be done equally by the man and the woman. But with the great majority of couples it is still the woman who actually does most of the household tasks.

Environment

Interest in the environment has been increasing, with membership of organisations concerned with it exceeding 3 million in 1988 – more than four times the level in 1971.[395] A Department of Environment survey reported high and rising levels of concern about a wide range of environmental issues.[62] In a different survey, in 1989,[396] 73 per cent felt that government should give a higher priority to environment policy, even if it meant higher prices for some goods. However, in another poll in the same year[397] 62 per cent opposed any restriction on the use of private cars and 63 per cent favoured a heavy programme of road building.

Role of government

Over many years surveys have shown a general view in Britain that among the functions of government are the promotion of full employment, the control of inflation, the provision of health, education and other social services and the reduction of differences in income between rich and poor, but there have been shifts in the emphasis given to each.

A survey in 1983 found that 69 per cent of respondents thought the highest priority should be given to keeping down unemployment, as opposed to 27 per cent giving top priority to keeping down inflation; by 1986 the former majority had increased to 75 per cent against 20 per cent;[388] but in 1989, with unemployment down and inflation rising, an opinion poll[396] found 43 per cent giving priority to the control of inflation against 36 per cent to the reduction of unemployment.

In 1979 37 per cent favoured spending more on health, education and welfare services, even if that meant higher taxes, while 37 per cent favoured cutting taxes, even if that meant spending less on health, education and social services;[398] by 1987 the proportions had changed, 66 per cent wanting higher spending on services and only 11 per cent wanting tax cuts; while in 1989 two different polls showed majorities of 58 to 21 and 71 to 20 in favour of higher public spending.[396,399] International comparative surveys undertaken in 1985[390] found that the proportions of people in Britain wanting higher government spending on health, pensions and education (88, 75 and 75 per cent respectively) were substantially higher than in the other countries studied – West Germany, Austria, Australia and the United States.

Despite (or because of) dissatisfaction with the present state of the health service, the service has been the area most highly and consistently favoured for more public spending (followed by education and pensions) in a series of polls and surveys.[388,389,397,399]

International

In a recent poll,[397] 42 per cent believed Britain's influence in the world had declined over the past decade, as opposed to 31 per cent thinking it had increased. There was diminished enthusiasm for defence spending, overwhelming enthusiasm for President Gorbachev as the most outstanding world politician of the 1980s, but still a majority for retaining the British nuclear deterrent.

Forty-three per cent now expect there will be a United States of Europe before the end of the century, as against 37 per cent who do not; and 63 per cent think Britain should be part of a greater European confederation including Eastern Europe.

Review of the decade

In an opinion poll in 1989[400] 39 per cent said they felt better off at the end of the decade than at the beginning, and 40 per cent worse off; 47 per cent felt their quality of life had improved, against 27 per cent who felt it had declined. In another survey in 1989[401] reviewing the changes over the decade, 58 per cent said they believed over the previous ten years Britain had become more prosperous, but 84 per cent said we had become more arrogant, 78 per cent more selfish, 70 per cent less honest, 69 per cent less tolerant and 57 per cent less happy. To sum up, 55 per cent agreed with the proposition that the country was heading in the wrong direction and major changes were needed, while 35 per cent agreed with the proposition that the country was heading in the right direction with no major changes needed.

These attitudes are mixed, changing and at times contradictory; and they will not necessarily be reflected in voting in elections. Nevertheless, they suggest that some of the major changes of the past decade have been widely welcomed and are now accepted as fixed foundations from which to make further progress in the coming decades; but that others have been introduced against the grain of public opinion, have become less accepted with the passage of time, and may well be checked or reversed in the future.

Underlying many debates on policy in Britain are two sets of attitudes. One is individualistic, stressing the merits of initiative and self-reliance and the advantages for society stemming from the drive of enterprising individuals for self-advancement. The other is collectivist, emphasising the virtues of community mindedness and social concern and the advantages of public provision of common services. During the 1950s, 1960s and 1970s the balance of public opinion moved now towards one of these sets of attitudes, now towards the other, and government policies reflected these oscillations, but mostly within the bounds of a broad band of consensus around the middle of this spectrum of attitudes.

In the 1980s there was a break from this consensus approach, with a sharp and vigorous shift of policies towards the individualistic end of the spectrum. The evidence of attitude surveys and opinion polls suggests that public attitudes have not moved along with this change of direction and that there is a growing feeling that some policies have gone too far. It may therefore be inferred that in the course of the next two decades electoral pressures are likely to cause policies to move back towards the previous longstanding balance between individualistic and collectivist attitudes.

This tendency is likely to be reinforced by the increasing degree of involvement in the European Community where, despite sharper changes in individual countries, in the Community as a whole there has never yet been any prospect of an outright majority for policies reflecting either end of the spectrum, and policy decisions have normally reflected a compromise consensus around the middle.

In the next chapter we look at the economic implications of three broad approaches to policy which reflect different tendencies in social attitudes: individualistic, market-oriented policies; more collectivist and interventionist policies; and strategies reflecting strong concern for environmental protection and a shift in production and consumption patterns towards more 'sustainable' development.

BRITAIN in 2010

T *hree Scenarios*

Three Scenarios

Previous chapters have presented a 'most probable' view of Britain's development to 2010, analysing the various factors influencing events in order to arrive at the outcome which seems the most likely. However, there are many uncertainties in this, in particular in the areas where outcomes may be greatly affected by changes in government policies.

This chapter is different from the previous chapters in that it explores 'alternative scenarios' designed to illustrate some of the consequences of different policies. The scenarios are different in that they are illustrative of *hypothetical* policy changes, not *forecasts* of what is most likely to happen. In order to keep within a manageable length, it has been necessary to consider the alternative scenarios in broad-brush outline only; and, from the large number of possible combinations of policy, to select three 'bundles' of policies, each chosen to reflect the characteristic features of one of the main streams of policy aspirations.

Practical alternatives

Over much of this century differences in policy aspirations have been largely along the lines of the traditional 'left-right' political antithesis. On the 'right', policy aspirations have tended to reflect ideals and ideas associated with individual independence, self-reliance, private ownership, use of market forces, low taxation and the keeping of government activity and intervention to a minimum. On the 'left', aspirations have tended to reflect ideals and ideas associated with public ownership, social equality, better welfare services, higher taxes, and intervention by government to regulate the economy and provide social services. It has been an essentially bi-polar division, with alternating governments seeking to change things in one direction or the other along a single axis.

More recently, a third set of aspirations has emerged, reflecting ideals and ideas associated with the preservation and enhancement of the environment and concerned, for example, about air, land and water pollution, about global warming, about the ecology of the countryside and the preservation of species, and about noise and traffic and nuclear safety;

and these have generated a debate about alternative policies for addressing these issues – whether to rely on regulation, or on taxes, incentives or other market-based mechanisms. Concern about these kinds of issues is not necessarily incompatible with the two traditional sets of aspirations, and it is not at present given expression in Britain in the form of a major political party. Nevertheless, these concerns have become a distinct political force, tending to change the traditional bi-polar antithesis into a three-way pull of competing policy aspirations.

The aspirations of the idealists and ideologues in any political movement tend to be unlimited – and hence unrealistic. For, in practice, what can actually be done by any government, even over a period as long as a decade or two, is circumscribed by a number of practical constraints – for example, by the position it starts from, by administrative problems and inertia, and by the attitudes and actions of other countries. The area of serious political debate is therefore not normally about ultimate aims, but about what will be practicable in the constrained circumstances of the real world.

In addition to the practical constraints, there are also political ones. In a democracy any party wanting to put its policies into effect needs first to win an election; and any government wishing to continue with its policies needs to ensure the policies command majority public support. They therefore need to take some account, at least in the middle ground, of the aspirations of others – practical politicians of the 'left' need to go some way to meet the aspirations of those inclining to the 'right' or to a 'green' view of things, and conversely for those seeking support for 'right' or 'green' policies. Thus the centrifugal aspirations of the most committed supporters tend to be moderated by countervailing political pressures arising from the need to win support from at least a proportion of less committed voters in the centre.

Hence it normally happens that the policies that go into party manifestos and, even more, the policies actually implemented by governments, tend to fall short of the aspirations of the enthusiasts, and the *effective* area of policy choice is within a more limited area. Even so, the differences between alternative policies are substantial and the differences in possible outcomes important.

While it is not feasible to examine these alternatives in exhaustive detail, it *is* possible to bring out some of the more important differences by postulating a number of policy changes indicative of each of the different policy approaches and using the Cambridge Econometrics model to illustrate in outline the kinds of economic consequences that may be expected to follow from them over the period to 2010.

Market scenario

This scenario is designed to illustrate the effects of 'right' policies intended to give freer play to market forces, with more deregulation and

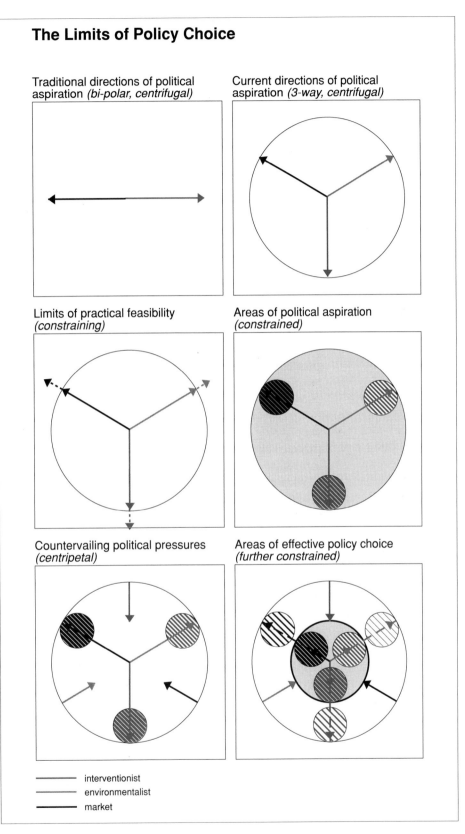

The Limits of Policy Choice

Traditional directions of political aspiration *(bi-polar, centrifugal)*

Current directions of political aspiration *(3-way, centrifugal)*

Limits of practical feasibility *(constraining)*

Areas of political aspiration *(constrained)*

Countervailing political pressures *(centripetal)*

Areas of effective policy choice *(further constrained)*

interventionist
environmentalist
market

Environmental issues are tending to give political choices a third dimension. The scope for effective policy choice is constrained, but remains important.

privatisation, lower taxes and substantial further cuts in government expenditure. The assumptions used to illustrate this bundle of policies are:

- *income tax*
  standard rate cut in stages from 25 per cent in 1990 to 20 per cent in 1995 and subsequently;

- *government spending*
  current expenditure on goods and services reduced by 1 percentage point a year below the levels in the base projection;

- *consumers' spending*
  private spending on education increased by 1.5 percentage points a year above the levels in the base projection, spending on pharmaceutical goods by 2 percentage points a year and spending on health by 3 percentage points a year (these changes are assumed in response to government incentives and/or reduced provision of public services);

- *supply-side changes*
  measures designed to reduce restrictive practices, intensify competition and improve the efficiency of the working of the market. (These changes are estimated to result in increasing labour productivity in manufacturing and business services by 0.25 percentage points a year above the growth rate in the base projection in the period 1991-2000, and by 0.35 percentage points a year in the period 2001-2010.)

These assumptions, run on the same *Cambridge Econometrics* model used for the main forecasts in Chapter 16, give an increase in gross domestic product which is not significantly different from that with the base projection used in the main forecast. However, there are a number of differences in the main components of gross domestic product.

Imports rise rather faster than in the base projection, but exports rise by half as much again, resulting in a stronger current account balance, particularly towards the end of the period.

Current government consumption rises more slowly and by 2010 has increased by only half as much as in the base projection. The effect of this on the Exchequer is broadly offset by the effects of lower tax rates, with the negative public sector borrowing requirement (net saving) rather lower than in the base projection in the first decade (when the tax cuts are already in full effect); but it becomes greater in the second decade (when they are more than offset by the increasing impact of continuing cuts in government expenditure).

The higher personal incomes resulting from lower tax rates are partly absorbed by higher private spending on education, health and pharmaceutical goods, but consumer spending is also higher than in the base projection on a number of other items such as cars, travel, eating out, furniture, furnishings and household goods.

After the first few years the annual rise in consumer prices is less than in the base projection. In most years the rate of inflation is between one third and one half of a percentage point below that in the base projection, and after 1995 inflation remains below 4 per cent a year.

Probably the most marked difference from the base projection used in the main forecasts is in employment. In the base projection unemployment falls fairly steadily after 1991 to about 800,000 by 2010. In the market scenario, employment is reduced by rising labour productivity and by a shift to less labour-intensive parts of the economy with the result that unemployment remains at or above the 1.8 million level until 2005, subsequently falling only to 1.4 million by 2010.

Interventionist scenario

This scenario is designed to illustrate the effects of the adoption of 'left' policies intended to give the government a bigger role in the management of the economy and to increase the public provision of social services. The assumptions used to illustrate this bundle of policies are:

- *income tax*
  standard rate increased in stages from 25 per cent in 1990 to 30 per cent in 1996 and subsequently (equivalent in the model to the raising of higher rates of tax and the introduction of new bands);

- *government spending*
  higher spending on health and education resulting in total government current expenditure on goods and services being increased by 1.25 percentage points a year above the levels in the base projection;

- *research and development*
  greater incentives for higher spending on R & D are assumed to lead to increases in both the unit value and volume of exports of manufactures of 0.25 percentage points in 1996 and 0.4 percentage points a year from 1997 onwards;

- *training schemes*
  numbers on government training schemes increased by 25 per cent each year in 1993, 1994, 1995 and 1996. (This,

together with the increase in R&D, is assumed to lead to increases in labour productivity in all industries of 0.25, 0.5 and 0.75 percentage points above the rates in the base projection in 1995, 1996 and 1997 respectively; of 0.8 percentage points a year between 1998 and 2000; and of 0.35 percentage points a year between 2001 and 2010.)

The assumptions used for this scenario result in a growth rate of gross domestic product which is faster than in the base projection used in the main forecast, but only marginally so. However, there are a number of differences in the components of gross domestic product.

As with the market scenario, imports rise slightly faster than in the base projection, and exports substantially faster, bringing an earlier and stronger improvement in the balance of payments.

In contrast with the market scenario, government current consumption rises by half as much again as in the base projection. Tax revenue also rises, but not by enough to cover fully the increase in government expenditure. Hence the negative public sector borrowing requirement, which in the base projection reduces almost to nothing in the last years of the period, disappears a few years sooner and by 2010 the annual borrowing requirement has risen to nearly 2 per cent of gross domestic product.

The increases in income tax result in a slightly slower growth in consumer spending – a total increase by 2010 of about 43 per cent, compared with 47 per cent with the base projection and 53 per cent with the market scenario. The slightly slower rates of increase are spread over most kinds of consumer spending, and are most marked with cars, durables and household goods.

With this scenario, as with the market scenario, the annual rise in consumer prices falls below that in the base projection after the first few years, with inflation below 4 per cent a year after about 1997.

The government intervention scenario, like the market scenario, differs from the base projection most markedly in the level of unemployment – but in the opposite way. Whereas with the market scenario unemployment remains much higher than in the base projection, with the interventionist scenario unemployment is reduced by the increased numbers in training schemes and by the shift to more labour-intensive public services, with the result that unemployment falls more quickly to about 1.2 million by the turn of the century and remains lower than in the base projection until the last few years of the period.

Environmentalist scenario

This scenario is designed to illustrate the effects of policies designed to give a higher priority to protecting and improving the environment.

It should be noted that this scenario does not depend on the assumption of the election of a 'Green Government' formed by a 'Green Party'. More likely, given the electoral system and electoral behaviour in Britain, stronger environmental policies would be implemented by a government formed by one or other of the present two main parties, either alone or in coalition with other parties, as a result either of its being converted to the merits of environmental issues, or persuaded of the electoral popularity of a more environmentally-oriented stance, or obliged to take action by external pressures – for example, compelling new scientific evidence, or targets for reductions in emissions of pollutants and CO_2 agreed by the European Community or wider international conferences.

The assumptions used to illustrate the bundle of policies which may be associated with a more robust approach to environmental issues are:

- *Carbon tax*
  a tax escalating by 10 per cent a year on the consumption of fossil-fuel-based primary energy, starting in 1991 (ie tax at a rate of 10 per cent in 1991, 20 per cent in 1992, 30 per cent in 1993, and so on up to 200 per cent in 2010). It is assumed that this tax will be implemented by the imposition of specific duties on coal, oil and gas, calculated each year according to the carbon content of each fuel. (It is estimated that taxes at these rates will result in sufficient reductions in emissions of greenhouse gases to meet the Toronto target of reducing emissions to 20 per cent below 1988 levels by the year 2005. In the event of demand proving to be more (or less) elastic to changes in price than has been assumed, the rates of the tax could be adjusted upwards (or downwards) until a rate was found which had the required effect on consumption. It should be noted that the Toronto target is more ambitious than the current government target of reducing emissions to 1990 levels by 2005, but is much less ambitious than the IPCC's estimated requirement of a 60 per cent reduction.);

- *other taxes*
  it is assumed that the carbon tax will be inflation-neutral (ie it will be offset by reductions in other taxes, or increases in government expenditure, or both). For the purpose of the calculations it has been assumed that this offset takes the form of appropriate reductions in VAT, and hence is spread widely across the economy, although if desired it could take other forms instead;

- *water industries*
  it is assumed a major investment programme will be

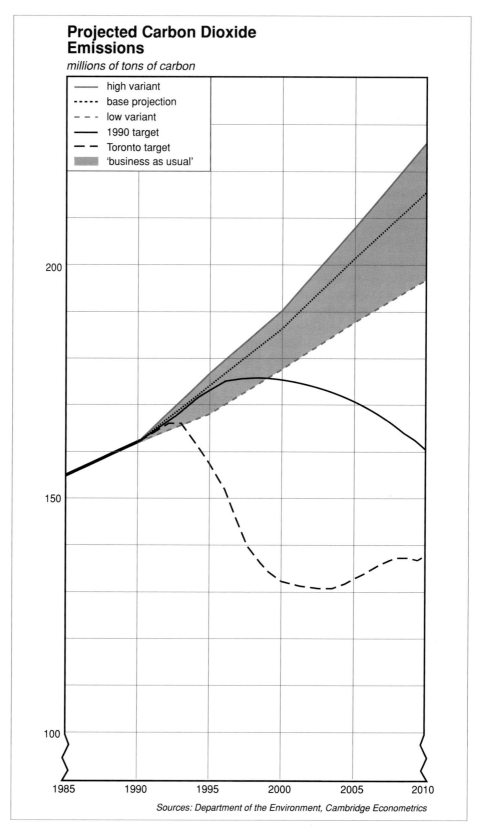

Projected Carbon Dioxide Emissions

millions of tons of carbon

- —— high variant
- ····· base projection
- – – low variant
- —— 1990 target
- — — Toronto target
- ▨ 'business as usual'

Sources: Department of the Environment, Cambridge Econometrics

Restoring carbon dioxide emissions to the 1990 level by 2005 would bring a substantial reduction in emissions as against carrying on with 'business-as-usual'. The Toronto target would secure a reduction nearly twice as large.

undertaken by the water services industries to improve water quality, and that this will be paid for by higher water charges to consumers;

♦ *industrial pollution*
tighter regulation of polluting industries is introduced, leading to a four-fold increase in the amount they spend on environmental protection over the eight-year period 1993-2000. Estimates of the costs of the investment required for pollution control, and of the improvements in the efficiency in the control industry to be expected at higher levels of activity, are based on an expert report on the industrial costs of pollution control.[402]

The assumptions used to illustrate this scenario result in growth in gross domestic product only marginally different from the base projection and the other two scenarios, for the macroeconomic effects of the carbon tax are broadly balanced by the offsetting reductions in VAT. There are, however, major structural changes within the overall total.

By the end of the period the escalating carbon tax and the cost of higher investment in water supply result in consumer prices substantially higher than in the base projection for water, two-thirds higher for electricity and more than one-and-a-half times as high for petrol, gas and coal. On the other hand, prices are lower than in the base projection for many other areas of consumer expenditure, particularly less energy-dependent ones such as health, education, and recreational services. There is a similar pattern of change in industrial prices.

These differential price changes bring a sharp fall in demand for energy and water and an increase in demand for items less affected by energy prices, and this in turn leads to major industrial restructuring with, by the end of the period, water output about 15 per cent lower than in the base projection, electricity output about 20 per cent lower, petroleum products output about 40 per cent lower and coal output about 75 per cent lower. At the same time, output of gas is double the level in the base projection, due to its substitution for coal and petroleum to take advantage of the lower level of carbon tax on gas (on account of its lower level of emission of greenhouse gases). With this scenario there is also a shift from some kinds of manufacturing to less energy-dependent parts of the service sector.

These structural shifts are accompanied by marked changes in the distribution of employment, with declines (relative to the base projection) in coal, electricity, and some manufacturing industries, but increases (relative to the base projection) in gas supply and parts of the service sector. Since the sectors declining relative to the base projection tend to be more capital intensive, and those increasing to be more labour intensive, the effect of the structural shifts in this scenario is to bring a faster fall in unemployment, which by 2005 comes down to about 900,000, compared with about 1.3 million with the base projection. However, it is assumed that (in the absence of effective incomes policies) further falls in unemployment are likely to generate inflationary pressures, that deflationary measures would be introduced to check this, and by 2010 the level of unemployment would be much the same as with the base projection.

With this scenario exports rise marginally more quickly, and imports marginally more slowly, than in the base projection, with the result that a current account payments deficit persists during the middle part of the period, but the deflationary measures assumed to be introduced after 2005 have the effect of checking the rise in imports and bringing overseas payments into balance by about the end of the period.

Whereas with the base projection the public sector borrowing requirement remains negative right through to 2010, with the environment scenario it comes into balance in the 1990s and the borrowing requirement rises steadily in the first decade of the next century – although not to the levels reached in the 1970s.

A further, unintended, effect of a carbon tax may be a shift in effective income away from low-income families, who typically spend a higher proportion of their incomes on heating, who often use less energy-efficient heating systems and who tend to be less well placed to go over to more economic systems. It would, however, be possible to use part of the proceeds of a carbon tax to compensate them, while making smaller reductions than otherwise in VAT or other taxes.

In short, then, with this scenario total economic growth is little different from the base projection, but the sharp differential movements in prices bring major structural changes, with a shift from more to less energy-dependent activities.

It should be noted that this scenario is based on the assumption that similar measures are adopted in other competitor countries. On the whole, it seems that these kinds of policy are much more likely to be adopted in circumstances where other countries are acting similarly than where they are not; water improvement measures are most likely to be undertaken with a view to meeting European Community standards, and heavy carbon taxes are most likely to be introduced in the context of a need to meet internationally-agreed targets for reduced emissions of greenhouse gases.

It should also be noted, however, that they are not *dependent* on this assumption. In the event of these measures being introduced *unilaterally* in Britain, it looks as if the macroeconomic consequences would not be greatly different. The main potential difference would be in the balance of payments effects. Higher water costs would have a major effect on only a relatively narrow range of industries, but very high carbon taxes would increase greatly the costs of the more energy-intensive industries. This could be expected to make them much less competitive internationally, leading to lower sales at home and in export markets; and this in turn could be expected to reduce greatly their profitability, leading to the possibility of some of them in time relocating to other countries with cheaper energy.

At the same time, however, the escalating carbon tax could be expected to bring about a major reduction in UK petroleum consumption;

and this in turn (assuming other countries were not adopting similar policies and were accordingly maintaining their oil consumption) would result in a substantially greater surplus of oil exports (or smaller deficit of oil imports). It is estimated that the positive effect of this on the balance of payments would be sufficient to offset the negative effect of the reduced competitiveness of the energy-dependent industries.

Implications

It must be stressed that these three scenarios are no more than *illustrative*. While the model on which they have been tested is large and sophisticated, and the calculations involved are complex, it is of course subject to the limitations of all econometric models, and cannot be expected to do more than indicate the likely macroeconomic consequences of the various assumptions specified. Hence the figures should be seen as *tentative first approximations*, not as definitive predictions, and used as indicators of the *kinds* of consequence to be expected, not the fine detail. That said, the illustrative scenarios do appear to suggest a number of points of potential importance.

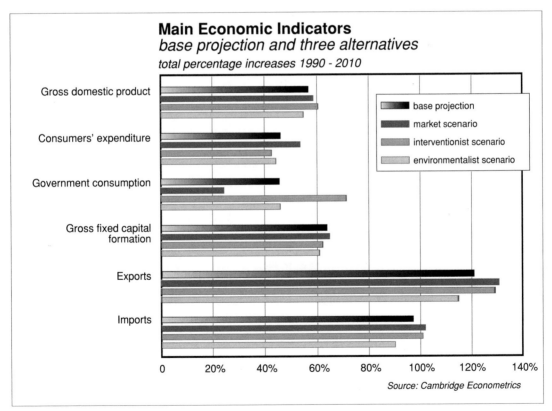

Main Economic Indicators
base projection and three alternatives
total percentage increases 1990 - 2010

Source: Cambridge Econometrics

Differences between the three scenarios in rates of growth of gross domestic product appear to be marginal.

First, the impact of both the market policies and the interventionist policies on *economic performance,* particularly on economic growth as measured by gross domestic product, does not seem likely to be as great as is commonly supposed. In choosing between them it may therefore be sensible not to give predominant weight to their possible economic advantages or disadvantages, but to give more attention to their relative attractions on other scores – whether there is potentially more merit in greater self reliance, lower taxes and less interference from government, or in reduced social divisions and better provision for public services and social security?

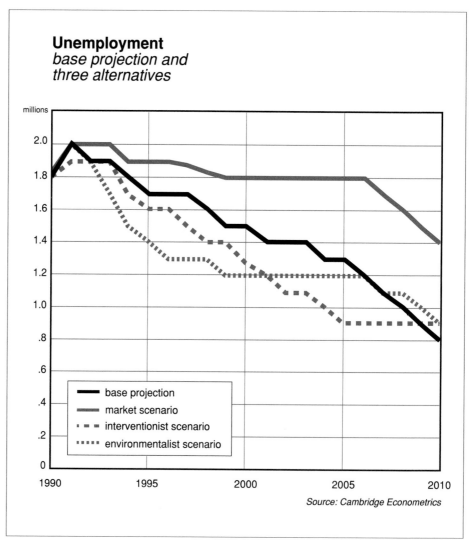

Differences between the three scenarios in their implications for unemployment appear to arise mainly from whether they bring a shift into more labour-intensive activities or less labour-intensive activities.

Second, the adoption of strong environmentalist measures does *not* seem likely to reduce economic growth (as measured by gross domestic product). Moreover, this conclusion is *not* dependent on any specific assumption in the figures which might need to be revised later in the light of better information or fuller calculations. For the economic effect of a carbon tax would be quite different from the effect of the jumps in petroleum prices in the 1970s. The OPEC price increases involved a direct transfer from consuming countries to exporting countries, with damaging effects on the economies of the former. A carbon tax, in contrast, would involve a shift from more-energy-intensive sectors to less-energy-intensive sectors *within the same country*. Since the deflationary effects of the carbon tax would be offset by reductions in other taxes (or increases in public expenditure, for example on energy conservation), there is no reason to expect the net effect on the economy as a whole to be deflationary. Hence the view that a carbon tax, even if desirable in itself, cannot be contemplated, because it would have unacceptably damaging effects on economic growth, would appear to be misplaced.

Other studies which have concluded that measures of these kinds need not be seriously damaging to economic growth include: one in Britain;[403] one in Australia[404] (GDP growth rate cut by less than 0.1 per cent); one in Norway[404] (GDP growth cut by 0.4 per cent a year, with two-thirds of the loss offset by gains in health and other benefits); and the National Environmental Policy Plan in the Netherlands.[405]

Third, a high carbon tax and other environmental-improvement measures, while unlikely to make much difference to total economic growth, as measured by gross domestic product, would nonetheless be likely to bring about major structural changes in the economy – in price differentials, in consumption patterns and life-styles, in industrial structure and in the distribution of employment. These changes would not be painless and would involve dislocation and transitional costs, particularly if the measures were brought in late and did not allow adequate time for adjustment. The basis for choice would therefore seem to be, not whether we can afford slower economic growth, but whether the benefits of a better environment are worth the costs of getting it, and whether risks of global warming are serious enough to justify the changes needed for reducing emissions of greenhouse gases.

19. Summary & Conclusions

The purpose of the exercise has been to make a systematic and objective assessment of the factors likely to influence future developments in order to arrive at a well-founded view of the most probable changes in Britain by 2010. The aim has been to identify the broad shape of the wood, not to specify the details of individual trees within it; even so, the argument has necessarily extended over many pages. It is therefore useful to bring together some of the main findings that have emerged and to sum up some of the more important implications for public policies.

INTERNATIONAL CONTEXT

Over the next two decades Britain will be increasingly affected by developments in the rest of the world, both in particular regions, especially Europe, and in areas of economic, environmental and security policy which are global in their impact.

Regional developments (Chapters 6-9)

Over the next 20 years the United States is likely to remain the world's strongest military power and also the largest economy; it will continue to be major partner for Britain in trade, investment and technology transfer. Japan will continue to grow in economic strength, but at a slightly less rapid rate, will provide keen competition in world markets and may continue to be a source of inward industrial investment in Britain. China may emerge as a giant new economic force – but probably not until after 2010.

Some countries in the Third World will acquire the characteristics of the 'developed' countries; but others will continue to face extremely serious problems, including widespread poverty. The major factor will be population growth, which is still expected to level off at some time, but is now expected to do so more slowly than was previously forecast. As a result total world population is now forecast to grow by about 90 million people (one-and-a-half Britains) each year, and by a total of about 2 billion people (another China and another India) by 2010.

This increase will in many areas bring pressures on food, water and other resources, environmental problems, overcrowding, political tensions, and the possibility of migration or war. It will also bring demands for more aid from the richer countries: since 1984 there has been a net transfer of resources of more than £40bn a year *from* the less developed countries *to* the more developed ones.

End of the Cold War (Chapters 3, 12)

The collapse of communism has already brought fundamental political and economic changes in the former satellite countries of Eastern Europe, and will increasingly do so in the Soviet Union itself, with the probability that several of the constituent republics will acquire local autonomy or outright independence. The Soviet Union faces enormous difficulties in making the transition to a market economy and plural political system, and years of turbulence are likely before perestroika shows economic successes.

Ideological change and economic reform is being accompanied by a considerable weakening of the military position, with major force reductions, effective dissolution of the Warsaw Pact alliance, withdrawal from Eastern Europe, and growing internal security problems within the Soviet Union. So it is not merely a matter of declared *intentions* to avoid war: there will soon no longer be the *capability* to mount an invasion of Western Europe – and economic weakness, technological backwardness, physical distance and political difficulties at home will ensure that this remains so.

Thus there will be no resumption of the Cold War. This will help reduce tensions worldwide, and the replacement of superpower rivalry with cooperation will help solve many previously intractable Third World conflicts. In Western Europe it will bring a fundamental reappraisal of defence needs. No doubt a substantial defence capability will still be considered necessary, but it will not be on anything like the scale previously considered necessary for repelling an invasion by the Red Army. The potential 'peace dividend' is therefore likely to be considerable. For example, if over the 20 years to 2010 British defence expenditure falls to half its present level, instead of rising roughly in line with economic growth, the saving by 2010 will be roughly of the order of £20bn a year – equivalent to an extra sixth in the increase in consumers' expenditure expected by then, or to the doubling of government expenditure on health and education, or to a fifteen-fold increase in expenditure on overseas aid.

World environment (Chapter 5)

The end of the Cold War will remove one world problem; the threat of global warming will pose another of no less magnitude. Air, river and sea pollution, acid rain, nuclear fall-out and ozone depletion have all attracted international concern and brought international responses. Global warming raises far more difficult problems which have yet to be addressed.

The governments of the world set up a panel composed of virtually all the leading scientists in this field to assess whether increased emissions of 'greenhouse' gases from deforestation, the burning of fossil fuels and other causes was causing damaging changes in world climate. The panel has recently reported its unanimous finding that increased emissions are causing the earth's temperature to rise by 0.3°C a decade (with an uncertainty range of 0.2°-0.5°C).

The probable effects on particular parts of the globe are not yet known, and are unlikely to be clarified before the turn of the century. However, the consensus among scientists is that, in the absence of measures to check the rise in emissions, in time they will lead to severe floods, storms and droughts, desertification of some regions, and threats to the homes, food supplies and livelihoods of millions of people; within a century or two they will make the earth hotter than at any time in the past 2 million years; and eventually they could make it too hot to be habitable at all.

The scientists estimate that to stop the build-up it will be necessary to cut greenhouse gas emissions by at least 60 per cent worldwide – implying cuts even bigger than this for the richer countries, which use more fossil fuel energy, in order to allow room for continuing development in the poorer countries. Also the poorer countries will need help in finance and technology in order to secure their cooperation.

Thus the stakes are high, with the prospects of major changes being needed in the generation and use of energy and in transport, and international cooperation will be essential for an effective response. So far no agreement has been reached on *targets* for reductions and negotiations are sure to be long and difficult. The gravity of the threat, the scale of the response required, and the conflicts of interest between different countries (and between different groups within countries) will ensure that this is a central issue in international relations right though the next two decades and beyond.

Global economy (Chapter 4)

The reductions in barriers to trade and to movements of capital and people, the revolutions in transport and communications, the changes in financial institutions, the growth of multinational companies, the increases in international transfers of technology, and the convergence in patterns of consumption have combined to bring great increases in world trade and financial flows, in international investment, and in global sourcing of production. These changes are likely to continue, with additional stimulus from the Uruguay round of tariff cuts, the Single Market and eventual Monetary Union in Western Europe, the change to market economies in Eastern Europe and further developments in transport and communications.

Thus the world is increasingly developing an integrated economy, with competition on a global scale. This will offer many benefits to consumers and to the more successful producers – but bigger problems for the *less* successful ones.

European union (Chapter 11)

The European Community has embarked on plans for closer economic and political union and, if they go ahead, the prospect is that by the turn of the century there will be in place most of the elements of a common monetary and economic policy, together with strengthened supranational institutions to operate them and a strengthened European Parliament to exercise democratic control over them. This may well produce a momentum that will lead to further moves, possibly going by 2010 a large part of the way to a 'United States of Europe' – most probably with Britain a member.

At the same time as closer links are developed between existing EC members, the Community is likely to be extended through the joining of new members: probably in the 1990s by Sweden, Norway, Finland and Austria and later by Switzerland, Czechoslovakia and Hungary. Poland and others may also be members by 2010.

These changes may be expected to bring a bigger market, sharper competition, faster growth, lower inflation and some harmonisation of social policies – probably also a need for regional policies to help areas, sectors and social groups which find themselves in difficulties in the new circumstances.

Interdependence (Chapters 2-8, 11)

Most of these changes, particularly the moves towards closer union in Europe, will have the effect of increasing international interdependence and of constraining the scope for separate action by national governments. To an ever greater extent national governments will be unable adequately, on their own, to control the exchange rates of their currencies, to determine macroeconomic policies and interest rates, to negotiate favourable international trade deals, to control the location decisions of multinationals, to control the flow of information by satellite and digital communications links, to protect the physical environment of their countries.

The price of economic isolation is too high, and the possibility of physical isolation no longer exists in an era of intercontinental missiles, acid rain, ozone depletion and global warming. Accordingly, the purposes governments wish to achieve, but can no longer achieve adequately on their own, they will increasingly need to seek to achieve together through international cooperation. This will take many forms: working though existing international organisations such as GATT, the IMF, the World Bank, the ILO, the OECD; using more ad hoc inter-government links such as the 'group of seven' financial countries and the various international research projects and conferences addressing environmental problems; and, in Western Europe, through development of the mechanisms of the European Community.

If, in increasingly many areas, the *means* of effective progress will be the devising of arrangements for international cooperation, it follows that the *price* of progress will be the taking of more decisions, and hence power, by the international organisations developed or created for this purpose. A major aim of public policy in the next two decades will therefore be to ensure that the international arrangements, particularly those of the European Community, are designed in ways which best meet the needs of people in member countries.

A key issue for the UK and other members of the Community is likely to be the principle of 'subsidiarity' (devolving decisions to the lowest level feasible); will this be the best way of ensuring unity without uniformity, of securing the benefits of central control where it is advantageous (for example, in some areas of economic policy and in technical standards), while settling for a looser compatibility where local choice and variety have advantages (as in most areas of social policy)?

And in so far as the tendency is likely to be for an increasing role to be taken by the institutions of the Community, another key issue is likely to be: how should they be brought under effective democratic control – *indirectly* through committees of the governments of member states, or *directly* through elections to a more powerful European Parliament?

BRITAIN IN 2010

Developments in the rest of the world will set the context for what happens in Britain; what are the developments expected within Britain itself?

Population changes (Chapter 12)

Total population is forecast to grow by about 2.6 million (4.6 per cent) by 2010, which is about half as much again as in the previous two decades, but is expected to level off in the decades after 2010. There is, however, the possibility that total population will grow by nearly twice as much by 2010; or that it will not grow at all.

The expected total increase will not in itself be large enough to cause problems but, in combination with internal movements, is likely to contribute to increasing housing pressures in the more popular parts of Southern England.

The number of children is not expected to change greatly and the number of teenagers (aged 15-19), which has recently been falling, will fall only a little further, and by 2010 is expected to return to slightly above the present level.

There will be a drop of 2.4 million (nearly one fifth) in the number of young adults aged 20-34, although about half of this drop will be offset by increases in the numbers of people in the older working age groups.

The number of older people aged 65-79 will not change greatly, but the number aged over 80 is forecast to increase by about 600,000 (more than one quarter). This will put extra strains on the health and social care services, although the expected increase is in fact *less* than has already been experienced in the past two decades. In the decades after 2010, however, there will be greater increases in the numbers of people above the present pension age, both absolutely and relative to the numbers in the working age groups, and at some point the question will have to be addressed: should the level of pensions be *reduced*? Or should the age of retirement be *increased*? Or should those still at work be expected to make higher contributions for the pensions of those already retired?

Employment prospects (Chapter 13)

Some further rise in the percentage of women in the labour market in the main age groups is expected to be slightly more than offset by a drop in the participation rates of both sexes in the upper age groups, leading to a marginal decline in the overall participation rate for the population as a whole. However, this is expected to be more than offset by population changes, leading to an increase in the total potential workforce of between 2 and 3 million.

The number of young adults aged 25-34 in the workforce is expected to fall by about 15 per cent, and the number of older people aged over 65 is expected to fall by a half, but these declines should be more than offset by increases in the main working age groups.

If by 2010 the proportion of young people in full-time education and training is doubled (as arguably it needs to be), then the number of young people aged under 25 in the workforce will be substantially less than in these forecasts, and it is likely that there will be a *decline* in the potential labour force of about 1 million.

The total of available jobs is expected to rise rather faster than the potential workforce, by a total of 3 to 4 million, with the implication that unemployment may come down over the period to less than 1 million.

The main sectoral shifts expected in employment are from manufacturing and agriculture (both of which, however, are expected to continue to have substantial increases in *output*, due to rising productivity), into parts of the service sector, in particular into business and professional services. Within manufacturing there will be further reductions in employment in almost all industries, but they will mostly be *smaller* than the reductions between 1970 and 1990, particularly in industries such as electronics and vehicles where large increases in output are expected.

More important than changes in total *numbers* are likely to be changes in the *kinds* of jobs. The trend away from unskilled manual jobs towards more highly skilled and professional occupations is expected to continue under the influence of increased use of new technologies, rising quality standards and keener competition in the Single European Market and beyond.

This will bring into sharper focus existing weaknesses relative to some of Britain's main competitors – inadequate numbers of industrial engineers and scientists (and failure to reward them well or promote them to top positions), limited typical qualification levels of managers and, crucially important, the low proportion of young people staying in full-time education or training after the age of 16.

Improvements in the extent and relevance of education and training are likely to be essential requirements for competitiveness in the more demanding markets ahead, and it is likely that in the next two decades the key factor determining the size of unemployment will be the extent to which people have the qualifications, including new skills and multiple skills, to take up the new kinds of job opportunities which will become available.

Environment needs (Chapter 14)

In the past two decades there has been a shift of population from North to South, and from the big cities and conurbations to smaller towns and rural areas. Both tendencies are likely to continue, further stimulated by the development of the European Community and the construction of the Channel Tunnel and high-speed rail links, but are likely to be constrained by increasing overcrowding in the South East and, perhaps, by planning policies in rural areas.

The countryside has been changing greatly, both visually, with new agricultural methods, and socially, with movement *out* of many agricultural families (no longer needed to work on the land because of greatly increased productivity) and movement *in* of many people coming from the cities in search of more agreeable rural homes for long-distance commuting or for retirement.

Changes in prospect in agriculture involving less intensive methods and diversification of activities are likely to release land for other possible uses and increase existing pressures for housebuilding and for tourism and recreational developments. This will threaten the distinctive features of areas of natural beauty and wildness and the peaceful qualities of rural communities.

There will therefore be difficult trade-offs to make in land use planning decisions. Also, tourism, country recreational activities and long-distance commuting are all highly car-dependent and therefore vulnerable to the greatly increased motoring costs likely to be involved in long-term measures to cut emissions of greenhouse gases.

The cities and conurbations have been changing as a result of the movement out from the centres of for manufacturers and, more recently of some offices also, to escape congestion and high land costs. A further important development has been the recent tendency of shopping centres to move to suburban locations and for new 'shopping cities' to be built right away from existing towns with a view to providing shopping and recreational facilities for a regional catchment area. There are many new proposals in the pipeline and whether or not they go ahead will have a major impact on the future character of Britain's cities.

Experience in North America, where the process has gone much further, suggests that these developments in retailing, if they go ahead, are likely to undermine existing city centres, to erode the financial basis of city governments, to extend traffic congestion to the suburbs and to times outside the commuting rush hours, and to increase dependence on private cars at a time when, as part of the response to global warming, it may be necessary to reduce motoring. It therefore seems likely that greater advantage will be seen in the course followed by most continental European cities (and an increasing number of North American ones) of curbing development at out-of-town and suburban locations and concentrating instead on improving existing city centres with new shopping and leisure complexes, weather-proof arcades over existing shopping streets, pedestrian precincts, and improved public transport facilities.

Although the increase in household formation is expected to become slower, an additional 1.3 million households are expected to be needing homes by 2001, and more in the first decade of the next century. One of the main problems is likely to be where to put them – available urban sites are limited in the more popular parts of the South, and building in green belts, small towns or rural areas is liable to involve damage to the amenity of existing populations. The other main problem will be how to provide for the quarter of households expected to need rented accommodation – the sale of council houses, sharply reduced council building, and the decline of the private rented sector have combined to reduce drastically the stock of homes available for rent, particularly those available at 'social' (ie subsidised) rents.

The natural environment in which we live is a crucial element in the overall quality of life, but can be at risk because the impact of industrial production on the environment is not directly reflected in product and service costs, and therefore is likely to be taken account of only if there are specific interventions through public policies.

Improvement in water quality is an area where problems are growing. Pollution of supplies by agricultural chemicals can be reduced by changes in agricultural practices, but future changes will not prevent continuing pollution for many years by chemicals already leaching down to the water table. Plant to remove these chemicals from drinking water will be expensive, as will also measures to remove contamination from hydrocarbons and lead in water pipes.

The recent agreement to discontinue the dumping of raw sewage at sea will also involve expensive treatment plant, as will measures to provide more satisfactory methods of disposal of liquid and solid toxic waste products of various kinds.

Personal mobility is a keenly sought after goal for most people and the rapid growth in car ownership and use in past decades has brought great benefit to many people. However, it has also brought environmental problems in the form of road accidents, noise, air pollution and traffic congestion, which has so far defied all measures taken to alleviate it: average traffic speeds in central London are now down to 12 miles an hour – only four miles an hour faster than was achieved with horses and carriages a century ago.

North American experience suggests that no amount of road building will be sufficient to accommodate the pent-up demand for road space in and around the main cities; and measures to attempt to do so tend to have more effect in damaging local amenity than in speeding traffic circulation. In this area, as in shopping, it is likely that continental European experience will prove to be a more suitable model, with the emphasis on improving public transport and facilities for cyclists and pedestrians and restricting the use of private cars in central areas.

The growing problem of air pollution from vehicles is being met by the requirement to fit catalytic converters to future models. A further consideration which is likely to be of growing importance is the contribution made by cars to emissions of greenhouse gases – in cities typically more than four times as much per passenger mile as buses and more than ten times as much as trains. This may be expected to lead to measures to discourage car use, such as higher petrol prices, charging for central area road use, and removal of the favourable tax treatment of company cars.

The problem of air pollution has also led to plans to reduce emissions of the gases that cause acid rain by the fitting of cleaning plant to some of the largest power stations, by making greater use of imported low-sulphur coal, and by building new gas-fired power stations.

The threat of global warming is also likely to lead to major changes in energy generation and use in other areas as well as transport. There is likely to be a shift to power stations fuelled by natural gas which emits less greenhouse gases than the same energy generated from coal or petroleum. There is also likely to be increased R&D and investment in the various potential sources of renewable energy, particularly in those like wind power and wave power where costs are already lower than for nuclear energy. Finally, there will be emphasis on the considerable savings which are achievable by conserving energy and using it more efficiently – in many cases measures which will pay for themselves and are worth doing regardless of the scale of the threat posed by global warming.

Some of the most important and complex decisions in public policy will be in determining what level of cuts in greenhouse gas emissions will be appropriate to aim for, and what combination of measures will be the most satisfactory for achieving it.

Many of the issues affecting the environment are interdependent, and the extent of the interactions means that environmental issues are not a number of discrete and separate problems but different aspects of a single problem. With most of them the key factor will be the policies adopted by governments over the next 20 years. Since the issues are interdependent, the policies for addressing them will need to take account of this; a single issue with many aspects will require a single policy strategy applied consistently across the whole range of areas involved.

Some of the possible policy measures are cheap and easy to implement, but some involve expensive public investment and long lead times. This will make it important to get the priorities right between different projects – again implying the need for a single integrated policy strategy.

The need to cut emissions of greenhouse gases may raise new sorts of policy problems. For example, the policies of energy undertakings have in the past been geared to increasing their sales and market shares. But in a greenhouse world the paramount need may be to *reduce* consumption. Will marketing managers be instructed to seek *falling* sales and *reduced* market share? What incentives will be appropriate and what form can competition usefully take? It may well be that many approaches which have worked well in the familiar world will need to be stood on their heads in the greenhouse world where conservation, not expansion, will be the yardstick of success.

Technology applications (Chapter 15)

During the second half of this century scientific knowledge has been expanding at a very rapid rate, and there have also been impressive advances in the technologies for putting it to practical use. In assessing future prospects it is important to distinguish between the *potential* of the various developments ahead and the extent to which the potential is likely to be *realised* in the form of practical applications.

Further rapid advances are certain in microelectronics, software, computing, and telecommunications; and are also to be expected in biotechnology, new materials, environmental sciences and energy technologies, and possibly in superconductors. Developments will be marked by growing convergence between different scientific disciplines and technologies and by the rapid pace of development, but also by the constraints in the way of immediate commercial exploitation, such as public concerns over safety and ethical issues, the need to meet criteria of commercial scale, cost and utility, inadequacies in supporting infrastructure, and underlying problems where levels of R&D in Britain are lower than in other competitor countries. Half of R&D expenditure in Britain is devoted to defence (a far higher proportion than in most other countries); and civilian R&D is concentrated mainly in a few high-tech sectors, leaving other sectors more thinly covered. On the other hand, early take-up will be encouraged in cases where new technologies bring marked gains in performance, quality or production costs. Moreover, environmental concerns will provide a strong stimulus to the take-up of new technologies, many of which can contribute to increased energy efficiency, waste minimisation and pollution control.

In agriculture there will be further applications for IT in farm management and for biotechnology in improving plants and livestock. The take-up of biotechnological innovations in agriculture (and in medicine) is likely to be gradual, constrained by strict regulatory regimes and by public concerns over safety and ethical issues.

In manufacturing there will be further applications of microelectronics and advanced computer-based systems; and in some industries also important applications of new materials, fibre-optics and biotechnology. There will also be important advances through innovations which are not technology-based, such as just-in-time production methods, total quality control systems and improved human relations policies.

In offices there will continue to be more widespread use of IT systems, but not to the point of the arrival of the all-electronic, paperless office.

In shopping and banking there will be further use of automated systems, with more bar scanner checkouts and the introduction of EFT/POS (Electronic Funds Transfer at the Point of Sale) to settle transactions instantly and without the need for completing or processing cheque or credit card forms. There will probably also be wider use of 'smart' cards (plastic cards with microchips embedded in them) to store and process records of financial transactions and other kinds of personal information. However, the growth of home banking will probably be limited by the inability to handle cash; and the growth of home shopping by the problem of delivery of the purchases and the social nature of much shopping. Tele-shopping and tele-working may well be promoted, however, over the long term by constraints on the use of private transport in response to the problem of global warming.

There are also likely to be important applications of new technologies in education, training, health and care services, transport, space, energy, environmental protection, crime prevention and in the home – although the fully computerised house is likely to remain the preserve of the enthusiast.

Effective use of new technologies is becoming an increasingly important factor in the expansion of the economy and the improvement of living standards. The extent to which this can be achieved will depend largely on securing more and better directed R&D, in training more people with the necessary special skills and, in some areas, in the government taking the initiative in setting standards, providing pump-priming finance to promote technology diffusion.

Economic growth (Chapter 16)

Over the past three decades there have been three distinct periods with different rates of economic growth in each. Between 1960 and 1973 economic growth (measured in terms of gross domestic product) averaged 2.9 per cent a year. In 1973 world oil prices quadrupled and in Britain, as in most other industrial countries, growth was much slower – an average of only 1.3 per cent a year in the six year period 1973 to 1979. In 1979 there were further oil price increases and a change of government in Britain brought radically new economic policies. In the period from 1979 to 1990 growth has averaged 2.2 per cent – roughly mid way between the two previous periods.

During this latter period major supply side changes have brought faster improvements in productivity in manufacturing but not, to any extent, in the economy as a whole, because of the smaller increases in productivity in the service sector and the increase in unemployment. A matter of concern during the later years of this period has been the re-emergence of the balance of overseas payments as a constraint on growth.

During the early 1980s there was a deterioration in the balance on non-oil trade (due mainly to continuation of a long-term decline in the trade performance of manufacturing industry), but this was more than offset by very large oil surpluses (from the rise in world oil prices and the coming on stream of North Sea production) and increased surpluses from invisibles (earnings from overseas assets, tourism, insurance, financial services and so on). In the later 1980s the deterioration in trade in manufactures continued further, but the oil surplus disappeared (with lower prices and some fall in North Sea output) and invisible earnings fell back also, with the result that oil and invisibles no longer offset the worsening balance in non-oil trade. In consequence the overall deficit on current account has risen to unprecedented levels.

A large oil surplus is unlikely to reappear (increases due to disruption of Gulf supplies are not likely to persist in the longer term); future invisible earnings are uncertain; and major improvements in export performance require the reversal of a trend that has been worsening over a long period of years. The balance of payments is therefore likely to be a significant constraint on faster growth, at least in the next few years; and there is little evidence from the main economic indicators of output, exports, investment, etc that the economy is now fundamentally stronger than before and poised for better performance in the future than in the past. It would therefore seem unrealistic to expect future economic growth rates to be significantly faster than previous ones.

The forecast, using the model of Cambridge Econometrics, is that economic growth (as measured by gross domestic product) will average about 2.3 per cent a year over the next two decades – a rate similar to that of the past decade. This will bring a total increase of a little over one half by 2010, with consumers' expenditure and government consumption rising by a little less and fixed investment by rather more.

Imports of goods and services are forecast to double over the 20 year period, and exports to more than double (to pay for the higher imports and clear the deficit). Thus the share of imports in total consumption will go up from 21 per cent in 1970 and 33 per cent in 1990 to 42 per cent in 2010 – an indication of the way that in Britain, as in most other industrial countries, trade is rising much faster than output, a measure of the extent to which the world is moving towards a single global economy.

Manufacturing's share of total output, which fell from 41 per cent in 1970 to 34 per cent in 1990, is forecast to recover to 37 per cent of the total by 2010, reflecting in part higher sales in export markets. The share of non-government services, which doubled between 1970 and 1990, is forecast to continue to increase, but less rapidly, from 17 per cent of the total in 1990 to 21 per cent in 2010; and the share of transport and communications is also expected to grow a little. Other sectors, while growing absolutely, are forecast to account for reduced shares of the total.

The forecast for total economic growth and the sectoral forecasts assume a stronger performance by manufacturing industry. Whether this is in fact achieved will depend mainly on the extent of improvements in management efficiency and of investment in new plant, R&D and training (both possibly helped by increased inward investment by foreign companies), and on the speed with which the labour market adapts to the need for convergence of inflation rates towards the EC average following the decision to join the European Exchange Rate Mechanism.

Life in Britain in 2010 (Chapter 17)

In some ways life in Britain in 2010 will be very different from now, but in others it will not have changed very much. Work, for instance: the most important thing is that there will still be plenty of it – 3 or 4 million more jobs than now. Pay will be higher, hours shorter and working conditions generally better, and probably human relations also, with more participation and autonomy in many workplaces. In general, skill needs will be higher, with more multi-skilled and professional jobs, and the education and training qualifications needed will in consequence be higher also. There is also likely to be an increase in self-employment and in the tendency for people to retire through various stages of part-time work, or to retire early and take up a second career on a part-time basis.

Earnings are likely to continue to rise, on average, at a rate similar to that experienced in the past decade, so that, typically, they are about a half higher than now by 2010; but recent changes in the pattern of income distribution are less likely to continue. Since 1979 the gap between upper and lower earnings has widened substantially; pensions and other benefits have been pegged to the cost of living index, so that in real terms they have not increased in line with other incomes; and tax changes have been more advantageous to high incomes than to low ones.

It can be calculated that if the changes since 1979 were continued to 2010, the earnings of the top decile would go up by more than 10 times the percentage of the bottom decile; median earnings would increase by a half while most social security benefits would not increase at all in real terms; and the upper half of incomes of all kinds would go up by nearly eight times the percentage of the lower half of incomes, while the lowest incomes would not increase at all. Such sharply widening differentials would give rise to insoluble problems in preserving incentives to work or save while keeping means-tested benefits above the barest poverty levels; and they could also be expected to generate increasing social division and tensions. It may therefore be expected that the pattern of future changes will be less unequal.

Housing standards are likely to increase further, with people spending a higher proportion of their incomes on their homes, and equipping them with more and better furniture and appliances. Outside they are likely to change less than inside; five out of every six of the houses and flats people will be living in 2010 have been built already, and most of the new ones will use current designs and materials.

Food consumption will not increase in volume, and will account for a smaller share of total consumer spending than now, but people will tend to be more health-conscious, eating less sugar, meat and dairy produce, and more fish, fruit and vegetables, and 'organic' foods. At the same time consumption of convenience foods is also expected to increase, and people will eat out and use take-aways more, and drink more wine and soft drinks, but smoke fewer cigarettes.

Spending on clothes and shoes is expected to continue rising, despite the reduced numbers of young people with money to spend on fashion goods.

On average people in Britain watch television for about 25 hours a week – far more than in most other countries. High viewing levels are likely to continue, along with other home-based activities such as listening to the radio, or to tapes or records, or watching video, reading books, gardening and home repairs and do-it-yourself work. Other activities likely to remain popular are going out for a meal or a drink and going on foreign holidays.

Other activities which are at present less widespread, but are expected to increase in the coming two decades include: visits to theatre, opera, ballet and cinema; visits to museums and historic sites and buildings; and participation in dancing and sports; but attendance at most spectator sporting events is expected to continue to decline. Demographic changes will favour the less active sports over the more strenuous ones; educational changes will favour more cultural activities; and income increases will encourage further growth of car-borne activities, although this may be offset later in the period by the expected increase in motoring costs.

Health care will be improved by the use of new diagnostic systems, new surgical techniques and new drugs, and these will tend to keep people alive for longer and in better condition, but they will not extend the normal life span of 80 years or so. The high costs of some of the new techniques, together with the higher number of very old people will increase health costs. At present both public spending and total spending on health care account for a smaller proportion of gross domestic product in Britain than in other countries such as France, Germany, Italy and Sweden, and popular opinion appears to favour higher levels of spending. The future policy issue is likely to be how health care is to be organised and financed.

With social care the problem is likely to be not that there will be an increase in the numbers of people in need of care, but that those who in the past have carried the main burden of providing the care – daughters and other women relatives, friends and neighbours – are likely to be available in smaller numbers as more women have jobs, and wish to continue in them, than in previous generations.

Marriage is still a very popular institution in Britain (the second highest rate in the European Community); but so also is divorce (also the second highest). The divorce rate in Britain is still rising and it has been calculated four out of ten marriages in 1987 will end in divorce. However, the majority of divorces are followed by remarriage. The increase in divorce is partly explained by the greater ease of obtaining one; but it is also probably because people now expect more of marriage than they used to, in a partnership of shared interests, activities and responsibilities.

Cohabiting without (or, frequently, in advance of) marrying has also been increasing. At the same time the number of births outside marriage has risen steeply. The increases in divorce and in births outside marriage have resulted in an increase in the number of lone-parent families.

If these trends were to continue, by 2010 the *great majority* of couples would cohabit before marrying and divorce after marrying, and then remarry; and *all* births would be outside of marriage well before 2010. Certainly, some further increases are to be expected, but the rates of increase are likely to slow down.

The nuclear family of two adults, with or without dependent children, will still be the norm by 2010, but marriage will less commonly be seen as a lifetime commitment and there will be more children in lone-parent families, often as a temporary condition in the period between divorce and remarriage. Within partnerships there is evidence of increasing equality in the sense of a belief that most household tasks should, in principle, be shared equally, but actual behaviour still seems to lag far behind. The gradual move towards greater equality between marriage partners seems likely to continue.

The extended families in close-knit local communities which once were common will in future be superseded, often by dispersed extended family patterns, with relatives living farther apart, travelling by car to meet from time to time, and with family links supplemented by circles of friends, often also geographically dispersed.

Surveys suggest that some of the political and social changes of the past decade have been widely welcomed and are now accepted as the fixed foundation from which to make further progress in the coming decades; but that others have been introduced against the grain of public opinion, have become less accepted with the passage of time, and may well be checked or reversed in the future.

During the 1950s, 1960s and 1970s the balance of public opinion alternated between two sets of attitudes: the one individualistic, stressing the merits of initiative, self-reliance and the advantages for society stemming from the drive of enterprising individuals for self-advancement; and the other more 'collectivist', emphasising the virtues of community and social concern and the advantages of public provision of common services. In the 1980s there was also a strong development in environmental concern, notably among more affluent sectors of the population; this is likely to continue, with a gradual rise in environmental awareness throughout British society.

The emphasis of government policies also alternated between these two sets of attitudes, but mostly within the bounds of a broad consensus around the middle. In the past decade there has been a break from this consensus, with a vigorous shift of policies towards the individualistic end of this spectrum. There is increasing evidence that public attitudes have not moved along with this change of direction and that there is a growing feeling that things have gone too far from the consensus area around the middle of this spectrum of attitudes. It may therefore be inferred that in the course of the next two decades electoral pressures will probably tend to shift the emphasis of policies back into the central zone of consensus – a tendency likely to be reinforced by closer involvement in the European Community where there has never been an outright majority for either end of the spectrum and policy decisions have normally reflected a compromise around the middle.

Three scenarios (Chapter 18)

The main forecasts are on a 'most probable' basis. Inevitably, they involve taking a view on the balance of probability in many areas of great uncertainty, and it must be stressed that even the best informed and most systematic assessment, while much more useful than superficial speculation, still cannot be guaranteed to provide wholly reliable forecasts. Indeed, the one thing that can be predicted with certainty is that some of the forecasts will turn out to be wrong.

Some of the greatest uncertainties are in areas where outcomes are largely determined by government policy decisions – which can be changed abruptly in ways not easy to predict. While it is not feasible in a report of limited length to set out alternative forecasts for all the areas of uncertainty, it is possible to illustrate some of the implications of different *policy choices*, by postulating three hypothetical *scenarios* based on three bundles of policies designed to reflect broad differences in political approach. Some of the possible economic implications of each have been tested, in tentative outline, with the use of the Cambridge Econometrics model.

The first scenario illustrates a *market-oriented* approach, with lower income tax, reduced government spending and supply-side changes to improve the efficiency of the market and raise labour productivity. The model suggests this scenario would be likely to give a faster rise in consumers' expenditure; a slower fall in unemployment; an earlier improvement in the balance of payments; and total economic growth over the two decades to 2010 similar to that in the main forecast.

The second scenario illustrates a more *interventionist* approach, with higher income tax, higher government spending on social services, and expansion of R&D and training schemes to improve productivity. The model suggests this scenario would be likely to give a slower rise in consumers' expenditure a faster fall in unemployment, an earlier improvement in the balance of payments; and, as with the first scenario, total economic growth similar to that in the main forecast.

The third scenario illustrates a more *environment-oriented* approach, with major investment to improve water quality, measures to reduce industrial pollution, and a carbon tax escalating by 10 per cent a year from 1991 (ie rising to 200 per cent by 2010) to cut emissions of greenhouse gases to 20 per cent below the 1988 level by 2005, with offsetting cuts in VAT. This target for greenhouse gases is the one set by the international conference in Toronto in 1988. It is tougher than the present proposal of the government to bring emissions back to 1990 levels by 2005, but much less stringent than the 60 per cent cut proposed by the scientists of the Intergovernmental Panel on Climate Change.

With this scenario the model suggests the likelihood of major structural changes, with much higher prices for water, electricity, petrol, gas and coal, but lower prices for many other categories of expenditure, particularly less energy-dependent ones such as health, education and most recreational services. It suggests that these price changes would bring major shifts in demand, and hence in output, with by 2010 water output about 15 per cent lower than in the main projection, electricity output about 20 per cent lower, petroleum products about 40 per cent lower and coal output about 75 per cent lower; but with higher output of gas (substituted for other fuels because of its lower rate of emission of greenhouse gases), and a shift from some kinds of manufacturing to less energy-dependent parts of the service sector.

With this scenario the model suggests that while structural shifts would be considerable, *total* economic growth would be likely to be much the same as with the main forecast, the deflationary effect of the carbon tax being broadly offset by the reductions in VAT, and the declines in the energy-intensive sectors being broadly offset by increases elsewhere.

These calculations are on the assumption that similar measures were adopted in other countries. However, if the measures were adopted *unilaterally*, the effect on total economic growth would probably be similar: the worsening of the balance of payments due to the more energy-dependent industries becoming less internationally competitive being broadly offset by the lower level of oil imports needed when consumption levels were reduced by the carbon tax.

Conclusion

Implicit in the form taken by this assessment of the prospects for Britain in 2010, with its complex interactions between many different causal factors, each of them subject to major uncertainties, is the possibility that any of the forecasts of what is 'most probable' may turn out to be substantially *wrong*. Nonetheless, they are more likely to be substantially *right* than a simple projection of past trends or a consideration of each area in isolation. And there are grounds for confidence in the validity of the general finding that in the course of the next two decades there will be many changes, some of them important, but they will mostly be *incremental* and *evolutionary*, not discontinuous and dramatic. There is little reason to expect breakthroughs in science, economics, politics or other areas of a kind likely to produce fundamental changes over a relatively short period.

Hence there are reasons for confidence also in the validity of the general picture of Britain in 2010 that emerges, changed in a great many ways, but still not unrecognisably different from the Britain of today. This finding may seem unexciting, but should not be surprising; indeed, it would be more surprising if it were suggested that the changes in the *next* two decades would be altogether more momentous than the steady but, on the whole, unspectacular changes that occurred in the *past* two decades, or the two decades before them.

Among all the inevitable uncertainties involved in looking into the future, one thing particularly important to remember is that many of the greatest uncertainties are in areas where the key factors are government decisions – which may change abruptly in ways that are hard to predict. In these areas the future is not something that we can try to foresee but cannot hope to change; on the contrary, the course of events will be influenced by the decisions which are taken, and the future is what we choose to make it. If we are to make the most of the potential opportunities, it is important to think clearly and choose well.

Thus one purpose of studying future possibilities is to get the best available view of what is most likely to happen, so as to provide a considered context for people who have long-term decisions to take. The other, and perhaps more important, purpose is to identify the potential areas of choice and illumine the issues involved. It is hoped that this book will have gone some way to meet its dual aims of narrowing the range of uncertainty and informing the areas of choice.

References

4 World Economy

1. Martin Wolf, 'The economic indicators that matter most', *Financial Times*, London, 26 September 1989, quoting figures from IMF and GATT.
2. 'UK and Main Manufacturing Countries' Exports of Manufactures', *Monthly Review of External Trade Statistics*, Central Statistical Office, London, April 1990, December 1986 and Annual Supplement 1980.
3. Barry Bosworth, 'America's Global Decline: Implications for the International Economy', Exploring the Future: Trends and Discontinuities, a joint conference of the Strategic Planning Society and the Royal Institute for International Affairs, London, 5-6 October, 1989.
4. S. Kuznets, 'Quantitative aspects of the growth of nations, level and structure of foreign trade: long-term trends', *Economic Development and Cultural Change*, January 1967, Vol.15, No.2.
5. General Agreement on Tariffs and Trade, *International Trade 1985-1986*, GATT, Geneva, 1986.
6. William J. Beeman and Isaiah Frank, *New Dynamics in the Global Economy*, Committee for Economic Development, Washington D.C., 1988.
7. *Economic Report of the President*, U.S. Government Printing Office, Washington D.C., February 1988.
8. Ralph Bryant, *International Financial Intermediation*, The Brookings Institution, Washington D.C., 1987.
9. John G. Heimann, Speech to the Forum de l'Expansion, Paris, May 1987.
10. Richard Cooper, 'The United States as an Open Economy', in *How Open Is the U.S. Economy?*, R.W. Hafer (Ed.), Lexington Books, Lexington, MA., 1986.
11. J.J. Nogues, A.Olechowski, and L.A. Winters, 'The Extent of Nontariff Barriers to Industrial Countries', *The World Bank Economic Review 1*, No.1, September 1986.
12. Raymond Vernon, 'Global Interdependence in a Historic Perspective', in *Interdependence and Cooperation in Tomorrow's World*, OECD, Paris, 1987.
13. Robert B. Reich, 'The Rise of Techno-Nationalism', *The Atlantic Monthly*, Washington D.C., May 1987.
14. Katherine Marton, 'Technological Transfer to Developing Countries via Multinationals', *The World Economy*, December 1986.

5 World Environment

15. *Hansard*, HMSO, London, 30 November 1988.
16. 'N-Waste Cost Shock', *The Environment Digest*, No.19, 1988.
17. Fred Pearce, 'Whatever happened to Acid Rain?', *New Scientist*, London, 15 September 1990.
18. *Environment in Trust: Air Quality*, Department of the Environment, London, 1989.
19. Mary Fagan, 'Bank of trapped CFCs is higher than 1989 output', *Independent*, London, 6 June 1990.

20. Nigel Williams, 'Hole in ozone layer grows', *Guardian*, London, 13 October 1990.

21. Paul Brown, 'World unites on ozone deal', *Guardian*, London, 30 June 1990.

22. Nicholas Schoon, 'Ozone destruction conference faces division over aid', *Independent*, London, 28 June 1990.

23. The Climatic Research Unit, University of East Anglia, quoted by Geoffrey Lean and Polly Ghazi in 'Sizzling 1990 the hottest year on record', *Observer*, London, 21 October 1990.

24. J. Hansen, 'Global Climate Changes: a Forecast by Goddard Institute for Space Studies Three-Dimensional Model', *Journal of Geophysical Research*, Vol.93, 1988.

25. National Research Council, *'Current Issues in Atmospheric Change'*, National Academy Press, Washington D.C., 1988.

26. L. B. Lave, 'The Greenhouse Effect: What Government Actions are needed?', *Journal of Policy Analysis and Management*, Vol.7, 1988.

27. I. Mintzer, 'Living in a Warmer World: Challenges for Policy Analysis and Management', *Journal of Policy Analysis and Management*, Vol.7, 1988.

28. D. Everest, *The Greenhouse Effect: Issues for Policy Makers*, Joint Energy Programme, Royal Institute of International Affairs and Policy Studies Institute, London, 1988.

29. Department of the Environment, *Global Climate Change*, Department of the Environment in association with the Meteorological Office, HMSO, London, 1989.

30. Report of the Intergovernmental Panel on Climate Change, United Nations Environment Programme and World Meteorological Organisation, 1990.

31. 'Busy bacteria may reduce the risk of a runaway greenhouse', *New Scientist*, London, 28 July 1990.

32. Jan Sinclair, 'Global warming may distort carbon cycle', *New Scientist*, London, 26 May 1990.

33. Peter Killworth, Hooke Institute of Atmosphere Research, Oxford, quoted by William Brown in 'Flipping oceans could turn up the heat', *New Scientist*, London, 25 August 1990.

34. David Drewry, British Antarctic Survey director, quoted by Charles Clover in 'Global warming adds 1 °C at pole', *Daily Telegraph*, London, 24 May 1990.

35. Peter Wadhams, Scott Polar Research Institute director, quoted by Robin McKie in 'Warmer world skates on even thinner ice', *Observer*, London, 22 July 1990.

36. John Gribbin, 'Methane may amplify climate change', *New Scientist*, London, 2 June 1990.

37. Steve Connor, 'The greenhouse time bomb', *Independent on Sunday*, London, 27 May 1990.

38. Martin Parry, senior agricultural advisor on IPCC report team, quoted by Tom Wilkie in 'Danger to bread-baskets from global warming spelt out', *Independent*, London, 25 October 1990.

39. Richard Warrick, Climatic Research Unit, University of East Anglia, quoted by Pearce Wright in 'Rise of 1 °C unstoppable', *Times*, London, 18 September 1990.

40. Pier Vellinga, chairman of the coastal impacts working group of the IPCC, quoted by Jan Sinclair in 'Rising sea levels could affect 300 million', *New Scientist*, London, 20 January 1990.

41. World Resources Institute, Washington, quoted in 'Disappearing forests fan fears over tropical action plan', *New Scientist*, London, 23 January 1990.

42. P. M. Kelly, *Halting Global Warming*, Climatic Research Unit, University of East Anglia, Norwich, 1990

43. F. Krause, W. Bach, J.Koomey, *Energy Policy in the Greenhouse, International Project for Sustainable Energy Paths*, El Cerrito, CA, 1990.

44. Jeremy Leggett, *Global Warming: the Greenpeace Report*, Oxford University Press, Oxford, 1990.

45. Sue Bowler, 'The politics of climate: a long haul ahead ', *New Scientist*, London, 27 October 1990.

6　United States

46. U.S. Department of Defence figures quoted in *New York Times*, 20 May 1988.

47. Daniel Bell, 'The World and the United States in 2013', *Daedelus*, Vol.116, No.3, American Academy of Arts and Sciences, Cambridge, Mass., Summer 1987.

48. *Direction of Trade Yearbook*, 1962-1964, IMF, Paris.

49. David Hale, 'America's economy: 1890 is a glance at the future', *The World In 1990*, Economist, London, 1989.

50. Eileen Applebaum, 'The Growth in the U.S. Contingent Labour Force', paper presented at conference on The Impact of Structural and Technological Change on the Labour Market, Wissenschaftszentrum, Berlin, 1988.

7   Japan

51. *Main Economic Indicators*, February 1990, Organisation for Economic Co-operation and Development, Paris, 1990.

52. G.D. Hobbs, 'The Commercial, Social and Political Implications of Future Demographic Change', Exploring the Future: Trends and Discontinuities, a joint conference of The Strategic Planning Society and The Royal Institute of International Affairs, London, 5-6 October 1989.

8   Third World

53. Nafis Sadik, *The State of World Population, 1990*, United Nations Population Fund, New York, 1990.

54. *The Newly Industrialising Countries*, Organisation for Economic Co-operation and Development, Paris, 1988.

55. World Bank figures quoted by Jim MacNeill in 'Strategies for Sustainable Economic Development' in *Scientific American*, New York, 1990.

56. Charles Leadbeater, 'World Industrial Review', *Financial Times*, London, 8 January 1990.

57. 1989 Report of the chairman of the Development Assistance Committee, OECD, quoted by Michael Prest in 'OECD says democracy vital for development' in *Independent*, London, 6 December 1989.

58. D. Gale Johnson, 'World Food and Agriculture' in *The Resourceful Earth*, Julian L. Simon and Herman Khan (Eds.), Basil Blackwell Inc., New York, 1984.

59. Gerald O. Barney (Ed.), *The Global 2000 Report to the President of the U.S.*, Pergamon Press, New York, 1980.

11   Western Europe

60. P. Cecchini, *The European Challenge 1992: the Benefits of a Single Market*, Wildwood House, London, 1988.

61. Amin Rajan, *A Zero Sum Game*, The Industrial Society, London, 1990.

62. Delors, *Report on Economic and Monetary Union in the European Community*, Commission of the European Communities, Brussels, 1989.

63. John Eatwell, *Economic Policy in the New Europe – the Problem of the German Surplus*, Manchester Statistical Society, Manchester, 1990.

64. MacDougall, *Report of the Study Group on the Role of Public Finance in European Integration*, Commission of the European Communities, Brussels, 1977.

12   Population

65. Stephen P. Schnaars, *Megamistakes: Forecasting and the Myth of Rapid Technological Change*, Macmillan, London, 1989.

66. Office of Population Censuses and Surveys, *Population Projections, 1987-2027*, PP2 No.16, HMSO, London, 1989.

67. 'The unsolved riddle of why people age', *Economist*, London, 10 January 1981.

68. WHO statistics, reported by David Brindle in 'Poor lookout for the old', *Guardian*, London, 7 November 1988.

69. Hilary Henson, 'Plugging the health gap', *Listener*, London, 4 February 1988.

70. Central Statistical Office, *Annual Abstract of Statistics 1990*, HMSO, London, 1990.

71. Emily T. Smith, Kevin Kelly and Corrie Brown, 'Aging: Can it be slowed?, *Business Week*, USA, 8 February 1988.

72. Gail DeGeorge, 'Wanna be a Methuselah?, Step Right Up', *Business Week*, USA, 8 February 1988.

73. WHO statistics reported by Chris Mihill in 'The AIDS age of apocalypse', *Guardian*, London, 27 January 1990.

74. OPCS Monitor, PP2, quoted by David Brindle in 'Aids likely to kill 100,000 men in 10 years', *Guardian*, London, 15 February 1989.

75. Institute of Actuaries AIDS Bulletin quoted by Celia Hall in 'Aids has "doubled the chances of men dying early"', *Independent*, London, 2 March 1989.

76. Public Health Laboratory Service Working Party Report quoted by Liz Hunt in 'Death from Aids "will be half the number forecast"', *Independent*, London, 3 February 1990.

77. Jonathan Mann, head of WHO Global Programme on AIDS, 'The global lesson of AIDS', *New Scientist*, London, 30 June 1990.

78. Roy Anderson, 'Prospects for the UK: the AIDS epidemic in the UK; past trends and future projections', paper at symposium on *HIV and AIDS: an assessment of current and future spread in the UK*, UK Health Departments Health Education Authority, London, 24 November 1989.

79. The National Study of Sexual Attitudes and Lifestyles, reported on by Phyllida Brown in 'Is sex too important to keep quiet about?' in *New Scientist*, London, 2 June 1990.

80. Chris Mihill, 'AIDS campaign will highlight victims', *Guardian*, London, 23 October 1990.

81. Sharon Kingman, 'Aids and the social outcast', *New Scientist*, London, 10 March 1988.

82. 'Drugs use spreads AIDS in Scotland', *Independent*, London, 19 July 1990.

83. Celia Hall, 'Addicts fail to change AIDS-risk behaviour', *Independent*, London, 12 April 1989.

84. 'Danger of alarmist AIDS warning', *Independent*, London, 5 September 1989.

85. Celia Hall, 'AIDS cases among heterosexuals have doubled in a year', *Independent*, London, 12 April 1990.

86. Roy Anderson, Professor of Epidemiology at Imperial College, London, quoted by Liz Hunt in 'Heterosexuals face big increase in AIDS cases', *Independent*, London, 25 October 1990

87. Christopher Joyce, 'Success stops trial of AIDS drug', *New Scientist*, London, 26 August 1990.

88. Aileen Ballantyne, 'Doctors may tame AIDS', *Guardian*, London, 10 June 1989.

89. Tom Wilkie, 'Modified HIV virus could be used as AIDS treatment', *Independent*, London, 19 February 1990.

90. 'A vaccine ready by the end of the decade', *New Scientist*, London, 30 June 1990.

91. Office of Population Censuses and Surveys, *Social Trends 20*, HMSO, London, 1990.

92. Home Office, *Social Trends 20*, HMSO, London, 1990.

93. Statistical Office of the European Communities, *Social Trends 20*, HMSO, London, 1990.

13   Employment

94. H. Joshi and E. Overton, *The Female Labour Force in Britain 1971-1991*, Centre for Population Studies, London, Research Paper 84-1, 1984.

95. J. Ermisch, 'Work, jobs and social policy', in R. Klein and M. O'Higgins (Eds.), *The Future of Welfare*, Basil Blackwell, Oxford, 1985.

96. Department of Employment, 'Labour force outlook to 1995', in *Employment Gazette*, London, March 1988.

97. R. Cawley, *The Economic Implications of Demographic Change in the European Community 1975-1995: A Critique*, Commission of the European Communities, Brussels, 1987.

98. B. Casey and F. Laczko, *Recent Trends in Labour Force Participation of Older Men in Great Britain and their Implications for the Future*, paper presented to the workshop 'Le Vieillissement Démographique en Europe: Tendances, Enjeux et Stratégies', organised by Futuribles Internationales and held in Paris on 4-5 October 1988.

99. R. Cawley, *The Changing Age Structure of the Working Population in Europe 1950-2025*, paper presented to the workshop 'Le Vieillissement Démographique en Europe: Tendances, Enjeux et Stratégies', organised by Futuribles Internationales and held in Paris on 4-5 October 1988.

100. M. White, 'Educational policy and economic goals', in *Oxford Review of Economic Policy*, Autumn 1988.

101. Jim Northcott, *Industry in the Development Areas: the experience of firms opening new factories*, PEP, London, 1977.

102. J. H. Goldthorpe, *Social Mobility and Class Structure*, Clarendon Press, London, 1980.

103. J. H. Goldthorpe and C. W. Payne, 'Trends in intergenerational class mobility in England and Wales 1972-83', *Sociology*, 1986.

104. M. White, *Long-term Unemployment and Labour Markets*, PSI, London, 1983.

105. M. White and S. McRae, *Young Adults and Long-term Unemployment*, PSI, London, 1989.

106. Institute for Employment Research, *Review of the Economy and Employment: Occupational Assessment*, University of Warwick, 1989.

107. Richard Pearson, Geoff Pike, Alan Gordon and Clare Weyman, *How Many Graduates in the 21st Century? The Choice is Yours*, IMS Report No.177, The Institute of Manpower Studies, Brighton, 1989.

108. M. White and D. Gallie, *Employers' Policies and Individuals' Life Chances*, forthcoming.

109. M. Rigg, P. Elias and S. Johnson, *An Overview of the Demand for Graduates*, HMSO, London, 1990.

110. M. White, *Employers' Wage Strategies and Unemployment*, paper presented to the Conference on Labour Market Research, jointly organised by Nuffield College and PSI, held at Nuffield College, Oxford, 7 October 1988.

111. M. Trevor and I. Christie, *Manufacturers and Suppliers in Britain and Japan: Competitiveness and the Growth of Small Firms*, PSI, London, 1988.

112. M. Rigg, I. Christie and M. White, *Advanced Polymers and Composites: Creating the Key Skills*, Training Agency, Sheffield, 1989.

113. J. Gershuny, *After Industrial Society: the Emerging Self-Service Economy*, Macmillan, London, 1978.

114 J. Gershuny and I. Miles, *The New Service Economy: the Transformation of Employment in Industrial Societies*, Frances Pinter, London, 1983.

115. Commission of the European Communities, *Employment in Europe 1989*, Office for Official Publications of the European Communities, Luxembourg, 1989.

116. H. Braverman, *Labour and Monopoly Capital: the Degradation of Work in the 20th Century*, Monthly Review Press, New York, 1974.

117 H. Benyon and N. Hedges, *Born to Work*, Pluto Press, London, 1982.

118. J. Downing, 'Word Processors and the Oppression of Women' in *The Microelectronics Revolution*, Tom Forester (ed.), Basil Blackwell, London, 1980.

119. Jacques Servan-Schreiber, head of The World Centre for Computer Sciences and Human Resources, quoted in *Computerworld*, Fromingham, Mass., 24 May, 1982.

120. S. Nora and A. Minc, *L'Information de la Societe*, La Documentation Française, Paris, 1978.

121. Siemens, *Office 1990*, Unpublished Report.

122. *Business Week*, 'Changing 45 million Jobs', article based on a study by Booz, Allen and Hamilton Inc., USA, 3 August 1981.

123. C. Jenkins and B. Sherman, *The Collapse of Work*, Eyre Methuen, London, 1979.

124. T. Stonier, 'The Impact of Microprocessors on Employment' *The Microelectronics Revolution*, Tom Forester (ed.), Basil Blackwell, London, 1980.

125 Jim Northcott and Petra Rodgers, *Microelectronics in Industry: What's Happening in Britain*, PSI, London, 1982.

126. Jim Northcott and Petra Rodgers, *Microelectronics in British Industry: the Pattern of Change*, PSI, London, 1984.

127   Jim Northcott, *Microelectronics in Industry: Promise and Performance*, PSI, London, 1986.

128.   Jim Northcott and Annette Walling, *The Impact of Microelectronics: Diffusion, Benefits and Problems in British Industry*, PSI, London, 1988.

129.   Jim Northcott, Petra Rodgers, Werner Knetsch and Bérengère de Lestapis, *Microelectronics in Industry: an International Comparison: Britain, France and Germany*, PSI, London, 1985.
       (German and French language editions also available from VDI-VDE TZ and BIPE).

130.   Ian Christie, Jim Northcott and Annette Walling, *Employment Effects of New Technology in Manufacturing*, PSI, London, 1990.

131.   M. White, *IT and the Changing Structure of Employment*, (working paper), National Economic Development Office, London, 1986.

132.   Jim Northcott, Colin Brown, Ian Christie, Michael Sweeney and Annette Walling, *Robots in British Industry: Expectations and Experience*, PSI, London, 1986.

133.   S. Watanabe, 'Labour-saving versus work-amplifying effects of micro-electronics', *International Labour Review*, Vol.125, No.3, Geneva, 1986.

134   Jim Northcott, Michael Fogarty, Malcolm Trevor, *Chips and Jobs: Acceptance of New Technology at Work*, PSI, London, 1985.

135.   M. White, *Case Studies in Wage Payment Systems in the Electrical Engineering Industry*, European Foundation for the Improvement of Living and Working Conditions, Dublin, 1984.

136.   W. W. Daniel, *Workplace Industrial Relations and Technical Change*, Frances Pinter for PSI, London, 1987.

137.   Jim Northcott, *Factors in Diffusion of Technologies: Evidence from Surveys of Use of Microelectronics*, paper presented to the conference on Technology and Investment: Crucial Issues for the 90s, jointly organised by The Royal Swedish Academy of Engineering Sciences, The Swedish Ministry of Industry and The Organisation for Economic Co-operation and Development, held in Stockholm, 21-24 January 1990.

138.   Werner Knetsch und Mario Kliche, *Die industrielle Mikroelektronik-Anwendung im Verarbeitenden Gewerbe der Bundesrepublik Deutschland*, Berlin, VDI-VDE Technologiezentrum Informationtechnik GmbH, 1986.

139.   Bérengère de Lestapis, *Diffusion de la Micro-Electronique dans l'Industrie*, Bureau d'Informations et de Prévisions Economiques (BIPE), France, 1985.

140.   Olof Löfgren, *Microelectronics in Swedish Industry*, National Industrial Board, Stockholm, 1988.

141.   Ulrik Jorgensen and K. S. Vilstrup, *Spredning af Informationsteknologi i Dansk Industri 1987*, Institut for Forbrugs-og Holdningsanalyser, Copenhagen, Denmark, 1988.

142.   Robert Bowie and Alan Bollard, *The Diffusion of Microelectronics through New Zealand Manufacturing*, NZ Institute of Economic Research, Wellington, 1987.

143.   J. Constable and R. McCormick, *The Making of British Managers*, British Institute of Management, London, 1987.

144.   C. Handy, *The Making of Managers*, National Economic Development Office, London, 1985.

145.   G. Crockett and D.P.B. Elias, 'British Managers: A study of their education, training, mobility and earnings', *British Journal of Industrial Relations*, Vol.22, No.1, London, 1983.

146.   J. H. Goldthorpe et al, *Social Mobility and Class Structure in Modern Britain*, Clarendon Press, Oxford, 1980.

147.   J. Butcher (Chairman), *The Human Factor: the Supply Side Problem*, First Report of the IT Skills Shortage Committee, Department of Trade and Industry, London, 1984.

148.   M. Harrison, 'Britain must expand education for engineers', *Independent*, London, 28 February 1989.

149.   Department of Education and Science, *Social Trends 20*, HMSO, London, 1990.

150.   YTS Follow-up Survey, *Social Trends 20*, HMSO, London, 1990.

151.   Department of Education and Science, *Social Trends 20*, HMSO, London, 1990.

152.   S. Prais, *Productivity and Industrial Change*, Cambridge University Press, Cambridge, 1981.

153. S. Prais and K. Wagner, 'Productivity and Management: the Training of Foremen in Britain and Germany', *National Institute Economic Review*, No.123, London, February 1988.

154. M. Rigg, *Training in Britain: Individuals' Perspectives*, HMSO, London, 1989.

155. Christopher Ball, *Aim Higher: Widening Access to Higher Education*, Royal Society of Arts, London, 1989.

156. George Parker-Jervis, 'Jobs', *Observer*, London, 18 February 1990.

157. Statistical Office of the European Community, *Social Trends 20*, HMSO, London, 1990.

14   The Environment

158. R. Kershaw, *Long Term Trends in the Distribution of the Population of England*, FACT/Department of the Environment, London, 1988.

159. P. Hall, 'The Industrial Revolution in Reverse', *Planner*, London, January 1988.

160. Cambridge Econometrics and Northern Ireland Economic Research Centre, *Regional Economic Prospects*, Cambridge Econometrics, Cambridge, 1990.

161. G. Steely, 'How to cope with growing demand', *Town and Country Planning*, London, September 1988.

162. Champion et al, 'Housing, labour, mobility and unemployment', *Planner*, London, Vol.73, 1987.

163. A. E. Green and A. G. Champion, 'The Booming Towns of Britain: the geography of economic performance', *Geography*, London, Vol.72, 1987.

164. A. E. Green, *The North-South Divide in Great Britain: an examination of the evidence*, Institute of Employment Research, Warwick University.

165. M. J. Weiner, *English Culture and the Decline of the Industrial Spirit, 1850-1980*, Cambridge University Press, Cambridge, 1981.

166. H. Newby, *Green and Pleasant Land: Social Change in Rural England*, Temple Smith, London, 1979.

167. K. Young, 'Interim Report: Rural Prospects' in *Social Trends 1988*, HMSO, London.

168. D. Cross, quoted in 'More flee cities to rural retreat', in *Guardian*, London, 8 January 1988.

169. 'Farms lost to homes boom', *Independent*, London, 11 November 1988.

170. T. Champion and A. E. Green, *Local prosperity and the North-South divide*, Institute of Employment Research, University of Warwick, 1988.

171. *Affordable Rural Housing: Need and Supply*, Acre, Cirencester, 1990.

172. 'Lest the Villages Decay', *Economist*, London, 13 February 1988.

173. P. Lowe et al., *Countryside Conflicts*, Gower, Aldershot, 1986.

174. B. Bloom, 'Aid for farms to combat pollution replaces capital grants scheme', *Financial Times*, London, 29 November 1988.

175. 'Rural Tourism: Consuming and Conserving', *Planning*, London, 25 November 1988.

176. 'MAFF's Farm Woodlands, Diversification and Extensification Plans', *UK CEED Bulletin* No.15, The UK Centre for Economic and Environmental Development.

177. Association of District Councils, *The Future for Rural Communities*, Association of District Councils, London, 1988.

178. A. Speller, 'Migrant interests and local needs', *Housing Review*, Vol.37, London, 1988.

179. A. Slade, 'Taking time out in the national parks', *Planning*, London, 15 July 1988.

180. 'Rural tourism: consuming and conserving', *Planning*, London, 25 November 1988.

181. G. Lean, 'Nature sites next for Ridley sell-off', *Observer*, London, 4 December 1988.

182. Geoffrey Lean and Jerry Connolly, 'The Great Land Grab', *Observer*, London, 23 October 1988.

183. R. Schiller, 'Retail Decentralisation – The Coming of the Third Wave', *Planner*, London, July 1986.

184. R. Davies and E. Howard, 'Issues in Retail Planning within the United Kingdom', *Built Environment*, Vol.14, London.

185.   S. Hampson, 'Danger ahead without retail planning', *Town and Country Planning*, London, September 1987.

186.   R. Davies, 'The High Street in Britain; Choices for the Future', R. Davies and E. Howard, 'Issues in retail planning in the United Kingdom, *Built Environment*, Vol.14, London, 1988.

187.   'Development Economics, Out-of-Town Retailing Shopping Centres', *Architects Journal*, 4 December 1987.

188.   H. Gilette, 'Evolution of the Planned Shopping Centre in Suburb and City', *APA Journal*, London, Autumn 1985.

189.   Ron McCarthy, *Leisure and retailing: a case study of Meadowhall*, paper given at conference on Britain in 2010: future patterns of shopping, held by Royal Society of Arts in London, 22 June 1989.

190.   Stuart Hampson, *Planning for shopping*, paper given at conference on Britain in 2010: future patterns of shopping, held by Royal Society of Arts in London, 22 June 1989.

191.   Hillier Parker, *Out-of-town regional shopping centres in the pipeline*, Hillier Parker, London, 1989.

192.   K. Treister, 'Historical perspective invaluable in planning rebirth of lively cities', *National Mall Monitor*, No.11, Clearwater, Fl.

193.   John Roberts, *The European experience*, paper given at conference on Britain in 2010: future patterns of shopping, held by Royal Society of Arts in London, 22 June 1989.

194.   London Planning Advisory Committee, 1988, *Strategic planning advice for London*, London Planning Advisory Committee, London, 1988.

195.   J. Hillman, *A new look for London*, Royal Fine Arts Commission, HMSO, London, 1989.

196.   P. Hall, paper delivered to Town and Country Planning Association conference, quoted in *Guardian*, London, 1 December 1989.

197.   M. Carley, *Housing and neighbourhood renewal*, PSI, London, 1990.

198.   Department of the Environment, *Social Trends 20*, HMSO, London, 1990.

199.   Department of the Environment, English House Condition Survey, *Social Trends 20*, HMSO, London, 1990.

200.   Department of the Environment, General Household Survey, *Social Trends 20*, HMSO, London, 1990.

201.   John Ermisch, *Fewer babies, longer lives*, Joseph Rowntree Foundation, York, 1990.

202.   National Audit Office, *Homelessness*, HMSO, London, 1990.

203.   Department of the Environment and Scottish Development Department, in *Social Trends 20*, HMSO, London, 1990.

204.   *Investigation of Pesticide Pollution in Drinking Water in England and Wales*, Friends of the Earth, London, 1988.

205.   'Forty-year fertiliser legacy comes home to roost', *Guardian*, London, 30 January 1989.

206.   John Carvel, 'Water clean up will be delayed', *Guardian*, London, 20 January 1989.

207.   Derek Miller of the Water Research Centre, quoted by Richard North in 'Scientist defends standards of Britain's drinking water', *Independent*, London, 22 September, 1989.

208.   John Mather, chief geochemist of the British Geological Survey, quoted in 'Fertiliser threat to drinking water', *Independent*, London, 9 September 1988.

209.   Mary Fagan in 'Rivers facing threat from algae caused by pollution', *Independent*, London, 1 March, 1990.

210.   Tom Addiscott, 'Farmers, fertilisers and the nitrate flood', *New Scientist*, London, 8 October 1988.

211.   Tim Radford, 'Water nitrate cut will take decades', *Guardian*, London, 17 November, 1988.

212   Water Authorities Association, *Water Pollution from Farm Waste*, Water Authorities Association, London, 1989.

213   The Department of the Environment, *The Nitrate Issue: a study of the economic and other consequences of various local options for limiting nitrate concentrations in drinking water*, HMSO, London, 1988.

214   John Knill, chairman of the Natural Environment Research Council quoted by Pearce Wright in 'Only a fraction of chemicals are monitored', *Times*, London, 7 February, 1990.

215.   John Ardill, 'Cancer risk water pipes could cost billions to clean' *Guardian*, London, 27 October 1988.

216.   Richard North, 'Britain will end dumping in North Sea by 1998', *Independent*, London, 6 March 1990.

217.   Paul Brown, 'Britain left isolated on pollution', *Guardian*, London, 9 March 1989.

218.   Richard North, 'Government failing to act over toxic waste' *Independent*, London, 15 October, 1988.

219.   *Toxic Waste, Second Report of the Environment Committee, 1988-89*, House of Commons Paper 22-1, HMSO, London, 1989.

220.   John Ardill, 'Tory MP leads attack over near disaster on waste', *Guardian*, London, 9 March 1989.

221.   Department of Transport, *Transport Statistics Great Britain 1979-1989*, HMSO, London, 1990.

222.   Department of Transport, *National Travel Survey*, HMSO, London, 1989.

223.   Department of Employment, *Family Expenditure Survey*, HMSO, London, 1988.

224.   Department of Transport, *Road Traffic Forecasts*, London, 1985.

225.   David Black, 'London speeds up 3mph since 1912', *Independent*, London, November 30, 1989. Source: Department of Transport London Travel Survey.

226.   Adam Raphael, 'The monster we love is strangling us', *Observer*, London, 16 July 1989.

227.   Terence Bendixson, 'Better a road toll than a death toll', *Observer*, London, 29 January 1989.

228.   Shyama Perera, '£1bn scheme to widen M25 scorned as wrong solution', *Guardian*, London, 2 March 1989.

229.   Centraal Bureau voor de Statistiek, *de mobiliteit van de Nederlandse bevolking 1989* (Netherlands National Travel Survey 1989), the Hague, 1990, and Department of Transport, *National Travel Survey 1985/6*, HMSO, London, 1988.

230.   Ken Creffield, 'On-yer-bike Danes to get a free ride', *Observer*, London, 30 September 1990.

231.   Paul Webster, 'Paris pushes motorists off the streets', *Guardian*, London, 11 October 1989.

232.   'Europe makes tracks for faster connections', *New Scientist*, London, 4 February 1989.

233.   David Black, 'Radical route planned for EC's fragmented railways' *Independent*, London, 20 November 1989.

234.   Department of Transport, *Road Accidents Great Britain 1988: The Casualty Report*, HMSO, London, 1989.

235.   Adam Raphael, 'Company cars – the hidden cost to Britain', *Observer*, London, 7 January 1990.

236.   Brian Jenks of accountants Touche Ross, 'What the company car perk is worth', *Observer*, London, 26 August 1990.

237   Nicholas Schoon, 'Sharp rise in drivers passing stop warnings', *Independent*, London, 11 March 1989.

238.   Julie Wolf, 'Exhaust limit accord struck', *Guardian*, London, 10 June 1989.

239.   Ian Anderson, 'Smog-bound Los Angeles to ban petrol driven cars' *New Scientist*, London, 1 April 1989.

240.   Richard Gould and John Gribbin, 'Greener cars may warm the world', *New Scientist*, London, 20 May 1989.

241.   Department of Energy, *Digest of United Kingdom Energy Statistics 1989*, Department of Energy, HMSO, 1989.

242.   Nicholas Schoon, 'Nuclear power decline forecast', *Independent*, London, 17 November 1989.

243.   Roger Milne, 'Smaller stations better suited to clean coal', *New Scientist*, London, 5 November 1988.

244.   Patrick Donovan, 'Britain lags behind Europe', *Guardian*, London, 10 November 1989.

245. Pierre Tanguy, chief inspector for nuclear safety of Electricité de France, quoted by Paul Brown in 'One in 20 chance of nuclear accident', *Guardian*, London, 19 March 1990.

246. Michael Harrison and Colin Hughes, 'N-power stations pulled out of electricity sell-off', *Independent*, London, 10 November 1989.

247. Walt Patterson, 'Energy issues another challenge', *New Scientist*, London, 28 January 1989.

248. Paul Brown, 'Wave power undercuts nuclear cost', *Guardian*, London, 19 March 1990.

249. Association for the Conservation of Energy, memorandum to Energy Committee of House of Commons, Memoranda of Evidence, Volume II, *Energy Policy Implications of the Greenhouse Effect, Sixth Report, Energy Committee of the House of Commons*, HMSO, London, 1989.

250. *Energy Policy Implications of the Greenhouse Effect, Sixth Report, Energy Committee of the House of Commons*, Volume I, report and proceedings, HMSO, London, 1989.

15   Science and Technology

251. T. Forester (ed.), *Computers in the Human Context*, Blackwell, Oxford, 1989.

252. Ian Miles et al, *Information Horizons*, Edward Elgar, Aldershot, 1988.

253. Michael Cross, 'Japanese memory chips win another round', *New Scientist*, London, 27 January 1990.

254. Mary Fagan, 'Possibilities of gallium arsenide', *Independent*, London, 26 April 1988.

255. Angeli Mehta, 'The sure-fire bet of RISC', *Independent*, London, 24 April, 1989.

256. William Gosling, 'The foreseeable future', *National Electronics Review*, 1988.

257. Terry Dodsworth and Louise Kehoe, 'Leaping ahead on a surface of silicon', *Financial Times*, London, 26 June 1988.

258. Greg Wilson, 'Computing in parallel', *New Scientist*, London, 11 February 1988.

259. Greg Wilson, 'The superchips of tomorrow', *Independent*, London, 13 June 1988.

260. David Hebditch and Nick Anning, 'Parallel thinking for powerful chip', *New Scientist*, London, 28 April 1988.

261. Michael Cross and Susan Watts, 'Wafers herald new era for computing', *New Scientist*, London, 25 February 1989.

262. Peter Large, 'On its way – the jumbo chip', *Guardian*, London, 28 June 1988.

263. Mary Fagan, 'Microchips put themselves to the test', *New Scientist*, London, 28 January 1988.

264. John Senior, 'Computing with light', *New Scientist*, London, 30 May 1985.

265. 'Superfast transistor bids goodbye to semiconductors', *New Scientist*, London, 24 March 1988.

266. Robert Matthews, 'Cold chip revolution has scientists in state of excitement', *Times*, London.

267. 'British scientist develops "thinking" computer chip', *Guardian*, London, 13 September 1989.

268. Dr. Edwin Galea, 'Supercomputers and the need for speed', *New Scientist*, London, 12 November 1988.

269. Mary Fagan, 'Advanced material for data storage', *Independent*, London, 23 February, 1988.

270. Bryan Silcock, 'The light fantastic computer', *Sunday Times*, London, 18 March 1984.

271. Tom Wilkie and Michael Cross, '"Brain cell" circuits for computers may oust silicon chips', *Independent*, London, 8 February 1988.

272. Angeli Metha, 'Brainy computer learns to solve real problems', *New Scientist*, London, 25 August 1988.

273. Angeli Metha, 'Clarification by fuzzy logic', *Independent*, London, 30 June 1989.

274. Robert Whymant, 'Japanese press the new technology panic button', *Daily Telegraph*, London, 27 March 1990.

275. Ian Anderson, Michael Cross and John Lamb, 'Listening computers broaden their vocabulary', *New Scientist*, London, 4 August 1988.

276. Mary Fagan, 'British breakthrough in speech-wise computers', *Independent*, London, 10 October 1989.
277. PA Consulting Group, *Evolution of the UK Communications Infrastructure*, HMSO, London, 1988.
278. E. M. Briscoe, 'A new era for engineering ceramics', in *Journal of the Royal Society of Arts*, London, November 1984.
279. 'Strong wood enters the concrete jungle', *New Statesman*, London, 1 September 1988.
280. Michael Cross, 'Japan puts its money into two-faced materials', *New Scientist*, London, 24 February 1990.
281. Michael Cross, 'Japan shapes a superconducting future', *New Scientist*, London, 8 September 1988.
282. Chris Evans, *The Mighty Micro*, revisited by Tony Allan in 'The world transformed', *Guardian*, London, 10 August 1989.
283. Michael Kenward, 'Science stays up the poll', *New Scientist*, London, 16 September 1989.
284. Mary Fagan, 'Britain "far behind as high-tech innovator"', *Independent*, London, 8 September 1989.
285. George Parker-Jervis, 'Research and Development Snapshot', *Observer*, London, 28 January 1990.
286. Alan Cane, 'Business ignoring scope in computers', *Financial Times*, London, 14 September 1989.
287. Alan Cane, 'Information technology potential "untapped"', *Financial Times*, London, 17 May 1988.
288. Alan Cane, 'Boardroom attitudes to computers "an enigma"', *Financial Times*, London, 6 March 1990.
289. Terry Dodsworth, 'Electronics industry faces harsh home truths', *Financial Times*, London, 26 June 1988.
290. Robert Heller, 'No sunrise in the West', *Independent*, London, 22 July 1988.
291. Mary Fagan, 'Nedo starts action group to rescue British electronics', *Independent*, London, 20 July 1988.
292. Christopher Huhne, 'The public issues that lie behind the private deals', *Guardian*, London, 11 January, 1989.
293. Mary Fagan, 'UK technology "lacks direction"', *Independent*, London, 16 March 1989.
294. Richard Evans, 'British software trade in danger of extinction by foreign domination', *Times*, London, 17 June 1986.
295. Sir John Cassels, 'Success in electronics: shortening the odds', *National Electronics Review*, London, 1988, (1987 Mountbatten Memorial Lecture).
296. Peter Marsh, 'Industry "fails to match" rate of foreign innovation', *Financial Times*, London, 8 December 1987.
297. Andrew Cornelius, 'Report highlights threat to industry', *Guardian*, London, 29 November 1989.
298. Pari Patel and Keith Pavitt, 'European Technological Performance: results and prospects', *European Affairs*, Summer 1989.
299. Cabinet Office, *Annual Review of Government-funded R&D 1989*, HMSO, London, 1989.
300. Michael Kenward, 'Government funds for R&D continue to fall', *New Scientist*, London, 4 November 1989.
301. Advisory Board for the Research Councils, *Science and Public Expenditure 1989*, ABRC, London, 1989.
302. Select Committee on Science and Technology, *Civil R&D*, HMSO, London, 1989.
303. John Matthews, 'A new approach to agricultural economics', *National Electronics Review*, National Electronics Council, 1990.
304. Steve Connor, 'Genes on the loose', *New Scientist*, London, 26 May 1988.
305. Jane Ford, 'Sheep will grow woollier on a bioengineered diet', *New Scientist*, London, 10 March 1988.
306. Debora MacKenzie, 'Science milked for all it's worth', *New Scientist*, London, 24 March 1988.

307. E. Yoxen, *The Impact of Biotechnology on Living and Working Conditions*, Office for Official Publications of the European Communities, Luxembourg, 1987.

308. J. Peterson, 'Hormones, heifers and high politics: biotechnology and the Common Agricultural Policy', *Public Administration*, Vol.67, No.4, London, Winter 1989.

309. 'The Genetic Alternative: A Survey of Biotechnology', *Economist*, London, 30 April, 1988.

310. Commission of the European Communities, FAST series report 22, *New Technology and Development in Employment*, Office for Official Publications of the European Communities, Luxembourg, 1988.

311. PA Consulting Group, *Manufacturing into the late 1990s*, HMSO, London, 1989.

312. J. Northcott, I. Christie and A. Walling, *Information Technology and Management Awareness, Vol.I:Open Systems*, HMSO, London, 1990.

313. Jim Levi, 'Enter the age of the portable office', *Observer*, London, 25 February 1990.

314. 'Fax: a threat and an opportunity', *Financial Times*, London, 21 March 1988.

315. Jonathan Green-Armytage, 'The office escapes in a small box' *Observer*, London, 10 April 1988.

316. John Marti and Anthony Zeilinger, *Micros and money: new technology in banking and shopping*, PSI, London, 1982.

317. Peter Rodgers, 'Debit cards aim to bounce cheques out of business', *Guardian*, London, 21 April 1988.

318. Robert Peston, 'Three banks join in new electronic shopping project', *Independent*, London, 21 April 1988.

319. Merion Jones, 'Consuming gold', *Guardian*, London, 11 February 1988.

320. Sunny Bains, 'Lasers out-think the smart credit cards', *New Scientist*, London, 29 October 1988.

321. Wendie Pearson, 'The politics behind a card that's smart', *Times*, London, 10 December 1985.

322. Teresa Hunter, 'The smart card that's not in the pack', *Guardian*, London, 8 August 1987.

323. Patrick Hosking, 'Banking by phone fails to connect', *Independent*, London, 9 January 1990.

324. Peter Large, 'Armchair shopping apathy', *Guardian*, London, 15 November 1988.

325. Glenn D. Rennels and Edward H. Shotliffe, 'Advanced computing for medicine', *Scientific American*, October 1987.

326. Gillian Cribbs, 'Health Service sets off gold rush for computer remedies', *Independent*, London, 26 September 1988.

327. Susan Watts, 'Robots to ease the burden in hospitals', *New Scientist*, London, 28 January 1989.

328. 'Disabled workers use IT to win over employers', *New Scientist*, London, 26 May 1988.

329. Kathleen Frenchman, 'Physical challenges beaten at the push of a button', *Observer*, London, 10 April 1988.

330. David Brindle, 'Claimants to be paid by "plastic"', *Guardian*, London, 28 February 1989.

331. Jan Forrest and Sandra Williams, *New technology and information exchange in social services*, PSI, London, 1987.

332. Ian Miles, *Home Informatics*, Frances Pinter, London, 1988.

333. M. Brocklehurst, 'Homeworking and the New Technology: the reality and the rhetoric', *Personal Review*, Vol.18, No.2, 1989.

334. John Lamb, 'At home in the electronic cottage', *New Scientist*, London, 5 May 1988.

335. 'Autoguide promises to point motorists in the right direction', *New Scientist*, London, 24 December 1988.

336. Mary Fagan, '£50m computerised theft highlights debate on hacking', *Independent*, London, 10 October 1989.

337. Lindsey Nicolle and Tony Collins, 'The computer fraud conspiracy of silence', *Independent*, London, 19 June 1989.

338. Peter Large, 'Computer frauds "costing £30m"', *Guardian*, London, 19 January 1987.

339. Angella Johnson, 'Electronic tag plan for first offenders', *Guardian*, London, 19 July 1988.

340. William C. Thompson and Simon Ford, 'Is DNA fingerprinting ready for the courts?', *New Scientist*, London, 31 March 1990.

16   The Economy

341. Central Statistical Office, *United Kingdom National Accounts*, 1990 (and earlier), HMSO, London, 1990.
342. *Industry and the British Economy to the Year 2000*, Cambridge Econometrics, Cambridge, 1990.
343. *UK Budget Statement*, Treasury, HMSO, London, March 1990.
344. Nicholas Oulton, 'Labour productivity in UK manufacturing in the 1970s and 1980s', *National Institute Economic Review*, London, May 1990.
345. Geoffrey Maynard, 'Britain's economic revival and the balance of payments', *Political Quarterly*, London, April-June 1989.
346. Charles Feinstein and Robin Matthews, 'The growth of output and productivity in the UK: the 1980s as a phase of the postwar period', *National Institute Economic Review*, London, August 1990.
347. Julia Darby and Simon Wren-Lewis, 'Manufacturing productivity in the 1980s', *National Institute Economic Review*, London, May 1989.
348. David S. Turner, *Does the UK face a balance of payments constraint on growth? A quantitative analysis using the LBS and NIESR Models*, Macroeconomic Modelling Bureau Discussion Paper No.16, University of Warwick, September 1988.
349. M. Landesmann and A. Snell, 'The consequences of Mrs Thatcher for UK manufacturing exports', *Economic Journal*, March 1989.
350. Cambridge Econometrics, *Industry and the British economy to the year 2000: spring report*, Cambridge Econometrics, Cambridge, May 1989.
351. Organisation for Economic Co-operation and Development, *Economic Survey United Kingdom 1988-1989*, OECD, Paris, 1989.
352. Central Statistical Office, *Economic Trends*, August 1990 (and earlier), HMSO, London, 1988.
353. Central Statistical Office, *Monthly Digest of Statistics*, August 1990 (and earlier), HMSO, London, 1990.
354. Central Statistical Office, *Annual Abstract of Statistics*, 1990 (and earlier), HMSO, London, 1990.
355. *Projections to 2010*, Cambridge Econometrics, Cambridge, 1990.

17   Life in Britain in 2010

356. Jonathan Gershuny, 'Time use, technology and the future of work', *Journal of the Market Research Society*, Vol.28, No.4, October 1986.
357. Department of Employment, quoted in *Social Trends 20*, HMSO, London, 1990.
358. Statistical Office of the European Communities, quoted in *Social Trends 20*, HMSO, London, 1990.
359. Paul Osterman, *New Technology and Work Organisation*, paper presented to conference on Technology and Investment: Crucial Issues for the 90s, Royal Academy of Engineering Sciences, Stockholm, 1990.
360. Central Statistical Office, *United Kingdom National Accounts* 1990 (and earlier), HMSO, London, 1990.
361. Department of Employment, *New Earnings Survey 1989 (and earlier)*, Department of Employment, London, 1989.
362. Department of Social Security, *Households below average income: a statistical analysis 1981-1987*, Department of Social Security, London, 1990.
363. Department of Social Security, quoted in *Social Trends 20*, HMSO, London, 1990.
364. Central Statistical Office, *Social Trends 20*, HMSO, London, 1990.
365. Broadcasting Audience Research Board and British Broadcasting Corporation, quoted in *Social Trends 20*, HMSO, London, 1990.
366. British Videogram Association, quoted in *Social Trends 20*, HMSO, London, 1990.

367. British Phonographic Industry Yearbook, quoted in *Social Trends 20*, HMSO, London, 1990.

368. Andrew Feist and Robert Hutchison, *Cultural Trends 1990*, PSI, London, 1990.

369. National sporting organisations quoted in *Social Trends 20*, HMSO, London, 1990.

370. Office of Health Economics, *Compendium of Health Statistics*, seventh edition, Office of Health Economics, London, 1989.

371. R. Doll, 'Major Epidemics of the 20th Century: from Coronary Thrombosis to Aids', in Central Statistical Office, *Social Trends 18*, HMSO, London, 1988.

372. D. Taylor, *British Medicines Research 1988*, ABPI, London, 1988.

373. D. Wetherall, 'Molecular cell biology in clinical medicine: Introduction', *British Medical Journal*, 295, 1987.

374. HM Treasury and Department of Health, (unpublished figures) London, 1989.

375. N. Bosanquet and A. Gray, *Will You Still Love Me?*, National Association of Health Authorities, Birmingham, 1989.

376. C. Ham et al, *New Horizons in Acute Care*, National Association of Health Authorities, Birmingham, 1989.

377. OECD, *Financing and delivering health care*, OECD, Paris, 1987.

378. Office of Population Censuses and Surveys and Lord Chancellor's Department, quoted in *Social Trends 20*, HMSO, London, 1990.

379. J. Haskey, 'The proportion of marriages ending in divorce', *Population Trends 27*, HMSO, London, 1983.

380. J. Haskey, 'Current prospects for the proportion of marriages ending in divorce', *Population Trends 55*, HMSO, London, 1989.

381. Office of Population Censuses and Surveys, quoted in *Social Trends 20*, HMSO, London, 1990.

382. J. Haskey, 'One-parent families and their children in Great Britain: numbers and characteristics', *Population Trends 55*, HMSO, London, 1989.

383. Michael Willmott, *Planning for Social Change, 1990*, Henley Centre for Forecasting, London, 1989.

384. P. Willmott and M. Young, *Family and Kinship in East London*, Routledge and Kegan Paul, London, 1957.

385. P. Willmott, *Social Networks, Informal Care and Public Policy*, PSI, London, 1986.

386. P. Willmott, *Kinship in Urban Communities: Past and Present*, Ninth H.J. Dyos Memorial Lecture, Victorian Studies Centre, University of Leicester, 1987.

387. P. Willmott, *Friendship Networks and Social Support*, PSI, London, 1987.

388. Roger Jowell, Sharon Witherspoon and Lindsey Brook (Eds.), *British Social Attitudes: the 1987 Report*, Social and Community Planning Research, London, 1987.

389. Roger Jowell, Sharon Witherspoon and Lindsey Brook (Eds.), *British Social Attitudes: the Fifth Report*, Social and Community Planning Research, London, 1988.

390. Roger Jowell, Sharon Witherspoon and Lindsey Brook (EDs.), *British Social Attitudes: the sixth report*, Social and Community Planning Research, London, 1989.

391. Isobel Allen, *Doctors and Their Careers*, PSI, London, 1988.

392. Susan McRae (Ed.), *Keeping Women In*, PSI, London, 1990.

393. Gerald Chambers with Christine Horton, *Promoting Sex Equality*, PSI, London, 1990.

394. Embassies of European countries, quoted in *Social Trends 20*, HMSO, London, 1990.

395. Environmental organisations, quoted in *Social Trends 20*, HMSO, London, 1990.

396. Guardian/ICM poll on political attitudes, reported in *Guardian*, London, 18 September 1989.

397. Observer/Harris Poll of the 80s, reported in *Observer*, London, 31 December 1989.

398. I. Crewe, 'Has the electorate become Thatcherite?', in R. Skidelsky (Ed), *Thatcherism*, Chatto and Windus, London, 1988.

399. Peter Kellner, 'Thatcherite gospel leaves masses unmoved', *Independent*, London, 4 May 1989.

400. Peter Kellner, 'Growing gloom over welfare state', *Independent*, London, 28 April 1988.

401. Peter Kellner, 'For better, for worse', *Independent*, London, 2 May 1989.

18   Three Scenarios

402.   ECOTEC, *Industry Costs of Pollution Control*, Final Report to the Department of the Environment, ECOTEC Research and Consulting Ltd, 1989.

403.   S. Barrett, 'Pricing the environment: the economic and environmental consequences of a carbon tax', *Economic Outlook*, London Business School, 1990.

404.   Robert E. Marks, Peter L. Swan, Peter McLennan, Richard Schodde, Peter B. Dixon, David T. Johnson, 'The cost of Australian Carbon Dioxide Abatement', *Energy Journal*, Spring 1990.

405.   S. Glomsrod, H. Vennemo, T. Johnsen, *Stabilisation of emissions of CO_2: a computable general equilibrium assessment*, Discussion Paper No. 48, Central Bureau of Statistics, Oslo, 1990.

406.   Netherlands, Second Chamber of the States General, *National Environmental Policy Plan*, The Hague, 1989.